AF559294

Veronese

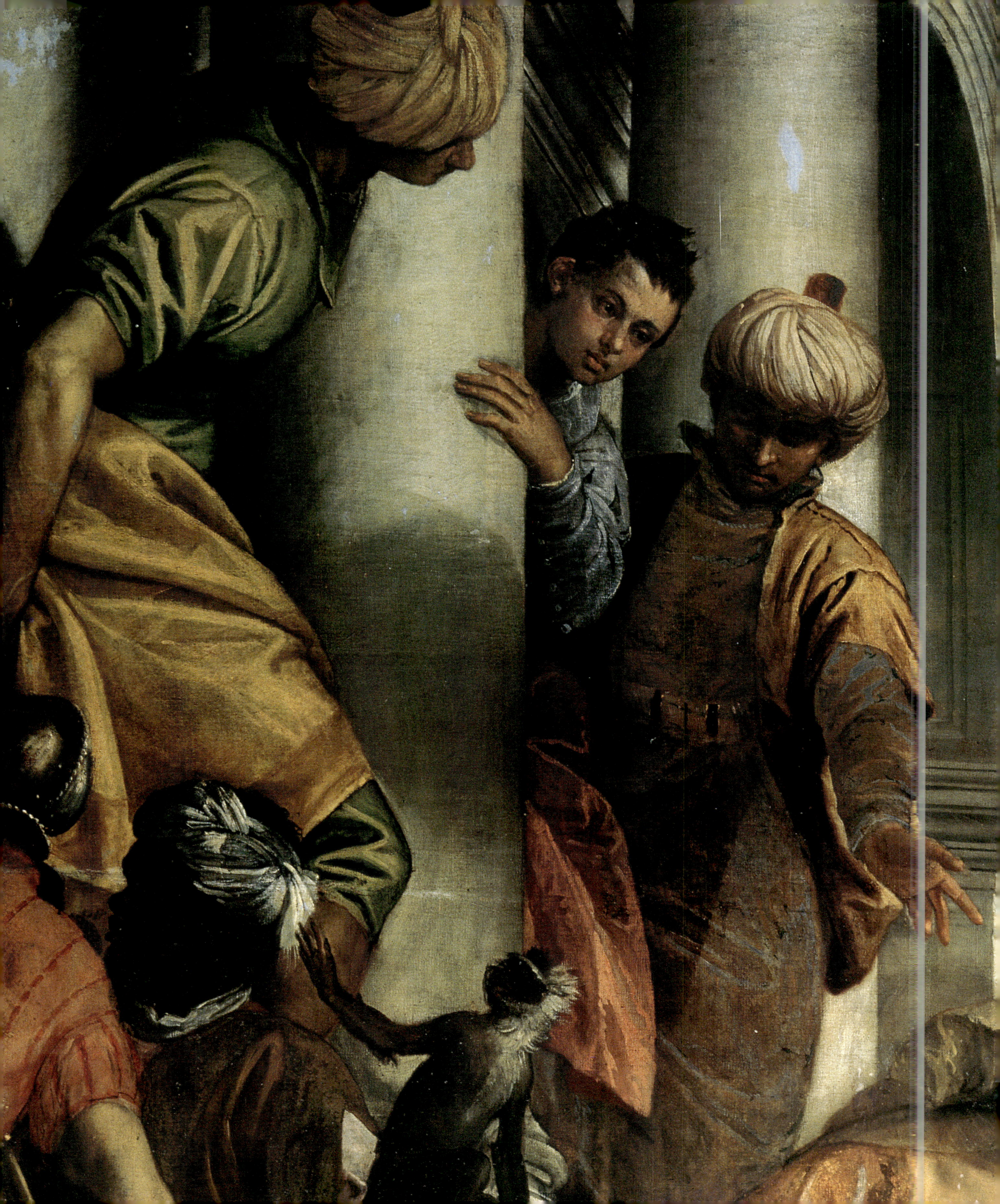

Andreas Priever

Paolo Caliari, called
Veronese

1528–1588

KÖNEMANN

Frontispiece

1 *Martyrdom of SS. Mark and Marcellianus* (detail of ill. 79)

Bonner Strasse 126, D-50968 Cologne

Publishing Manager and Art Director: Peter Feierabend
Project Coordination: Ute Edda Hammer, Jeannette Fentroß
Editing: Angela Wieland
Layout: Bärbel Messmann
Picture Research: Stefanie Huber
Lithography: CDN Pressing, Verona

Original title: *Paolo Caliari, genannt Veronese*

Translation from German: Paul Aston and Fiona Hulse in association with Cambridge Publishing Management
Editing: Susan James in association with Cambridge Publishing Management
Typesetting: Cambridge Publishing Management
Project Management: Jackie Dobbyne for Cambridge Publishing Management, Cambridge, UK
Project Coordination: Kristin Zeier and Nadja Bremse-Koob
Production: Stefan Bramsiepe

Printing and Binding: Neue Stalling, Oldenberg
Printed in Germany

ISBN 3-8290-2875-X

10 9 8 7 6 5 4 3 2 1

Contents

Judgment and Sentence – The World of the Image and the Image of the World

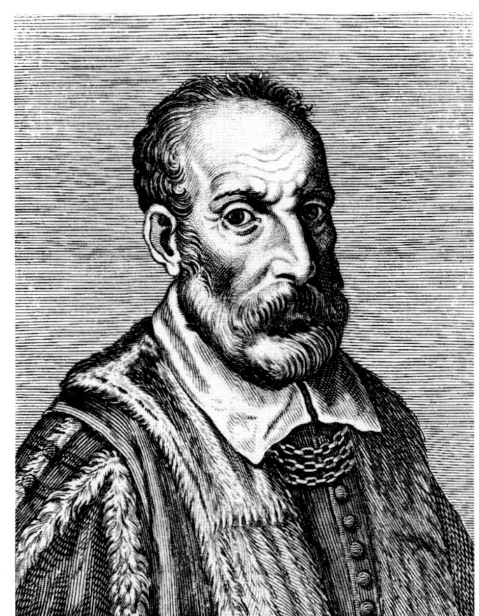

2 Giovanni Gregori
Paolo Veronese, pre-1648
Copper engraving from: Carlo Ridolfi, *Le maraviglie dell'arte ovvero le vite degli illustri pittori veneti e dello stato*, Venice 1648, vol. 1, p. 282
Staats- und Universitätsbibliothek, Göttingen

In 1648, the painter and art historiographer Carlo Ridolfi published an extensive biography of Veronese. This portrait introduces the painter's *Vita*, and is probably based on a self-portrait, now lost, then in the possession of Veronese's descendants in Venice in the second half of the 17th century.

3 *Feast at the House of Levi* (detail of ill. 96)

With his eloquent gesture, which is remarkably similar to that of Alexander the Great in the painting in the London National Gallery (ill. 84), the elegantly dressed Venetian accompanied by a page links the figures in the left arch with Christ as the focus of the picture, in terms of both form and content. Without being a self-portrait, the portrait-like, characteristic head with a high forehead and distinctive nose does not lack a certain resemblance to the portraits we have of Veronese himself.

"Paulino, whom I knew and whose exquisite works I have seen, would have deserved a great work in his praise, for his pictures show that no other painter was his equal; and this ignoramus skips over him in four lines." This marginal note, attributed to Annibale Carracci (1560–1609), the founder of the Accademia degli Incamminati in Bologna and great reformer of Italian painting around 1600, was discussing no less a figure than the Florentine painter and art historian Giorgio Vasari (1511–1574). Annibale's posthumous criticism, his displeasure at the overall rather sketchy accounts of the life and work of Paolo Veronese in the extended edition of the *Vite de' piu eccelenti pittori, scultori et architettori* (The Lives of the Most Excellent Painters, Sculptors, and Architects), published in 1568, reveals that within a short time after the Venetian painter's death there was a need to find out more about this exceptional artist and his works.

The first to realize what Annibale Carracci had been hinting at was Carlo Ridolfi (1594–1658), the biographer of Venetian artists. Originally a painter, he compiled the biographies of the most famous Venetian painters of the 16th and early 17th centuries, including one account that, despite several inconsistencies, is still considered to be one of the most important sources for assessing Veronese. It has made a decisive contribution to making the extensive artistic legacy of the painter from Venice and the Veneto known far beyond that state's borders. His training with the painter Antonio Vasillacchi (1556–1629), an occasional colleague of Veronese's, put Ridolfi in the position of being able for the first time to give closer accounts of the artist's character, his behavior and manners. Modesty, care for others, and thrift are some of the virtues we are told about. Paolo Veronese, it is reported, was informal in his dealings with other people, never made great efforts to achieve public office, kept all his promises, and placed value on his external appearance. While he wore valuable clothes made of expensive materials and velvet shoes, he otherwise apparently lived without any luxuries, was thrifty in his expenditure and therefore able to achieve some prosperity. We do not know very much more about Veronese the person. Apart from some letters in a business vein and cursory technical notes, which occasionally appear on drawings he made, he left no records behind. Despite this, there is a highly unusual event in his biography.

On July 18, 1573 Veronese was invited before the Venetian Inquisition, evidently following a denunciation, in order to justify his unconventional depiction of the Last Supper in the Dominican refectory in Santi Giovanni e Paolo in Venice. German mercenaries, a man with a nose bleed, the presence of a dwarf-like jester as well as other "foolishnesses" *(scurrilita)* with which, according to the Inquisition's tribunal the painter had offended against decorum, the law of appropriate artistic means, gave rise to the charge of "heresy". Veronese, who briefly answered the question about his occupation with the words "I paint and make figures" *(Io depingo et fazzo delle figure)*, and in imitation of a familiar quotation from the Roman poet Horace (65 B.C.–8 A.D.) attempted in vain to take up the cudgels for the freedom of art, defended himself cautiously, but self-confidently. The reference to the necessity of *ornamento* that filled the surface and his method of working – "I make paintings while considering what is seemly and what my intellect can grasp" *(Io fazzo le pitture con quella considerazione che'l è conveniente, chel mio intellecto puo capire)* – was of little benefit to the painter of figures. The Inquisition demanded corrections. The condition of reworking the queried depiction within three months at his own expense did not, however, result in any fundamental alterations, merely a compromise formula on the monumental painting in the Venetian Accademia which, in the form of a Latin inscription, is still visible today at a distance, and documents its change into the *Feast in the House of Levi* (ill. 96). Thus, Veronese merely altered the picture's title. Veronese's reputation as a painter was not harmed by this incident. Carefully guarded in the Inquisition's archives in Venice was the document (ill. 97) that records the unusual event and which was not made known to contemporaries or subsequent generations of critics. Not until 1867 were the minutes of the hearing rediscovered; all too soon, in many places, they were being used to brand the painter as an awkward, little-educated personality. All of a sudden there appeared to be confirmation for the

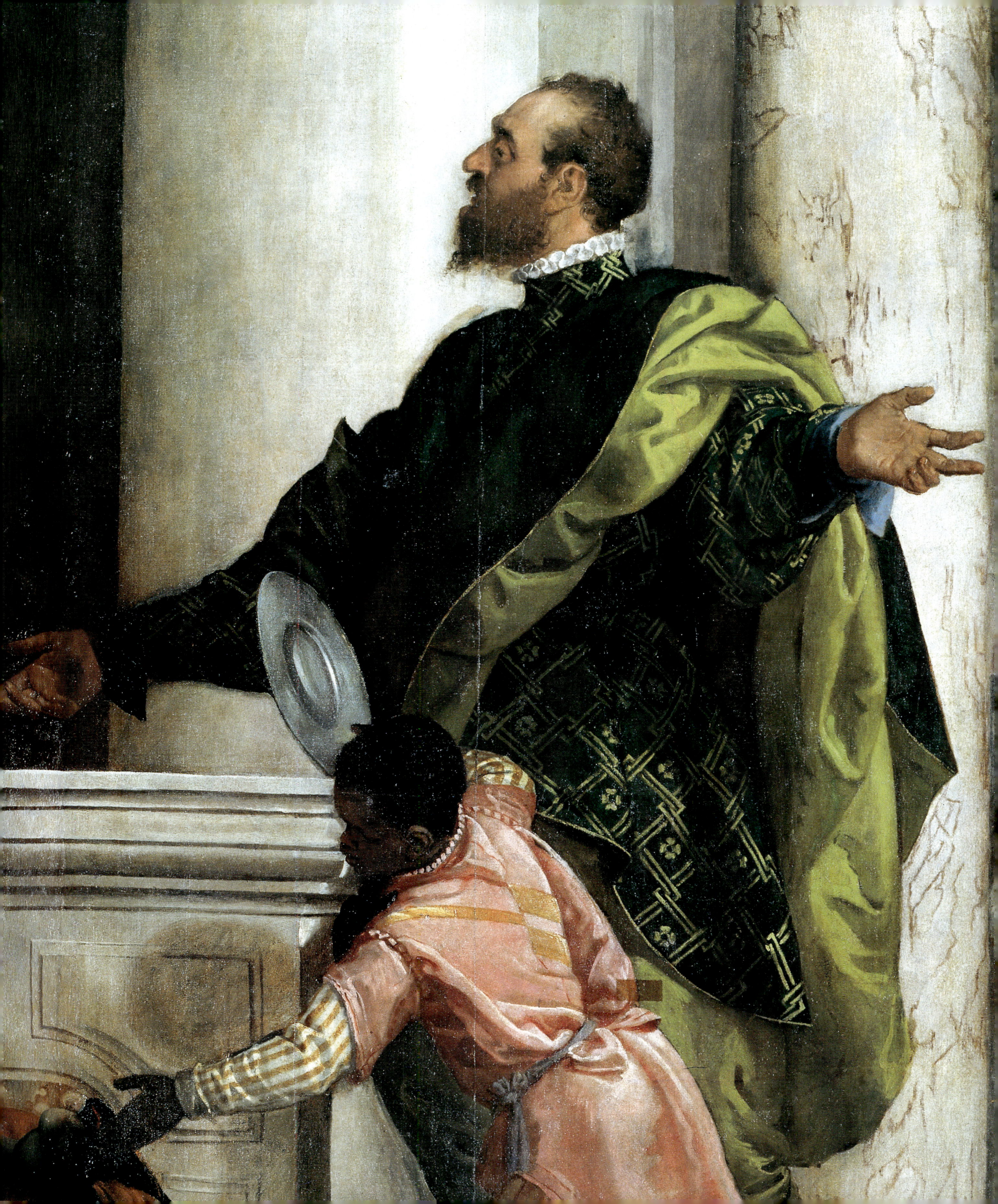

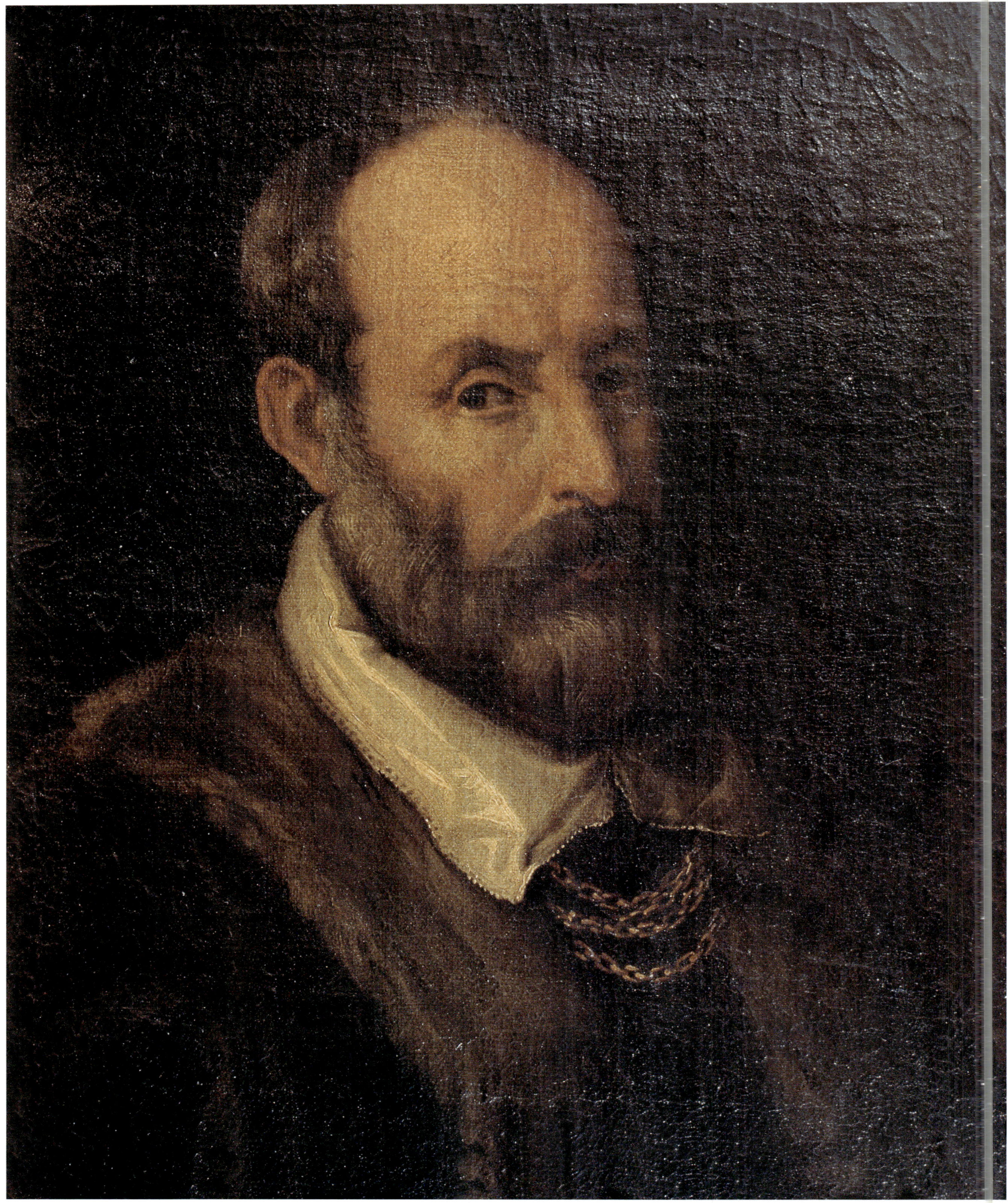

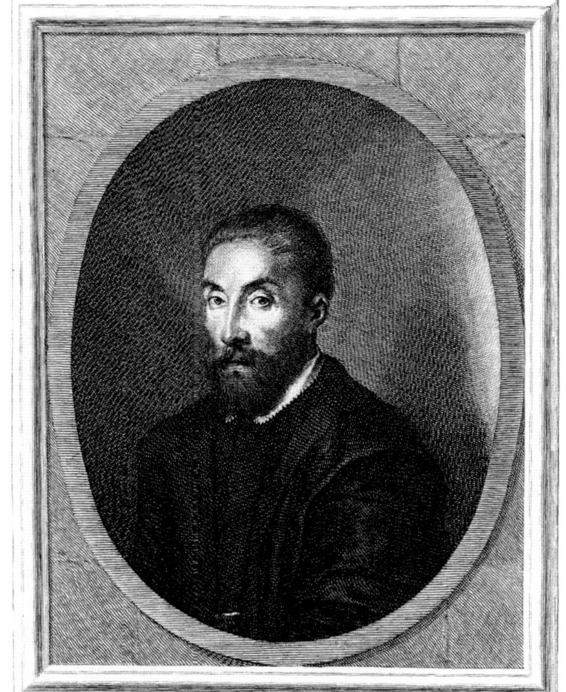

5 Jacobus Coelemans
Paolo Veronese, 1701
Copper engraving, 24 x 18 cm
Kupferstichkabinett, Staatliche Kunstsammlungen, Dresden

The engraving records a lost self-portrait by Veronese once owned by the Marquis d'Aguilles (1645–1709) in Aix. The Flemish engraver was commissioned to engrave around 118 reproductions of paintings in this once important collection, including works by Raphael, Andrea del Sarto, Titian, Tintoretto, and Annibale Carracci. They and the self-portrait of Veronese passed to the gallery collection of the *Recueil des plus beaux tableaux du cabinet de Messire Jean-Baptiste Boyer, seigneur d'Aguilles, conseiller au Parlement de Provence, à Aix* (Aix, 1709).

complaints voiced in the early 18th century by Francesco Algarotti (1715–1764) and other representatives of Neoclassical art criticism, which at times had considerably dampened the enjoyment of the celebrated colorist's paintings in contemporary critical circles in France, England and Germany: Veronese was considered a painter who allowed armed mercenaries, Levantines, and other bizarre figures to appear in his large religious Suppers, which in his historical and religious paintings always neglected decorum at the expense of the bright present moment by offering everything appropriate to a cheerful and sensual enjoyment of earthly existence: pleasant weather, marvelous buildings, crowds of cheerful, attractive figures, magnificent garments, valuable jewelry, and so on.

The apparent realism of this and other pictorial inventions was still celebrated by 17th-century critics as a painterly revelation and, as the 1652 *Trattato della pittura. Uso et abuso loro* by the Roman painter Pietro da Cortona (1599–1667) proves, was by no means misinterpreted, even outside Venice, as an offense against the laws of depiction of a religious theme; but in the 18th century this led to associations and interpretations of an unusual nature. Two succinct examples: when Admiral Francesco Cornaro held a magnificent feast in the harbor town of Livorno in January 1712, his contemporaries honored the material extravagance by mentioning that Veronese could not have done it more dazzlingly in his famous Supper. And in Venice, the art expert and librarian Antonio Maria Zanetti the Younger (1706–1778) could not, in 1771, have suspected that his – from today's point of view iconographically mistaken – attempt to identify the portraits of Charles V, Vittoria Colonna, Achmet II, Mary Tudor, Francis I and other famous historical figures of the second half of the 16th century on the depiction of the *Wedding at Cana* (ill. 73) was to give rise to curious interpretations. Before the eyes of an art public, extremely receptive to unusual novelties, the religious history changed into a historical account, the personality of the artist from a painter of histories to a master of ceremonies and chronicler of witty Venetian *joie de vivre*. For soon afterwards, Zanetti's words were followed by numerous copies containing marvelous "pictorial legends", extended by several anecdotes and a wealth of other portraits, which now provided the name of a prominent person for almost every one of the roughly 130 figures in the picture.

In France, Veronese's impressive realism has always been passionately discussed in academic circles. Charles-Nicolas Cochin (1715–1790), who traveled in Italy between 1749 and 1751, was enthusiastic about the inclusion of numerous portraits and contemporary heads; even further, he believed he could recognize *hommes véritables* (actually existing people) in Veronese's works. This was the start of a route which, in the historicizing 19th century, would lead to further misunderstandings. As the creator of splendid Venetian banquets and "magnificent portrait paintings", the Venetian painter advanced in the art criticism of the period to the level of genre painter. What had formerly been a fascinating colorful pictorial world, arousing admiration, was now experienced as the expression of the painter's, and Venetian society's, picture of the world. Artistic methods were linked to questionable contents, and from then on terms such as luxury, cosmopolitan carefreeness, theatricality, and ostentatious painting were, for a long time, to determine the one-sided view of his work.

Against the background of this development the question arises as to how Veronese saw himself. While his famous fellow painters Titian (c. 1488–1576) and Tintoretto (1518–1594) left impressive self-portraits, which are now part of the gallery of the imagination of any lover of Venetian painting of the Cinquecento, Veronese, inventor of magnificently colored paintings and frescoes, appears to retreat behind his work – his own self-portrait, several versions of which doubtlessly still existed in the 17th century, has not survived. Some clues are provided by the portrait (ill. 2) which Ridolfi used to introduce his readers to the painter's *Life*. The engraver evidently based his work on a self-portrait which was in the careful ownership of Veronese's heirs in 17th-century Venice. This lost painting survives in a copy (ill. 4) attributed to the Venetian painter Palma il Giovane (c. 1548–1628) owned by the Uffizi, which shows the portrayed man at an advanced age, dressed in a black jacket and fur-trimmed waistcoat. In both cases, the gold chain wound several times around his neck identifies the painter as a nobleman and alludes to the prize with which he was presented in the Sala Grande of the Biblioteca Marciana in 1557 for his allegory *Music* (ill. 41). A further portrait, on this occasion clearly identified as a self-portrait (ill. 5), which at the beginning of the 18th century was still

4 Palma il Giovane (attrib.)
Paolo Veronese, early 17th-century copy of a lost self-portrait
Oil on canvas, 45 x 38 cm
Galleria degli Uffizi, Florence

In the second half of the 17th century, both Leopoldo de' Medici and Grand Duke Cosimo III de' Medici tried in vain to obtain a Veronese self-portrait. When Cosimo was offered a portrait by the Venetian painter Palma il Giovane (c. 1548-1628), he snapped it up, but later still went on making inquiries because he wanted a painting by Veronese himself. Recorded in early 18th-century Uffizi inventories as a work by Veronese, this painting is now considered a copy of a lost original which also obviously acted as a model for Carlo Ridolfi's engraving (ill. 2).

6 Matteo Carneri
Paolo Veronese, pre-1631
San Sebastiano, Venice

The bust forms part of the plain tomb beside the organ in San Sebastiano in Venice, and was made, as the former inscription on the spot once made clear (PAVLI CALIARI EFFIGIES ÆT. SVÆ. 58), two years before Veronese's death. The terracotta model originally erected here was by the sculptor Camillo Bozzetti. In the early 17th century, Veronese's eldest son Gabriele Caliari (d. 1631) had the whole monument renovated. The bust by Bozzetti was replaced by a copy by the sculptor Matteo Carneri, with a new inscription: PAVLO CALIARO / VERONEN. PICTORI / NATURÆ ÆMVLO / ARTIS MIRACVLO / SUPERSTITE FATIS / FAMA VICTVRO. It alludes to the qualities of Veronese's art in adhering closely to nature, and declares that he conquered fate through his fame.

in the collection of paintings belonging to Jean-Baptiste d'Aguilles in Aix-en-Provence, and upon which the Flemish artist Jacobus Coelemans (1654–1732) based his engraving in 1701 before all traces of the work were lost, once again provides us with the image of a stern head with a powerful forehead and serious eyes with an almost distrustful expression. Refined restraint, reserve and distance, in addition to self-confidence, are communicated by this impressive portrait of the older Veronese. In both cases, it is the face of a clever, attentive observer that confronts us. Together with the portrait bust mounted over the painter's grave in the church of San Sebastiano in Venice (ill. 6), these works convey a reasonable idea of the appearance of a painter whose self-portrait was more desirable than any other in the circles of prominent Florentine collectors during the second half of the 17th century, and which gave rise to a wide range of speculation.

For example, Cardinal Leopoldo de' Medici and Grand Duke Cosimo III invested a lot of time and considerable sums of money in order to gain possession of a portrait of Veronese. Nonetheless, various efforts on the part of their art agents to locate a flawless original self-portrait, for the collection of self-portraits being built up in the Uffizi, were in vain. In the face of repeated new and frequently dubious offers which were made to the experienced Medici experts, in 1682 Cosimo finally had the head of the viola da gamba player in the *Wedding at Cana* (ill. 76), in the refectory of the monastery of San Giorgio Maggiore in Venice, copied for the purpose of comparison. According to a rather questionable local travel guide tradition, dating back no further than 1660, contemporaries and subsequent generations of experts believed the bearded musician in a white garment to be a self-portrait of Paolo Veronese. It is scarcely a coincidence that literary inventions of this type, which had little to do with Veronese but very much to do with the aesthetic debates of the 17th century, started to inflame the imagination of European intellectual travelers at a point in time when the painter's works were extremely popular in Venice and were considered to be amongst the city's chief attractions. Thus, it was considered imperative to be familiar with the great Suppers and, above all, the *Wedding at Cana* (ill. 73): anyone who had not seen this picture, it was said in the *Viaggio pittoresco* published in Venice in 1671 by the painter and copper engraver Giacomo Barri, had not seen anything of the city. Praise of this sort inevitably encouraged the creation of legends, which in the case of the *Wedding at Cana* was to be a cryptic success during the course of the 17th and 18th centuries.

Up to the present day it is the epic breadth of the marvelously detailed and inventive pictures, and the conception of individual figures with their portrait-like heads (ill. 3) permeated by a feeling of tangible reality, which persistently tempt experts and scholars alike to search for portraits in Veronese's work. Indeed, these qualities have a considerable part to play in the continuing fascination that the colorful pictorial world of the Venetian by choice still holds for us after more than 400 years. Originally from Verona, in his own way Veronese made a considerable contribution to the particular appearance of Venetian painting in the Cinquecento. Diversity, inventiveness and festive pictorial architectures are in many cases associated above all with his artistic legacy; they were, however, anything other than an end in themselves, but were rather the eloquent expression of a constantly developing individual artistic manner of thinking that was decisively determined by collaboration with the architects Michele Sanmicheli and Andrea Palladio, as well as encounters with Daniele Barbaro, Jacopo Sansovino and Titian. Only within this framework is it possible to judge to what extent the painter from Verona occupied a special position in Venice and, as Erik Forssman once accurately expressed it, was able to become "the architect of Venetian painting".

Roughly 400 paintings, followed by about [illegible]00 attributed works and an extensive body of drawings, mean that it is necessary to make a selection that will inevitably leave some questions open. While Paolo Farinati (1528–1590), Veronese's painter colleague and later witness at his marriage, in many cases signed and dated his paintings and in addition kept a type of diary in which he recorded contracts, expenditure and income with a positively pedantic precision, Veronese evidently appears to have considered these things to be quite unimportant. Few works are signed, the attribution and dating of many works is open to controversy, and made more difficult not least by the fact that the painter was quite capable of adjusting to the individual tastes of his sponsors. In addition there is another particular feature. Veronese's career in Venice is closely connected to the activities of his workshop, which, during his lifetime and particularly after the painter's death, routinely made use of his pictorial inventions and the suggestive power of his name, a name that promised quality. The choice of works and the intention to examine sources, influences and effects selectively will be carried out in an endeavor to remain true to these criteria.

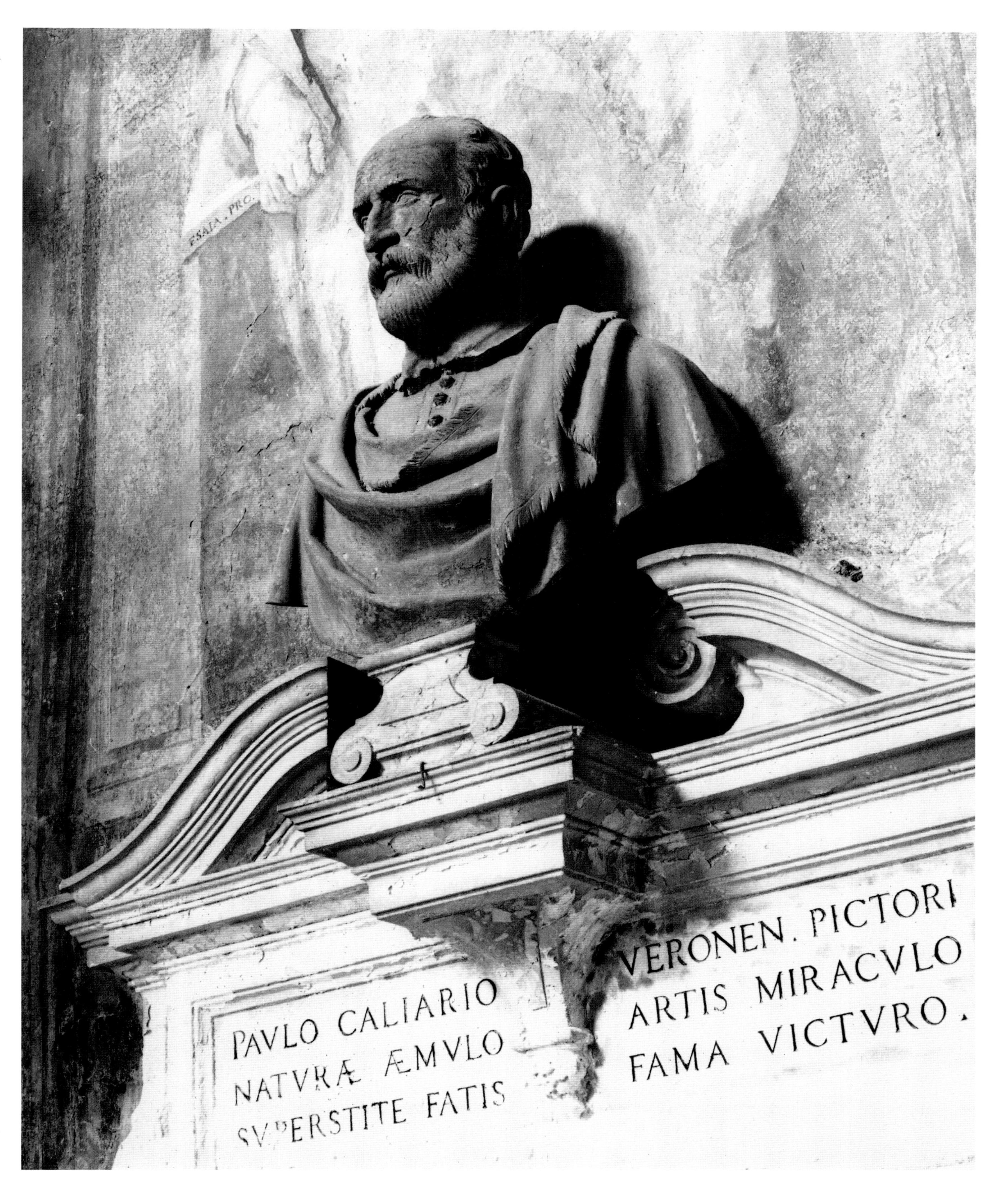
ESAIA . PRO.
PAVLO CALIARIO
NATVRÆ ÆMVLO
SVPERSTITE FATIS
VERONEN. PICTORI
ARTIS MIRACVLO
FAMA VICTVRO.

Verona – Training and Artistic Beginnings

7 Raising of the Daughter of Jairus, c. 1546
Oil on paper mounted on canvas, 42 x 37 cm
Musée du Louvre, Paris

First documented in 1662, in the collection of Secretary of State Loménie de Brienne the Younger, this is considered a *modello* for a now lost painting said by Carlo Ridolfi in 1648 to be in the church of San Bernardino in Verona. In 1697, the Franciscans secretly sold it to the painter Peter Strudel, who was visiting the city at the time, and replaced it with a copy. The picture shows Jesus visiting the house of the synagogue elder Jairus, whose 12-year-old daughter had just died. When he enters the sick girl's chamber, he asks the minstrels and the wailing women to leave the house. He then takes her hand and brings her back to life, saying: "Maiden, I say unto thee, arise." This miracle, told in the gospels of Matthew, Mark and Luke, is set by Veronese in the forecourt of a Renaissance palace. The viewer's eye is led through the arch to the musicians and wailing women, who were induced to leave the scene of the event.

Paolo Veronese was born in 1528 in the San Paolo di Campo Martio district of Verona, the son of Gabriele di Piero and his wife Caterina. Like his ancestors who had immigrated from Lombardy in the 15th century, Gabriele was a stonemason by profession and had no surname. At first this was also true of Paolo, his second eldest son, who even Vasari still called "Paulino pittore" in 1568, although at this point the painter had already adopted the name Caliari from a prominent patrician family in Verona. Paolo did not follow in his father's footsteps, but one ought to mention that Carlo Ridolfi reported the existence of *modelli di creta*, clay models, which had been produced under his father's supervision. Thus it could be assumed that, while he was young, the talented boy did indeed learn a technique which later in life enabled him to prepare complicated figural compositions using small sculptured models.

In Venice it was Tintoretto who repeatedly profited as a painter from this method of working, and in Veronese's case no less a figure than the 18th-century French lover of art Pierre-Jean Mariette (1660–1742) firmly believed that he owned just such a *modello*. He had indeed purchased a small terracotta *Venus and Adonis* group from the Parisian collector Pierre Crozat, a work which in turn was so similar to a painting by Veronese on the same theme engraved by Simon François Ravenet (c. 1706–1774) and at that time in the Dupille collection, that in 1772 Mariette stated in a letter to Tommaso Termanza that the small sculptures preceded the picture and that the Venetian painter liked them to such an extent that he subsequently painted them.

At the age of 14, Paolo is mentioned for the first time in the records of Verona. In 1541, he was an apprentice and assistant in the household of the respected local painter Antonio Badile (1518–1560), who was only ten years his elder. Educated on Titian and the pictorial tradition of Venice, Verona and Brescia, Antonio Badile conveyed the theoretical and practical fundamentals of the craft of painting to his young charge, and there is some evidence that the talented student owed what was probably his first public commission to his master's recommendation.

The work Paolo delivered was a "pendant" to Badile's *Raising of Lazarus* dating from 1546, in the cruciform chapel in the church of San Bernardino in Verona donated by the ancestors of Don Massimiliano Avanzi; it was the *Raising of the Daughter of Jairus* (ill. 7) a painting that Ridolfi explicitly acknowledged as an early work, but towards the end of the 17th century it was to fall victim to a criminal act. In 1697, when Veronese's works were highly sought after in European collectors' circles, the Viennese painter Peter Strudel (1660–1714) succeeded in persuading the all too business-minded Franciscan monks Bottari, Riva and Da Bergamo to sell the devotional picture. It secretly changed hands for 400 florins, without the agreement of the authorities, and was replaced by a copy produced by the otherwise unknown painter Giovanni Cagnato which still hangs there today. Sentences – the clerics were convicted and temporarily exiled from the Republic of Venice – did not, however, achieve the desired effect. The original, presumably transferred to Vienna, did not return to Verona and is still lost, its shape only to be inferred from the mediocre copy and Paolo's oil sketch (ill. 7).

As far as Paolo's artistic beginnings are concerned, this small sketch made on paper is informative in more than one respect. Mounted onto canvas at a later date and, as can be deduced beyond doubt from older French inventories, subsequently enlarged at the top, the painted sketch uses a diversity of motifs and stylistic ideas, and offers certain qualities that are the typical characteristics of his early period. Above all, it is the choice of colors and the direction of the light that are noticeable. In contrast to the warm brownish range of colors that Badile initially used in allusion to Titian, blue and red form a balanced interaction with weak broken shades of brown, pink and pale green to create an atmosphere reminiscent of the cool daylight colors of the Veronese painters Giovanni Caroto (c. 1488/89–1563/1566), Francesco Morone (1470/71–1529) and Cavazzola (1486–1522) – older local artists whose works Paolo came into direct contact with, and was able to study, in the Avanzi Chapel and the churches of Verona. The luminance of the colors is intensified by happy contrasts and by the

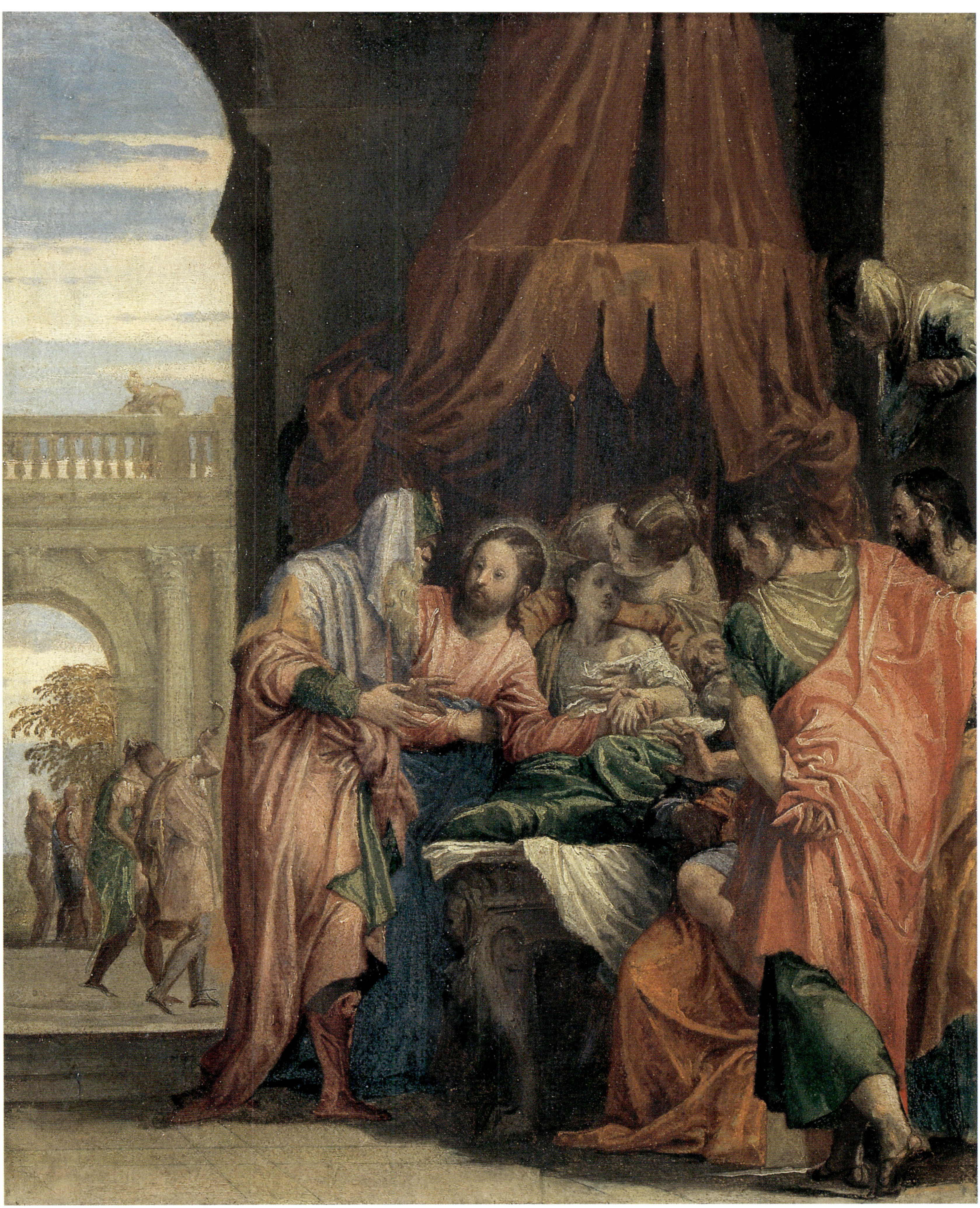

8 *Enthroned Madonna with Child, St. John the Baptist, St. Louis of Toulouse and donors (Pala Bevilacqua-Lazise)*, c. 1546–1548
Oil on canvas, 223 x 172 cm
Museo Civico di Castelvecchio, Verona

Despite several formal inconsistencies, the altar painting for the church of San Fermo Maggiore in Verona is an expression of Veronese's early mastery. It was apparently commissioned by Giovanni Bevilacqua-Lazise, and he and his deceased wife Lucrezia Malaspina are probably the donors in the picture. Among changes compared with the preparatory oil sketch (ill. 9) is the indicating gesture of John the Baptist, and overpaintings around the left arm can also be made out with the naked eye. Anxious to tone down inelegant intersections and divergent movements, the painter placed the saint's left hand on the cross staff that anticipates the Redemption. At the same time, he altered the angle of the Virgin's gaze, so that she is looking more noticeably at the donor and the Baptist as intermediary.

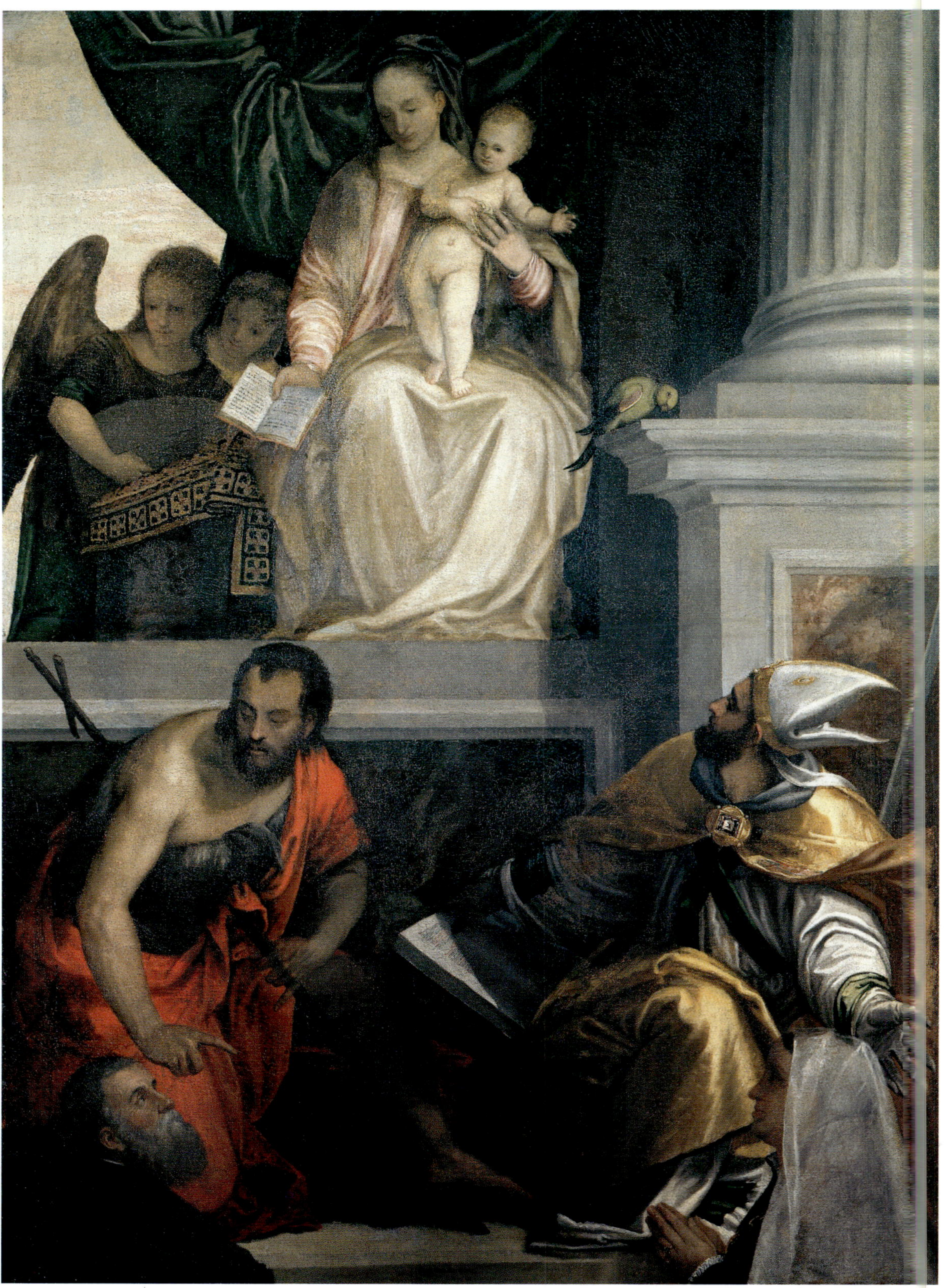

inclusion of painted architectures which mark the background of the scene against the light-blue sky dotted with clouds; these seem to herald the later pictorial architect Paolo Veronese.

In 1568, Vasari was the only biographer to write about Paolo's training in Giovanni Caroto's workshop. This report seems credible, partly because Vasari personally met the painter and architectural theoretician in 1538 while making sketches of classical buildings in Rome, and later continued the relationship. Caroto's experiences left their mark on a treatise that appeared in 1540, *De origine et amplitudine civitatis Veronae*, to which the artist, an important contributor to the development of the Veronese school of painting, contributed numerous reconstruction drawings, plans, views and records of architectural details on classical buildings. It may therefore have been Caroto who, during the 1540s, following the apprenticeship with Badile, opened the eyes of the stonemason's son to the unique collection of classical architecture and works of art which both then and now distinguished Verona from all other upper Italian towns. It is true that the classical monuments of Verona, on the banks of the Adige, were particularly important for another artist whose personality and work are intimately connected with the artistic beginnings and development of the young Paolo: Michele Sanmicheli (1484–1559). The gifted architect and student of Bramante's who, as Vasari later wrote, loved Paolo like his own son, signed as the person responsible for the design of the Cappella Pellegrini, built between 1527 and 1557 and joined to the church of San Bernardino by a round arch. Paolo was thus able to follow the progress of work on the central plan building at close quarters, though this did not lead him to adopt exactly the formally strict triumphal arch motif that Sanmicheli had already successfully put to the test in Verona, around 1530, on the façade of the *Palazzo Bevilacqua* (ill. 28), in his own aforementioned *Raising of the Daughter of Jairus* (ill. 7).

To take this point first, throughout his life, Paolo remained true to the principle of critically examining older and contemporary artistic models, taking up proven ideas, but creatively shaping them into something new. The group of the Madonna and Child in the *Pala Bevilacqua-Lazise* (ill. 8), created for the church of San Fermo Maggiore in Verona, does not deny that various local altar paintings produced by Badile between 1539 and 1543 have been studied. But the composition of the lifelike figures, their repertoire of expressions that are oriented towards Parmigianino (1503–1540), the harmonious inclusion of sculptural pictorial architectures as well as the materiality of the objects in the picture, all combine to suggest stylistic methods that go beyond the models and suggest individual qualities. The alter painting owes its creation to Lucrezia Malaspina's will of 1544, in which it is specified that a chapel should be donated. It is possible, by means of the ink drawing by his own hand in Chatsworth House, and the small oil sketch in the Uffizi (ill. 9), to follow the process extremely well by which the pictorial composition was determined, from the plan to the final version of the painting in the Museo Castelvecchio. The conspicuous stylistic relationship with the oil sketch of the *Raising of the Daughter of Jairus* (ill. 7), which was originally almost exactly the same size, suggests that the *modello* dates from about 1546. Paolo developed the portraits of the two donors step by step: in the two preparatory studies they do not as yet have any depth of field and simply function as place-markers. Depicted as half-length portraits, their position on the bottom edge of the picture seems a little old-fashioned, but the young painter was following a tradition of portrayal that was customary in Verona, and thus possibly corresponding with the client's requirements. If one follows the suggestion that the Church was completed in 1548, it may be possible to identify the bearded patrician wearing the black fur-trimmed jacket as Giovanni Bevilacqua-Lazise, accompanied by his deceased wife Lucrezia Malaspina.

Eager to learn, the painter was able to use other aids for his investigation of motifs. His later biographer

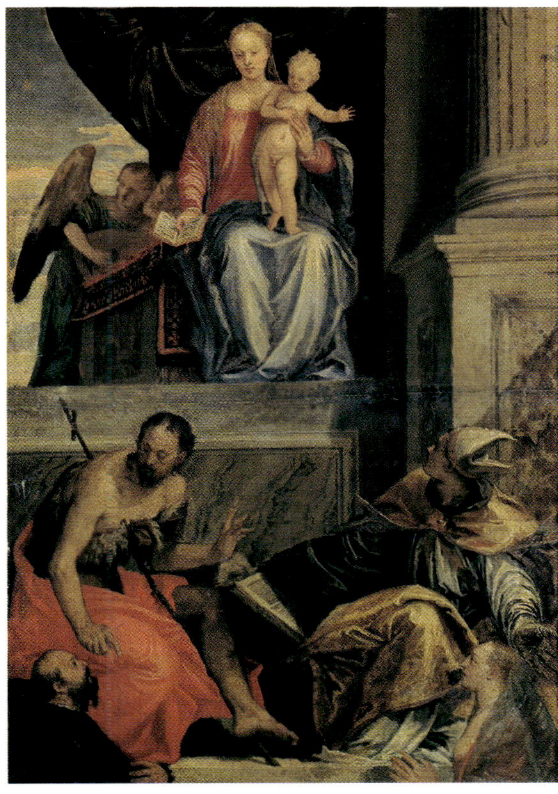

9 *Enthroned Madonna with Child, St. John the Baptist, St. Louis of Toulouse and donors*, c. 1546
Oil on paper, mounted on canvas, 50 x 36 cm
Galleria degli Uffizi, Florence

An inventory of the estate of Veronese's heirs dated 1682 lists not only pen and chalk drawings but also chiaroscuro drawings and paintings on paper (*dipinti in carta*). This oil sketch (only later mounted on canvas) must have been one such painting on paper. It was preceded by a preparatory chiaroscuro drawing (Devonshire Collection, Chatsworth).

Ridolfi, for example, noted his initial study of the printed graphics of Albrecht Dürer and the drawings of Francesco Parmigianino. While he was still in the workshop of Badile, who tended to sign his paintings with a signature modeled on Albrecht Dürer's monogram, Paolo would have become acquainted with, and copied, sheets by the Nuremberg master so esteemed in Italy. Woodcuts, copper engravings and etchings provided the contemporary painters of Verona with diverse opportunities for study, and it may therefore indeed, as has been suspected, have been a copper engraving based on Michelangelo's *Prophet Ezekiel* on the ceiling of the Sistine Chapel that provided the starting point for the figure of St. Louis of Toulouse on the *Pala Bevilacqua Lazise* (ill. 8). At first, there were no parallels for the astonishingly bold motif of movement of the saint in Paolo's early work. It is the painterly show of strength of a talented novice who is carefully beginning to try out Mannerist means of expression.

This impression is confirmed by looking at the *Conversion of Mary Magdalene* (ill. 10) in the London National Gallery, which was probably painted at the same time. Placed on a narrow stage, the figures fill the entire picture surface. They appear, in the smallest possible space, to be fulfilling the commandment of "copia et varietà delle cose" which appeared in Leon Battista Alberti's (1404–1472) treatise on painting *Della pittura*, published in Venice in 1547, a work that attained lasting programmatic importance for the pictorial arts. It required that painters of religious and secular histories used diversity and variety in their depiction, among others, of men, women, children, animals and architectures, and that they took care that figures were alternately standing, sitting or kneeling and that they expressed various emotions effectively.

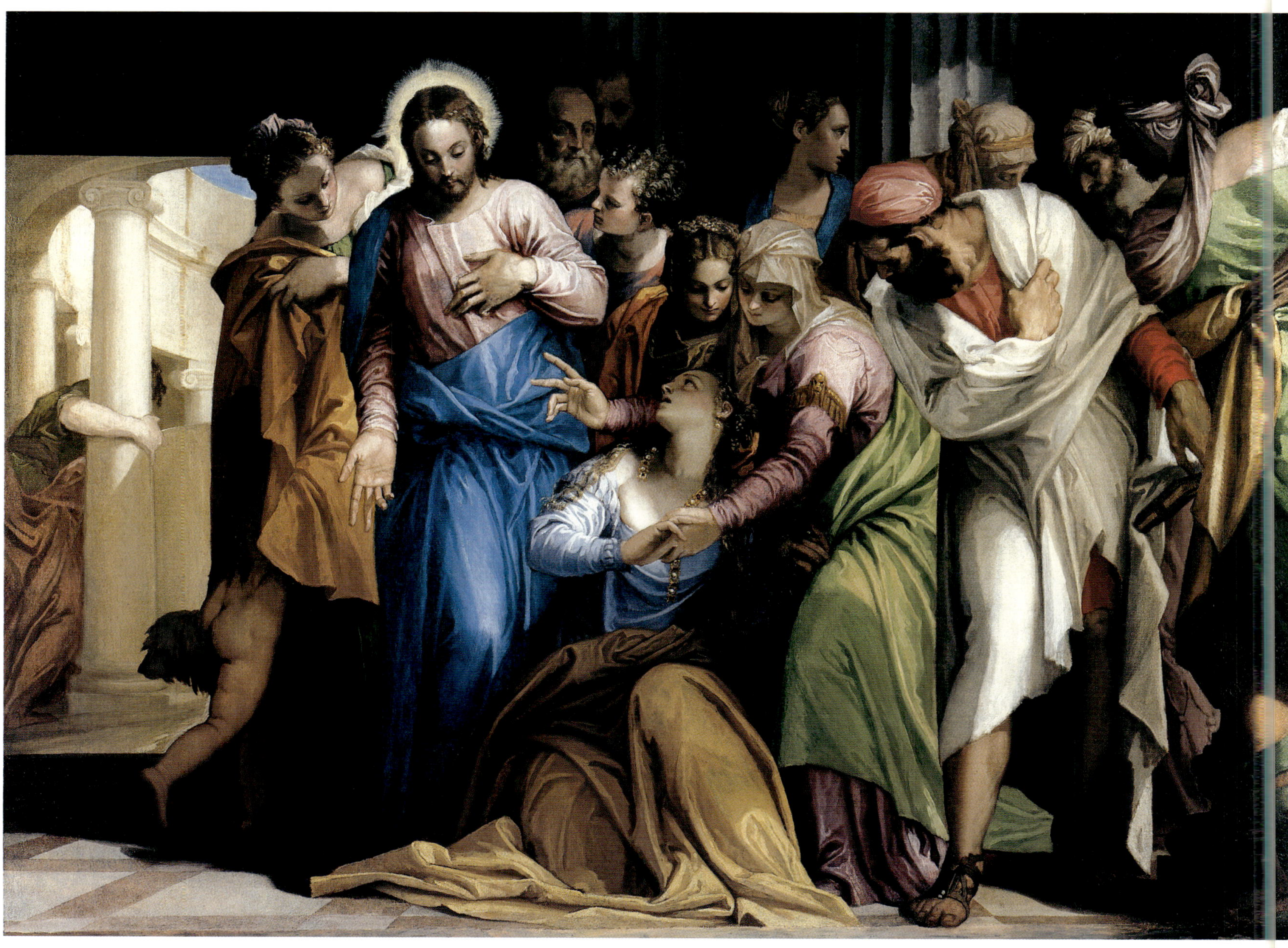

10 *Conversion of Mary Magdalene*, c. 1547
Oil on canvas, 117.5 x 163.5 cm
National Gallery, London

The interpretation of the subject is controversial. The Magdalene's usual attribute of a pot of ointment is missing, and therefore the crowded painting has been rather unconvincingly interpreted as *Jesus and the Woman Taken in Adultery* (St. John 8, 3–11) or even *The Healing of the Woman with the Issue of Blood* (St. Mark 5, 25-34). The scene of the adulteress caught *flagrante delicto* features in a painting by Veronese dated c. 1585, and is first listed under this title in the inventory of the De Croy Collection in 1613. It is now in the Kunsthistorisches Museum in Vienna. It sticks closely to the Biblical text and has little in common with the London picture. The story of the miracle of the woman with a hemorrhage who is healed after she touches Jesus's robe is also ruled out as a textual source.

If it were not for the problem of dating, one could almost gain the impression that Paolo had taken Alberti's advice literally. He presented a rapid sequence of pictures with a profusion of varying figures and garments, a complicated network of effects and dynamically divergent movements; even the head of a dog can be made out to the right of a small angel who, in turn, appears to be shyly looking for protection behind the folds of a garment. Apart from the unsolved question of the theme of the picture – most recently the iconographically unusual depiction has rather unconvincingly been interpreted as *The Healing of the Woman with the Issue of Blood* – this early work also offers stylistic methods which attest to the appeal of the elegant *maniera* of Parmigianino and his successors. Specifically, it is the conception of Mary Magdalene and the slim, elongated proportions of her female companions and Christ's dainty pose, as well as the profile of a female figure in the background framed by two mighty "fluted columns," that catch the eye and do not conceal their Emilian character. Finally, one's gaze is firmly guided to the bearded figure on the right, turning towards the beautiful sinner with a black look. With masterly balance, its plasticity, reminiscent of a sculpture, the figure faces the observer with a riddle: at the same time it reflects certain formal limits which Paolo did not succeed in overcoming in that the secondary figure, though executed in a perfectly craftsman-like manner, was not necessarily required and in connection to the restlessly swaying staffage of figures, bold perspectival foreshortenings and strong twists, was even detrimental to the picture's overall effect.

Even though Paolo did not make *varietà* part of his artistic program until a later date, the scene with many figures, bold shining shades of color and a marked horizontal format was nonetheless the expression of a new self-confidence. The painter's increasingly technical perfection is displayed, for example, by the *Lamentation over the Dead Christ* (ill. 12), last dated to about 1547; it is an early masterpiece which is extraordinarily delicate in terms of color, and today it is one of the treasures of the Museo Castelvecchio in Verona.

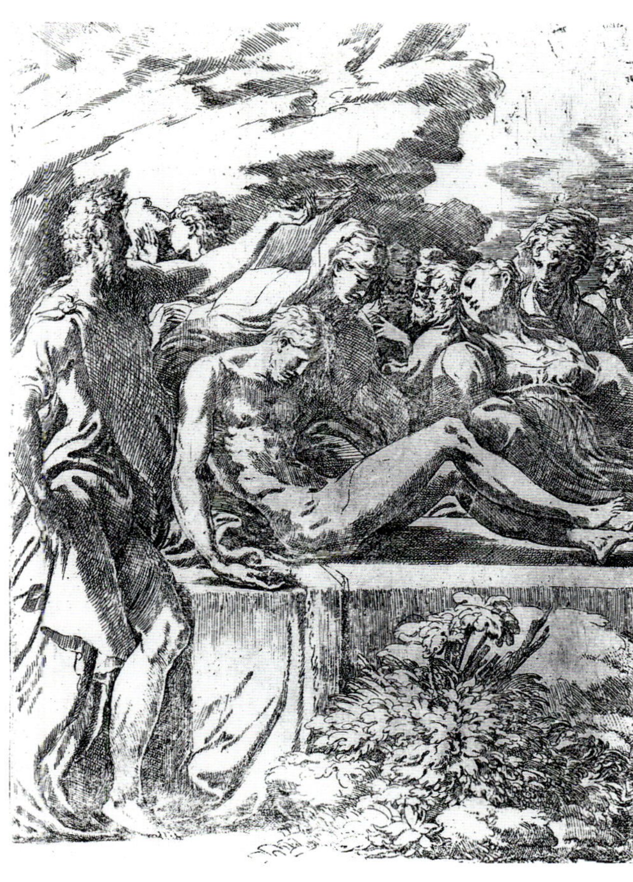

11 (left) Francesco Parmigianino
The Deposition
Etching (2nd condition), 33.1 x 24 cm
Graphische Sammlung Albertina, Vienna

Parmigianino's composition survives in several printing conditions. The second version shown here is the result of a reworking in his own hand. Characteristic of Veronese's free treatment of motifs and stylistic mannerisms is the way he adapts the gesture of Parmigianino's Joseph of Arimathaea and the emotional intensity of individual figures.

12 (below) *Lamentation over the Dead Christ*, c. 1547
Oil on canvas, 76 x 117 cm
Museo Civico di Castelvecchio, Verona

The unusual feature of the iconography is that it is not Joseph of Arimathaea that holds the body of Christ as would be customary, but Nicodemus, identifiable because he is younger, has a dark beard and wears turban-style headgear. His hands are covered to avoid direct physical contact. Joseph of Arimathaea on the other hand appears in the background as an old man with a white beard and hair in a well-chosen three-quarters profile. His features are undoubtedly presented as a portrait so that one could imagine him as a prominent member of the monastic community, perhaps even the patron who commissioned the devotional picture.
In view of the sketch-like, summary execution of some parts of this very well-preserved picture, it has been assumed that it was a preparatory oil sketch for a larger-format painting that was never carried out. An argument against this is the masterly, delicate palette of reds, yellows, greens and blues providing delightful contrasts with violet and pink.

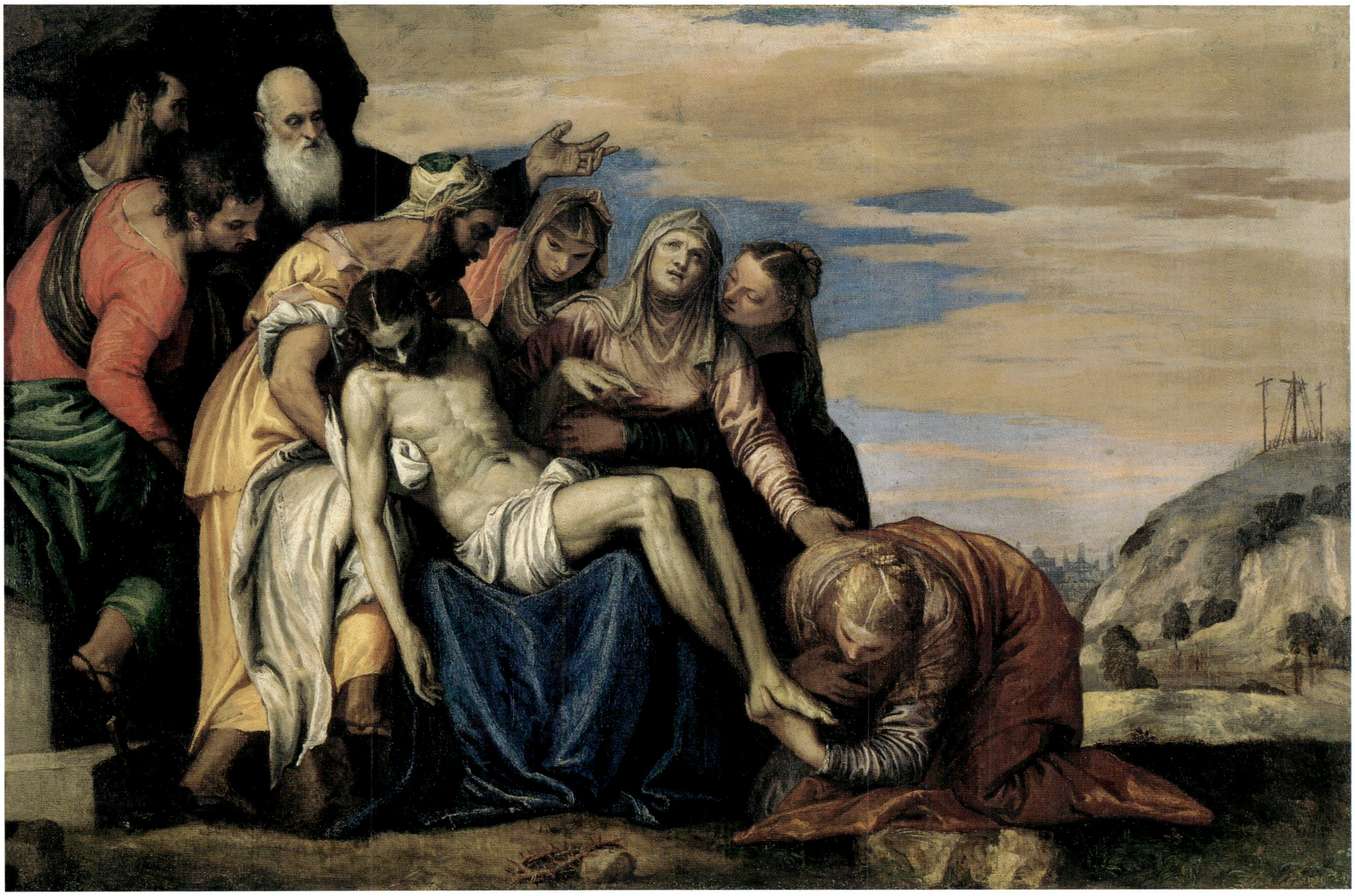

13 *Mystic Marriage of St. Catherine*, c. 1547
Oil on canvas, 57.6 x 91.4 cm
Loan of the Barker Welfare Foundation, Yale University Art Gallery, New Haven

This picture shows the Holy Family with St. Catherine of Alexandria and St. Anne. According to a 9th-century legend, St. Catherine was a princess converted to Christianity by a hermit. The child Jesus appeared to her later in a dream and handed her a ring as a sign of her engagement. Under the worried gaze of Joseph, the saint – dressed as an elegant Venetian woman – turns lovingly towards the child sitting in his mother's lap, who reacts with excited pleasure. The figure of St. Anne can be considered a response to the corresponding figure in the *Madonna della Perla* (ill. 15) by Raphael, which was much esteemed by contemporaries. According to his biographer Ridolfi, the young Veronese had made a prolonged study of the painting by Raphael, which was kept at the time in the Palazzo Canossa in Verona, and had copied it.

The painting originally came from the sacristy of the church of Santa Maria delle Grazie in Verona, which was dissolved in 1809 and no longer survives, and it was possibly commissioned by Lorenzo Busti da Zevio, the prior of the Jeronymite monastery between 1542 and 1548. The action is organized around a strict diagonal composition. Its center is formed by the corpse of Christ, resting in his mother's lap. In a manner similar to the *Conversion of Mary Magdalene* (ill. 10), Paolo moved the figures very close to the front edge of the picture and once again heeded the command to include *varietà*, but the narrative style has changed in accordance with the theme. The breadth of detail and drama of the *Conversion of Mary Magdalene* has given way to an epic presentational manner; and the desire to harmoniously use carefully matching postures and gestures to relate the figures taking part in the events to each other makes it possible to comprehend characteristics which impressively reveal the painter's creative imagination. The width of dominating effects ranges from the impotent Mary's gesture, gazing up to heaven for consolation, via the concerned expressions of the women who are facing her in silent sympathy, to the gesture of the aged councilor Joseph of Arimathea, which quite evidently derives from an idea of Parmigianino's in his *Entombment* (ill. 11). The latter is pointing pensively towards the place of execution located on a hill outside the city. The figure of Nicodemus in the golden-yellow shimmering garment shows how skilled and inventive the young Paolo already was in taking up and varying his own inventions. Upon closer observation, the relationship between the turban-wearing figure and the somewhat coarse bearded figure who holds the observer's attention in the *Conversion of Mary Magdalene* (ill. 10) becomes clear. It almost appears as if the painter, even if he did not use the very same living model, still used one of his own clay models, mentioned by Ridolfi, that enabled him to study complicated body positions and the effects of light and shade. Other slightly altered motifs, which were by no means new at the time the *Lamentation* (ill. 12) was created, indeed had already been tried out, were cited. For instance, the St. John and the figure in strict profile assigned to him appear as a further development of an ensemble of figures familiar from the *bozzetto* of the *Raising of the Daughter of Jairus* (ill. 7), which Paolo used to lead the observer into the right side of the composition.

Such repetitions and paraphrases were, of course, by no means unusual in the works of other contemporary painters. Apart from the necessity to pick up on one's own ideas and develop them logically, the inclinations of the clients and their esteem of particular figures and pictorial inventions may have played a part. Thus a

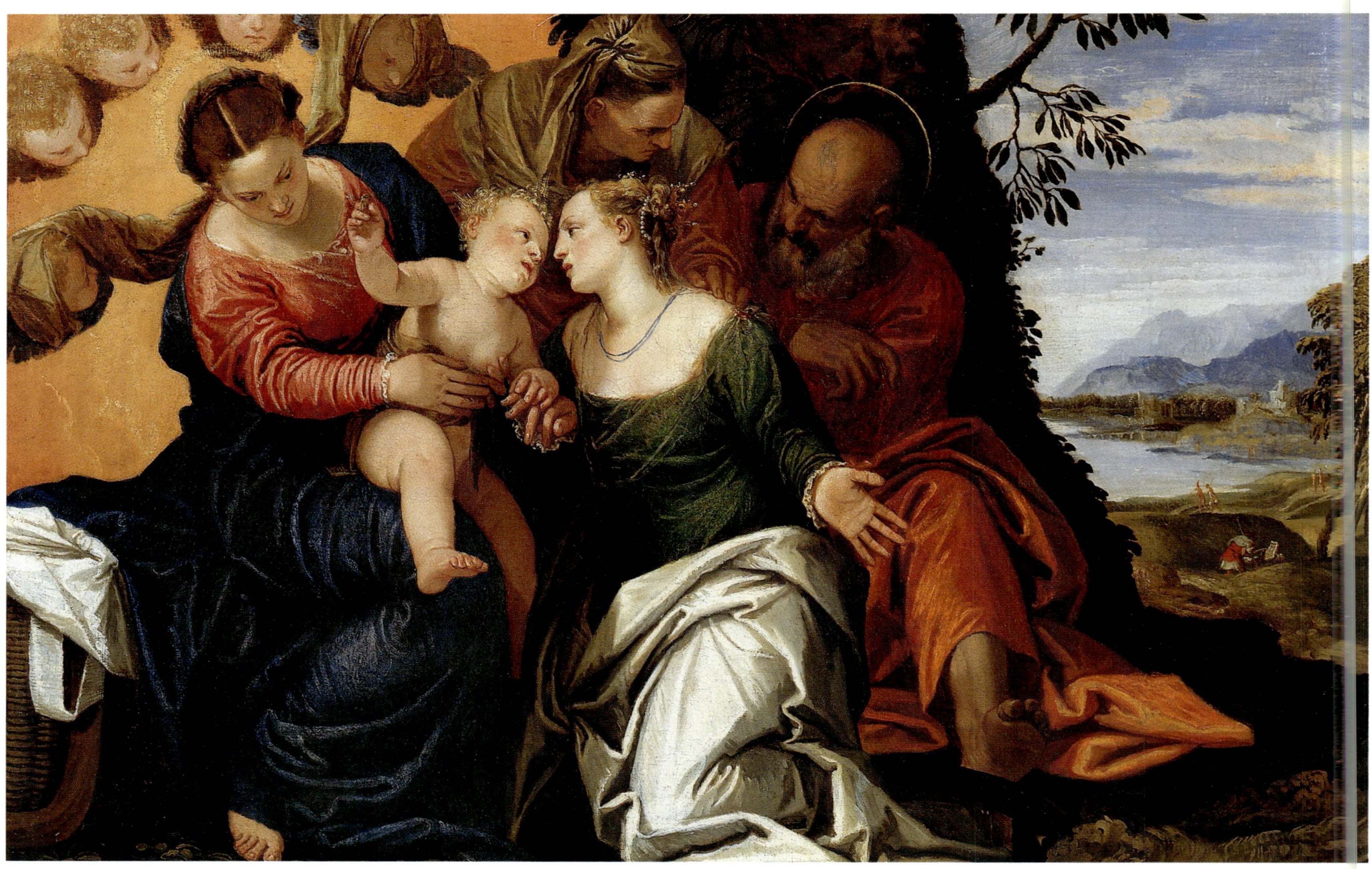

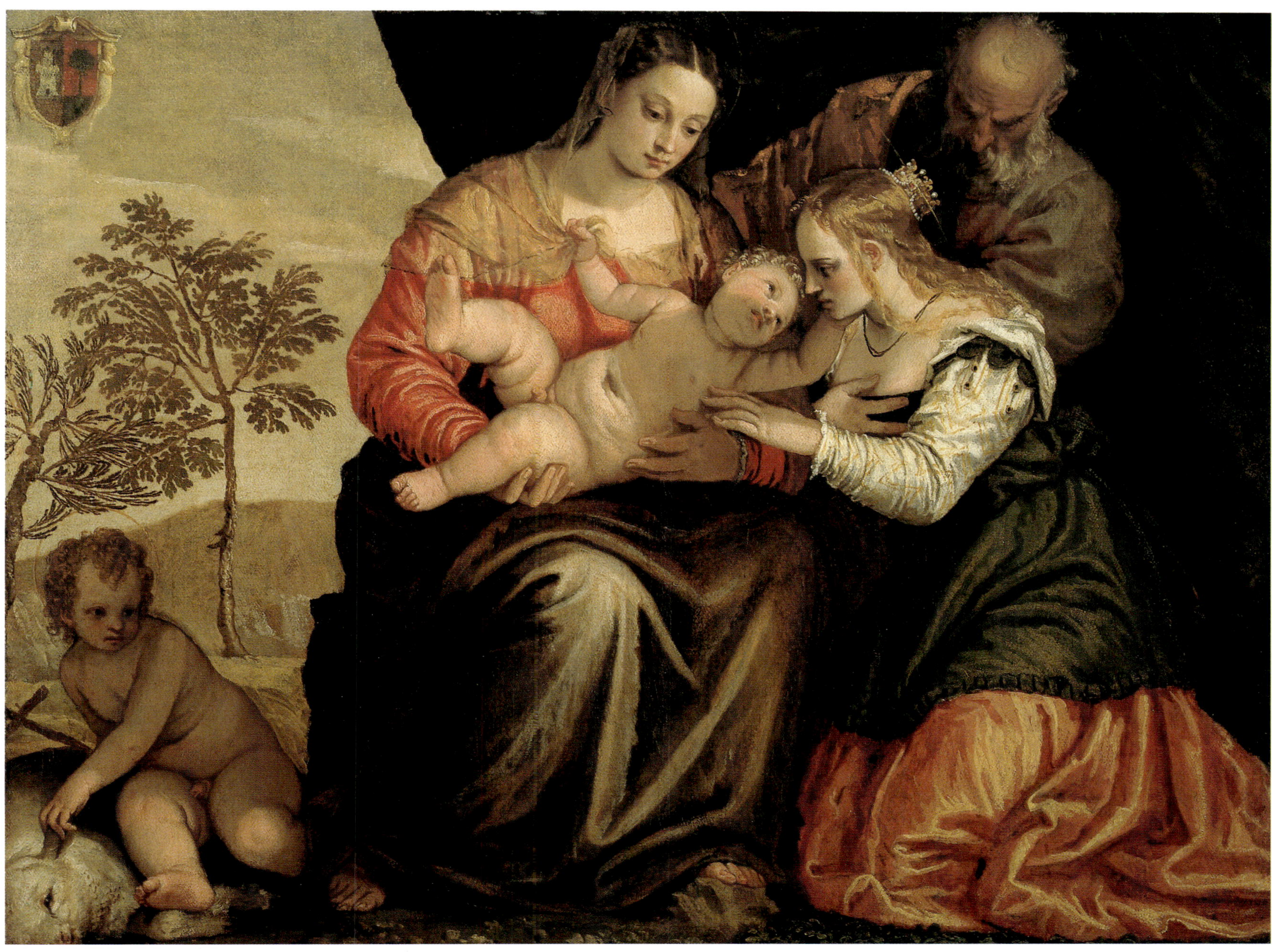

series of depictions of the Holy Family produced during the 1540s document the growing popularity of a succinct pictorial scheme which was clearly particularly valued amongst the circles of local clients, one which Paolo, by referring to Parmigianino and Raphael, was able to modify skillfully. The origins and context of creation of the devotional pictures, some of which are now in the museums of Amsterdam and St. Petersburg, are, almost without exception, unknown. This is also true of the *Mystic Marriage of St. Catherine* (ill. 13) in New Haven, whose provenance can only be traced back to 1767, at which point the painting was in the Liechtenstein Collection in Vienna. Nonetheless, it is informative to compare the work with the depiction of the same theme attributed to Giovanni Battista Zelotti (c. 1526–1578), now in Tokyo (ill. 14). It provides clues that the painting in the Yale University Art Gallery must have been created around or shortly before 1547. In the pine tree and tower that are drawn on an escutcheon, the *Mystic Marriage of St. Catherine* (ill. 14) depicts the combined coats of arms of the Pindemonte and Della Torre families, both highly respected in Verona. Both coats of arms are, as Diana Gisolfi has demonstrated, part of the furnishings of the corresponding family chapels in the churches of San Anastasia and San Fermo Maggiore in Verona. While the theme of the picture already suggests that this is a work produced on the occasion of a marriage, it is possible that Giambattista Pindemonte, who married Anna della Torre in 1547, is the donor. It is beyond question that Zelotti's work owed quite a lot to Veronese's painting. Born in about 1526 and, like Paolo, trained in Badile's workshop, here Zelotti reacted without reserve and rather conventionally to the picture created by his younger colleague who was just beginning to be successful.

Indeed our sketchy knowledge about Paolo's clients in Verona makes it difficult to judge his artistic beginnings. Collections of antiques, natural history specimens and paintings increased the fame of well-known

14 Giovanni Battista Zelotti
Mystic Marriage of St. Catherine, 1547
Oil on canvas, 84 x 100 cm
National Museum of Western Art, Tokyo

On the basis of the coat of arms (top left), the picture can be linked to the wedding of Anna della Torre and Giambattista Pindemonte in Verona in 1547. There are problems with the state of conservation of the picture. Paint has rubbed off in places, and corrections and overpaintings by other hands make it difficult to judge the original work. X-rays of the right-hand side revealed another figure in the curtain area that was possibly lost during an earlier restoration. In the past, the painting was often attributed to the young Veronese. It is however an exemplary documentation of the mutual links between him and a group of contemporary Verona-based painters that included not only Zelotti but also Battista dell Angelo del Moro, Paolo Farinati and Domenico Brusasorzi.

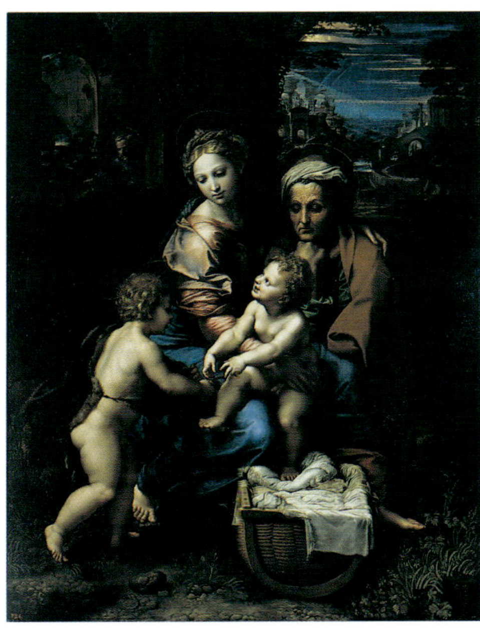

15 Raphael and workshop
The Holy Family with St. Anne and the infant John the Baptist (Madonna della Perla), c. 1518/19
Oil on canvas, 144 x 115 cm
Museo del Prado, Madrid

Acclaimed by Vasari and later authors as a work by Raphael himself but occasionally attributed by modern critics to his most gifted pupil Giulio Romano (1499–1546), the painting was presumably acquired during a stay in Rome and then housed in the Palazzo Canossa built by Michele Sanmicheli. There it was engraved by Battista dell'Angelo del Moro and copied by Veronese. A further copy was made by the contemporary Veronese painter Orlando Flacco at the request of Count Bevilacqua. Despite the condition that the famous painting should not be disposed of, Conte Galeazzo Canossa sold it in 1604 to the Duke of Mantua, Vincenzo Gonzaga. Between 1627/28, it subsequently passed from the collection of Carlo Gonzaga to that of Charles I of England, and following his execution it was sold to the Spanish ambassador in London Don Alonso de Cardenas acting on behalf of Philip IV, who used to describe the painting as his "pearl".

16 (opposite)
Isabella Guerrieri Gonzaga Canossa, c. 1547/48
Oil on canvas, 115 x 95 cm
Musée du Louvre, Paris

Long recorded as the portrait of an unknown woman, in 1648 the painting was in the possession of the Bevilacqua, who were related to the Canossa. It is one of the earliest of a series of patrician portraits, and documents the growing reputation of the young Veronese, who was the protégé of the Verona-based architect Michele Sanmicheli. Isabella became a widow in 1541. Her appearance and conspicuously plain dress testify to her position in life, and express the young painter's ability to empathize with his subject.

families at an early point. Painters sponsored by members of the Bevilacqua, Del Bene, Canossa, Della Torre, Nichesola, Giuliari, Pellegrini, Ridolfi and Sagramosa families would have included the young Paolo, alongside Paolo Farinati, Battista dell'Angelo del Moro and Domenico Brusasorzi. At an early age he evidently delivered a contribution to the genre of façade painting, so valued in Verona. In 1648 Carlo Ridolfi still knew of figural depictions in the Via Strova, but neither these works nor the copy made in the 1540s of the so-called *Madonna della Perla* (ill. 15) by Raphael, which in the 16th century was one of the Palazzo Canossa's treasures, have survived. And while it is furthermore extremely doubtful whether in about 1543/44, in other words when he was barely 15, Paolo indeed carried out various works in the demanding medium of fresco painting in the Sala di Ganimede and the Sala di Mosè in this palace, it is likely that at the latest by the time he had studied and copied the painting acclaimed by Vasari, he had already become acquainted with the person who was to become a friend and influential sponsor of Paolo's: Michele Sanmicheli. His acquaintance with Michele Sanmicheli and members of the Canossa family opened up new opportunities to the young Paolo and fundamentally altered the situation of the ambitious painter who until then had been employed in producing altar and devotional paintings in Verona.

There is some certainty that the earliest surviving, if not the very first portrait of the painter, owes its existence to a commission from *Isabella Guerrieri Gonzaga Canossa* (ill. 16). Born into a noble house closely connected to the Mantuan court, she was married to Conte Galeazzo Canossa, the nephew (died in 1541) of the Lodovico who presumably bought Raphael's *Madonna della Perla* (ill. 15) in Rome and shortly before his death commissioned Sanmicheli to build the city palace. The young woman's pose and clothing appear unusual. She appears self-confidently before the observer in front of an undecorated dark wall of cloth. Dressed in a simple white shirt and a black dress fastened in front of her bosom, Isabella appears to want to avoid any superficial display. Even the gold chains are displayed unpretentiously. She is evidently accompanied by one of her sons, a curly-haired boy who is attempting to secure a bone from the attentions of the approaching, all too curious dog. Sergio Marinelli, who succeeded in liberating the portrait from its state of anonymity with near-criminological detection skills, has interpreted the bone and the greyhound's head as an emblematic allusion to the coat of arms of the Canossa, and Isabella's appearance as a reference to her social status as a widow. Paolo used conspicuously muted colors reminiscent of the palette of his former teacher Badile in this simple portrait, which has little official character about it and was probably created in about 1547. Softly modeled, the face of the depicted woman also brings to mind depictions of the Madonna which was a favored subject for the painter in his early altar and devotional pictures. This portrait quite evidently corresponded to the requirements of his young client. From 1541, she self-confidently administered the family's estates and, to contemporary observers of her portrait, would have recommended herself as a responsible mother and widow who avoided excessive self-ostentation.

Paolo was able to pick up on this first experience as a portrait painter in his portraits of *Livia da Porto Thiene and her Daughter Porzia* (ill. 17) and *Iseppo and Adriano da Porto* (ill. 19). The latter, one of the most wealthy and influential figures in Vicenza, had, in about 1551/52, commissioned various stucco workers and painters from Verona to carry out the decoration of his town palace, which was then under construction. Large parts of these furnishings were lost during the course of the 18th and 19th centuries, including the works of the "excellent painter Paolo Veronese". These were carried out in unidentified rooms which Andrea Palladio (1508–1580), the famous architect of the palazzo on the Via San Gaetano, specifically emphasized in his *Quattro libri dell'architettura* (Venice, 1570) while looking back on this early work carried out in his native city. The two high-quality portraits are fairly certain to have been produced during this time. They visualize the client accompanied by his son Adriano, and his wife Livia with her daughter Porzia as full-length figures before a niche. The life-sized pairs of figures are framed on either side by slender door jambs. A preparatory portrait study showing *Iseppo and Adriano da Porto* (ill. 18) following up the drawing of the *Pala Bevilacqua* in Chatsworth, again lets Paolo appear as a drawer. In an endeavor to clarify proportions, plastic values and the effects of light and dark, he produced an ink drawing of the ensemble of figures that strongly emphasized contours. Later, in the painted version, Paolo altered the figure of the little Adriano. In terms of posture and the direction of his gaze, Iseppo's son was now more clearly related to his mother and sister, in order to achieve a unified pictorial effect.

As well as being responsible for the two portraits, Paolo also worked on the decoration of the Palazzo da Porto in Vicenza as a fresco painter. Indeed, fresco painting was a rich field of activity for the painters of Verona. In the mid-16th century, both the aristocracy of the province and the rich Venetian nobility discovered the villa, an extravagantly furnished country residence, as a distinguished architectural commission, way of life and object of prestige value. It was the recollection of the classical era, though above all economic considerations, that were significant in promoting this development, and that were also a decisive factor in the trend, from the beginning of the 1540s, for members of families rich in tradition to turn increasingly to the province, the *Terraferma,* in order to acquire huge estates there.

In 1551 the young Paolo Veronese's travels brought him to the area near Castelfranco Veneto. If Vasari is to be believed, he was, together with his assistant Giovanni Battista Zelotti, following the friendly invitation of Michele Sanmicheli, the builder of the Villa Soranza, to decorate it with frescoes. Only a few

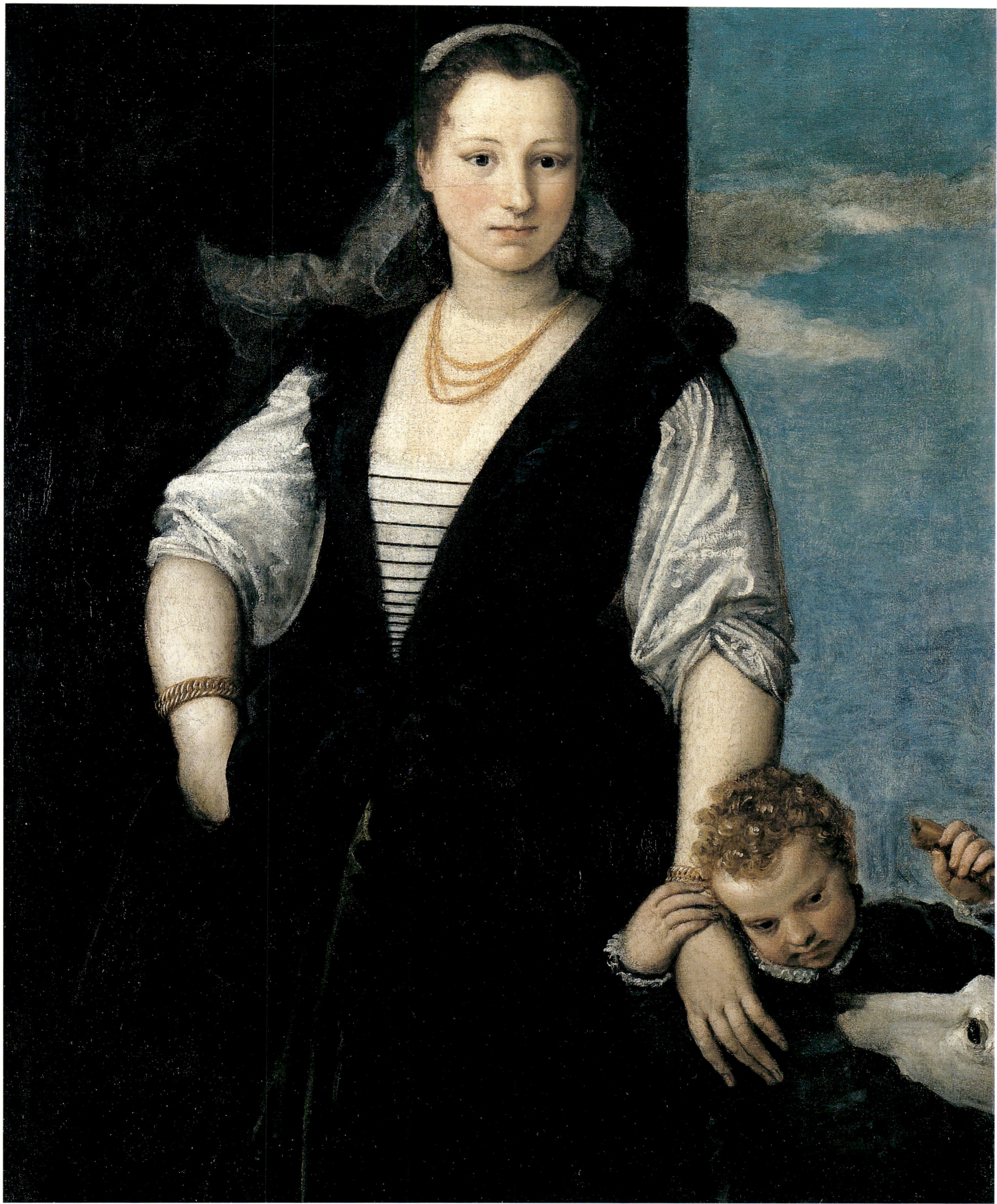

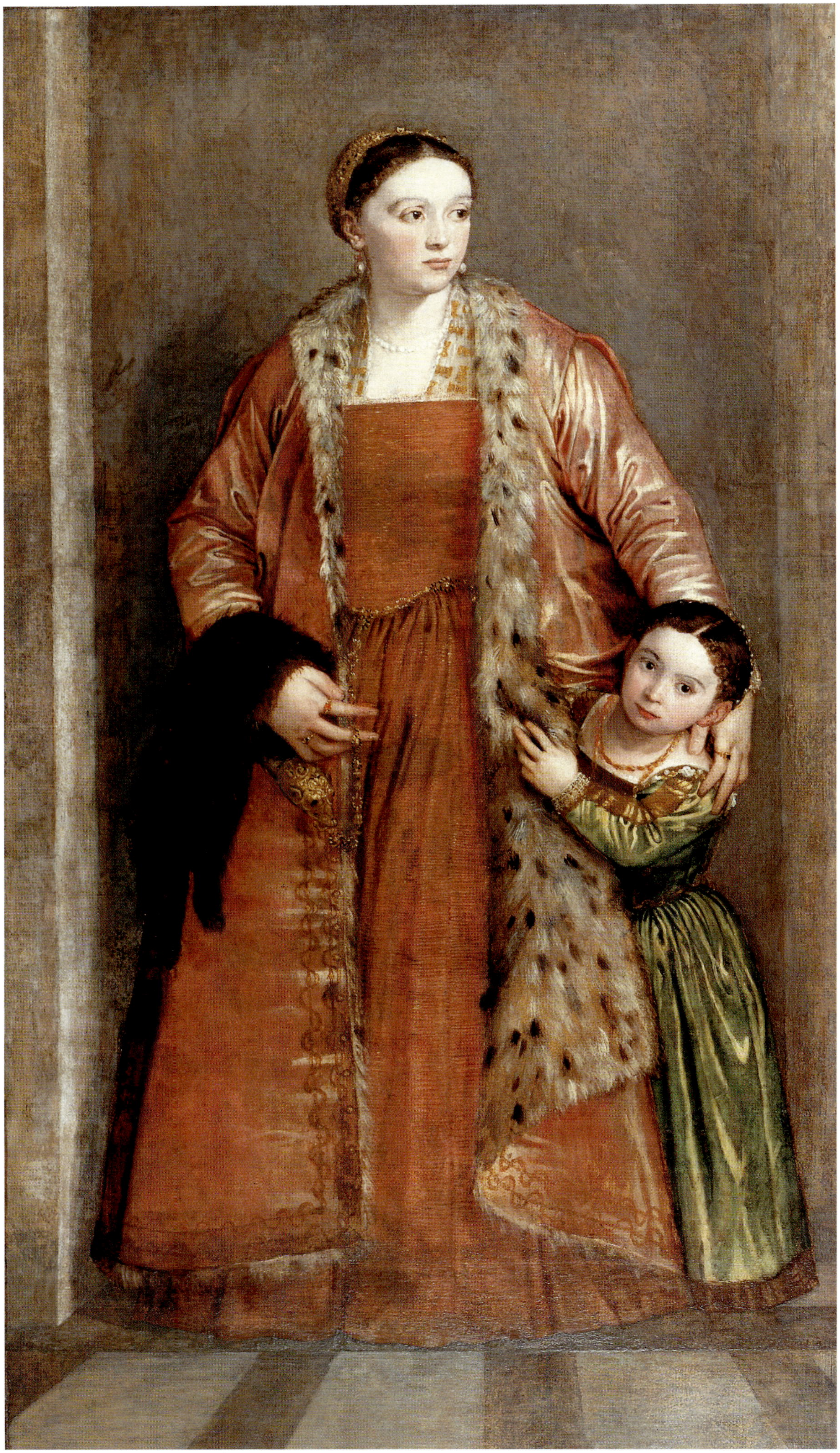

18 (below) *Iseppo and Adriano da Porto*, c. 1551
Pen and chalk on tinted paper, 34.2 x 18.1 cm
Département des arts graphiques, Musée du Louvre, Paris

This drawing documents the genesis of the Porto portrait (ill. 19) in Florence. Veronese first sketched the two figures with gray chalk, then in the next step moved on to work out and occasionally correct individual details in pen. As the sketch proceeded, he changed the posture and position of the head of the boy Adriano, in order to better match the figures in the pendant painting.

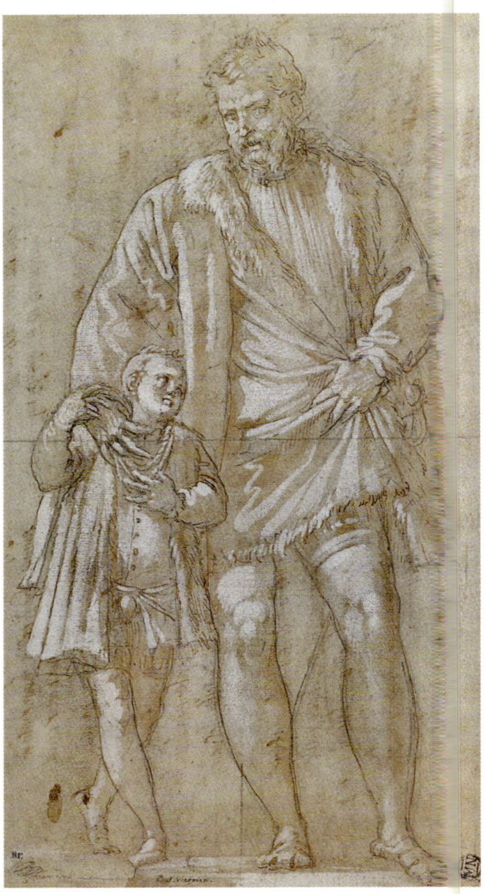

17 (left) *Livia da Porto Thiene and her Daughter Porzia*
c. 1551/52
Oil on canvas, 208 x 121 cm
Walters Art Gallery, Baltimore

19 (opposite)
Iseppo and Adriano da Porto, c. 1551/52
Oil on canvas, 207 x 137 cm
Galleria Palatina, Palazzo Pitti, Florence

With their sensitive depictions of the children, the two Da Porto portraits are among the finest creations of the young Veronese. The harmony of color and original construction of the seemingly natural poses are remarkable. By using full-length portraits, whose introduction Vasari ascribes to Titian, the painter was here trying out a type of portrait known to him not via Venice but from the Lombard painter Moretto da Brescia (1498–1554) and portraits in the style of his *Nobleman* (National Gallery, London) of 1526. Particularly charming is the painterly depiction of the exquisite materials of the robes.

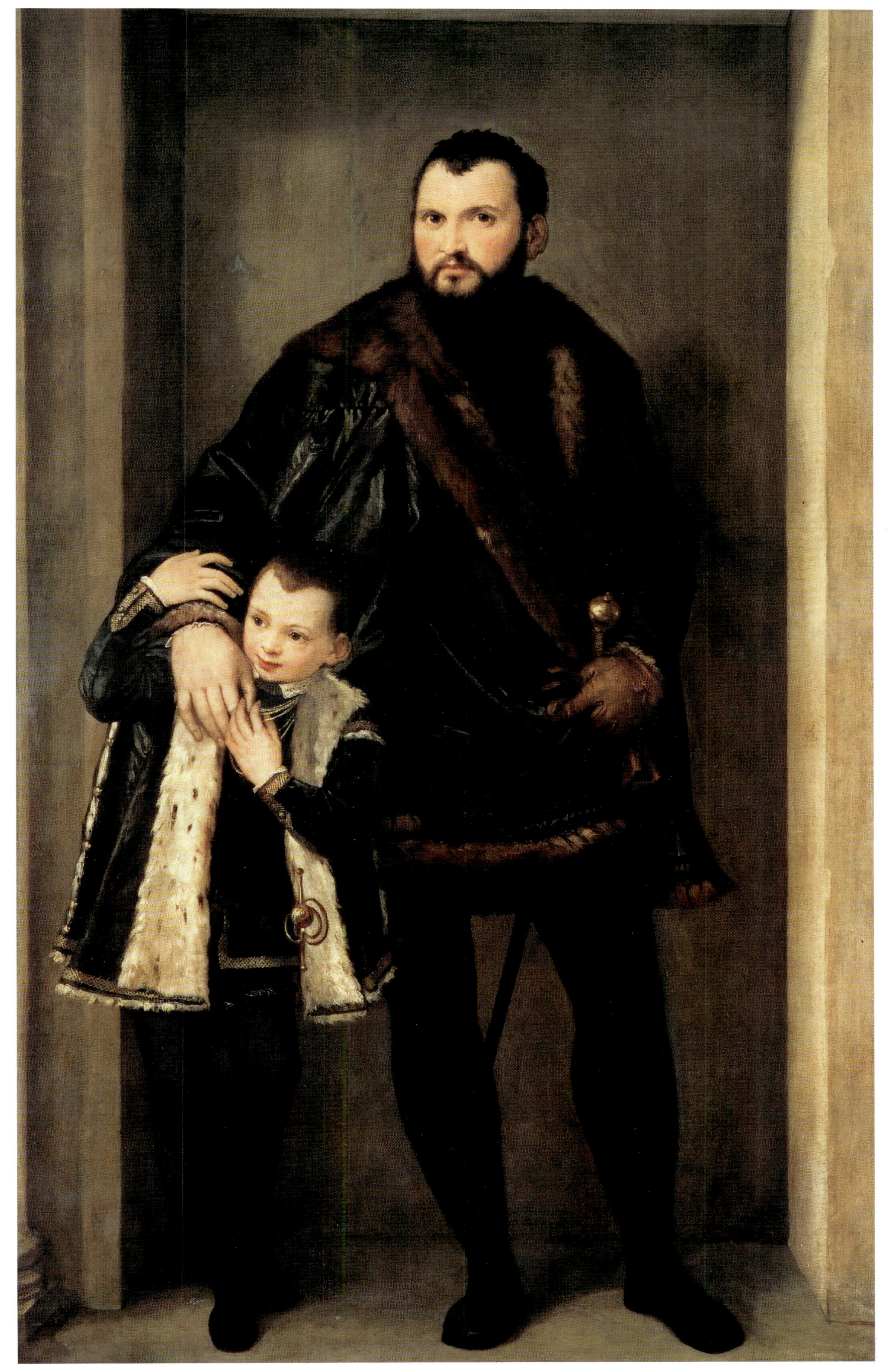

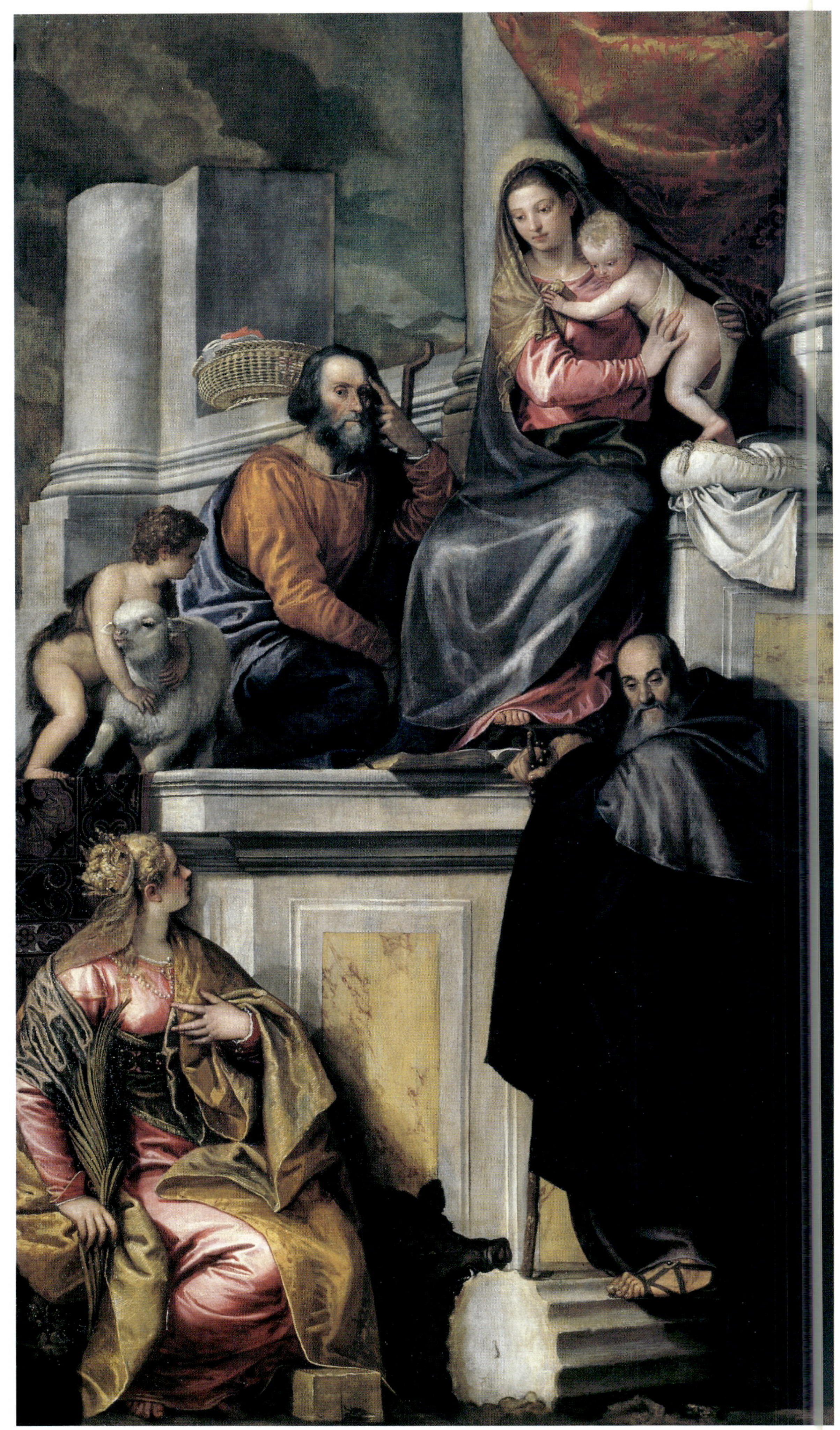

20 *The Holy Family with SS. Anthony Abbot, Catherine and the infant John the Baptist (Pala Giustinian)*, 1551
Oil on canvas, 313 x 190 cm
San Francesco della Vigna, Venice

Clearly contrasting cool colors in the service of precise, dramatically constructed forms are the main characteristics of Veronese's first altar painting for a Venetian church. Infrared reflectography recently brought to light a surprising technical finding: originally, parts of the pictorial architecture in the background of the picture were differently arranged. In an early phase, the column behind Mary was roughly in the center of the picture. As the painting proceeded, it was overpainted and moved right. Clearly not initially envisaged, therefore, was the awkward-looking pier fragment with its engaged half-column, whose relationship with the other architectural motifs produces inconsistencies of perspective. When Agostino Carracci copied the large painting around 1582 (ill. 22), one of the things that he corrected was the harsh arris at the top of the pier.

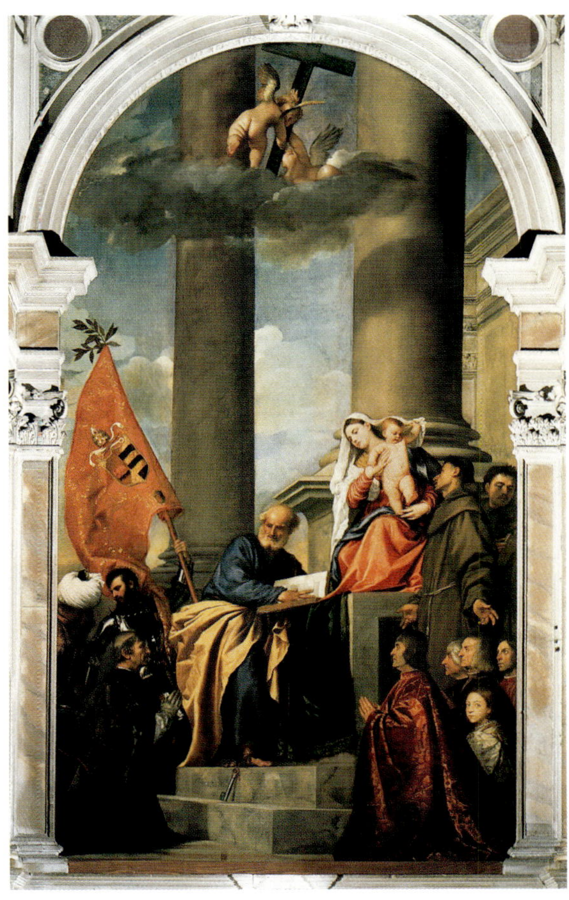

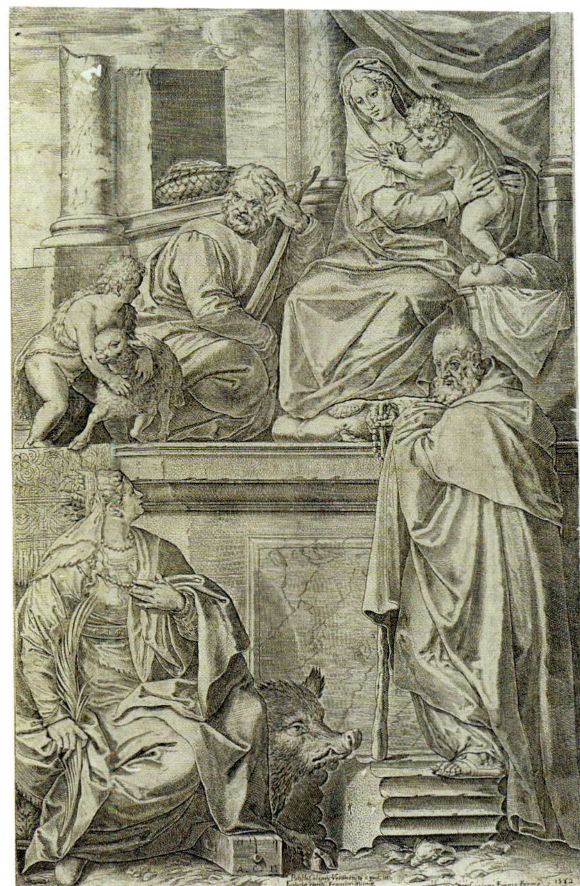

21 (far left) Titian
The Madonna of Ca' Pesaro (Pala Pesaro), 1519–1526
Oil on canvas, 385 x 270 cm
Santa Maria Gloriosa dei Frari, Venice

In commissioning this altarpiece, Jacopo da Pesaro, Bishop of Paphos in Cyprus, created a notable monument to himself and members of his family. Here, Titian deliberately dispenses with traditional formulations of the *sacra conversazione* type. The Madonna with the Child and saints is no longer incorporated in a hieratic, frontal pose such as was used for example in Giovanni Bellini's *pale*. Seen from the side and moved from the center to the right of the picture, she turns towards the donor, who kneels before her throne. This famous painting is both eloquent of Titian's endeavors to develop a new kind of altar picture and innovative in introducing the donor portrait, hitherto not customary in Venice. The depiction of Jacopo as the successful Commander of the fleet in the victory over the Turks in the Ionian Sea (1502) capitalizes on the claims of the Bishop and his family to self portrayal and representation.

22 (left) Agostino Carracci
The Holy Family with SS. Anthony Abbot, Catherine and the infant St. John, copy of Veronese, 1582
Copper engraving, 48.8 x 31.6 cm
Museo Civico Correr, Venice

The Bolognese painter and engraver Agostino Carracci visited Venice in 1582 and 1587. Like his brother Annibale, he had a very high regard for the paintings of Veronese. Following several altar paintings and devotional pictures in Venice and Padua, he made engravings that on closer inspection turn out to be critical copies. In the case of the engraving made from the Pala Giustinian (ill. 20), he made a minor correction to the actual format of the picture and other changes to the pictorial architecture. He also omitted the open book at the Madonna's feet. Particularly noticeable is the attempt to relate the figures to each other more strongly, altering the directions in which SS. Joseph and Anthony Abbot look, to attain a closed pictorial effect.

fragments of the once famous decorations, which Ridolfi described so passionately in 1648, survived the demolition of the villa in the early 19th century; they are now kept in the cathedral of Castelfranco and the art collection of the Seminario Patriarcale in Venice. At best, they suggest what progress the young painter from Verona had made when he painted walls and ceilings with allegories, mythological gods, scenes from the life of Alexander the Great and all sorts of landscapes, and created illusionistic painted extensions to rooms. There is much to support the view that, after he had completed his work in the Villa Soranza, Paolo went directly to Venice, for 1551 is also the year when he made his first official appearance as an altar painter in Venice.

The *Pala Giustinian* (ill. 20) in the church of San Francesco della Vigna was commissioned by Lorenzo (died 1553) and Antonio Giustinian (died 1565), and was probably the first stage in furnishing the newly built Franciscan church with a series of high-quality altarpieces. High dignitaries and influential figures in public life were members of the brothers' family circle. For example, they were related to the doges Andrea Gritti and Francesco Donà, to Daniele and Marcantonio Barbaro, and to the Grimanis who also owned chapels in this church. It may once again have been Michele Sanmicheli who made it possible for a painter, as yet unknown in Venice, to enter the influential circles of this patriciate, especially as the Veronese architect had already been in contact with Giovanni Cornaro in 1542 and only a few years later was commissioned by him to carry out the Palazzo Corner on the Campo San Polo. It is known that Paolo's depiction of the *Holy Family with Saints Anthony Abbot, Catherine and the young St. John*, his contribution to one of the most popular themes in Venetian painting of the Cinquecento, was closely based on Titian's *Pala Pesaro* (ill. 21) in the Frari church. But this dialogue with a famous model gave rise, not to a feeble copy, but to a creative interpretation. At first, Paolo decided not to include the donors. In this case, Titian's model was not the accepted thing and was probably not revived in Venice at a later date as such an exaggerated form of representation evidently no longer harmonized with the aristocratic rule of a more reserved form of self-portrayal. In contrast, Paolo continued the asymmetrical pyramidal composition as well as elements in the pictorial architecture which, in both cases, primarily fulfilled symbolic and narrative requirements without at the same time being clearly defined in spatial terms. Paolo also adjusted the composition to comply with specific theological interests. Adapting Titian's compositional scheme made it easier for him to place the figure of Joseph slightly above the center of the picture, in this way underlining his role as titular and patron saint of the altar. In terms of coloration, the painter from Verona also very much went his own way. He translated Titian's atmospherically dense, warm colors into cool, shining tones: pink, orange, green and violet in various shades are countered on the right side by the dark gray of the cloak belonging to St. Anthony Abbot, whose all too generous folds of cloth appear to conceal what will, at the latest, become apparent when one examines more closely the relationship between the

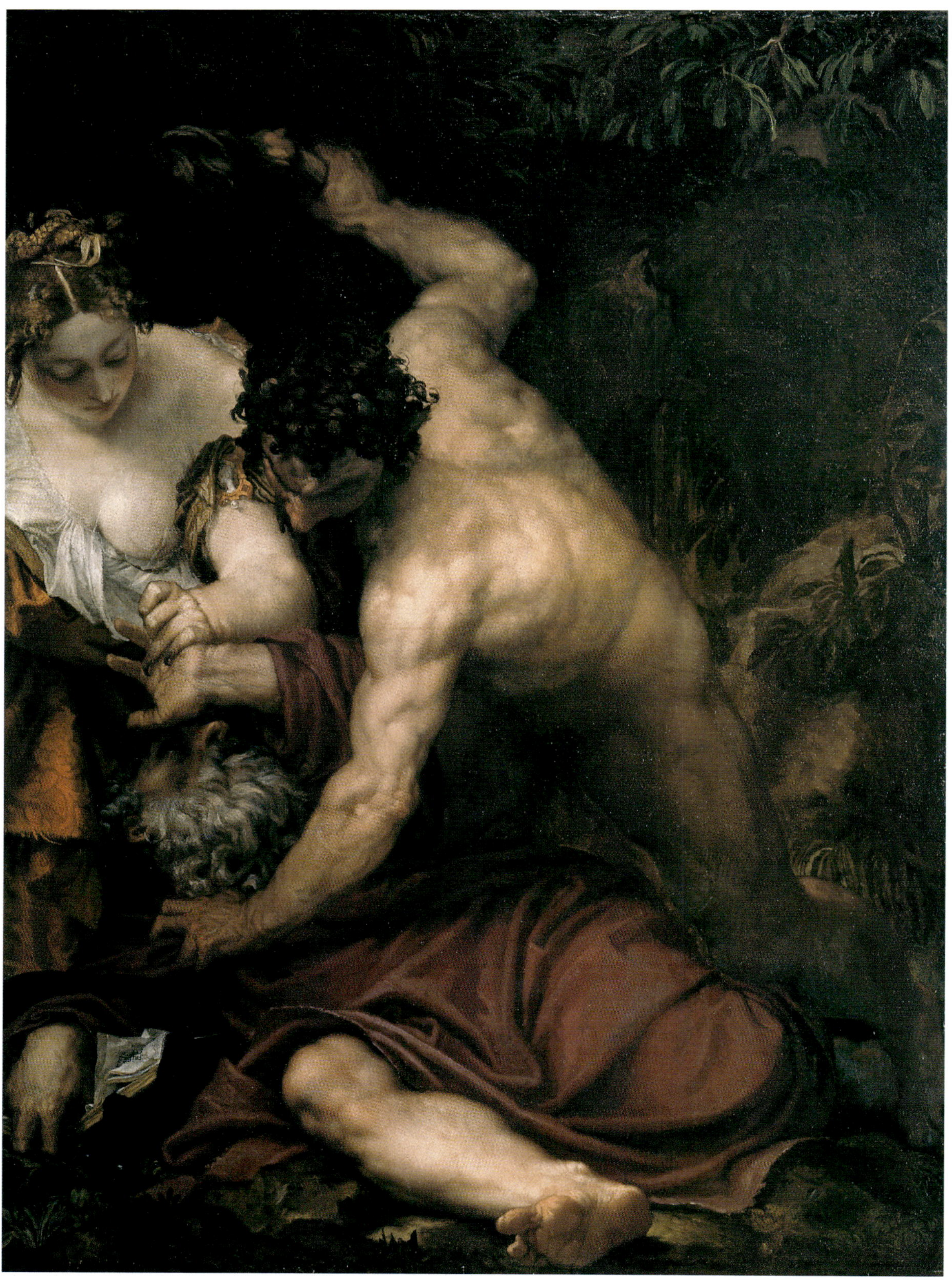

23 (left) *Temptation of St. Anthony*, 1552
Oil on canvas, 198 x 151 cm
Musée des Beaux-Arts, Caen

Painted in 1552 as a commission by Cardinal Ercole Gonzaga for the cathedral of San Pietro in Mantua, the altarpiece illustrates in almost square format an episode from the life of St. Anthony of Egypt, who from 286 to 306 retired to an isolated fort in the desert near Thebes. There he was exposed to numerous fearful temptations by the devil and his demonic accomplices, in the shape of seductive women. The artistic resources employed match the dramatic subject. Foreshortened perspectives and *torsioni*, carried off with virtuosity, abound in this pictorial confection. The atmospheric coloration and employment of warm colors are reminiscent of the paintings of Correggio, which Veronese may have seen in Mantua

24 (opposite)
Temptation of St. Anthony, 1552
Pen and chalk on paper, 41.4 x 35.6 cm
Département des arts graphiques, Musée du Louvre, Paris

As early as the 17th century, when this drawing was part of the collection of Everard Jabach in Paris, it was considered the work of Veronese. We can only guess at the purpose of the drawing. The often-voiced suspicion that it was a never implemented *modello* for the painting in Caen cannot be rejected out of hand, in view of Cardinal Gonzaga's art policies. As a strict man of the Church who had spent time in Bologna and Rome, Ercole was a passionate advocate of the reforms of the Council of Trent, and indeed from 1561 he was its presiding cardinal. It was under his patronage that Giulio Romano renovated the Cathedral of San Pietro in the manner prescribed in the Catholic reforms, and further churches and monasteries in the diocese of Mantua were to follow. It is possible that the lyrical, bucolic character of the scene did not please the Cardinal, so that Veronese was forced to drop the design and rework the religious story with a more obvious message.

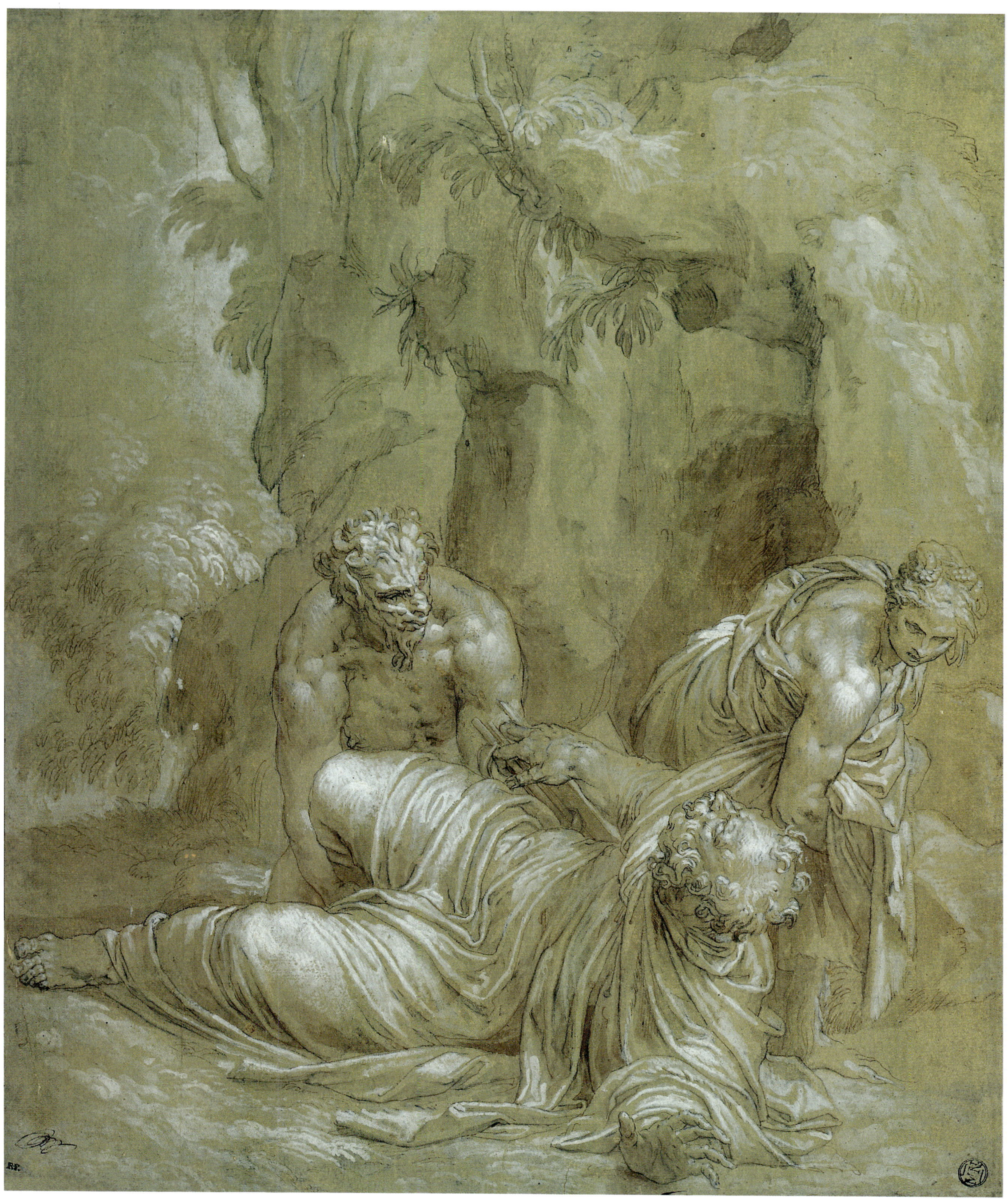

head and body. The anatomy of the figure clearly provided the painter with some difficulties. Agostino Carracci, who produced a copper engraving (ill. 22) based on the painting in 1582, appears to have taken this and other weaknesses as an opportunity to make some careful corrections, but his academic criticism cannot hide the fact that, towards the end of the 16th century, he was one of the first non-Venetian artists to recognize the special status of the *Pala Giustinian.*

Soon after Paolo had returned from Venice to Verona, Cardinal Ercole Gonzaga (1505–1563) commissioned an altarpiece from him for the cathedral of San Pietro in Mantua, whose interior had been refurbished by Giulio Romano from about 1545 onwards in the Renaissance style. Other commissions had gone out to a group of ambitious contemporary Veronese painters with comparable artistic styles, all of whom reacted in very similar ways to the challenge of the central Italian Mannerism as shaped by Raphael and Michelangelo. They were Paolo Farinati, Battista dell'Angelo del Moro, and Domenico Brusasorzi. The *Temptation of St. Anthony* (ill. 23) must already have been finished by the end of 1552, especially as the above-mentioned painters politely asked the cardinal in a letter dating from March 11, 1553 to collect and pay for their works. Paolo himself signed this letter as "Paullo spezap[re]da" (i.e. stonemason), proof indeed that he did not adopt the surnames Caliari and Veronese until his move to Venice at a later date. In 1797, at the command of Napoleon, the *Temptation of St. Anthony* was brought to Paris and shortly afterwards given to the museum in Caen; it is beyond doubt one of the main works of Veronese's early period and even filled Vasari with astonishment. He paid enthusiastic homage to this picture as the best of the four altarpieces, thus laying the foundations for the benevolent criticism of numerous successive art historians. What, therefore, is the special charm of a work in which there is no trace of the artist's encounter with Titian and Venetian painting, which had taken place just a few months previously?

Once more, it seems, Paolo was pulling out all the stops in order to find a way of expressing his admiration for the stylistic methods of artists such as Parmigianino and Correggio, and combining this with his own ideas. The result is an extravaganza in paint. Before the dark mysterious backdrop of a sparsely lighted wooded landscape, the figures, seen unusually close up, develop a wealth of complicated movements. Pale moonlight pours forth generously over the muscular back of the diabolical accomplice and the beautiful temptress seeking to beguile the aged hermit, who has fallen backwards to the ground, with her charms. Her forward-bending posture, which results in the half shade on her bare breasts, is a complicated compositional method which from the start Paolo was able to use very skillfully. Combined with the far-reaching gesture of the demon – for which there was a wealth of formal ideas in Giulio Romano's colossal fresco in the nearby Palazzo del Tè – this trick makes a further contribution to filling the dramatic subject with life.

Evidently, though a little puzzlingly, there is a relationship between this painting and the exceptionally high-quality drawing (ill. 24) in the Louvre, which in the past has on several occasions been interpreted as a *modello* for the *Temptation of St. Anthony* (ill. 23).

Once again the action is determined by three figures, though in this case the figure of the hermit is moved into the center of the scene, giving rise to the impression when looking at the painting that Paolo was using the same model and simply making a radical change in the rotation of the body. If the pictorial drawing did indeed precede the painting, it is likely that the later version sought to avoid the ambivalent nature of the depiction. In contrast to the painted version, the lyrical tenor of the scene undoubtedly makes it more difficult to read the subject. The temptress is reminiscent of a nymph, and even the demon is not immediately recognizable as such, at first appearing to be a faun. As a man of the Church and an enthusiastic champion of the Catholic reforms, and someone who, following the death of Pope Paul V (1559), was for a while considered to be a candidate with good prospects for the highest ecclesiastical office, Ercole Gonzaga may have disliked the classical and mythological undertones of the design, so that Paolo was forced to use other artistic means in order to solve the pictorial task he had been set to his client's satisfaction. It is risky to see the figure of St. Anthony and the new, lyrical mood of the scene as a reaction to Titian's once famous *St. Peter Martyr* which burnt in the church of Santi Giovanni e Paolo in Venice in 1867. Nonetheless, the drawing at least appears to make the step, albeit timidly, that would soon be taken when Paolo moved to, and settled in, Venice.

25 *Temptation of St. Anthony* (detail of ill. 23)

It is only on closer inspection that the seductive beauty in the *Temptation of St. Anthony* is recognizable as a pliant accomplice of the devil. Her talons dig deeply into the gray-haired hermit's left hand. He has fallen on the ground outside his accommodation, defenseless and desperately trying to protect his face.

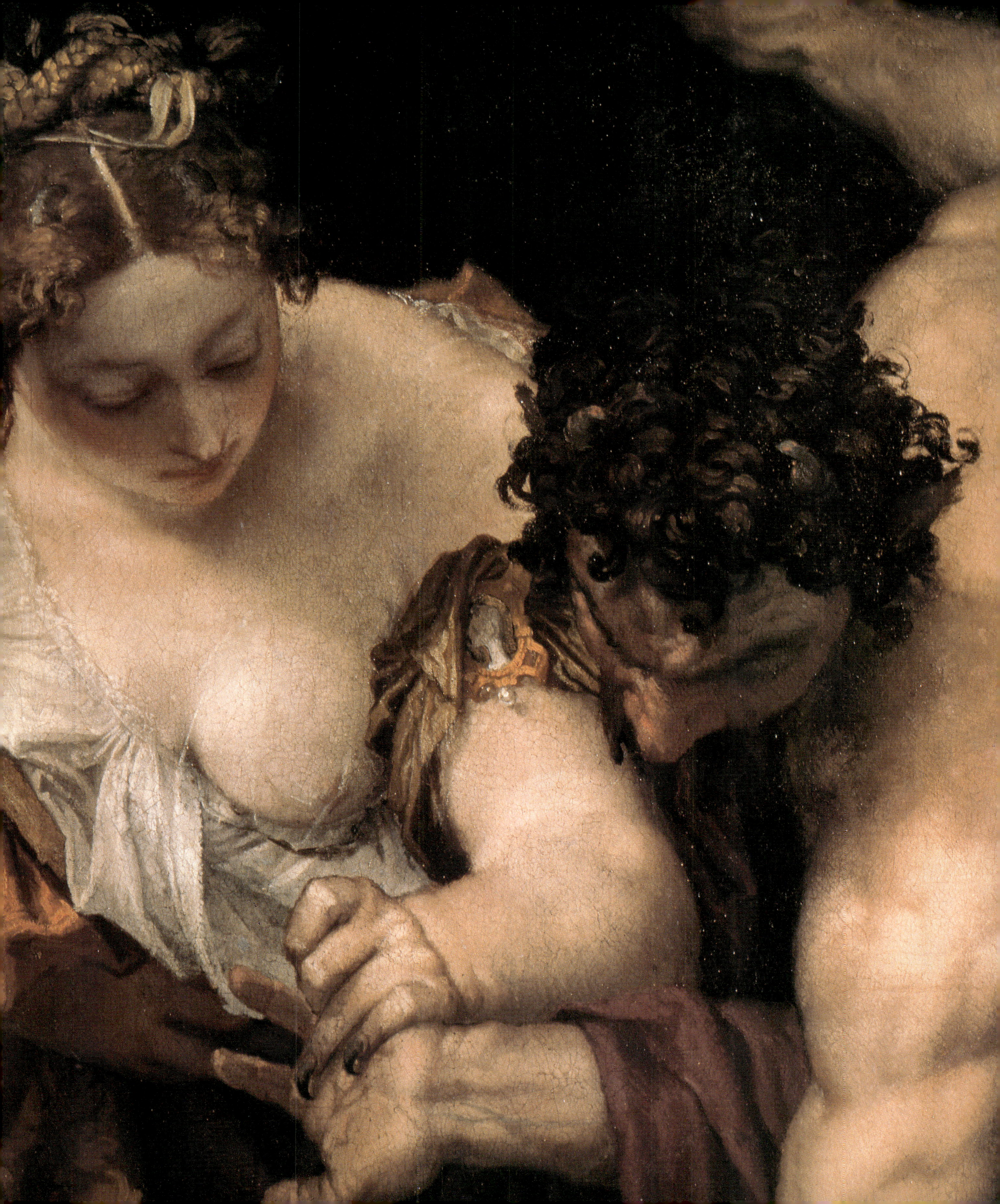

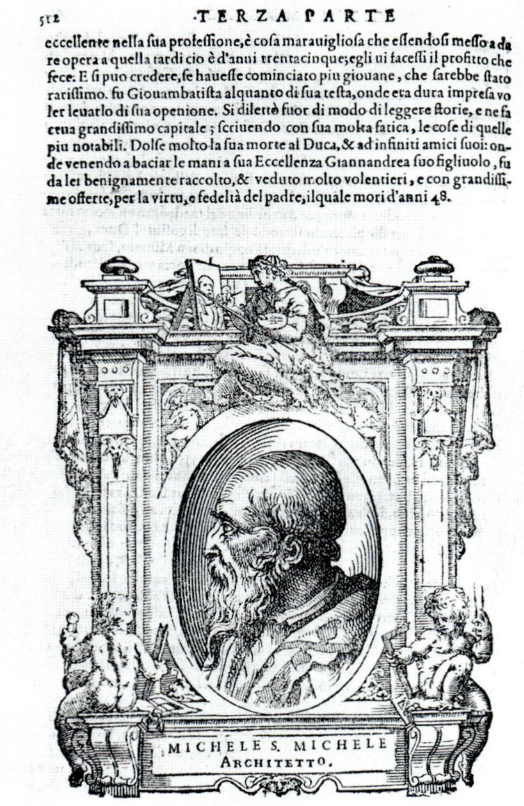

512 ·TERZA PARTE

eccellente nella ſua profeſſione, è coſa marauiglioſa che eſſendoſi meſſo a dare opera a quella tardi cio è d'anni trentacinque; egli ui faceſſi il profitto che fece. E ſi puo credere, ſe haueſſe cominciato piu giouane, che ſarebbe ſtato rariſſimo. fu Giouambatiſta alquanto di ſua teſta, onde era dura impreſa voler leuarlo di ſua openione. Si dilettò fuor di modo di leggere ſtorie, e ne faceua grandiſſimo capitale; ſcriuendo con ſua molta fatica, le coſe di quelle piu notabili. Dolſe molto la ſua morte al Duca, & ad infiniti amici ſuoi: onde venendo a baciar le mani a ſua Eccellenza Giannandrea ſuo figliuolo, fu da lei benignamente raccolto, & veduto molto volentieri, e con grandiſſime offerte, per la virtu, e fedeltà del padre, ilquale mori d'anni 48.

26 *Michele Sanmicheli*, 1568
Giorgio Vasari, *Delle vite de' più eccellenti pittori, scultori et architettori*, Florence 1568, Vol. 3, Part II, p. 512
Woodcut
Bayerische Staatsbibliothek, Munich

The head and shoulders portrait in strict profile appears in the biography of the Veronese architect and military engineer Sanmicheli (c. 1487–1559) published by Vasari in 1568. Pictura sits above the portrait oval as the personification of painting, working on a portrait on an easel. Two putti on brackets illustrate the tools and aids of the practicing architect, including the set square, lath, plumb line and chisel. The portrait of the bald architect matches a portrait dating from around 1550 (Conti Giuliari Collection, Verona) finally attributed to the Veronese painter Paolo Farinati.

"Verona, also called Theodoric's Berne, is one of the oldest, noblest, most beautiful and charming places in Lombardy, completely fortified and larger than Brescia, situated on a fertile plain and split into two halves by the Adige. Apart from the most beautiful buildings and magnificent palaces, which the city is full of, it also has pretty alleys and streets, also many and large squares [...]. The many antiquities that can still be seen in the city give a good impression that this city was not held in low esteem in classical times, but was powerful and famous."

[freely translated excerpt from *Eine Gesandtschaftsreise junger Zürcher nach Venedig* (An Embassy of Young Men from Zurich to Venice), 1608]

Verona's antiquities had captivated visitors for centuries. Originally an Etruscan settlement, then settled by the Gallic Veneti, the city on the banks of the Adige became a Roman colony in 89 B.C. Due to its location on an intersection of several important long-distance trade routes, the Via Postumia, Via Galliena and Via Claudia Augusta, it not only developed into an important trade center but also became one of the more strategically significant centers of government in upper Italy. Numerous classical monuments, including the huge amphitheater, the third largest layout of its kind in all Italy which the two Swiss ambassadors quoted above confirmed as having a capacity of about 23,000 people, the Porta dei Borsari, and the Arco dei Gavi, falsely attributed to the classical architect Vitruvius (1st century B.C.) during the Renaissance, still testify today to the honorable past of the metropolis. Until the early 12th century, the city was held by various rulers. A longer period of stability was provided from 1277 to 1387 by the rule of the Scaligeri dynasty, which had gained the upper hand in struggles within the city. Under their rule, the medieval municipal area grew considerably. In addition, San Fermo Maggiore, Santa Maria della Scala and Santa Anastasia were important church buildings that were either renovated or rebuilt, and the imposing Castelvecchio, now used as the city museum and built at the head of the Adige loop between 1354 and 1356 by Prince Cangrande II, was the last residence of the Della Scala. They were succeeded by the Visconti. For their part, they continued developing the city as a military base, but had to concede rule to the Republic of Venice in 1405. From then on, Verona belonged to the Venetians, whose rule lasted until 1796 and was only interrupted for a short period between 1509 and 1517, when the Republic was at war with the League of Cambrai.

When the architect Michele Sanmicheli returned to his native city during the winter of 1526/27, the political situation had already eased. The troops of Emperor Maximilian I (1459–1519) who had attempted to stop Venice's expansion on the mainland, had withdrawn. The Venetians in turn immediately took extensive action in order to secure the city, which in 1502 already had about 40,000 inhabitants, by strengthening the defenses. The experience that Sanmicheli had gained in Rome in the circle of the architect Bramante (c. 1444–1514), in Orvieto as the cathedral architect and as a military engineer meant that the architect, so respected by Vasari (ill. 26), was considered an expert ideal for this task. From then on, working for the Serenissima, he showed great expertise in directing the building of, amongst others, military bastions on Corfu, in Legnano, Venice and Verona itself, where the Porta Nuova, constructed between 1531 and 1541, was a powerful rusticated city gate which, due to its being the first example of a fully executed Doric order of columns as inspired by classical Roman gateways, was able to meet both aesthetic and military requirements. Sanmicheli also used rusticated ashlar in the Porta Palio, constructed in about 1547. On the side facing onto the fields, the generous façade forms a representative portico structured by fluted three quarter columns arranged in pairs. A characteristic aspect of the architect's work is the frequently observed combination of generous strict forms with small decorational elements.

Sanmicheli also made a name for himself in Verona as a church architect. As early as 1527, a sensation was caused by the Cappella Pellegrini, donated by Margherita Pellegrini. Conceived in imitation of the Roman Pantheon and the ideas of Bramante, the light central plan building connected to the church of San Bernardino is captivating due to its architectural structure, which is full of detail yet still clear. Further important stages are marked by the choir stalls in the cathedral, arranged in a semicircle, the west façade of the church of Santa Maria in Organo, and the dome and belfry of the church of San Giorgio in Braida. While the latter are prominent highlights in the city view of Verona, the church of Madonna di Campagna started in 1559 outside the city gates is one of the architect's main works. It was left to his student Bernardino Brugnoli to complete this church.

Soon after his arrival in Verona, Sanmicheli also carried out a series of important town palaces. In about 1530 he came into contact with Count Lodovico Canossa (1475–1532), one of the most influential figures in the city. Lodovico had regularly visited Rome as a diplomat to the Papal court of Leo X (1475–1521), and was also related to the Gonzaga and the Castiglione in Mantua. In Rome, circa 1518/19, he had bought Raphael's *Madonna della Perla* (ill. 15); as a collector in the Roman mold, his actual interest was in medallions and sculptures. It was for him that Sanmicheli, from 1530, worked on the *Palazzo Canossa* (ill. 27) on the River Adige, the extended version of which was not completed until 1667. The two-story façade is largely based on Bramante's Palazzo Caprini in Rome, but its detailed structure tends towards Mannerism. It may well have been Giulio Romano's (1499–1546) well-fortified Palazzo de Tè in neighboring Mantua that was the force behind the tall ground floor decorated with rusticated bands of varying widths. In contrast to the copper engraving in Valesi's publication, composite coupled pilasters structure the upper story of the magnificent building, and at the beginning of the 1540s Battista dell'Angelo del Moro played a leading role as a fresco painter in decorating the interior. Before 1534, Sanmicheli tackled the renovation of the Palazzo Bevilacqua (ill. 28). The main feature of the façade, which once again was composed to create a strong three-dimensional effect, is the harmonious balance of the ground floor and *piano nobile*, in which strong horizontal accents are created both by the gallery separating the stories, and the powerfully protruding cornice which forms the upper conclusion to the two-story façade. The lavish façade ornamentation – the genius of which is expressed in the spandrels of the large windows, lions' heads and grotesque figures – as well as the alternating triangular and segmental pediments, and the triumphal arch motif borrowed from the neighboring Porta dei Borsari, all testify to the vivid interest in classical forms of decoration and architecture.

Both palaces, which were to be followed by others in Verona and Venice, not only contributed to an improvement on the Via Postumia, now the Corso Cavour, leading up to the Porta Palio, but also formed a delightful counterweight to the painted façades created by Girolamo dai Libri, Giovanni Maria Falconetto and other important and less-important native painters, which had once made a major contribution to the special appearance of one of the most beautiful cities of the Venetian mainland.

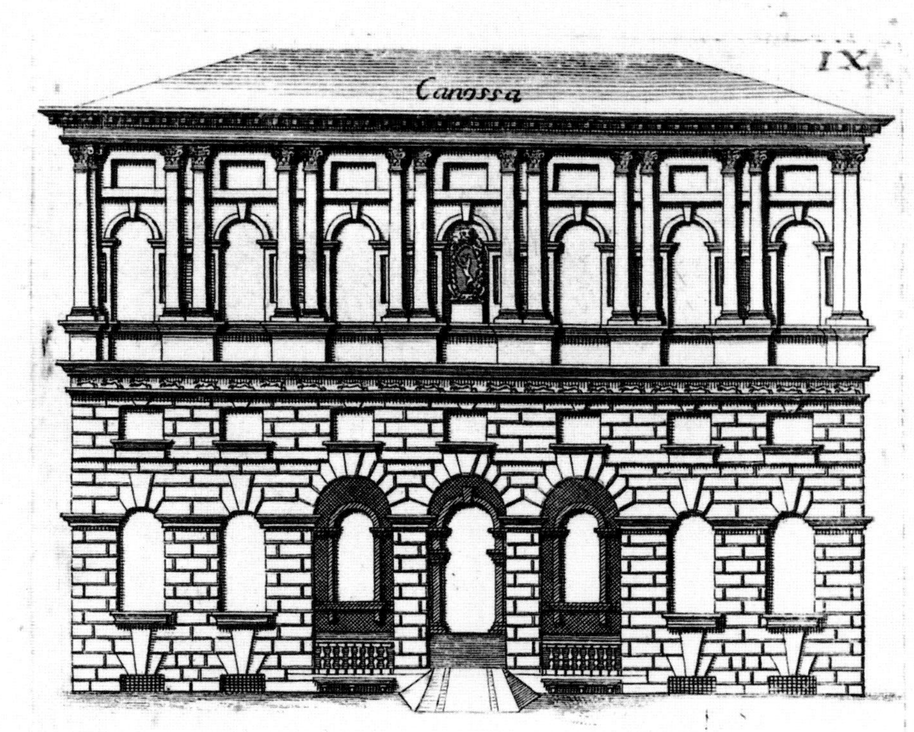

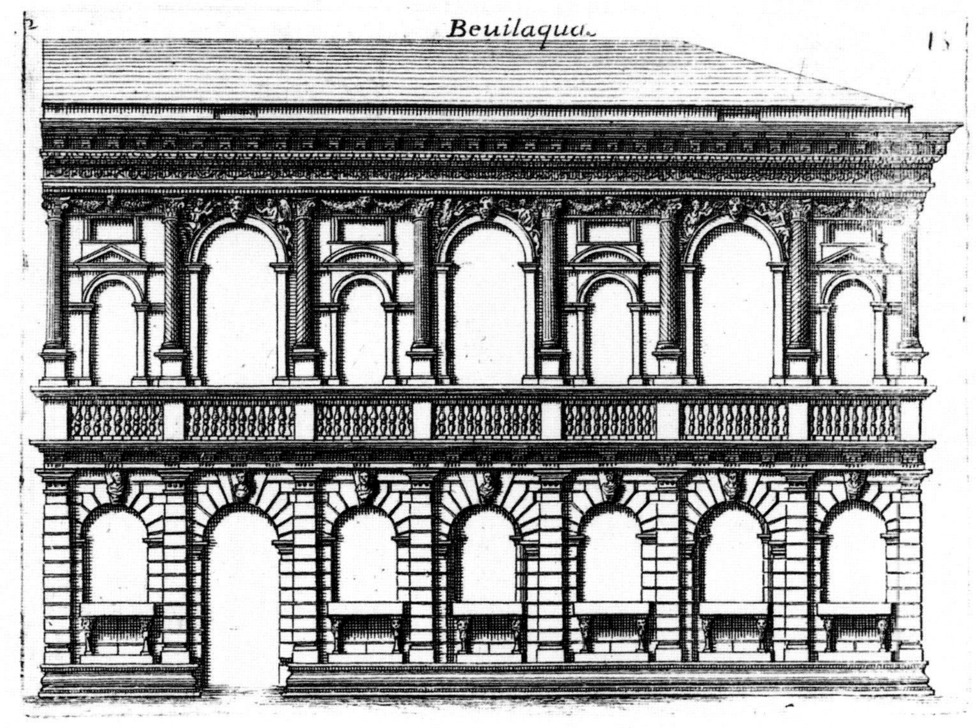

27 (top) Michele Sanmicheli
Palazzo Canossa, c. 1530–1537
Copper engraving from: Dionisio Valesi, *Varie fabriche antiche e moderne della città di Verona con alcune statue e busti della Galleria Bevilacqua non che del Museo Muselliano*, 1753, Plate IX
Biblioteca Hertziana, Rome

Commissioned by the Conti Canossa in Verona, the palazzo is among the masterpieces of the celebrated architect Michele Sanmicheli, and reveals the stylistic influence of the Roman architect Bramante.

28 (above) Michele Sanmicheli
Palazzo Bevilacqua, pre-1534
Copper engraving from: Dionisio Valesi, *Varie fabriche antiche e moderne della città di Verona con alcune statue e busti della Galleria Bevilacqua non che del Museo Musélliano*, 1753, Plate X
Biblioteca Hertziana, Rome

Originally conceived on a much larger scale, the Palazzo Bevilacqua in Verona shows the architect using quite a different style. A particular feature is the rich decoration of the façade, and the application of the triumphal arch motif, drawing on the pattern of surviving classical buildings in Verona.

Heaven on Earth – Early Ceiling Paintings in Venice

29 *Jupiter Hurling Thunderbolts at the Vices*,
c. 1554–1555/56
Oil on canvas, 560 x 330 cm
Musée du Louvre, Paris

This oval ceiling painting was originally the central picture gracing the ceiling of the Sala delle Udienze (Audience Chamber) in the Doge's Palace. In 1797 it was confiscated by the art commissars of Napoleon Bonaparte (1769–1821) and removed to Paris. In 1863 Jacopo di Andrea made a copy at the behest of the government, and this now replaces the looted original in Venice. The ceiling paintings in the rooms of the Consiglio dei Dieci (Council of Ten) were first mentioned in 1556 as *opera veramente di disegno & gentile*. With these words, Francesco Sansovino showed his high regard for the quality of draftsmanship and artistic execution. A principal feature of the picture is the bold use of foreshortened perspectives, of which the ceiling painter was a supreme master. The sculpturally rounded figures stand out dramatically against the blue of the sky.

When Paolo arrived in Venice in 1553 at the age of 25, he was very probably a witness to a vivid discussion that painters and art experts would be able to read about just four years later in the *Dialogo della pittura* by Lodovico Dolce (1508–c. 1568). This aesthetic debate had been started in 1550 by the Florentine painter Vasari, who idolized Michelangelo (1475–1564) and Raphael (1483–1520) and considered the art of drawing to be a decisive sign of quality in painting. In an effort to raise the value of color and the achievements of Venetian painting, Dolce, in his *Dialogo*, which was published in Venice in 1557, emphatically countered the one-sided canonization by subordinating drawing and line to color. His mouthpiece was no less than Pietro Aretino (1492–1556), the erudite man of letters who considered Titian to be the artist in whom painting in Venice had reached its ultimate perfection. Thus it was in this area of conflict between *disegno* (drawing) and *colorito* (coloration) and the synthesis of Roman–Tuscan and Venetian stylistic methods as recommended by Dolce that the young painter from Verona entered onto the stage of Venetian painting. In contrast to the native Venetian Tintoretto, for whom the basic principle "The drawing of Michelangelo and the color of Titian" had become an artistic program, Paolo followed his own course. The fact that he came from Verona, and that he had only become indirectly familiar with the principles of Roman formal culture in Parma and Mantua, saved him from the clever intellectual experiments with which well-known and less-known representatives of the *maniera* had, since the end of the 1530s, been inspiring their clients in Venice, and qualified him just as much as the aura of the *Pala Giustinian*, completed in imitation of Titian, for his appearance in the offices of the Consiglio dei Dieci (Council of Ten) in the Doge's palace.

Side by side with his moderately talented "alter ego" Giovanni Battista Zelotti, and the painter and cleric Giovanni Battista Ponchino (c. 1500–1570), who had been commissioned by Daniele Barbaro to direct the work, Paolo initially worked from 1554 onwards on the central ceiling painting in the Sala delle Udienze. The oval main picture with its depiction of *Jupiter Hurling Thunderbolts at the Vices* (ill. 29) is a reference, in the magnificently colored guise of mythology, to the legitimate judicial office of the Council of Ten, which, as a powerful legal body, was responsible for watching over the security of the state. It is framed on each side by four smaller oval and rectangular satellite pictures, including the allegories *Juno Showering Gifts over Venetia* (ill. 31), *Youth and Age* (ill. 32), and *Liberty*, which Paolo was once again responsible for.

When Francesco Sansovino first wrote, in passing, about the decorations, in the first edition of 1556 later to be reprinted several times, of the most important monuments and attractions in Venice, he praised the quality of the drawing and the pleasing nature of the works. The central picture in the coffered wooden ceiling, above all, must have corresponded to the expectations of the clients and experts as, in imitation of Giulio Romano, it presented a wealth of well thought-out perspectival foreshortenings in positively breathtaking density and dynamism. Small wax or clay models such as Carlo Ridolfi saw in Tintoretto's workshop in Venice may have been used by Paolo as aids when, even before beginning the actual process of painting, he had to rehearse the daredevil movements of the figures and their interactions.

Only a few yards separate these works from the independently executed decoration of the ceiling in the Sala della Bussola. The main picture of the *Coronation of the Virtues by St. Mark*, now kept in the Louvre, once again attests to the talented ceiling painter's predilection for bold foreshortenings. Despite Mannerist echoes which Sansovino benevolently honored with the term *gentile* (charming), the figures lack the histrionics that, for example, are typical of the deliberately emotional figures in the central octagon of the Stanza dei Tre Capi by Zelotti. Paolo contributed two ceiling paintings to the decorations in this room. These paintings also differ qualitatively from those of his painter colleagues in that here he succeeds with only a few figures in creating the illusion of a dramatic action. Also, there is color. Pure colors, flooded with light, shining and clearly distinguished from each other, determine his depictions of the *Triumph of Virtue over Vice* (ill. 30) and the *Triumph of Nemesis*. This palette must have been a genuine alternative in Venetian painting in

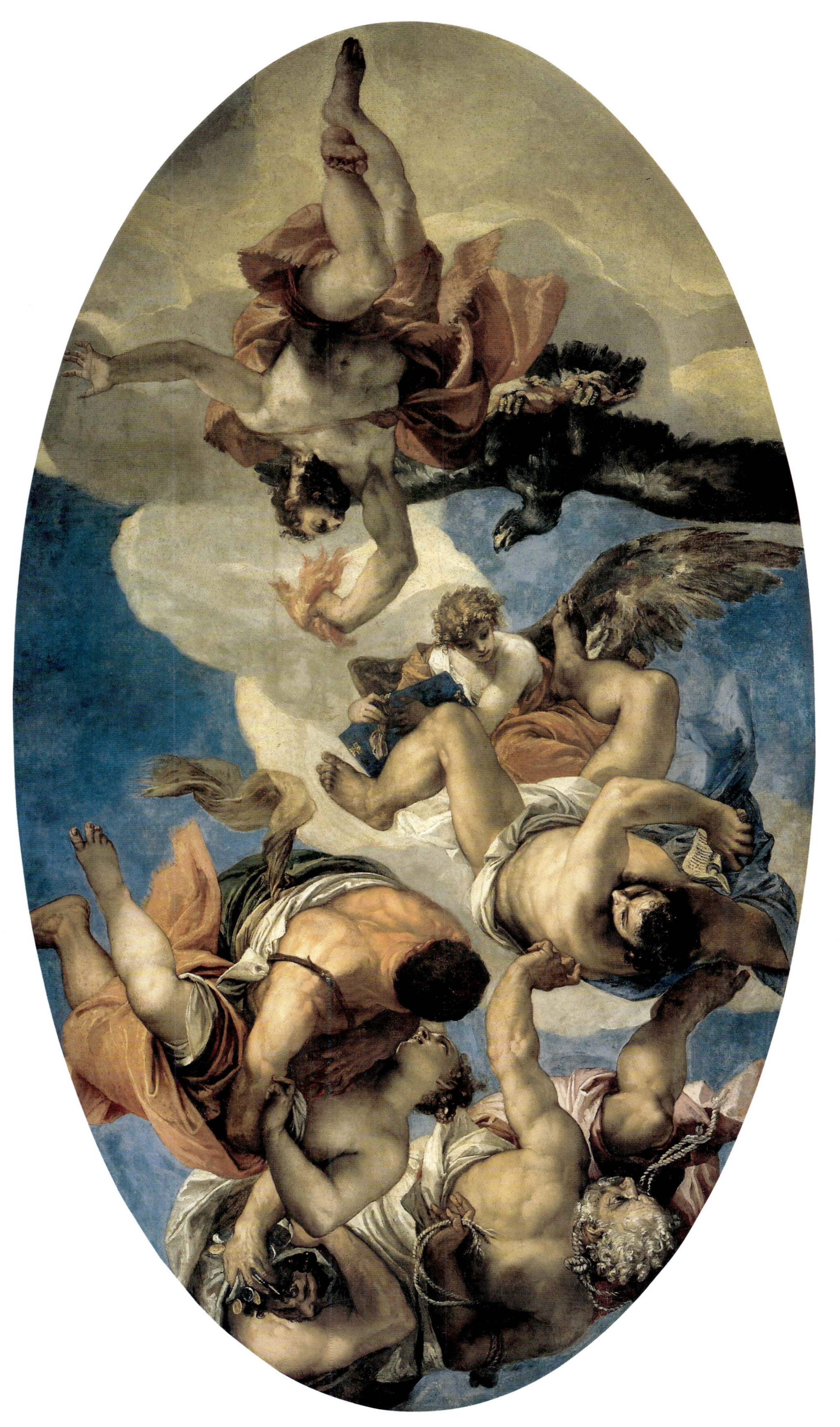

31 (right) *Juno Showering Gifts on Venetia*, c. 1554–1555/56
Oil on canvas, 365 x 147 cm
Sala delle Udienze del Consiglio dei Dieci, Doge's Palace, Venice

The goddess Juno, wife of Jupiter, is (like the personification of Venetia) shown in sharp bottom view. The gilt framework of the ceiling acts as the base of the composition, the frame being linked with the main central picture (ill. 29) by a narrow band.

30 (below) *The Triumph of Virtue over Vice*, c. 1554–1555/56
Oil on canvas, 295 x 165 cm
Stanza dei Tre Capi del Consiglio dei Dieci, Doge's Palace, Venice

Veronese supplied two allegories for the ceiling panel of the Stanza dei Tre Capi, the office of the three principal members of the Council of Ten. Laurel wreath and palm bough indicate that the brilliantly weighted Virtue has triumphed over Vice. The painter's response to the occasionally rather contrived movements of the figures in the central octagon by Giovanni Battista Zelotti was to use a calm, classical style. As with all the other ceiling paintings in the rooms of the Council of Ten, the *Triumph of Virtue over Vice* has a strongly moralizing tone. Like mute admonitions, the paintings remind the Council of Ten as guardians of order and decency of one of their main tasks – fighting vice.

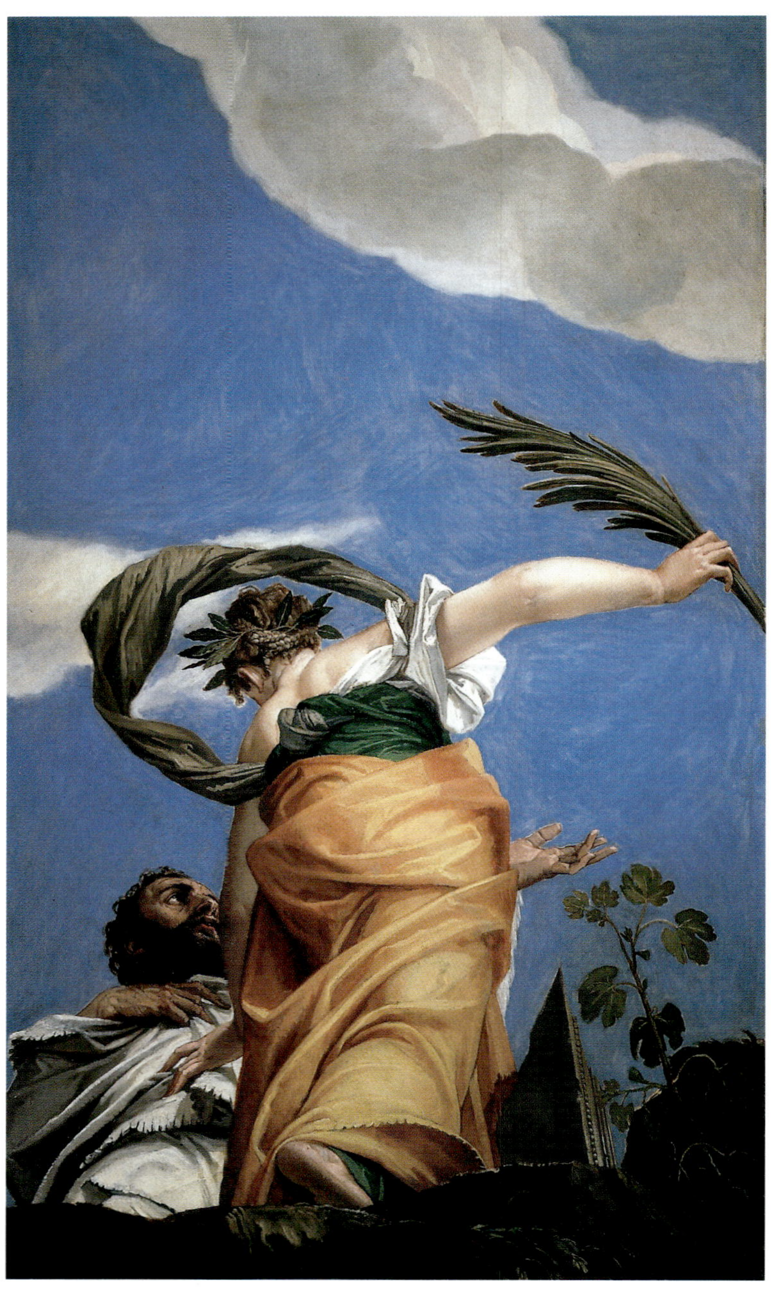

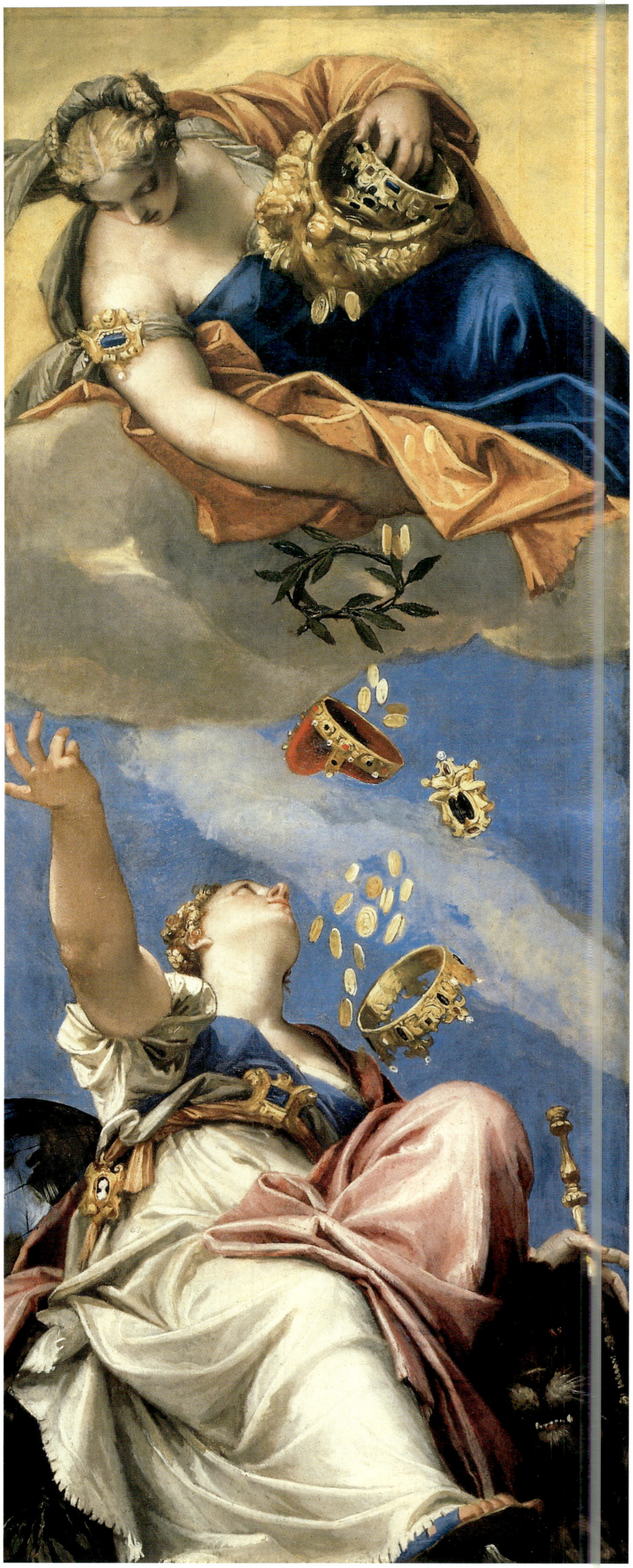

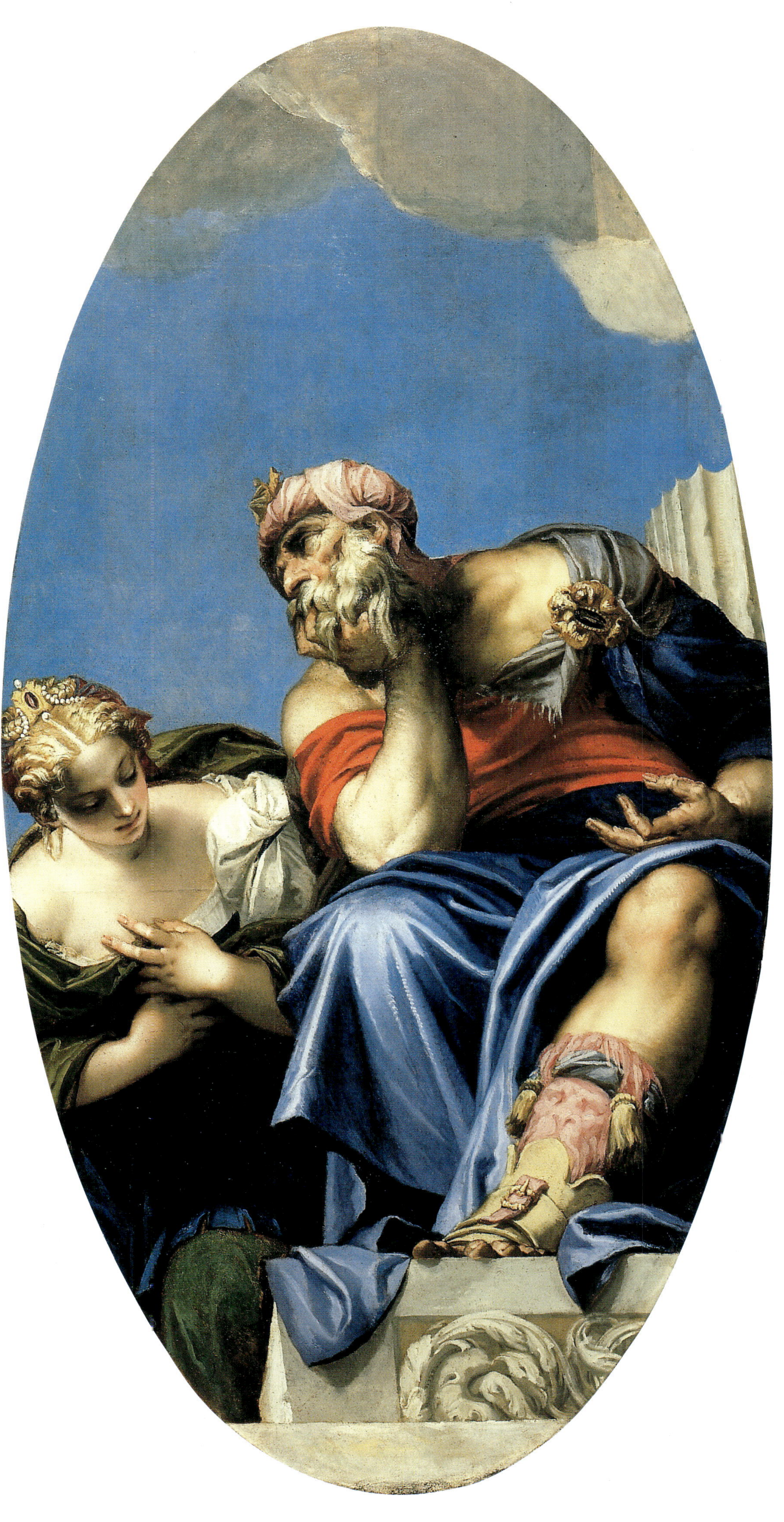

32 *Youth and Age*, c. 1554–1555/56
Oil on canvas, 286 x 150 cm
Sala delle Udienze del Consiglio dei Dieci, Doge's Palace, Venice

For the Venetian painter Palma il Giovane, the work on the left of the main picture (ill. 29) was a masterpiece of painting: in this, he considered Veronese had achieved something extraordinary, successfully blending the greatest advances made in antiquity with his own *maniera*. The subject of the picture is not known, the modern name being just for convenience. The bearded old man, sunk in thought on the ruins of ancient architecture, may have reminded Palma of pictures of classical philosophers. His delightful companion is derived from the figure in the *Temptation of St. Anthony* (ill. 23).

which only Titian had succeeded in creatively developing the atmospheric colors of Giorgione (c. 1477–1510).

Paolo's imaginative answer to the challenge of ceiling painting did not fail to meet with a response in Venice. In early 1555, Fra Bernardo Torlioni, from Verona and now prior of the Jeronymite monastery of San Sebastiano, commissioned his fellow countryman to paint the ceiling of the sacristy. The latter had, as "Paolo Veronese pictor", moved into the house of a certain Vincenzo Zen in the Santi Apostoli Quartier district during January. In the sacristy he was to lay the foundations for his life's work in the form of an extensive painted decoration which, towards the end of the 16th century, would bear comparison with the definitive Scuola Grande di San Rocco, which had been decorated by Jacopo Tintoretto.

The main picture in the *soffitto*, the *Coronation of the Virgin* (ill. 34), makes a rather restrained impression in contrast to the allegories in the Sala dei Dieci, almost timid in its choice of formal artistic means. Avoiding sweeping gestures and dynamic movements, Veronese placed particular value on the management of light and the painted description of the garments in which – starting with the primary colors yellow, blue and red – he tested the effect of complementary contrasts. In the figures in the satellite pictures, *St. John* (ill. 33), *St. Luke, St. Mark* and *St. Matthew*, the sophisticated formation of folds continues, but now it is the complex movements of the evangelists, who are fitted very skillfully into the narrow picture fields, that determine the pictures. The work on the sacristy ceiling had already been completed by November 1555. Its quality led to further commissions. Once again it was Torlioni who signed the new contract on December 1 and who provided the painter with the opportunity to prove his abilities on the ceiling of the nave of San Sebastiano.

Following initial preliminary studies (ill. 35), three scenes were depicted from the Book of Esther, the Old Testament heroine whose intercession succeeded in averting the persecution of the Jewish people planned by the king's minister Haman. She had fearlessly appeared before King Ahasuerus and, by interceding, had risked her own life. In late medieval edifying literature, her courageous action was considered to be a prefiguration of the Virgin's intercession before Christ on behalf of mankind. As an Old Testament model of Mary, the *Coronation of Esther* (ill. 36) is, on the one hand, typologically connected to the *Coronation of the Virgin* (ill. 34) in the sacristy. However, as early as the 9th century, Rhabanus Maurus (c. 780–856) had interpreted Esther as a symbol of the Church triumphant. The unusual iconography of the series, which starts with the *Banishment of Vashti* (ill. 37) but ignores the familiar scene of Esther's intercession before the throne of Ahasuerus, and finally culminates in the *Triumph of Mordecai* (ill. 38), appears to bear out the exegete's interpretation. Esther's foster-father Mordechai, who, during the late Middle Ages, was typologically compared with Christ's entrance into Jerusalem by being depicted as a rider, henceforth no longer just symbolized the victorious defeat of the conspiracy, but also the triumph of the Catholic Church over Luther and his new teachings.

The innovative character of the magnificently colored pictorial inventions was not lost on Paolo's contemporaries. Remembered with great praise by Vasari, Francesco Sansovino and later authors, the paintings were considered to be instructive masterpieces in terms of their figures and pictorial architectures, perspectival foreshortenings, mastery of space,

33 *St. John*, 1555
Oil on canvas, 85 x 240 cm
San Sebastiano, Venice

The *Coronation of the Virgin* (ill. 34) is framed by pictures of the four evangelists sitting, kneeling or reclining, accompanied by their symbols (eagle, ox, lion and angel), and, in their over life-size dimensions, they seem to burst out of the pictorial fields. In the picture of *St. John*, as in the others, the open book is a reference to the subject as writer of the gospel of the same name.

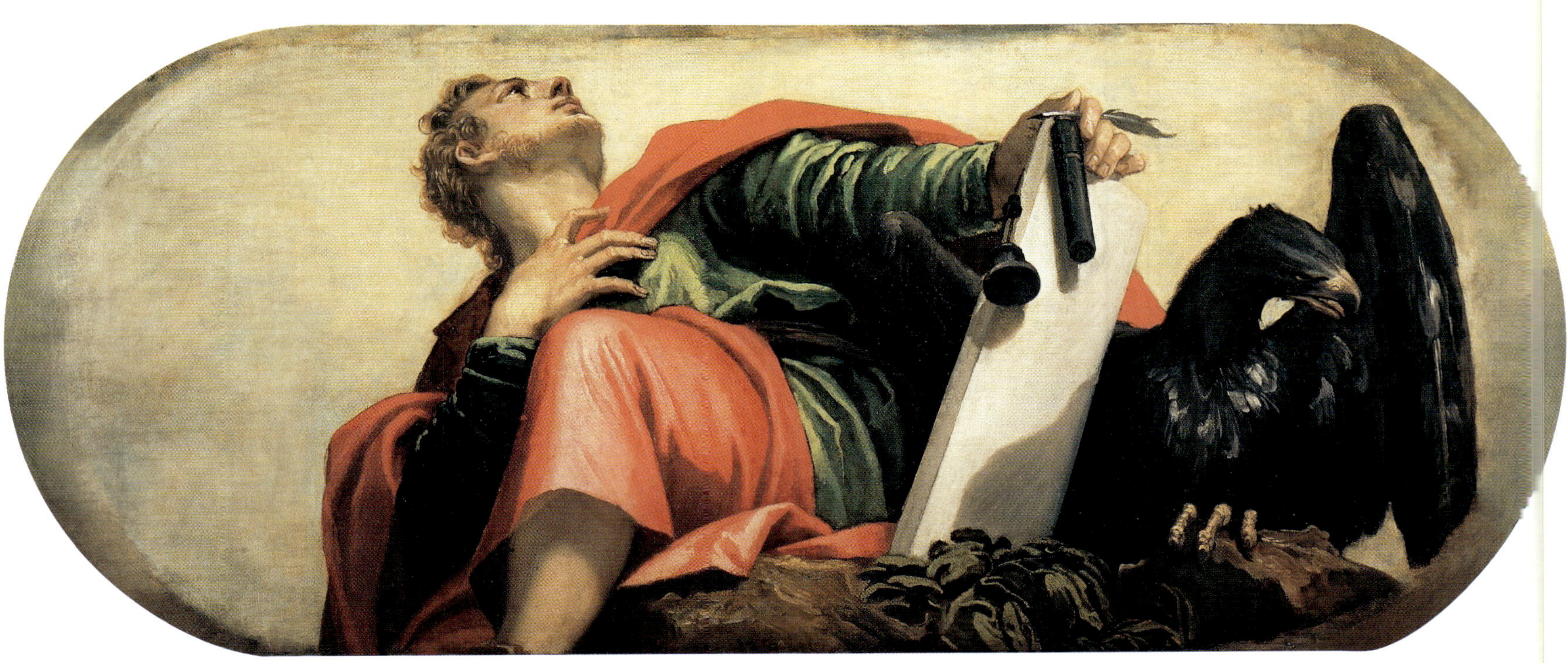

34 *Coronation of the Virgin*, 1555
Oil on canvas, 200 x 170 cm
San Sebastiano, Venice

This ceiling painting in the sacristy of San Sebastiano has an unusual iconography compared with older depictions. Mary is being crowned by Christ, while God the Father touches His Son's shoulder with his left hand. The date of completion of the ceiling painting is recorded in a book in one of the four corner tondos held by a winged angel. The inscription reads: M.D.L.V./ DIE XXIII/ NOVEMBER (November 23, 1555).

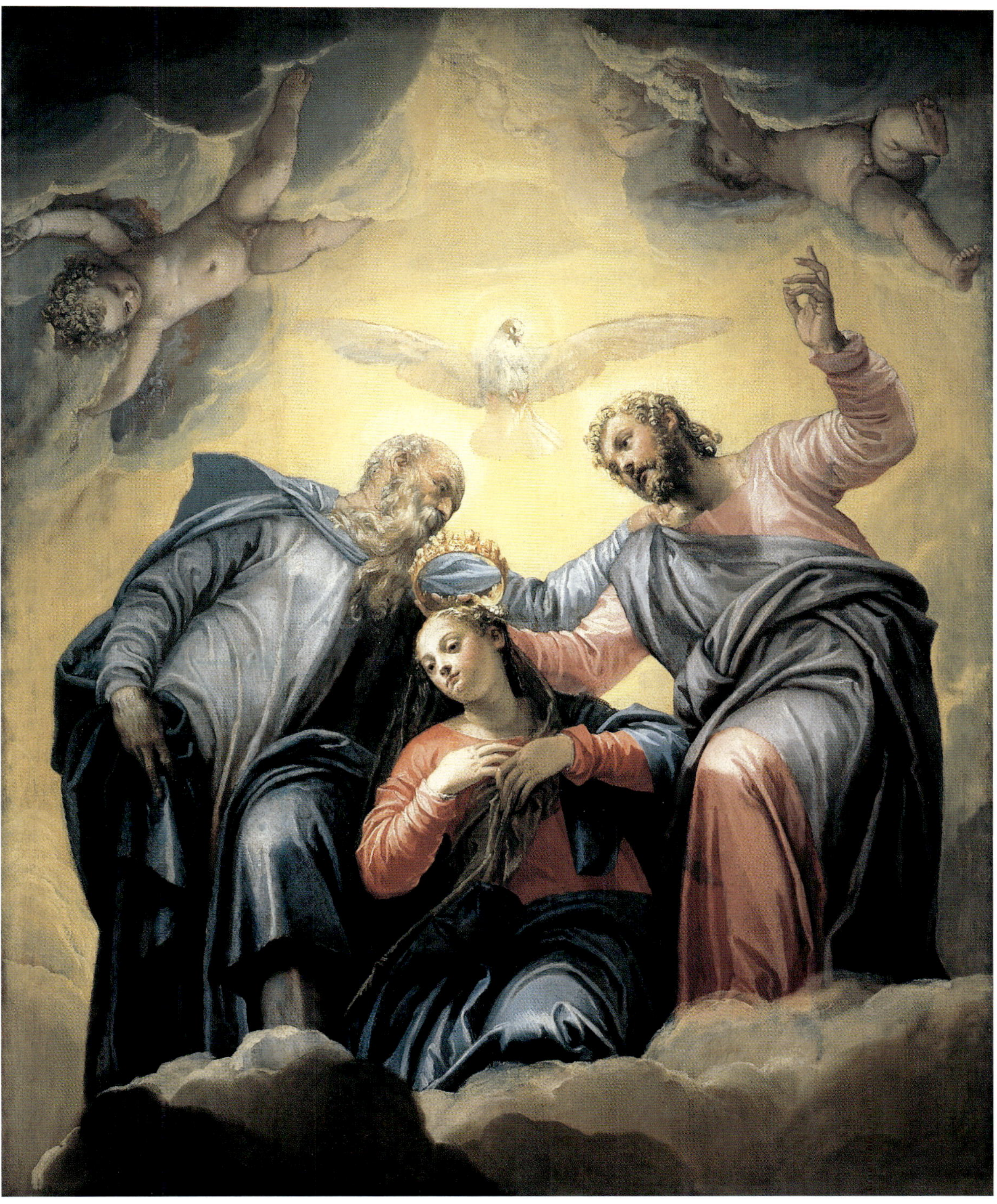

management of light, color and brushstrokes. When the painter and art theoretician Joachim von Sandrart (1606–1688) stopped off in Venice in 1629 and visited the church of San Sebastiano, he is said to have enthusiastically copied most of Veronese's paintings with a drawing pencil. About 30 years later, the arrival of Sebastiano Bombelli (1635–1719) of Udine meant that a painter and copyist entered the church nave who was more aware than almost any other Venetian artist of the necessity of studying the ceiling painting. His contemporaries reacted with stunned amazement to his painting technique, closely modeled on his predecessor, which used *tocchi*, short brushstrokes, to avoid undesired contours in favor of painterly effects. At this point in time the painted decoration of the church was considered, both north and south of the Alps, to be an exemplary way of decorating a room. The ceiling paintings in particular were among the preferred objects of study and painters that were eager to learn made detailed close-up studies of them with the aid of ladders. When the onslaught of copyists was threatening to get out of hand in the second half of the 17th century, the monks were forced to take countermeasures: on March 28, 1670 the Council of Ten started by forbidding the erection of ladders with the threat of punishment – three years later, on March 21, 1673, it was decreed that from then onwards only one copyist at a time would be admitted to the church to study the ceiling paintings.

Veronese's rich sense of color, and his ability to harmoniously attune figures and pictorial architectures to each other, reached a new level of quality in the

35 Studies for the *Triumph of Mordechai* and *Coronation of Esther*, 1555/56
Pen drawing, 15 x 17.7 cm
Département des arts graphiques, Musée du Louvre, Paris

Preliminary studies were very important for Veronese from the very first. In the case of the ceiling paintings of San Sebastiano, two drawings are known that provide insight into the genesis of the pictures. The sheet in the Louvre brings together studies for individual figures in Mordechai's retinue (ill. 38), by way of a first draft of ideas. A quick study of the later structure of the *Coronation of Esther* (ill. 36) occupies the right side. A noticeable feature is the differing gesture of King Ahasuerus compared with the painted version: he still has the scepter in his left hand, but the crown is scarcely visible. Obviously, Veronese was originally thinking of an event that came after the coronation ceremony. Esther had gone to see the king at great personal danger, whereupon the king stretched out his golden scepter as a sign of mercy and raised her to her feet. The later correction of this detail may have been prompted by Fra Bernardo Torlioni, the client who was responsible for the program of ceiling paintings.

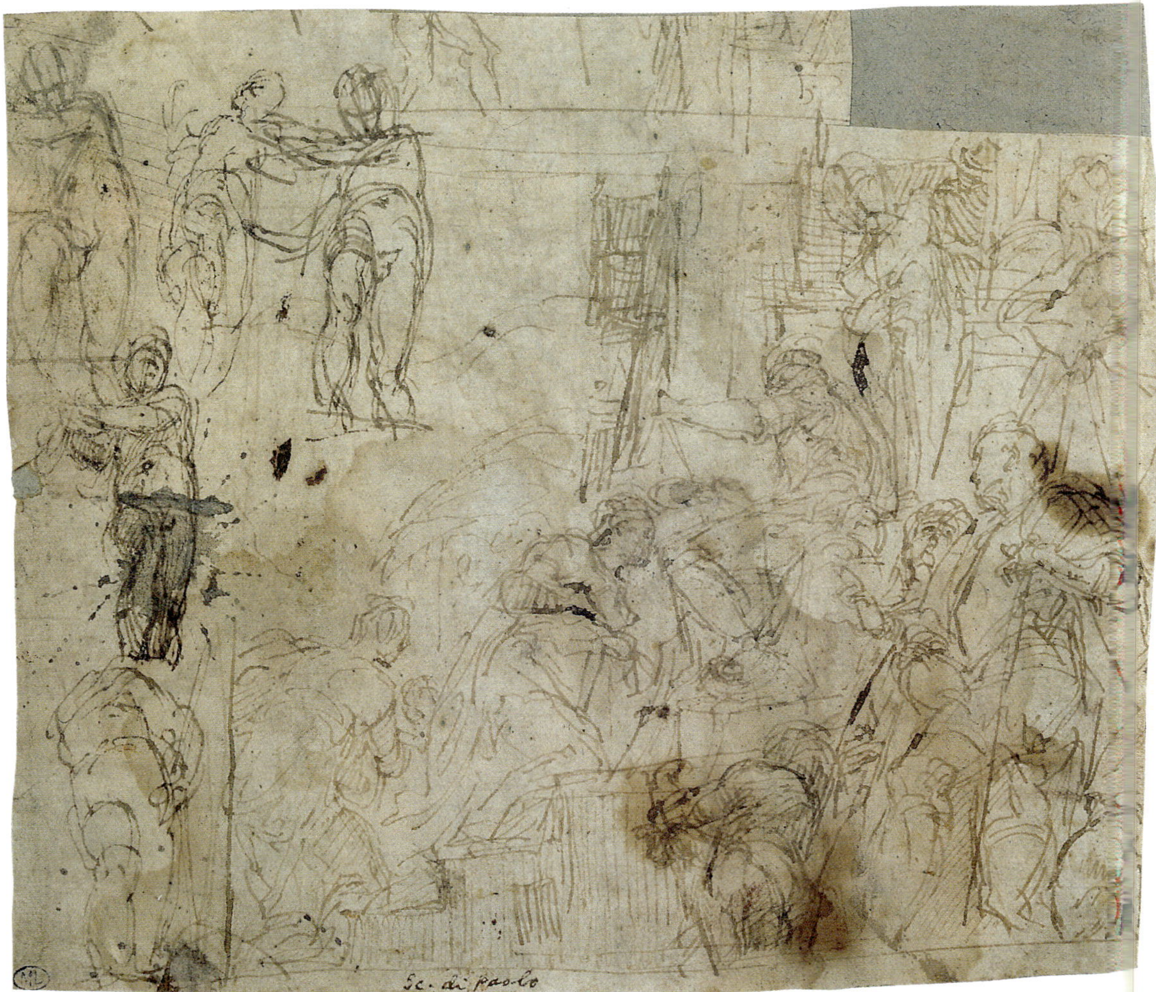

ceiling paintings of the Libreria Marciana, built by Jacopo Sansovino (1486–1570), and it is not therefore surprising if Vasari, when looking at these works, was once again prepared to overlook temporarily his prejudices against Venetian painting.

Authenticated by records and produced between August 1556 and February 1557 on behalf of the procurators responsible for the national library, the tondi visualize allegorical depictions of *Music* (ill. 41), *Music, Astronomy and Deceit* (ill. 39) and *Honor* (ill. 40). They owe their existence to an unusual competition. The painters who took part in it were Giuseppe Porta (c. 1520/25–c. 1575), Battista Franco (c. 1510–1561), Giulio Licinio (1527–after 1593), Andrea Schiavone (c. 1510/15–1563), Giovanni De Mio (1510/12–after 1570), and Giovanni Battista Zelotti, already mentioned on several occasions; each had been required to produce three adjacent allegorical depictions. The presence of Veronese in a group of moderately talented Mannerist painters in the Roman mold makes one suspicious, but it was scarcely a coincidence that he was summoned at this point in time. In the *Dialogo della pittura* by Lodovico Dolce, available in Venice in 1557, Aretino voiced his fear, addressed to young Venetian painters, that "the art of painting is once again going astray". While he considered Battista Franco, a Venetian trained in Rome who today is almost unknown, to be the only person on whom his hopes were pinned, Francesco Sansovino went one step further by declaring the painters taking part in the decorative work as being the best in Italy. It is a fact that Sansovino would have been thinking less about Veronese than about his competitors, whose vocation seemed to be to help the library get a "modern" decoration oriented on central Italian trends. Nonetheless, the competition produced a surprising result. The choice of the commission, which had to decide on the ceiling paintings and which included both the architect Jacopo Sansovino and Titian, was to opt for Paolo Veronese, who was subsequently awarded a gold chain by the procurators for his allegory of *Music* (ill. 41). Titian's intervention may indeed, as has been suspected, have been the result of tactical considerations, in order to weaken the influence of the *maniera* as it was successfully represented in Venice by Battista Franco, Schiavone and Tintoretto. On the other hand, it may by all means have been genuine sympathy for the alternative artistic manner of a young talent who had already delivered some very promising examples of his ability. During the period when he was establishing himself, this official recognition in addition to being honored by the most famous painter of the city, considerably strengthened the position of Paolo, the *forestiero* from Verona.

36 *Coronation of Esther*, 1556
Oil on canvas, 450 x 370 cm
San Sebastiano, Venice

The strict diagonal composition offers a wealth of narrative detail, and like all other pictures in the series, takes into account the *di sotto in sù* angle of vision, with its foreshortened perspectives, which pervades the space. The pictorial architecture provides a formal link between the pictorial fields. Columns, cornice and roof terraces form a continuous axis running through all three pictorial fields.

Technically, the light reflections on Haman's armor are particularly delicate: on closer inspection, they break up into spots of paint. Esther's gesture resembles the modest gesture of the Virgin in the *Coronation of the Virgin* (ill. 34), and emphasizes the typological nature of the picture series.

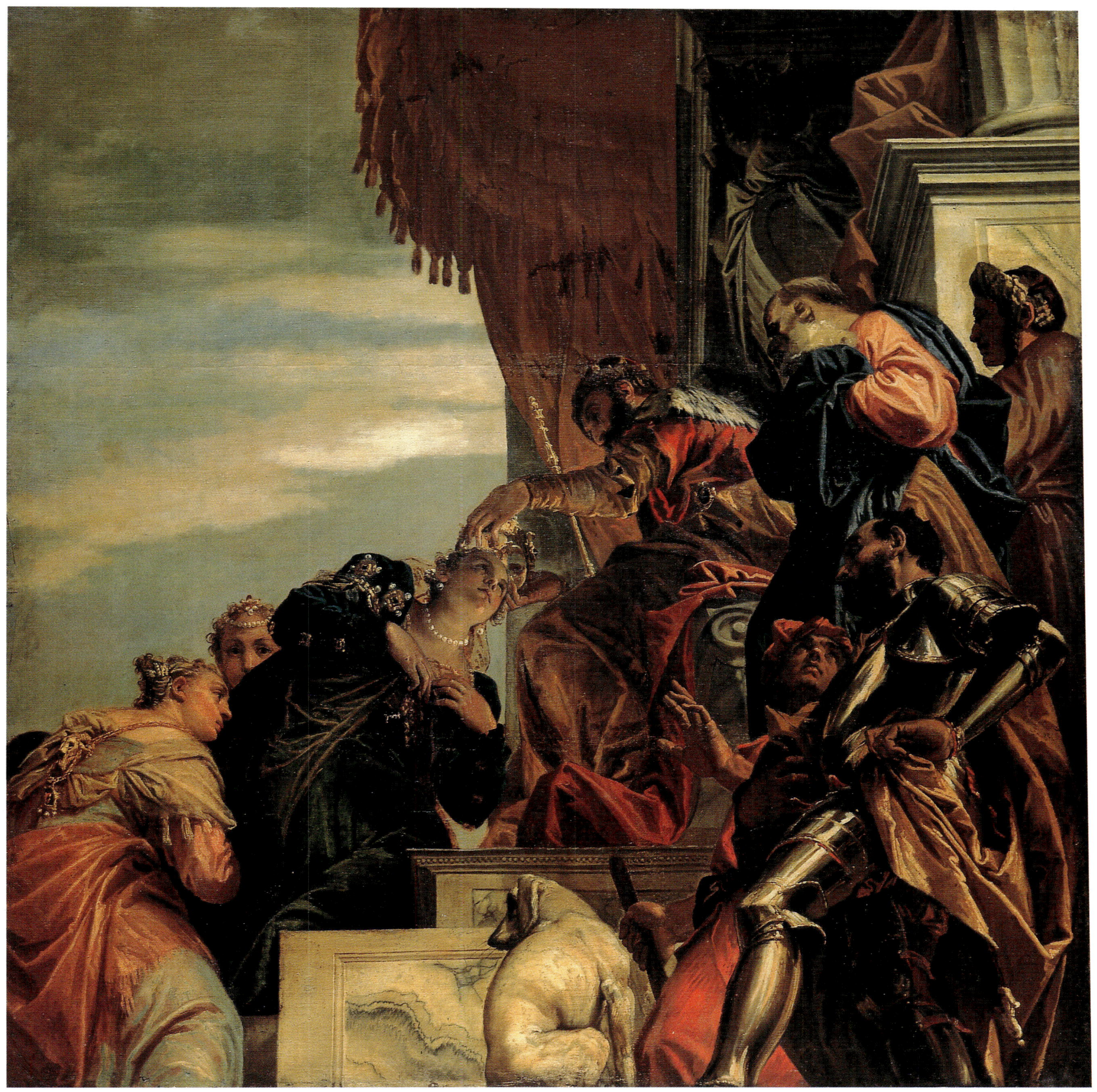

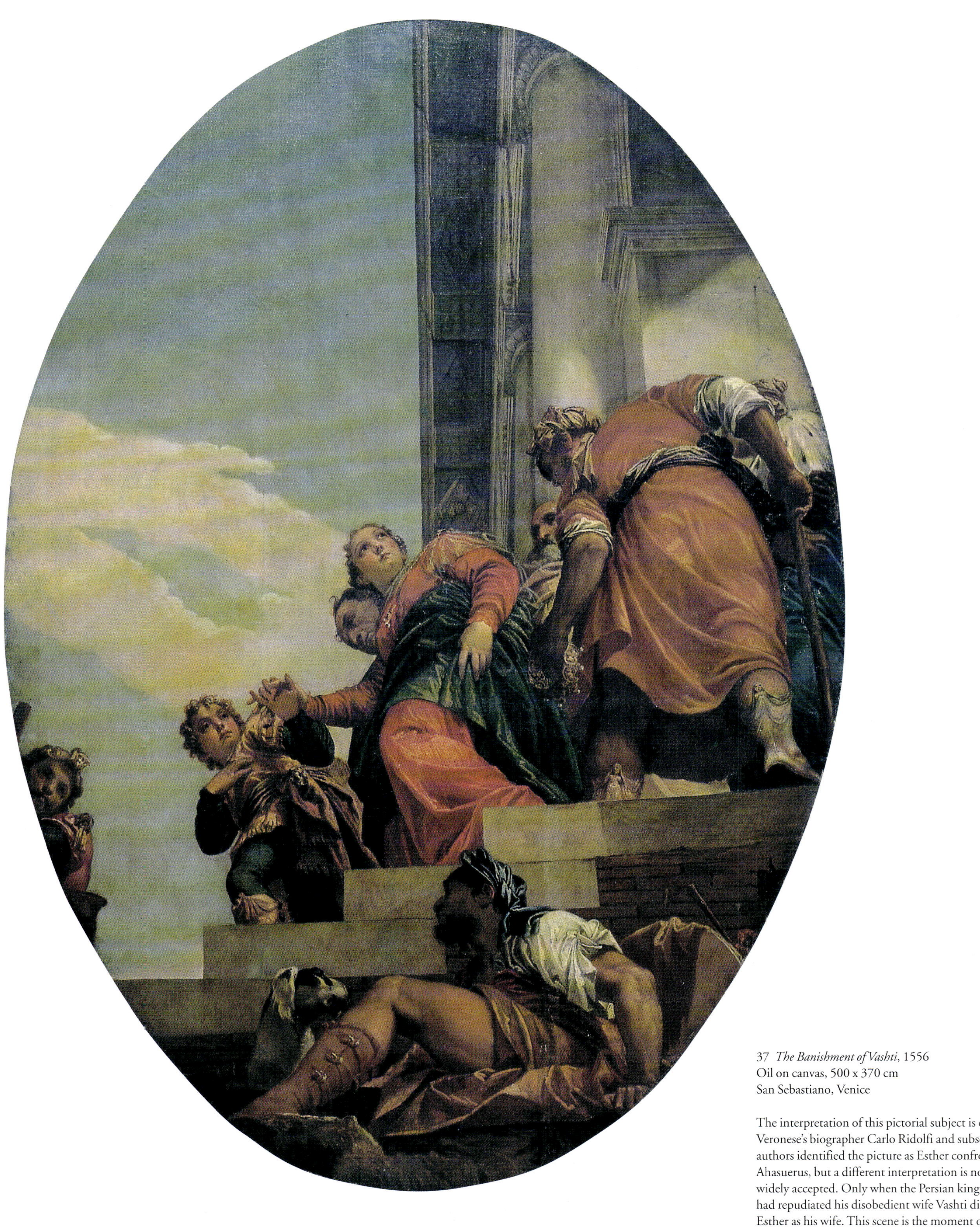

37 *The Banishment of Vashti*, 1556
Oil on canvas, 500 x 370 cm
San Sebastiano, Venice

The interpretation of this pictorial subject is controversial. Veronese's biographer Carlo Ridolfi and subsequent authors identified the picture as Esther confronting Ahasuerus, but a different interpretation is now more widely accepted. Only when the Persian king Ahasuerus had repudiated his disobedient wife Vashti did he choose Esther as his wife. This scene is the moment of repudiation. Relieved of her crown, Vashti leaves the royal palace with her retinue.

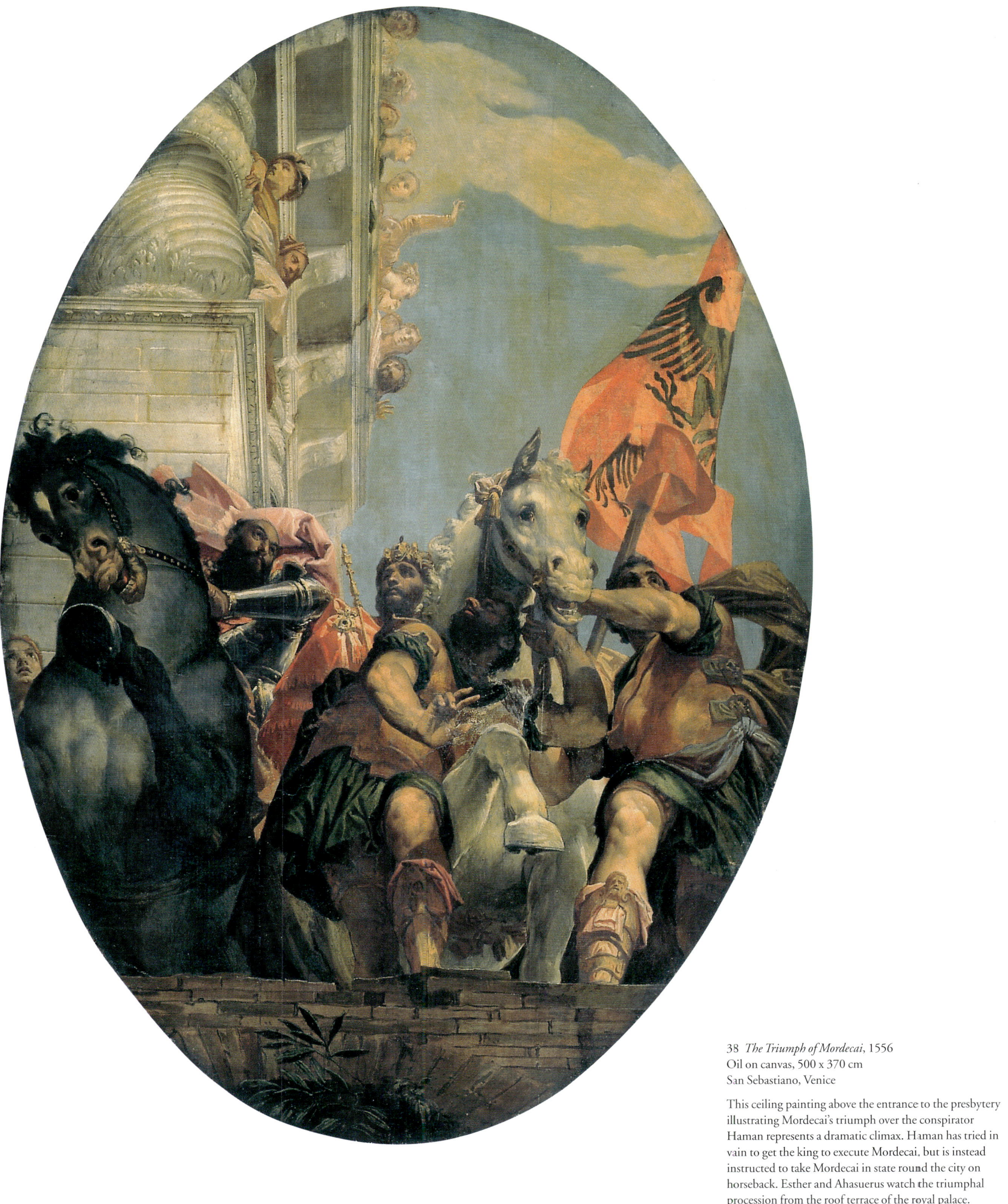

38 *The Triumph of Mordecai*, 1556
Oil on canvas, 500 x 370 cm
San Sebastiano, Venice

This ceiling painting above the entrance to the presbytery illustrating Mordecai's triumph over the conspirator Haman represents a dramatic climax. Haman has tried in vain to get the king to execute Mordecai, but is instead instructed to take Mordecai in state round the city on horseback. Esther and Ahasuerus watch the triumphal procession from the roof terrace of the royal palace.

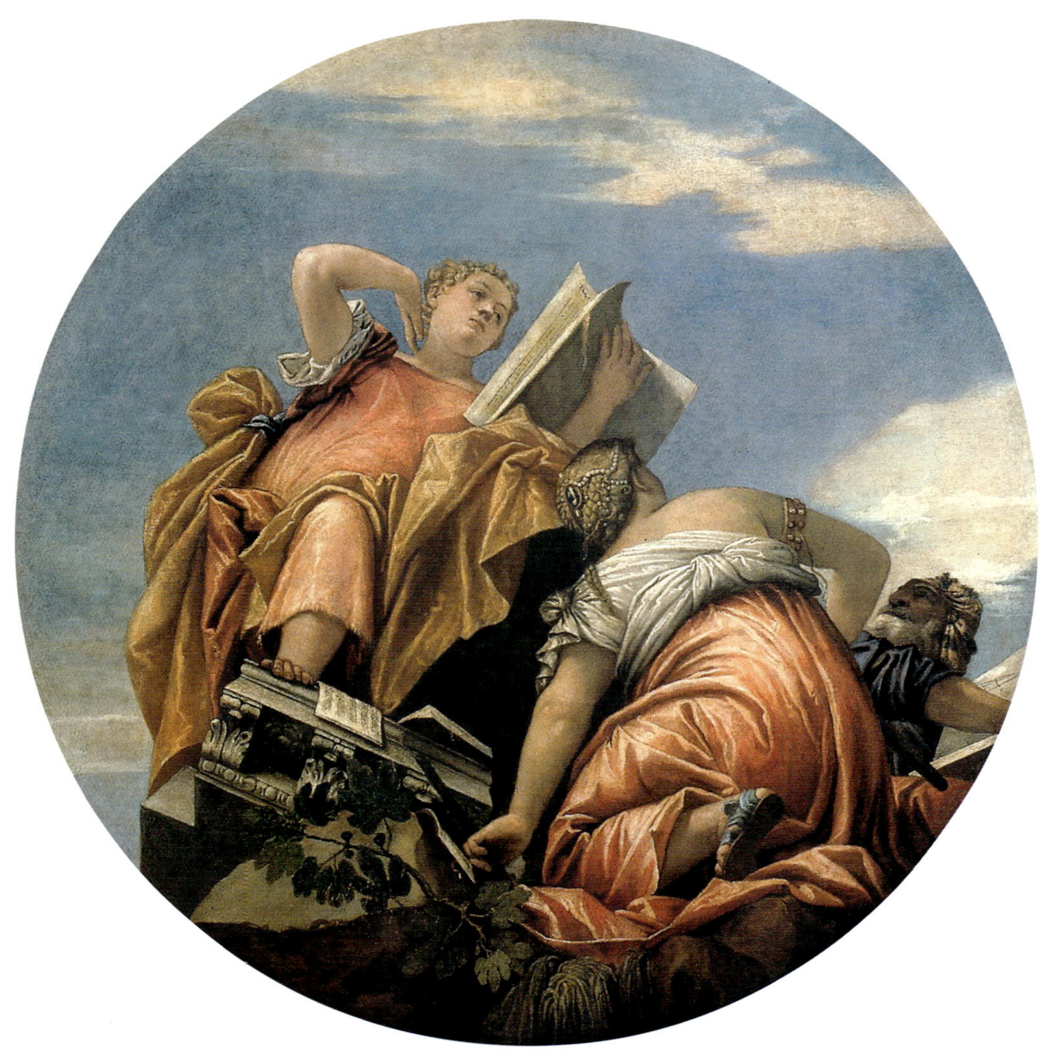

39 *Music, Astronomy and Deceit*, 1556/57
Oil on canvas, diameter 230 cm
Biblioteca Marciana, Venice

This central tondo is introduced by a kneeling female figure who, holding a flute in her left hand, turns her head to gaze upwards. Presumably, she represents music. Assigned to her is a young woman, who is studying a book with astronomical plates. Standing on a sheet of music, she appears to be listening to the sounds of heaven. On the right, the scene concludes with a woman examining a book with geometrical diagrams. The back of her head is covered by the mask of an old man. On the basis of the iconological handbooks of Francesco Marcolini *Le sorti intitolate giardino di Pensieri* (Venice, 1540), Charles Hope identifies this figure as Mensogna (Falsehood) and proposes the following interpretation: The study of the universe opens the way to divine harmony. Superior to earthly creations, harmony is not reconcilable with the fallacies of a science that denies higher wisdom.

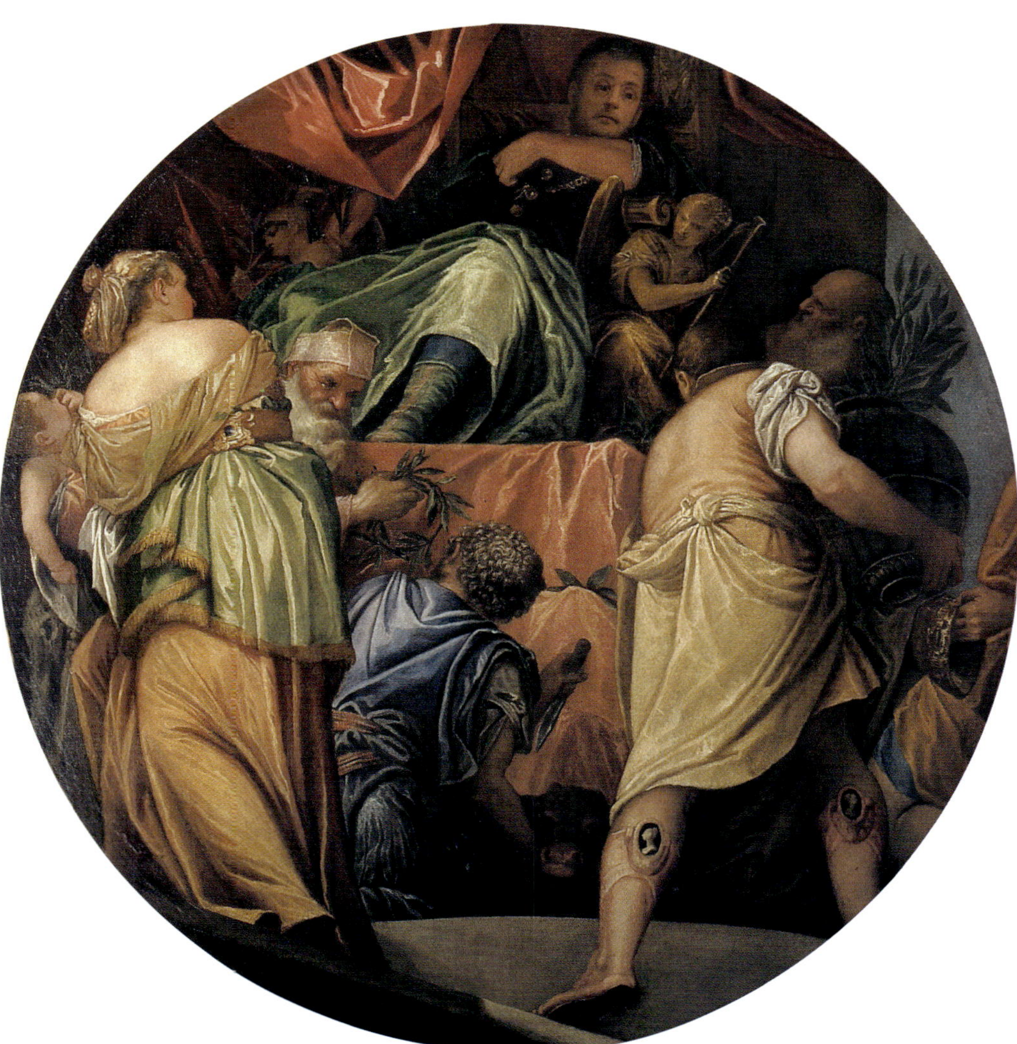

40 *Honor*, 1556/57
Oil on canvas, diameter 230 cm
Biblioteca Marciana, Venice

Even Vasari, who interpreted the ruler on the throne as *L'Onore*, i.e. the personification of Honor, got no further in 1568 than a mere description of this enigmatic scene. The ruler's throne is decorated on each side by small, carved figures. The one on his left holds a scepter, the tip of which forms an eye. Various figures present themselves in front of the throne, including a woman with a child (Caritas?), a kneeling figure bearing an animal sacrifice and a bearded old man with a crown woven of laurel boughs. A comparison of the tondi shows that Veronese supplied works of very differing approaches and quality. The harmoniously grouped figures in *Music* (ill. 41) translate the dramatic pictorial resources of the ceiling paintings of San Sebastiano into a calm, classic style. In contrast the two figures with their backs turned to us in *Honor* resound with Mannerist echoes. Veronese here applies Tintoretto's principle of divergence to the arrangement of moving figures.

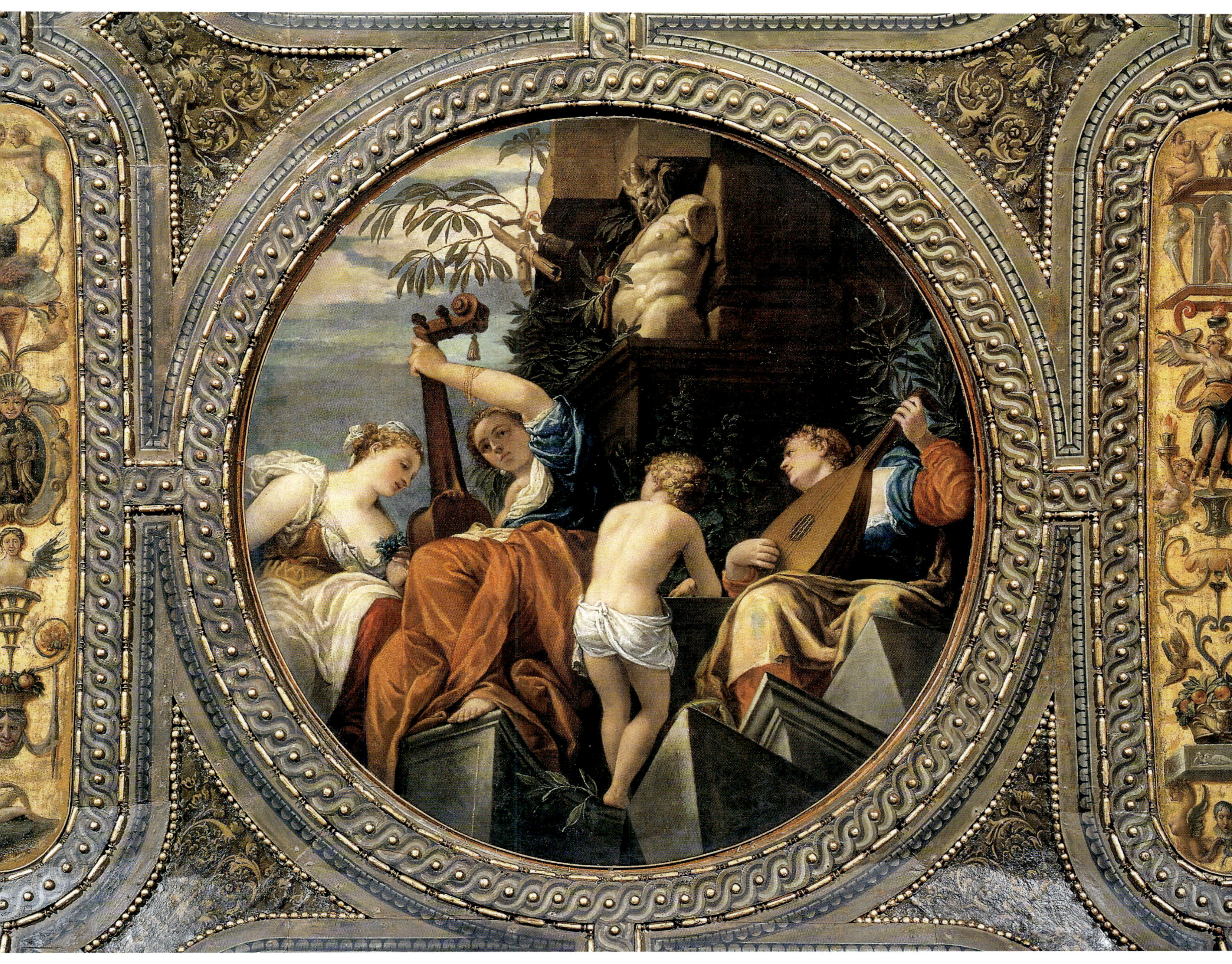

41 *Music*, 1556/57
Oil on canvas, diameter 230 cm
Biblioteca Marciana, Venice

Like *Music, Astronomy and Deceit* (ill. 39) and *Honor* (ill. 40), this tondo belongs to a series of 21 such circular pictures adorning the ceiling of the great room of the Libreria Vecchia. Sansovino and Titian awarded the work a golden chain as the best painting, the chain being later recorded in the estate of Veronese's heirs. The Libreria Vecchia housed not only reading and lecture rooms but also the offices of the procurators. It is not known whether a specific program and defined sequence underlay the decoration. Even the iconography of most of the pictures throws up puzzles.

Corresponding to the purpose of the room and function of the building, the pictures illustrate allegories of education, the arts and sciences. Contemporary commentators related the decoration to the good conduct of government and its foundations, which required not just a virtuous, but also an erudite ruler. Veronese probably owed his involvement in the project to the intervention of Antonio Giustinian who commissioned the *Pala Giustinian* (ill. 20). As *provveditore della fabbrica* (building inspector), Giustinian would have been the painter's paymaster.

New Clients and Sponsors

42 *Transfiguration of Christ*, 1555/56
Oil on canvas, 555 x 260 cm
Cathedral of Santa Maria, Montagnana

Accompanied by Peter, James and John, Jesus had gone to Mount Tabor to pray, where the disciples were witnesses to his transfiguration. In the Biblical account, Christ's face "did shine as the sun, and his raiment was white as the light. And behold, there appeared to them Moses and Elijah talking with him. While he yet spake, behold, a bright cloud overshadowed them: and behold a voice out of the cloud, which said, This is my beloved son, in whom I am well pleased, hear ye him" (St. Matthew 17, 5). Later, Jesus instructed the prostrate, fear-struck disciples to "show the vision to no man". Unlike Raphael's *Transfiguration* (Vatican, Rome) of 1519/20, in which the Transfiguration, Resurrection and Ascension are combined in the figure of Christ, Veronese's sticks to the text in emphasizing the mystic moment of transfiguration. Linked in a richly graded scale of color, Christ, Moses and Elijah greatly resemble the figures in the *Coronation of the Virgin* (ill. 34) in style. The angels tumbling from the clouds and the eloquent gestures of the prostrate disciples provide the dramatic touches.

In June 1555, while he was still working on the ceiling paintings in the church of San Sebastiano, Veronese was commissioned to paint the *Transfiguration* (ill. 42) for the main altar of the cathedral of Santa Maria in Montagnana. The deal was concluded in Francesco Pisani's villa, designed by Andrea Palladio. Located in front of the Porta Padova, the building must have been largely finished by this point in time. The work on the large altar painting was delayed, however, so that the clients were not able to take delivery of the painting, which was approximately 5.5 m. high, until the following year. Proudly indicating his origins, the painter signed the picture "PAVLO / VERO / P.", the first time it appears on an authenticated work.

In neighboring Padua, word must have soon got about what was all too evident in Montagnana and, above all, Venice. The *Martyrdom of St. Justina* (ill. 43), which is brilliant in terms of color, comes from the Benedictine monastery of Santa Giustina and the first record of its presence in the abbot's private chapel dates from 1642. Commissioned by an unnamed predecessor, the devotional picture was particularly esteemed in Benedictine circles, for when the local painter Giovanni Battista Bissoni (1575–1634) was summoned to Ravenna in about 1600 in order to produce a *Wedding at Cana* for the refectory of the Benedictine monastery of San Vitale there, he not only cited the monumental painting in the refectory of San Giorgio Maggiore in Venice, but also the devotional picture with which he was doubtlessly very familiar due to his contacts with the Benedictines of Santa Giustina. A comparison of the picture with the tondo of *Honor* (ill. 40), completed in Venice in February 1557, speaks for itself and confirms the authenticity of the year 1556, recorded on the copper engraving reproduction by Pietro Menarola, as the date the *Martyrdom of St. Justina* (ill. 43) was created. Painted at almost exactly the same time as the *Anointing of David* (ill. 45), both the tondo and the painting in Padua testify to Veronese's careful investigation of Tintoretto's *maniera* and his famous *Miracle of the Slave* (Gallerie dell'Accademia, Venice). In 1548, this painting had caused a complete sensation and given rise to passionate discussions in expert circles. Never before had movements and emotions in human figures been depicted so densely and acutely in Venetian painting. Veronese was thinking of Tintoretto's figure of the thug busy with his instruments of torture when he created his own exemplarily balanced figure with the pilgrim's staff seen from behind. Without copying his model, he temporarily came into competition with a painter who, eight years previously, through his unconventional dramaturgy, had successfully called local traditions into question.

In January 1556, Paolo had already come into contact in Verona with Don Mauro Vercelli da Verona, the abbot of the Benedictine monastery of Santi Nazaro e Celso, and the person who probably commissioned the *Feast in the House of Simon* (ill. 46). Payments made to the painter suggest that the painting was already being worked on at this point in time. It is not known why there was a delay in its completion. Stylistic parallels with the *Presentation in the Temple* (ill. 53) in San Sebastiano suggest that it was not finished until 1559/60. Both the demanding horizontal format and the location where it was to be displayed must have presented a special challenge, especially as it was necessary to match the depiction to the specific spatial conditions of the refectory in the Benedictine abbey. Surviving preparatory drawings (ill. 48) provide an idea as to how carefully Veronese prepared the work which was originally integrated with an illusionist fresco decoration.

While the frescoes he painted no longer survive, they can be roughly reconstructed by means of Ridolfi's description, a modest engraving reproduction by Giacomo Barri, and a copy drawing (ill. 49). According to these, two painted columns were used as a frame; they were evidently connected with each other by a fruit garland, and in terms of shape and size would certainly have made reference to the Corinthian order of columns of the painted columned portico reminiscent of Palladio. Finally, above the inwardly curved corner sections lay the two satyrs that Ridolfi, in 1648, particularly valued for their rustic quality. Two years later, the painting was bought by Giovanni Filippo Spinola for 7,000 Venetian ducats, transferred to Genoa and, probably in the same year, amended at the

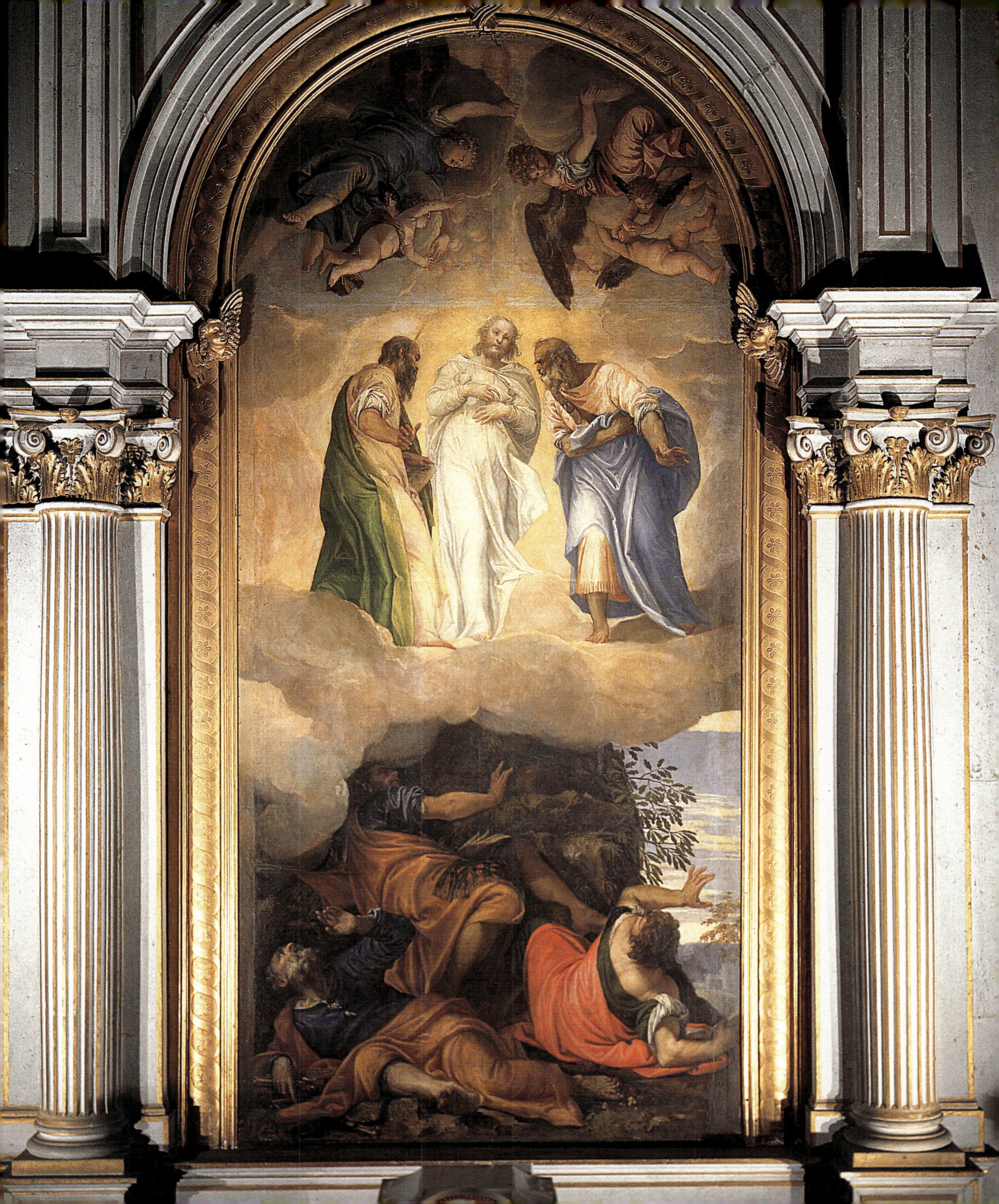

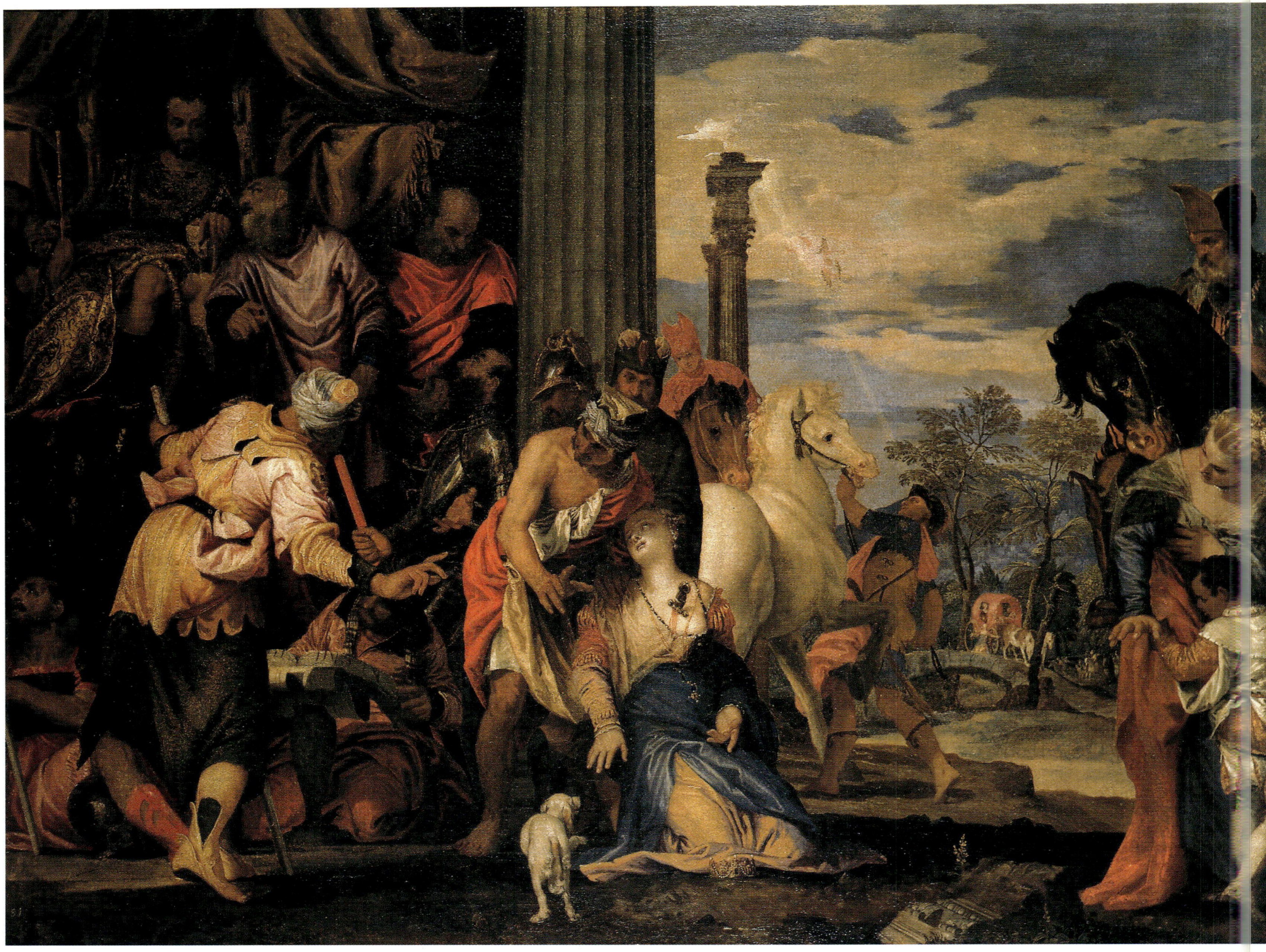

corners in order to help the spectacular new acquisition make an entrance worthy of a gallery picture.

Although the painting in its present condition no longer corresponds to its original state, it nonetheless becomes clear upon closer observation why it is considered to be one of the painter's most important works. It is the pictorial architect and later creator of feasts rich in figures who is making himself eloquently heard here. Once again it was Vasari who in 1568 expressly praised the figures drawn from nature and the marvelous perspectives, and thus immediately grasped where the special charm of the depiction lay. In a small space, Veronese succeeded in harmoniously connecting the figures together in terms of posture and movement, in combining them into groups and relating them excitingly to the clearly structured architectures. Intensely shining pure colors such as had already appeared in the *Martyrdom of St. Justina* (ill. 43) accompany the rhythmic rise and fall of moderately moving figures. In contrast to Tintoretto, who preferred to arrange the figures in his paintings according to the principle of divergence and usually chose deep pictorial spaces permeated by atmospheric shades of light and dark, Veronese recommended himself to his clients as a master of groups and clearly structured pictorial spaces. Over the following years, those monasteries of the Benedictine order that had joined the Paduan reform congregation of Santa Giustina continued to be among the painter's most important clients. His work for the Benedictines in Padua and Verona was, therefore, the prelude to a development favored by personal connections, which in Veronese's case were to lead to the patronage of the Benedictines of San Benedetto Po (1561/62), Santa Maria di Praglia (1562), San Giorgio Maggiore (1562/63) and Santa Giustina (1575).

Any attempt to define his artistic work of the 1550s as any one particular development would be premature and would be an inexcusable simplification. Thus in about 1557, in chronological proximity to religious histories such as the *Feast in the House of Simon*

43 *Martyrdom of St. Justina*, 1556
Oil on canvas, 104 x 138 cm
Museo Civico, Padua

After Justina had been baptized by Prosdocimo, the first bishop of Padua, she was brought up in the Christian faith. When the Emperor Maximilian came to Padua in 304, Justina heard of his persecutions of Christians, and immediately sought to instill courage in local believers. However, she herself was imprisoned, dragged before the emperor and instructed to sacrifice to Mars, the god of war. Her refusal to do so cost her her life. With its plethora of figures, the picture is a masterpiece of narration. The action begins in the background with a carriage drawn by two horses, which Justina has just left. She kneels on the bridge to pray, and is caught in a beam of heavenly light. The foreground is taken up with the scene of the martyrdom. Struck by the dagger, the prince's daughter yields humbly to her fate.

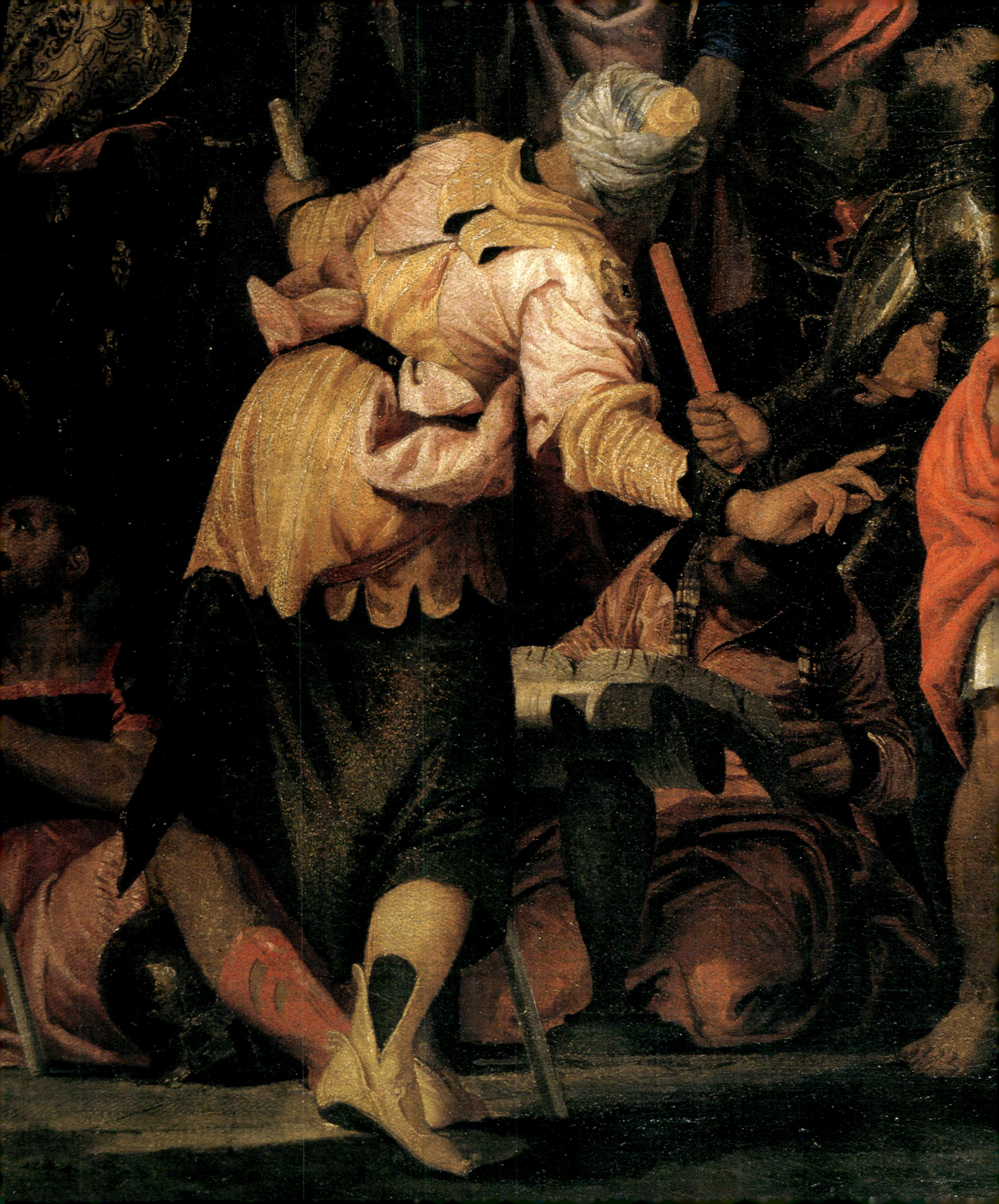

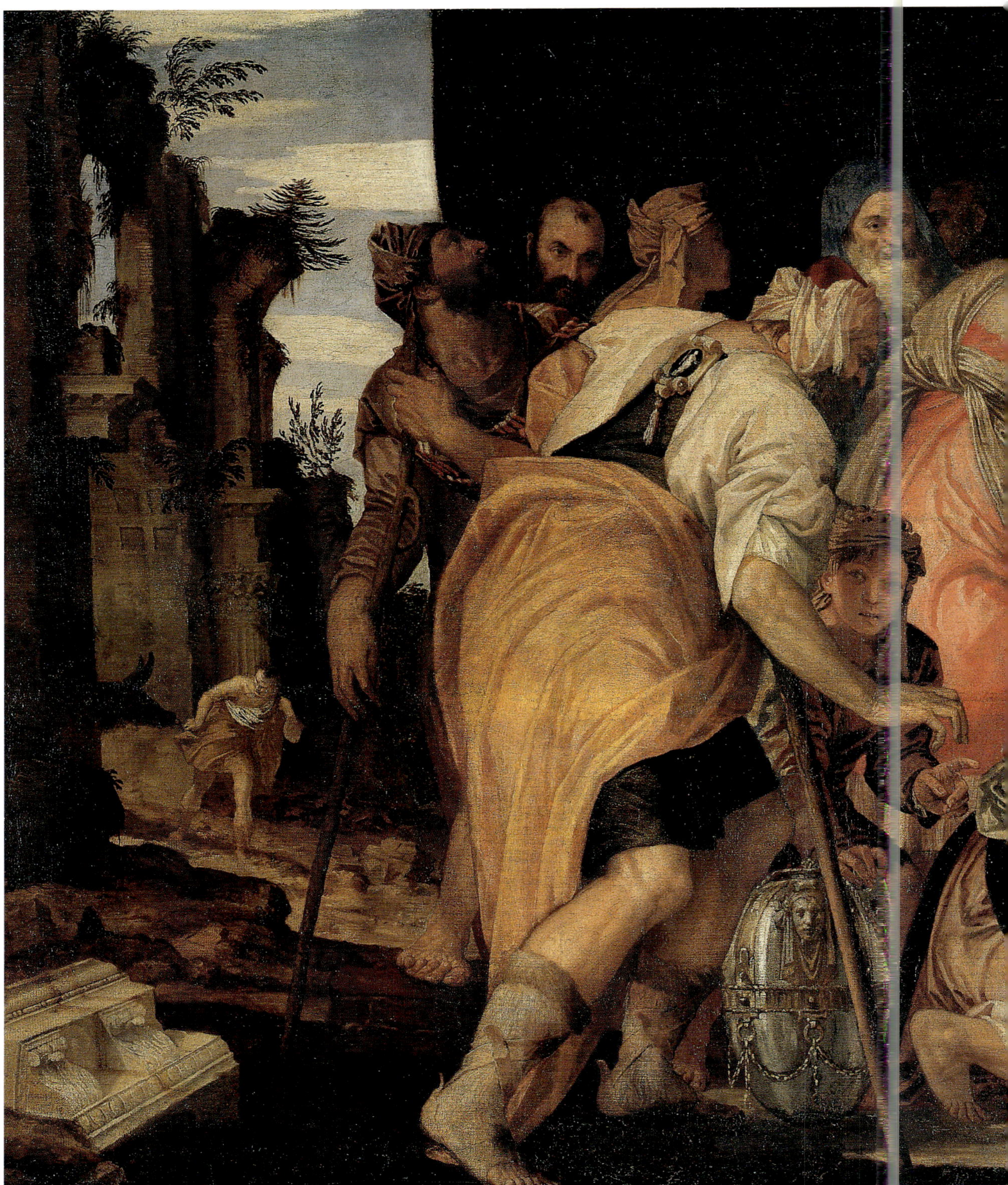

44 (previous page)
Martyrdom of St. Justina (detail of ill. 43)

Lent charm by a combination of finely graded yellow and pink tones, the complex movements of this figure with its back to us acts as a link between the Roman emperor, his retinue and St. Justina, while at the same time forming a counterpoise to the group of figures on the right. In this phase of his career, Veronese repeatedly experimented with the stylistic resources of Mannerism, though the depiction of complex movements and anatomical varieties of figures never became an end in itself. A date of origin around 1565 has been suggested, but this is incompatible with the date of 1556 on an engraved reproduction of the painting and the affinity of motifs with the *Honor* tondo (ill. 40) in the Libreria Vecchia in Venice, painted in 1556/57

(ill. 46), Veronese created a cycle of decorative ceiling paintings for the Palazzo Trevisan in Murano in which, after his first experiences in the Villa Soranza, he was again working as a fresco painter. Daniele Barbaro, to whom Ridolfi in his time attributed the design of the palazzo, may have been the go-between when Camillo Trevisan was looking for a suitable painter to carry out the decoration of the ceiling of the Sala dell'Olimpo on the ground floor. Severely damaged, the allegorical and mythological figures that still survive on site and the fragments in the Louvre that were transferred to canvas are only a pale reflection of something that once ennobled the place and repeatedly astonished the experts that succeeded Vasari. If the painter of figures had once again appeared here as a sensitive choreographer and master of foreshortenings, the painted decoration of the organs in the churches of San Geminiano and San Sebastiano in Venice was to require completely different artistic qualities.

The *Saints Geminianus and Severus* (ill. 52), *St. John the Baptist*, and *St. Mennas* (ill. 50), which once ornamented the casing of the organ in San Geminiano, share the same adventurous fate that befell so many other paintings by the Venetian painter which are now no longer at the location they were designed for. In 1807, the parish church on the west side of the Piazza di San Marco, which Jacopo Sansovino had magnificently renovated from 1557 onwards, was torn down at

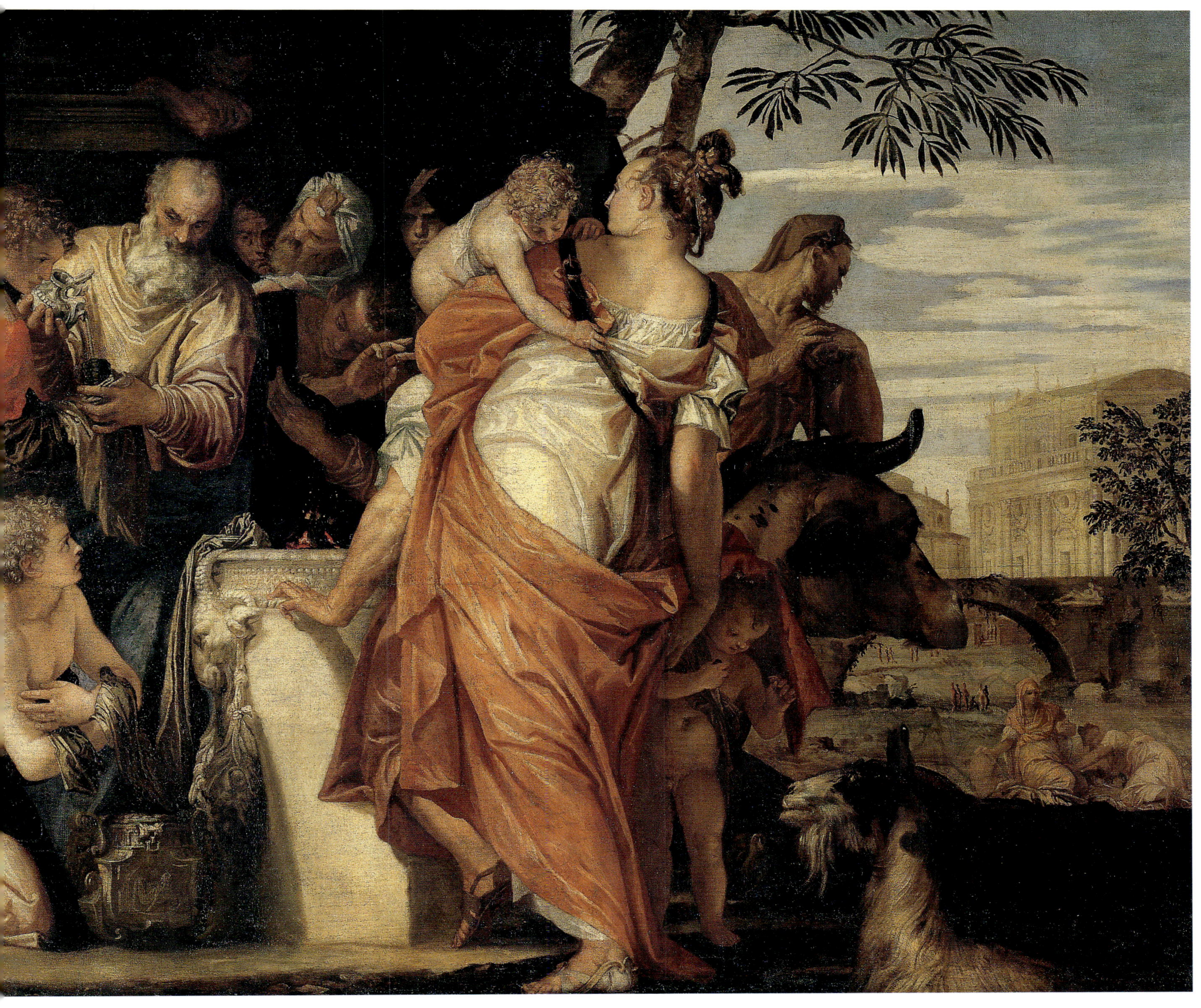

the command of Napoleon. Three years later, its place was occupied by the Ala Napoleonica. Only in Modena, where St. Geminianus held the office of bishop in the 4th century and is still venerated as the town's patron saint, were the three paintings finally reunited in 1924. It seems that Veronese returned from complicated to simpler things as a narrator. This step was determined by the original location of the works. The interior of the church was characterized by the strict formal idiom of the architect Sansovino; the pictures had to be matched to this. Veronese developed the three large figures with restrained movements, on the previously separated exterior wing, in front of an architecturally clearly structured niche with a round arch at the top. The only point in which he observed the commandment of *varietà* was that of detail; garments decorated with brocade and sophisticated colored and ornamental descriptions. But these visual charms are not the only thing that catch the observer's eye. Geminianus and Severus, who have taken a deacon with a book into their midst, owe their immediate presence to the way their gazes and movements are carefully matched to each other. The small deacon functions as a connecting link. The direction he is gazing in leads us to St. Severus, who is studying the open manuscript and, at the same time, pointing to the main altar of the church. While the two bishops only appeared when the wings of the organ were shut, when

45 *The Anointing of David*, c. 1554/55
Oil on canvas, 173 x 365 cm
Kunsthistorisches Museum, Vienna

The story of the shepherd boy David, who was anointed by the prophet Samuel after King Saul had been condemned by God, is told in I Samuel, 16, 1–13. To keep his plan secret from Saul, Samuel took a heifer with him and invited Jesse and his sons to the sacrifice. However, not all of them turned up. Only when Samuel asked whether Jesse had another son did David appear – he had been looking after the sheep. Samuel then took the horn of oil and anointed him, as commanded by God. As in the *Martyrdom of St. Justina* (ill. 43), presumably from the same period, the painter develops the action from the background to the foreground.

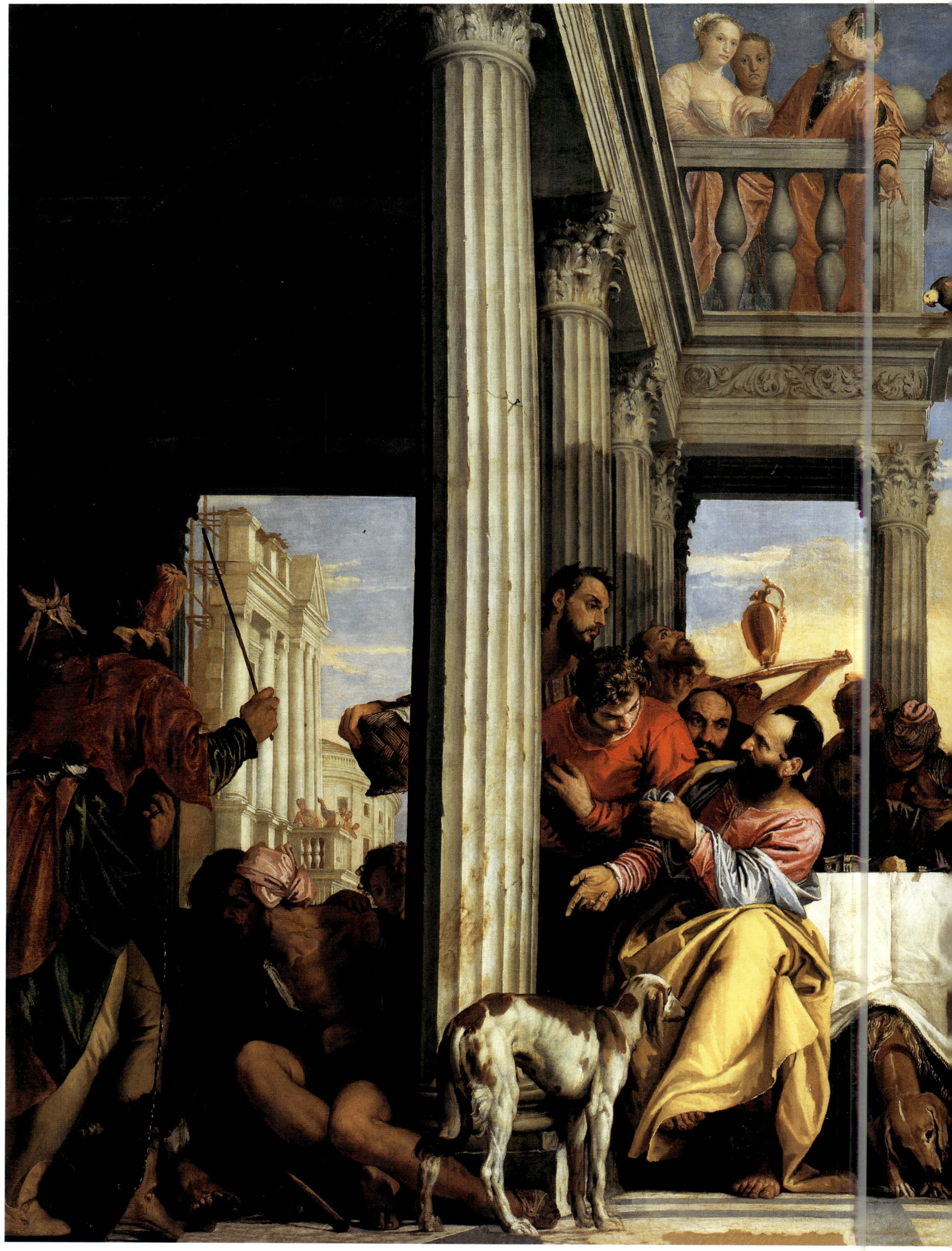

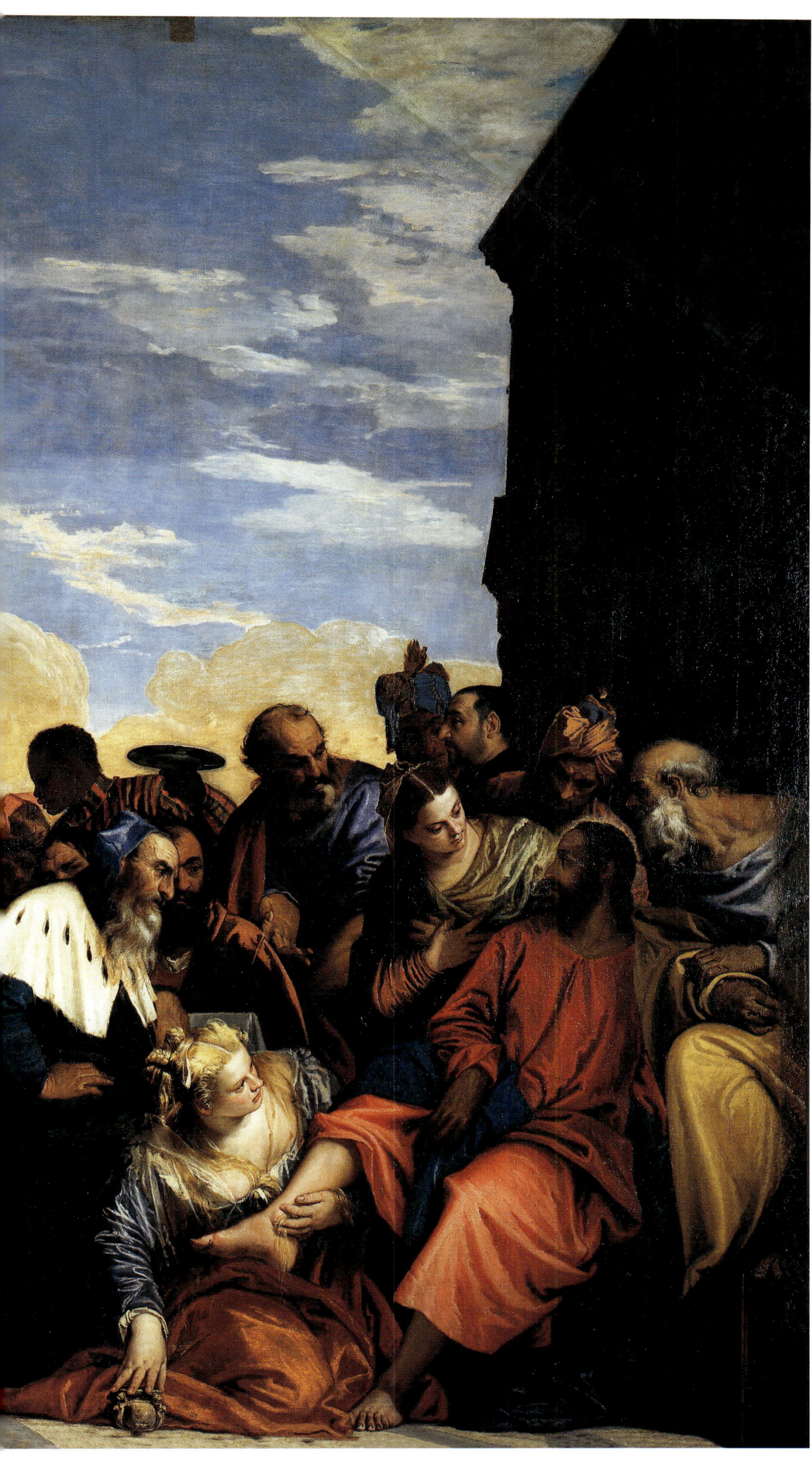

46 *Feast in the House of Simon*, 1556–1559/60
Oil on canvas, 315 x 451 cm
Galleria Sabauda, Turin

In contrast with the usual iconography, this banquet scene, originally painted for the dining room of the Benedictines in Santi Nazaro e Celso in Verona, is set not at the house of Simon but at the house of Lazarus and his sisters Martha and Mary (St. John 12, 1–11). The anointing of Jesus's feet by Mary, and Judas Iscariot's protest at the waste of the ointment form the dramatic poles between which Veronese's narrative unfolds. It is a work of hitherto unparalleled richness of detail and density. The great painting is the first in a series of banquet scenes (*cene*) that the painter did in the early 1570s for various monasteries in Venice and Vicenza. Veronese's biographer Carlo Ridolfi, who had copied the painting in 1629 as a study exercise, was commissioned to make another copy of it in 1650, when the Benedictines sold it to Giovanni Filippo Spinola from Genoa.

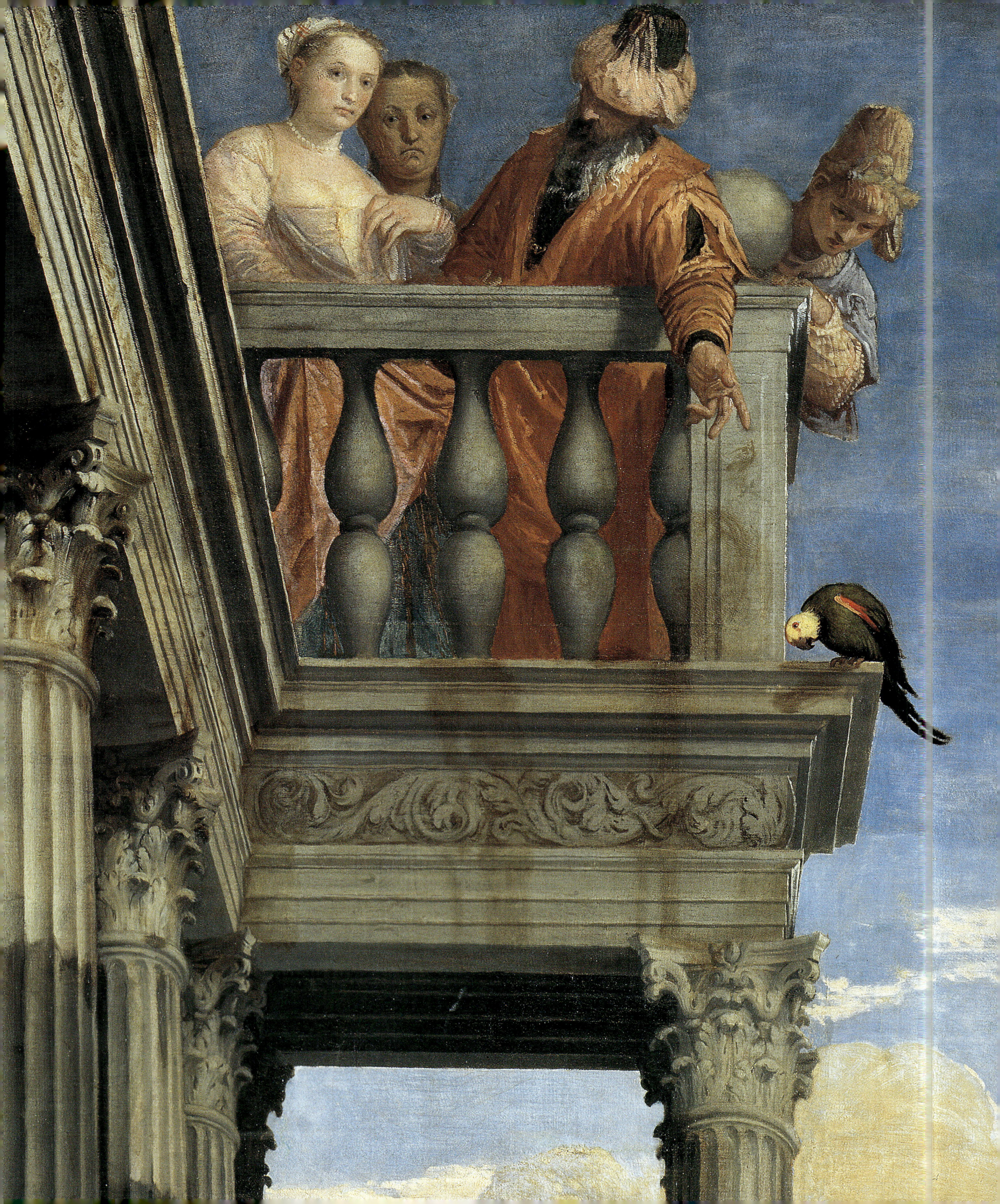

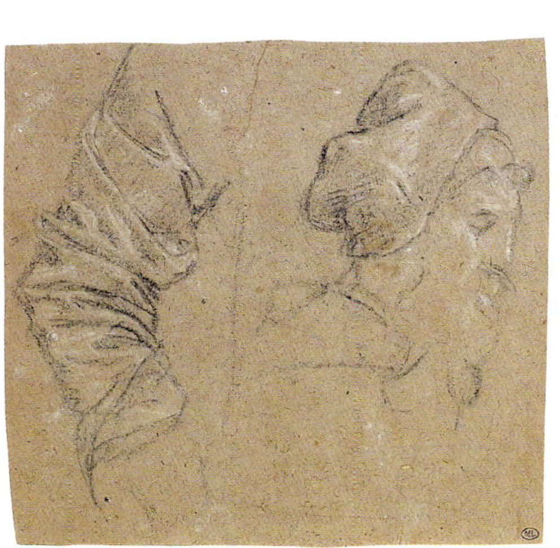

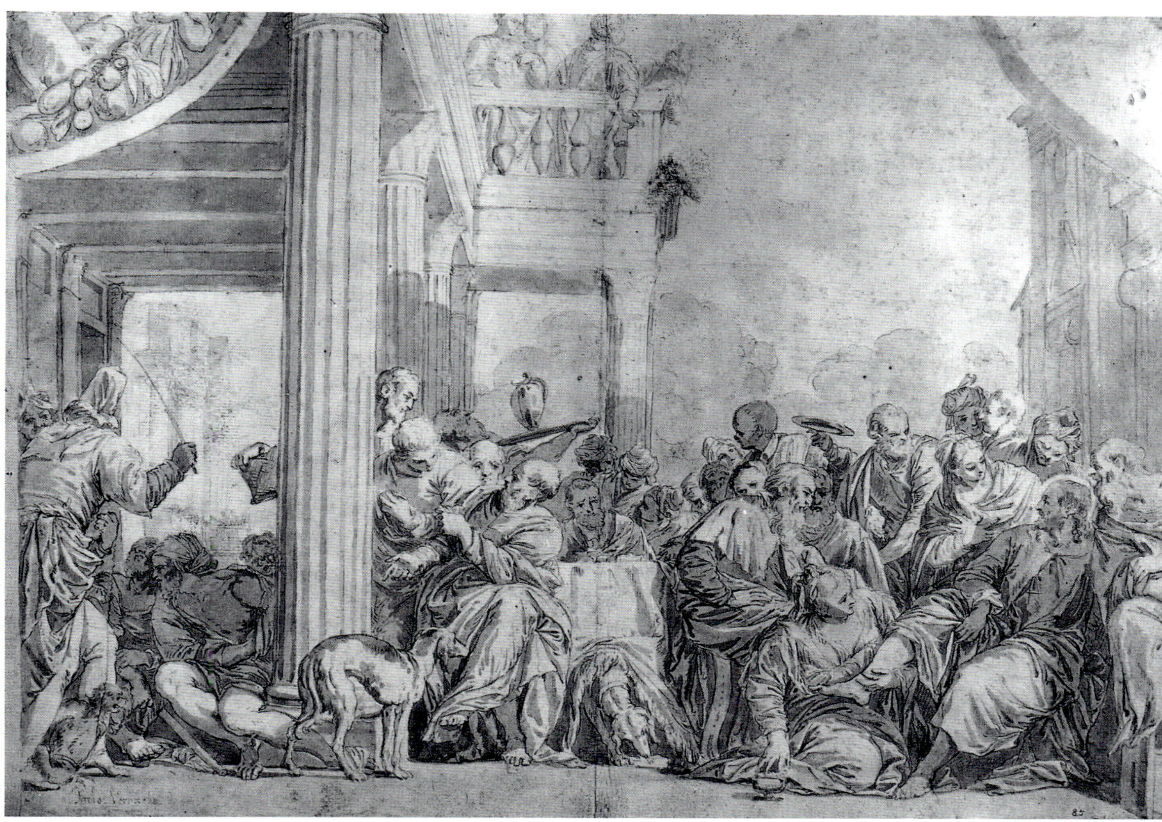

48 (above) Study for the *Feast in the House of Simon*, c. 1556
Black and white chalk on brownish paper, 16.5 x 18 cm
Département des arts graphiques, Musée du Louvre, Paris

This small sketch sheet has been identified by William R. Rearick as a preliminary study for the *Feast in the House of Simon* (ill. 46). At least the head of the host is developed enough to be recognizable. However, it is questionable whether the drapery study relates to this figure. It seems much more to anticipate the differentiated folds of Christ's left sleeve. Only after Veronese had settled in Venice did he occasionally try out the medium of chalk drawing, borrowing from Titian's drawing techniques. A further sheet (Département des art graphiques, Musée du Louvre, Paris) displays studies for two figures on the terrace.

49 (top right) Unknown artist
Feast at the House of Simon, copy of Veronese, before 1650
Red chalk drawing, 28.8 x 42.2 cm
Formerly Christie's, London, 1974, no. 141

We owe information about the original format of the *Feast at the House of Simon* (ill. 46) to this drawing by an unknown artist. On the left, the copyist recorded one of the two frescoed satyrs formerly painted above the curved corners of the painting. After the Benedictines sold the painting in 1650, the new owner transformed it into a gallery painting by restoring the corners.

47 (opposite) *The Feast at the House of Simon* (detail of ill. 46)
Pediments, colonnaded halls and roof terraces filled with onlookers are a notable feature of Veronese's great feast scenes. The bearded oriental who points to the scene of Christ being anointed ensures the multiple interweaving and dovetailing of pictorial architecture and figurative staffage so typical of Veronese.

it was open *St. John the Baptist* and *St. Mennas* (ill. 50) accompanied the music. In the latter figure of the Egyptian martyr, the idealism of St. John has given way to a memorable realism. The knight dressed in metallic shining armor has the features of a portrait, but it is more than questionable whether Veronese used his own features for the figure who gazes triumphantly towards us, thus conceitedly elevating it to a superficial allegory. His contemporaries at least did not consider the strongly expressive head to be a portrait. Nevertheless, the figure which was fitted into the undecorated niche in an apparently playful manner was noted. When Federico Zuccaro (c. 1540–1609), a Roman painter who was otherwise committed to completely different artistic ideals, visited the city of Venice in 1563, he made an ink copy of *St. Mennas* (ill. 51). The fact that in addition to this he devoted a drawn copy (Pushkin Museum, Moscow) to the organ casing in the left transept of the church of San Sebastiano testifies to the innovative character of these works.

While Veronese had not been granted the privilege of influencing the shape of the organ in San Geminiano, in San Sebastiano his design formed the basis for the work started in October 1558 by the carver Domenico Marangoni. The result is an expression of the "architectural way of thinking" of the painter and confronts us with a quite unusual solution: negating the classical sequence of architrave and typaneum, the round arch stretches far into the tympanum, in order to meet the framing Corinthian architecture at the pediment. The round arch itself forms the painted architectural framework for the almost 5.5 m. high *Presentation in the Temple* (ill. 53). On the painted inner sides of the organ wings, which when they are open connect directly with the organ casing, the painter also expertly structured the picture plane available to him with architectural features. The organ is now framed by a monumental Corinthian peristyle which sets the scene for the *Healing of the Lame at the Pool of Bethesda* (ills. 54, 55). The figures, developed out of the depths of the picture, make it clear that order and expressiveness in a picture need not exclude each other. Only at the front edge of the picture do the figures become full and complete, excitedly reaching out with their arms, hands and gazes towards the miracle of the healing. Neither in the emotional figures nor in the architectural features did Veronese remain caught up in his models. While, on first sight, the painted architecture is reminiscent of the formal language of Sansovino, even Ridolfi quite rightly remarked that Veronese had reproduced the visible world purely from his imagination. Thus, the composition of the picture and the sensitive use of architecture lacks the theatricality which is typical of numerous pictures created by successors in the 17th and 18th centuries. What 19th century critics rashly condemned as decorative and pleasant, as a product of the painter's all too free imagination, was nothing more than an artistically necessary means of expression that was subject to laws inherent to the picture. After all, they were not meant to be experienced in a museum or on one of the reproductive engravings which, in the 19th century, all too often substituted for a study of the original; instead, they were meant to be seen in the context of the complete furnishings of the church of San Sebastiano. Fra Bernardo Torlioni, who commissioned them, immediately recognized Veronese's qualities in 1555 and, for a period of about 15 years, bound the talented painter to himself and the church of San

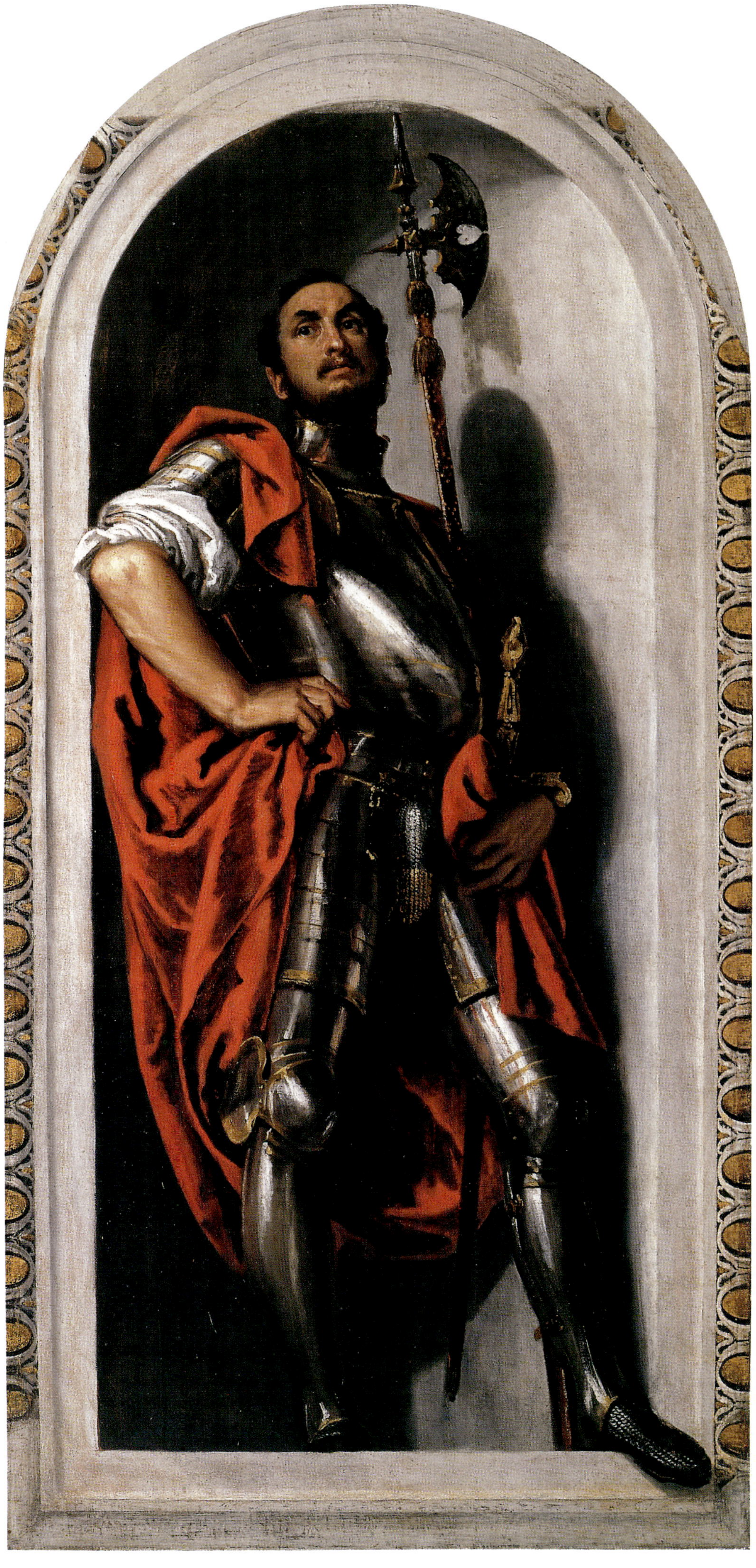

50 (left) *St. Mennas*, c. 1560
Oil on canvas, 247 x 122 cm
Galleria Estense, Modena

Mennas was an Egyptian Christian who served in the Roman army in Phrygia, later lived as a hermit and was beheaded c. 295 AD because of his faith. His undoubtedly striking presence is due to his self-assured pose. Supremely balanced, it seems as if the *miles christianus*, with his sword and halberd and gleaming armor, is about to step out of the niche.

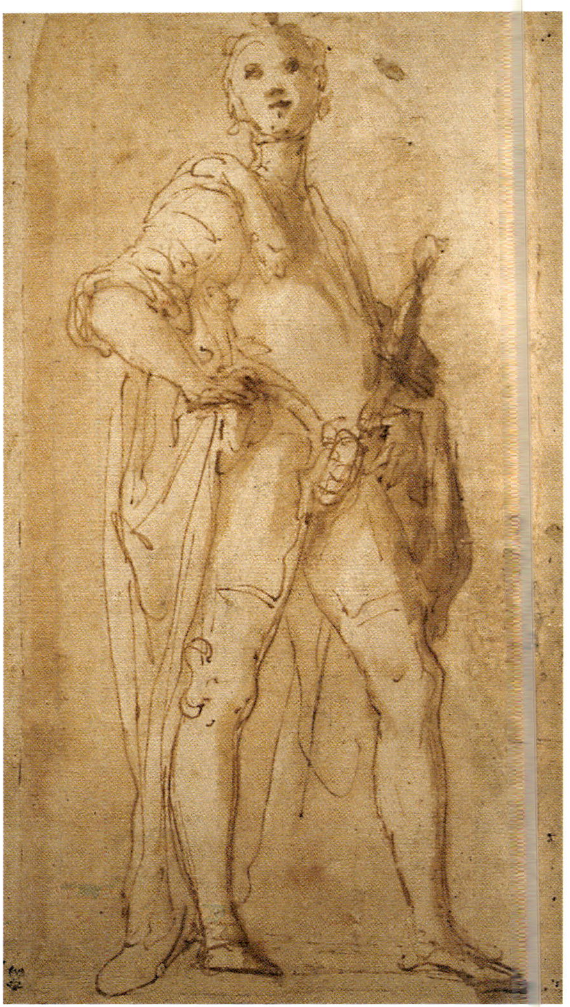

51 (above) Federico Zuccaro
St. Mennas, copy of Veronese, c. 1563 – 1565
Pen drawing, 24.6 x 14.4 cm
Musée des Beaux-Arts et de la Dentelle d'Alençon, Alençon

Federico Zuccaro (c. 1540 – 1609) visited Venice in 1563 and during his stay copied a number of Veronese's paintings. The drawn copies, in which he made a freely adapted version of the originals, served the painter as a reminder (*memoria*), and were once part of a sketchbook that was in the collection of Pierre Crozat in Paris until 1741.

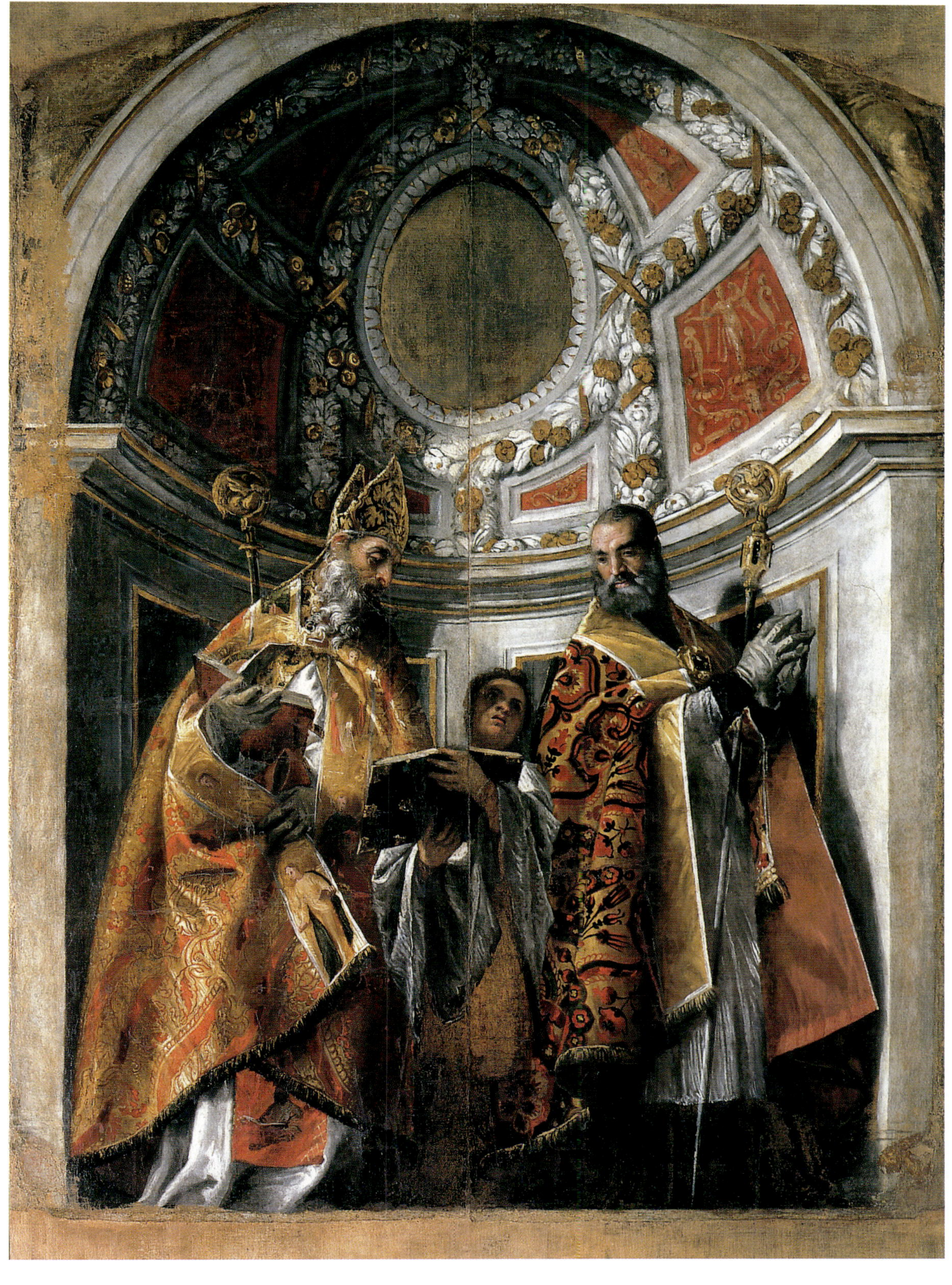

52 *SS. Geminianus and Severus*, c. 1560
Oil on canvas, 341 x 240 cm
Galleria Estense, Modena

This painting once belonged to the decorations of the organ in the church of San Geminiano in Venice, destroyed by Napoleon in 1807. In keeping with its function, it was once split down the middle. When closed, the two wings covered the pipes of the organ. When opened, they revealed St. John on the left and *St. Mennas* (ill. 50) on the right.

Sebastiano. By collaborating with Michele Sanmicheli and Andrea Palladio in Treville and Vicenza, carrying out commissions for churches and monasteries in Montagnana, Verona and Padua, and working in the Doge's palace and for private clients in Titian's, Sansovino's and Daniele Barbaro's circles, Veronese matured during the course of the 1550s into a sought-after interpreter of secular and religious themes.

In contrast, his activities in the field of portrait painting, which have not yet been adequately researched, remain largely in the dark. High-quality works, such as the *Portrait of a Young Man Wearing Lynx Fur* (ill. 56), which may have still been created in Verona, and the *Portrait of a Lady* (ill. 57) in the Louvre which for a long time was dubiously titled "La Bella Nani", can nowadays, for stylistic reasons, with some certainty be assigned to this period in his creative work.

In other portraits, which have frequently been attributed to Veronese on a trial basis, what the depicted persons have in common is a high degree of distance and refinement. The fact that both these qualities occasionally appear coupled with a peculiar melancholy

53 (following page)
Presentation in the Temple, 1560
Oil on canvas, 490 x 190 cm
San Sebastiano, Venice

This scene adorns the outside wings of the carved organ of San Sebastiano in Venice. Parts of the figurative composition largely repeat an earlier picture on the same subject in Dresden. Here, the structure is much more clearly articulated and harmonious and enclosed by a large round arch. A typical feature is the introduction of various subsidiary figures required less for the event itself than for formal reasons. Also, Veronese delighted in using painterly means to explore certain movements or the qualities of the color and appearance of expensive materials.

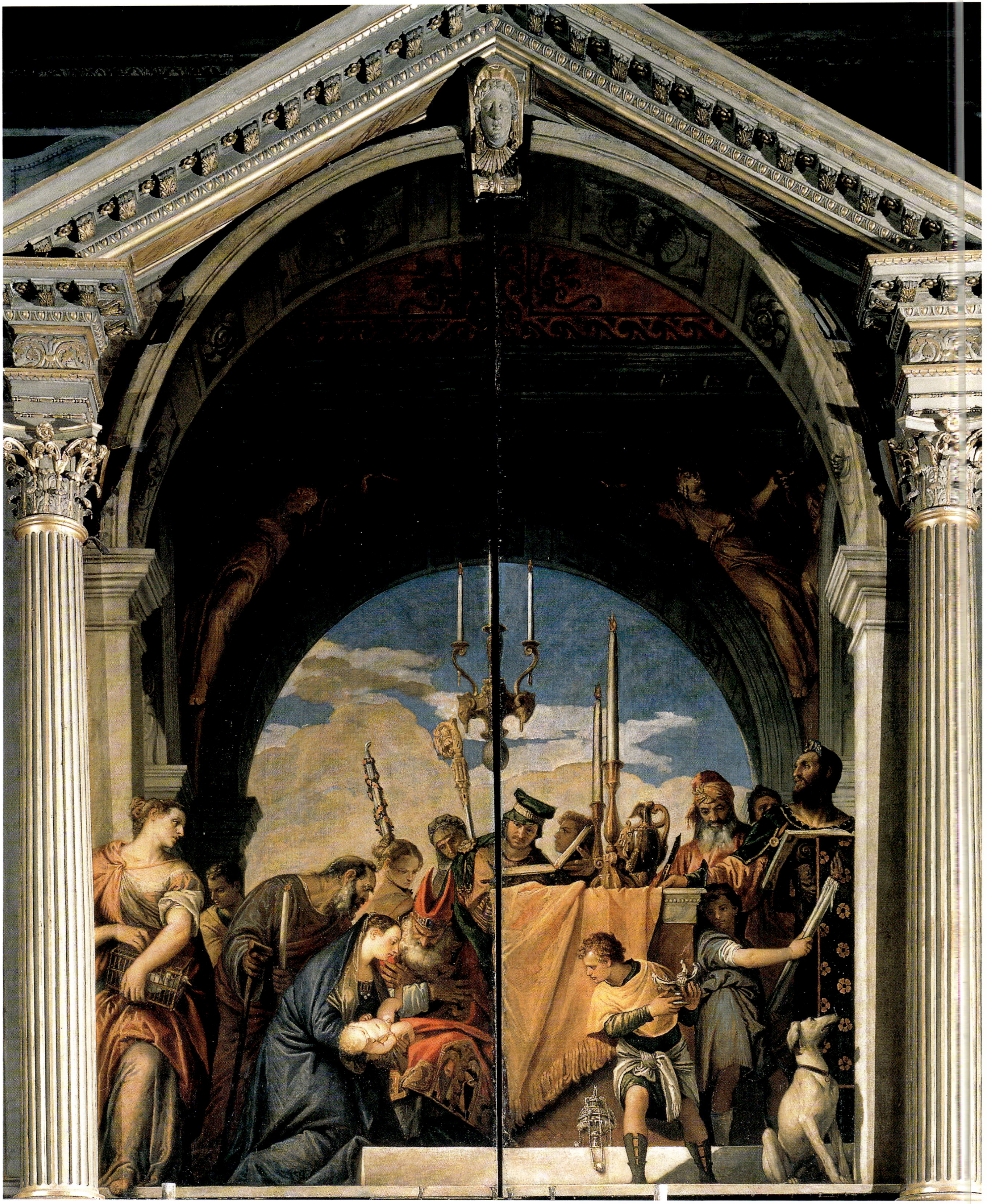

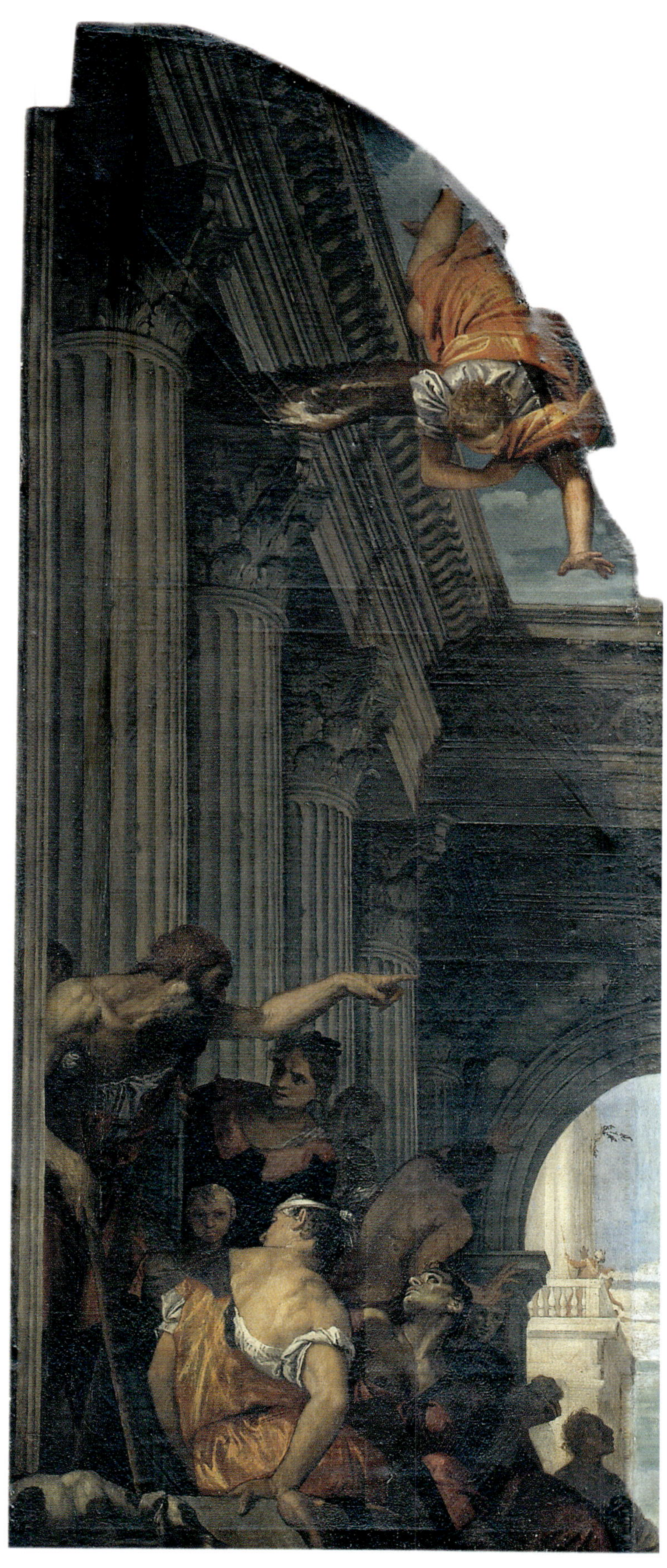

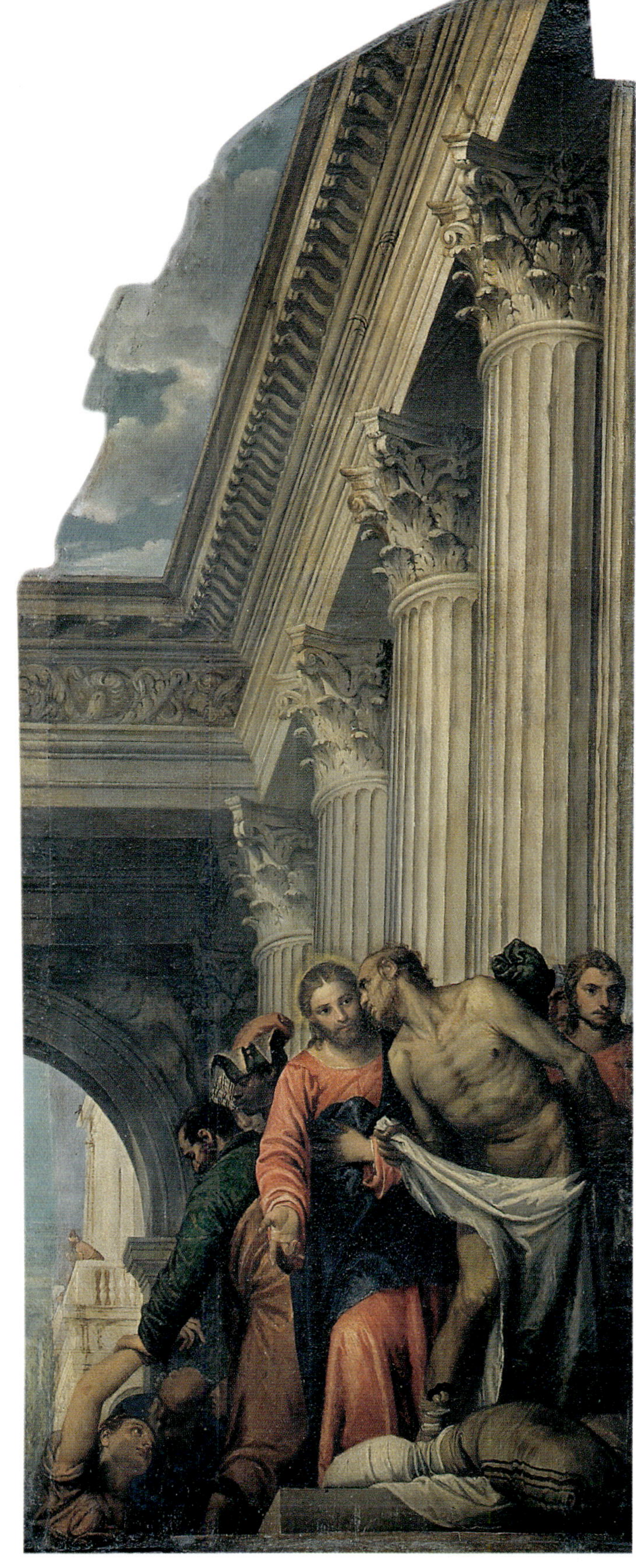

54, 55 *Healing of the Lame Man at the Pool of Bethesda*, 1560
Oil on canvas, 490 x 190 cm
San Sebastiano, Venice

When opened, the painted wings of the organ of San Sebastiano show an interior court surrounded by Corinthian colonnades. The latter allude to the mention of five porches around the pool in Jerusalem in the story as told in St. John 5, 1–8. In it "lay a great multitude of sick folk, of blind, halt and withered", waiting for the angel who "went down at a certain season into the pool and troubled the water". The first person to enter the water after the "stirring" was cured. The depiction is among the miracles of Christ: with the words, "Rise, take up thy bed and walk", he heals a lame man who is always too late to reach the water. Veronese's accommodation of the throng of moving figures to the architecture from the depth to the foreground is masterly.

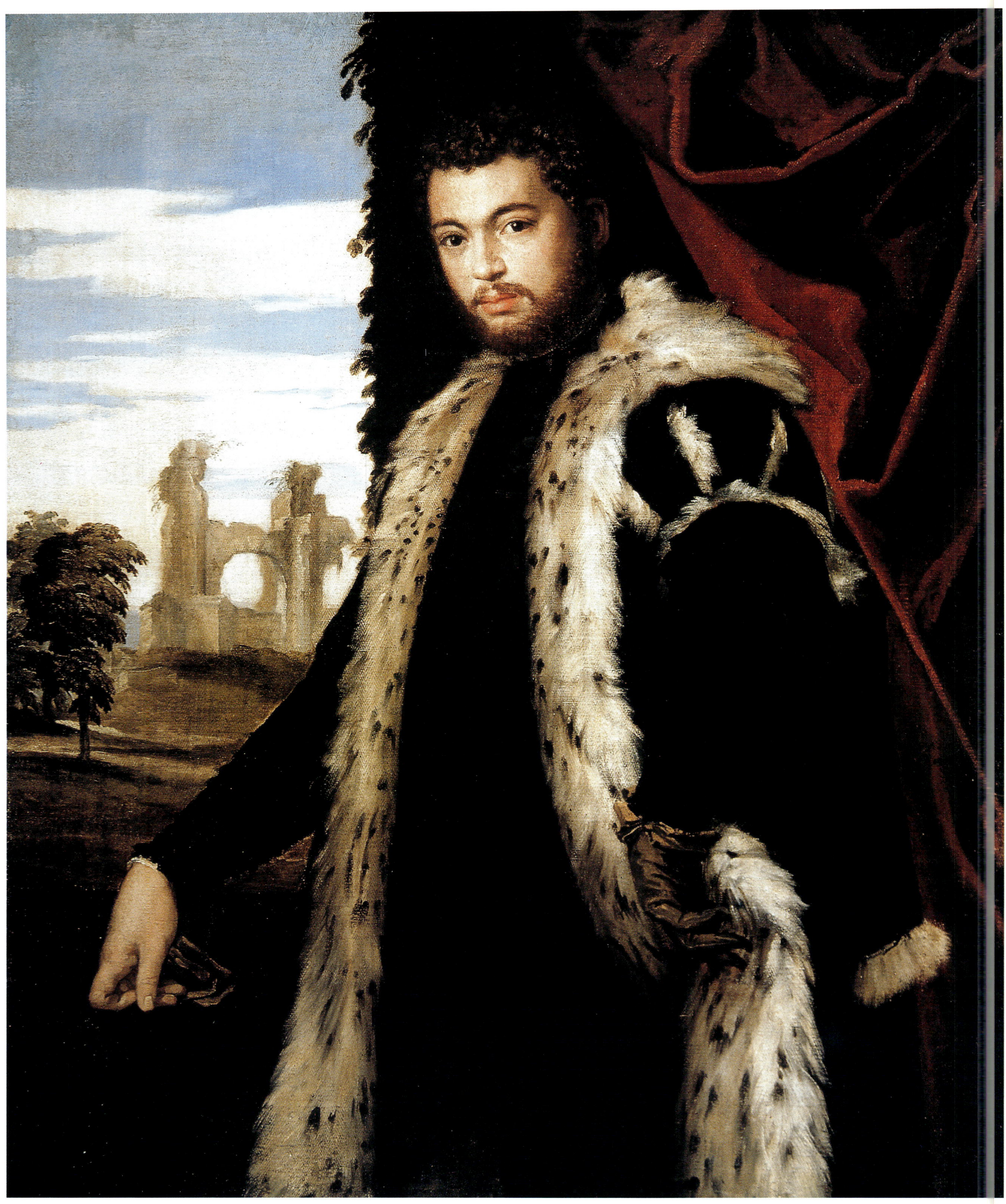

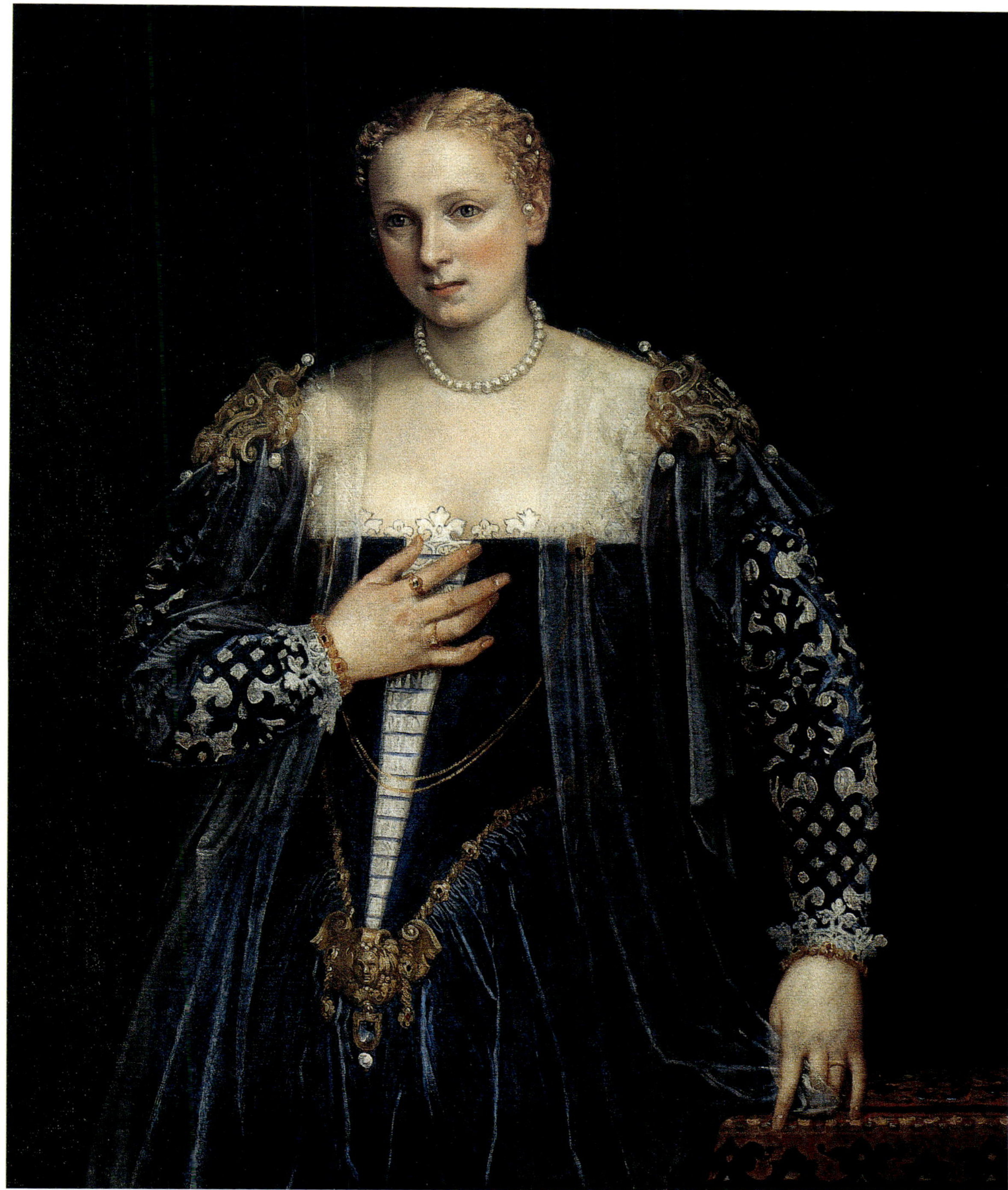

57 (right) *Portrait of a Lady (La Bella Nani)*, c. 1555
Oil on canvas, 119 x 103 cm
Musée du Louvre, Paris

This portrait has long been identified with a portrait by Veronese documented in 1660 without any further description at the Casa Nani in the Cannaregio quarter by the Venetian Marco Boschini. The provenance of the Louvre portrait can only be traced back into the early 19th century, when it belonged to the collection of the Venetian abbot Luigi Celotti. The dating is a matter of controversy, with suggested dates ranging from 1555 to 1561. The only clues are comparisons with the portrait of a lady in the *Supper at Emmaus* in the Louvre dated 1559 and the portrait of the eponymous subject in *Giustiniana Giustinian and her Nurse* (ill. 71). Though Veronese takes his inspiration for the rendering of the expensive dark-blue velvet gown from nature, the blond Venetian woman looks, like so many of his no-longer identifiable models, aloof, reserved and strangely uninvolved. The eloquent and elegant gesture of the hand to the breast makes little difference: it can be taken simply as a gesture of asseveration, vouching for the sincerity of the subject.

56 (opposite) *Portrait of a Young Man Wearing Lynx Fur*, c. 1551–1553
Oil on canvas, 120 x 102 cm
Szépmüvészeti Múzeum, Budapest

In its warm-color tones, this portrait recalls the works of the Lombard painter Moretto da Brescia (1499–1554), while its structure is reminiscent of late 1540s portraits by Tintoretto, which Veronese certainly must have seen even before his first visit to Venice in 1551. The luxurious lynx fur visibly documents the prosperity of the young *gentiluomo*. The architectural ruins in the background, possibly inspired by engravings published by the Antwerp engraver and graphics publisher Hieronymus Cock (1518–1570), have an emblematic, symbolic character. They remind us of the past greatness of Rome and at the same time draw attention to the breadth of the subject's education.

deserves our attention insofar as it is precisely this aspect of Veronese's portrait painting that was to become the object of correspondence between the English poet and soldier Sir Philip Sidney (1554–1586) and his friend Languet. According to this, in February 1574, Sidney sat for "one Paul of Verona" in Venice, after Tintoretto, "who holds by far the highest place in this art," had evidently not been available. As early as June 1574 the portrait was in Vienna, but Languet criticized the poor likeness, even thought he could recognize his friend's brother in the well-drawn portrait and asked him to consider that Sidney may well have looked like that when he was 10 or 12 years old, and that he also seemed a little distressed and sad. In the *Portrait of Sir Philip Sidney*, the existence of which can no longer be proven, Veronese may have created one of those portraits with a tendency towards idealization, which can occasionally be found in his *œuvre*. In contrast to Titian, whose brush brought masterpieces of extraordinary psychological penetration and abstraction to light, Veronese remained a sober observer for large stretches of his career as a portrait painter. What remained important was detail. This is demonstrated, perhaps most impressively, by the portrait of Daniele Barbaro (ill. 58), who was to become Veronese's most important sponsor towards the end of the 1550s, and, indeed, even became a key figure in his work.

58 *Daniele Barbaro*, c. 1561–1566
Oil on canvas, 121 x 105.5 cm
Rijksmuseum, Amsterdam

Around 1560/61, Veronese was commissioned by Daniele Barbaro to provide the interior frescoes for Barbaro's Palladian villa in Maser (ills. 65, 67–71). The artist and his client had probably been acquainted since the early 1550s. A dating of 1556 has been suggested, based on Barbaro's edition of Vitruvius published in 1556 and the two volumes of this edition lying on the table. However, in view of the rather more aged appearance of the subject, a dating to the first half of the 1560s looks preferable. The upended book in front of a globe depicts a small putto on the left pointing with a rod at a geometrical proportion drawing. As this figure appears in the corresponding illustration of the Vitruvius edition sideways on, slightly averted and also wholly without clothing, it might be presumed that it was Veronese himself who provided the drawing on which this illustration is based. Likewise, the volume on the table – the page open shows parts of the title page of the *Dieci libri* – alludes to the cleric's real sphere of activity. Though he had been appointed Patriarch of Aquileia, he devoted himself mainly to humanistic studies and architectural theory. Veronese catches the physiognomy of the subject and his apparatus in paint with unusual precision. This was evidently a response to his client, whose interest lay in precision in his own field of activity.

The name of Daniele Matteo Alvise Barbaro, who was born in Venice on February 8, 1514, is linked with an extraordinary career. In the 15th century, his family had already produced important scholars in the form of Francesco di Candiano Barbaro (1398–1454) and Ermolao Barbaro (1453–1493), and it is therefore not surprising that Daniele, following his early education in Verona, followed this tradition and entered the University of Padua at the beginning of the 1530s. In 1535 he was one of the students of the respected humanist Benedetto Lampridio, who acquainted him with the writings of Aristotle and encouraged him to study the classics in the original. With a wide variety of interests, Daniele devoted himself during the following years to the study of philosophy, mathematics, astronomy and optics. Shortly after he was made a doctor of *artes*, the young scholar was appointed as inspector of the newly constructed botanical gardens belonging to the University of Padua. His portrait created in 1545 (ill. 60) by Titian may have been produced on this occasion. During this period, he was close friends with outstanding figures in the circle of the *Accademia degli Infiammati,* including the man of letters Pietro Bembo (1470–1547) and the humanist Sperone Speroni (1500–1588), to whom Titian also devoted a portrait in 1544/45 (Museo Civico, Treviso).

However, Barbaro's period in office in Padua was short-lived. As early as 1549 he entered the service of the *Serenissima*, and after a period of just two years he was sent to represent the interests of the Republic of Venice as an ambassador to the English court. In the spring of 1550 Giovanni Grimani (c. 1500–1593), the incumbent patriarch of Aquileia, had suggested Daniele as his possible successor. On the one hand, the decisive factor in this recommendation was the close friendship between the Grimani and Barbaro families and the lack of a male heir, but the actual reason for this step was different. For as early as April 1549 something had started, which finally, 12 years later after tough negotiations, was to end up as the famous *causa Grimani,* the Inquisition's trial of the patriarch of Aquileia: controversial comments Grimani had made on divine pre-ordination had led to him being suspected of heresy. This occurred at a rather unfavorable point inasmuch as his name had been put forward by the Signoria in Rome in 1550 for promotion to cardinal. For political reasons, therefore, the Venetian senate was interested in nominating a Venetian of integrity for the patriarchy and demanded that Giovanni Grimani name a suitable representative in case he was appointed cardinal.

Daniele made the decision while he was still staying in England, and only after some hesitation did he accept the appointment, made on December 17, 1550. Giovanni Grimani nonetheless continued in office as the patriarch of Aquileia, and more: the man who was probably the most important collector of classical works of art in Venice, to whom we can trace the donation of the façade of the church of San Francesco della Vigna among others, survived his designated successor by more than two decades.

Largely free of his ecclesiastical and political duties, and financially independent, Daniele Barbaro from then onwards once more devoted himself very intensively to his academic studies. In the early 1550s he came into contact with the architect Andrea Palladio, and just four years later the opportunity arose to accompany the outstanding expert on classical architecture to Rome. The experience gained on this journey, which, bearing in mind the planned villa in Maser very probably included the study of classical villas, bore rich fruit. Based on his own preliminary studies, which, according to his own account, had begun as early as about 1547, he published the *I Dieci libri dell'architettura di M. Vitruvio* (ill. 59) in Venice in 1556, an annotated translation of the treatise *De architectura libri decem* written by Vitruvius. The treatise, written in about 25 B.C. by the Roman architect and engineer Vitruvius and dedicated to Emperor Augustus (63 B.C.–14 A.D.), is the only surviving book from the classical age to deal with the principles of architecture. It dealt both with questions of technique and materials and with aspects of the construction of cities and fortifications, and the orders of temples and columns. To these were added a theory of proportions and astronomical observations. While copies of the lost original text had already been circulating during Carolingian times, a critical discussion of Vitruvius did not begin until the writings of Italian theoreticians of the 15th and 16th centuries. In this way, Vitruvius's theory of proportions and his description of the architectural orders of the classical era became an integral part of architectural theory.

In imitation of older editions by Fra Giovanni Giocondo (Venice, 1511) and Cesare Cesariano (Como, 1521), the critical edition of the Vitruvius exegete Barbaro set new standards with regard to form and content. Two slightly reworked editions in Latin and Italian which were published in Venice in 1567 document the topicality of the work. Palladio worked in conjunction with Barbaro on the first edition, and possibly even Paolo Veronese as has recently been suggested. The latter at least referred to the first edition in his impressive portrait of the cleric and trained architectural theoretician (ill. 58). Andrea Palladio was not merely an expert advisor in questions of theory and technique, he also provided the drawings for the most important illustrations. Using Aristotelian views as its starting point, Barbaro published *La pratica della perspettiva* in 1568, another important treatise on the theory of art. This rulebook instructed painters, sculptors and architects in questions of perspective and proportion. In addition, for the first time, it contained a detailed scientific and analytical description of the *camera obscura.*

Daniele Barbaro died during the night of the of April 12–13, 1570. As an unpretentious cleric who had already

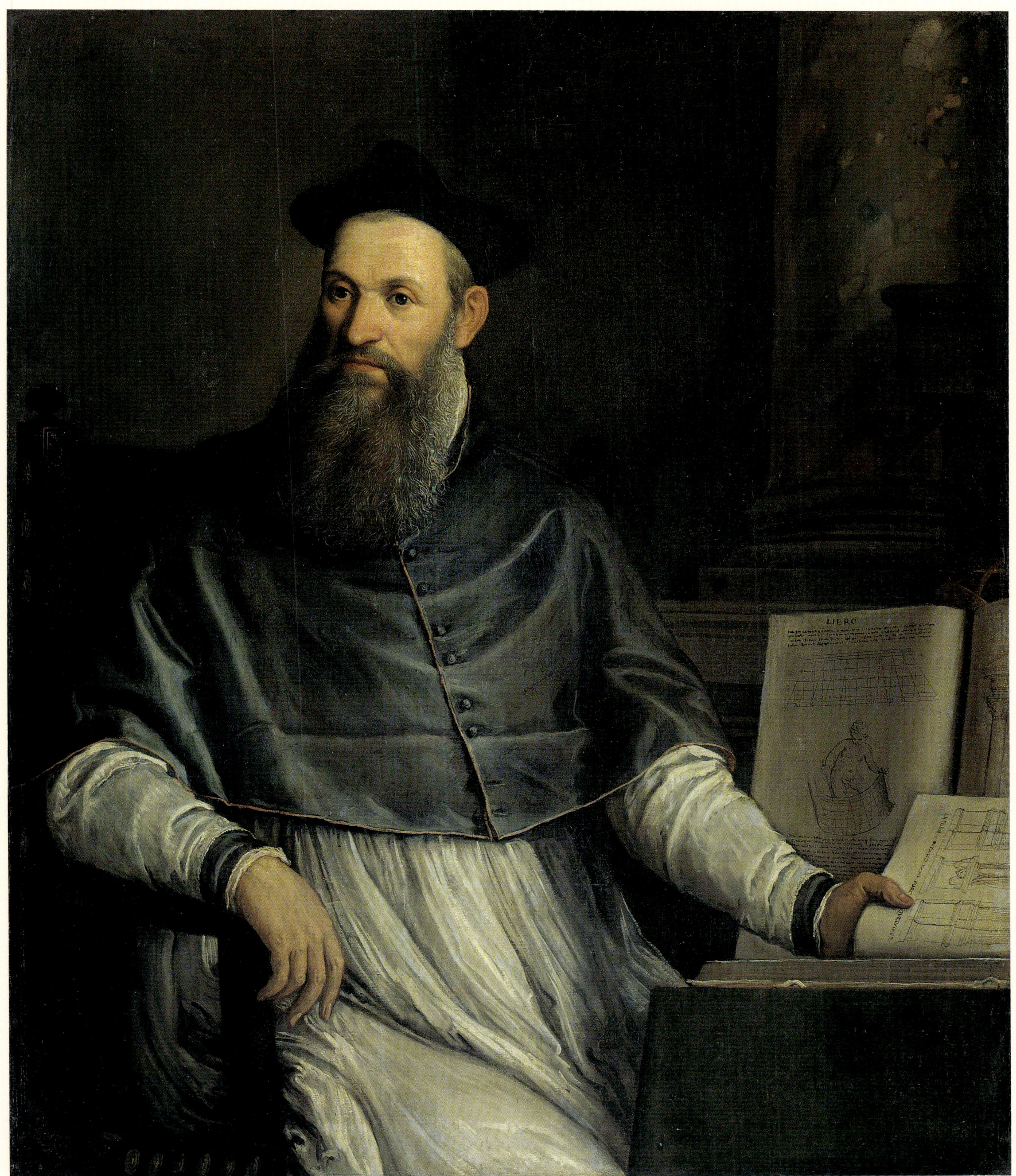

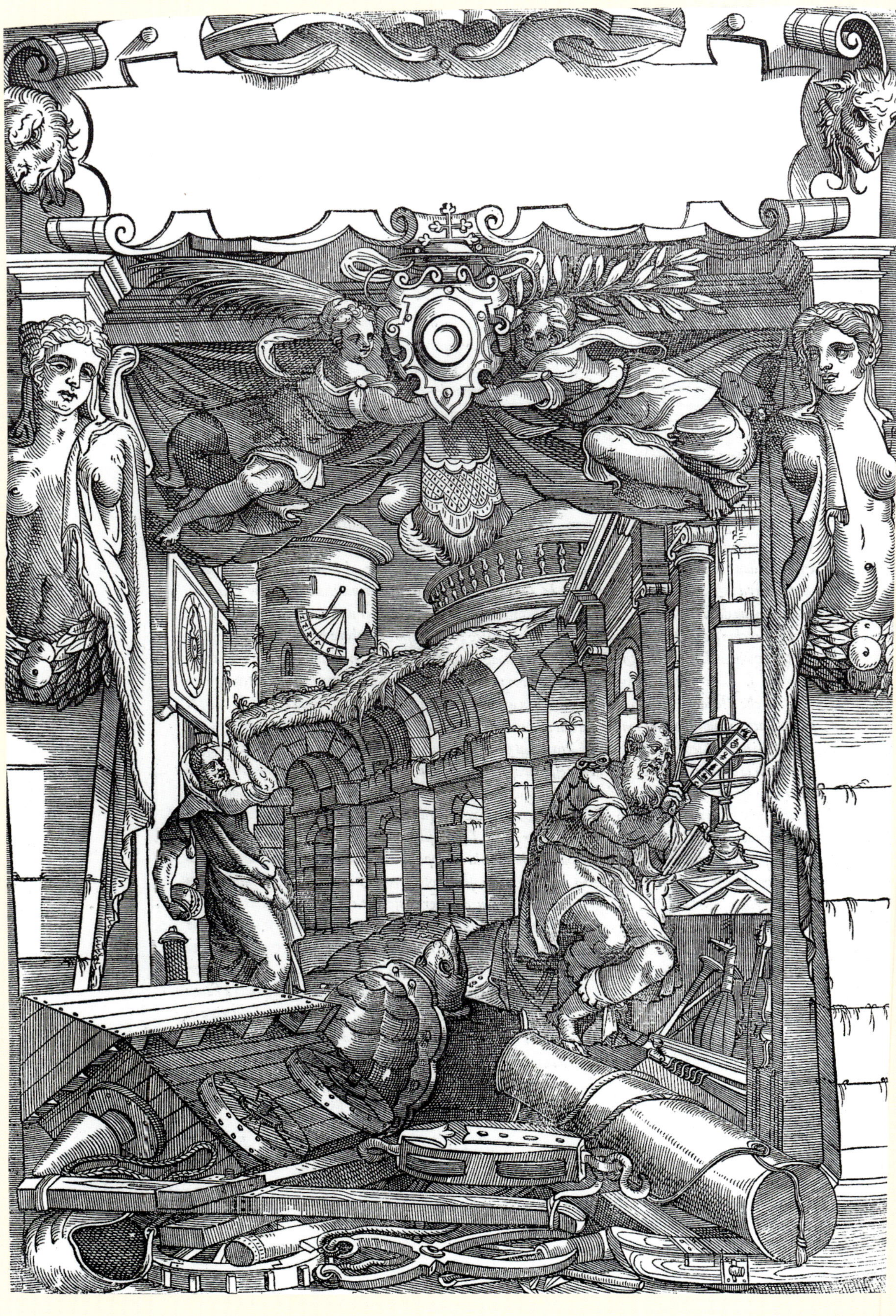

59 Daniele Barbaro
I Dieci libri dell'architettura di M. Vitruvio tradutti e commentati da Monsignor Barbaro, eletto patriarca d'Acquileggia, Venice 1556, frontispiece (verso)
Woodcut
Bayerische Staatsbibliothek, Munich

The woodcut opens Daniele Barbaro's edition of Vitruvius, published in 1556, mirroring Barbaro's views on architectural theory, and presumably shows the scholar himself in the middle of an accumulation of sundry appliances and instruments. Cog wheel, block and tackle and tongs allude to the practical activities of the architect. The tortoise and mobile assault shelter derive originally from the military sphere. They were for the Roman army's protection when advancing. Barbaro is here following an older tradition of Vitruvius exegesis, which describes the vault of the ancient basilica in Fano built by Vitruvius as analogous to the carapace of a tortoise. Translated into architectural terms, the mobile shelter became a pitched roof. In the background, arches and vaults as the epitome of classical architecture are contrasted with "modern" contemporary architecture, with the Ionic ascribed to Barbaro corresponding the order used in the façade of the mansion in Maser. An interest in architecture also meant, for Barbaro, studying astronomy. Its importance is underlined by the sundial, linking the earthly world with the stars and the sphere in front of the scholar.

60 Titian
Daniele Barbaro, 1545
Oil on canvas, 81 x 69 cm
Museo del Prado, Madrid

This portrait is considered to be a replica in his own hand of an almost identical portrait in the National Gallery of Canada in Ottawa, which identifies the subject as Daniele Barbaro in an inscription. The picture in Ottawa is probably that mentioned in 1545 in a letter from Pietro Aretino, which once belonged to the portrait collection of Paolo Giovio in Como. With the body turned slightly to the right and the grave, spiritual face framed by the beard and hair, Daniele Barbaro's gaze is fixed on the viewer. His black gown reveals scarcely anything except the left hand and the book, which, as an attribute of scholarship, alludes to Barbaro's humanistic education. Barbaro was hardly 30 years old at this date.

made very critical comments on the funerary monuments in churches in his commentaries on Vitruvius, he had declined a burial in the family's own chapel in San Francesco della Vigna in Venice and instead instructed in his will that he should have a simple burial in the cemetery of the Franciscan church. His will, which among other matters contains instructions about some astronomical instruments which he bought or built himself, is written in the words of an unassuming man and scarcely suggests that this was the last will and testament of the builder of probably the most famous villa in the Veneto, and the patron of Andrea Palladio and Paolo Veronese.

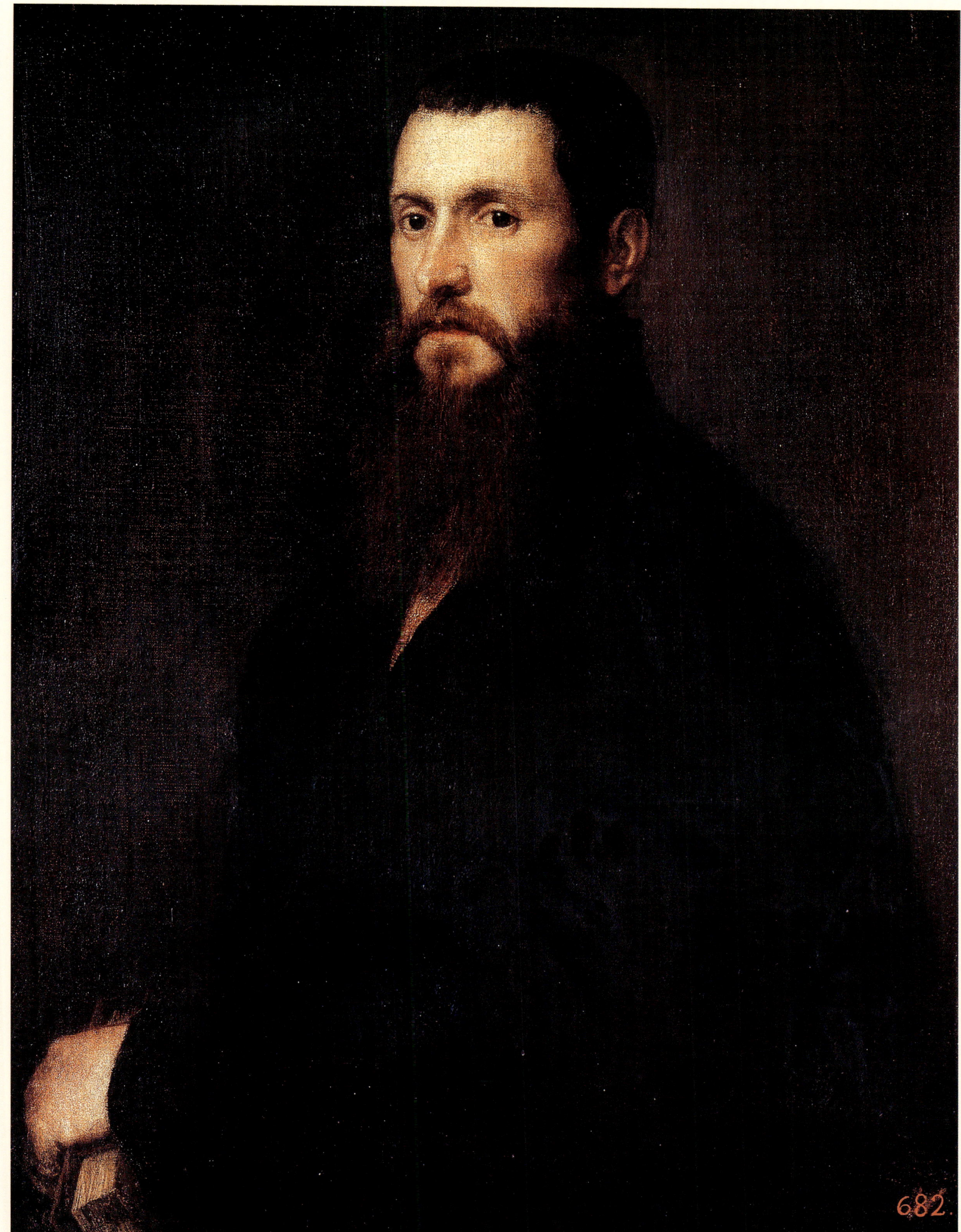
682.

Villa Barbaro in Maser – The Master of Spatial Illusion

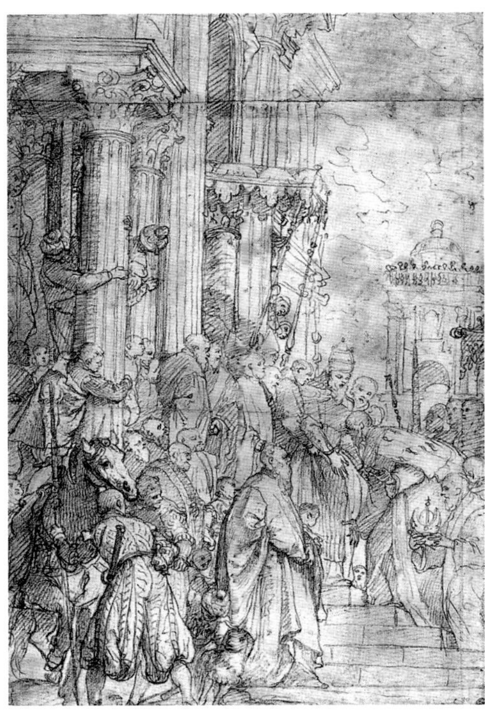

61 Federico Zuccaro
Frederick Barbarossa kissing the Hand of the Antipope Victor IV, copied from Veronese, c. 1563–1565
Pen drawing, 33.6 x 22.8 cm
János Scholz Collection, Pierpont Morgan Library, New York

The drawing is based on a picture by Veronese, which, commissioned in January 1562, was destroyed by fire in the Sala del Maggiore Consiglio at the Doge's Palace in 1577. When Federico Zuccaro was honored with the task of replacing the painting during the restoration work, he painted the *Humiliation of the Emperor Barbarossa* (Sala del Maggiore Consiglio, Doge's Palace), inspired by Veronese's lost painting. In 1648, Carlo Ridolfi records that it was the fame of the frescoes of the Villa Barbaro that brought Veronese the commission for the history painting.

62 (opposite) *Girl in the Doorway* (cf. ill. 64)

The picture shows a girl, presumably a member of the Barbaro household, apparently entering the Sala almost by chance, but it is in fact one of the painted *trompe l'œil* that still captivate visitors to the Villa Barbaro in Maser.

In the painting *Frederick Barbarossa kissing the Hand of the Antipope Victor IV*, Veronese's biographer Carlo Ridolfi paid homage in 1648 to a work that he himself had never seen in the original. Nonetheless, this picture had been described in detail by Vasari and copied on several occasions by contemporary painters (ill. 61) before it fell victim to a fire in December 1577 in the Sala del Maggior Consiglio in the Doge's palace. Probably just 6 m. high and more or less square, the work, which was commissioned on January 7, 1562, was Veronese's largest history painting until then. It contained the portraits of both the Doge and numerous Venetian nobleman and office bearers, including Lorenzo and Antonio Giustinian, the donors of the *Pala Giustinian*. Ridolfi mentions that this work owed its creation to the painter's reputation and the fame of his unique works in Maser.

According to this, Veronese's cycle of frescoes in the Villa Barbaro must have been completed by the end of 1561, and it remains surprising that the painter's extensive work in Maser has left no trace in either the writings of his client Daniele Barbaro or the *Quattro libri dell'architettura* written by his famous colleague Andrea Palladio. Palladio, who otherwise did not hesitate to mention assistants and colleagues and made no exception in Paolo Veronese's case where the decoration of the Palazzo Porto in Vicenza was concerned, remained silent when he wrote about the villa, located in the fertile Trevisan countryside close to Asolo, in his treatise (ill. 63) in 1570. Only a letter written to Daniele Barbaro by Giulia da Ponte in 1559 provides vague clues as to when the painter started work. It mentions the nymphaeum *(ninfeo)* surrounding the fountains to the north, which at this time was also complete and perhaps even already decorated with allegorical fresco paintings.

Planning of the overall layout had probably started in 1551. It was carried out by Palladio between 1556 and 1558, though certain peculiarities of the complex have led to the supposition that he was forced to make major concessions to the taste of his client, the amateur architect. Thus there are some suggestions that Daniele Barbaro was responsible for the design of the nymphaeum, lavishly decorated with small ornaments, while his brother Marcantonio, who regularly lived in the villa and occasionally did sculptural work, contributed some of the conspicuously coarsely modeled statues. As Norbert Huse has shown, the collaboration of client and architect also left unusual traces on the exterior of the manor house. To name just a few features, there is the round arch of the balcony door which, in contrast with Palladio's ideas, penetrates the entablature of the pediment on the first floor; also, the unusual ground plan of the manor house itself, which is drawn conspicuously further forward than the working quarters on either side, evidently in imitation of the *triclinium* of the classical Pliny villa in Laurentinum. Finally, it appears as if inside the central plan residence there has been a continuation, with different roles, of features all too evident in the exterior. Decorative sculptural elements such as door frames, plain fireplaces and the entablature that structures individual rooms have been executed in stucco – a material atypical of Palladio – and their detail is contrary to the architect's strict formal language. Instead, individual forms are re-encountered in the painted architecture of Veronese, who was perhaps indeed responsible for the entire interior decoration under the direction of the architect's client. Was it consequently the tense relationship between the sculptural and painted decorative forms on the one hand and the constructed architecture on the other that led the architect not to write a single word about the cycle of frescoes in his treatise in 1570? The question remains unanswered. More importantly, the esoteric iconography of the magnificently colored frescoes also appears to derive from the client. To parade their, in part, quite contradictory interpretations would be beyond the scope of this account. The *leitmotif* of the decorations embodies a concept of harmony which is developed in varying ways and is already discernible in Daniele Barbaro's coat of arms (ill. 59). Recorded on an escutcheon that is crowned by a cross, the ring echoes the shape of the circle. The circle is not merely a symbol of unity, perfection and, in this connection, of heaven and the spiritual as opposed to the material world, it is also the expression of an all-embracing concept of order and harmony. In the figural fresco paintings, which decorate a total of

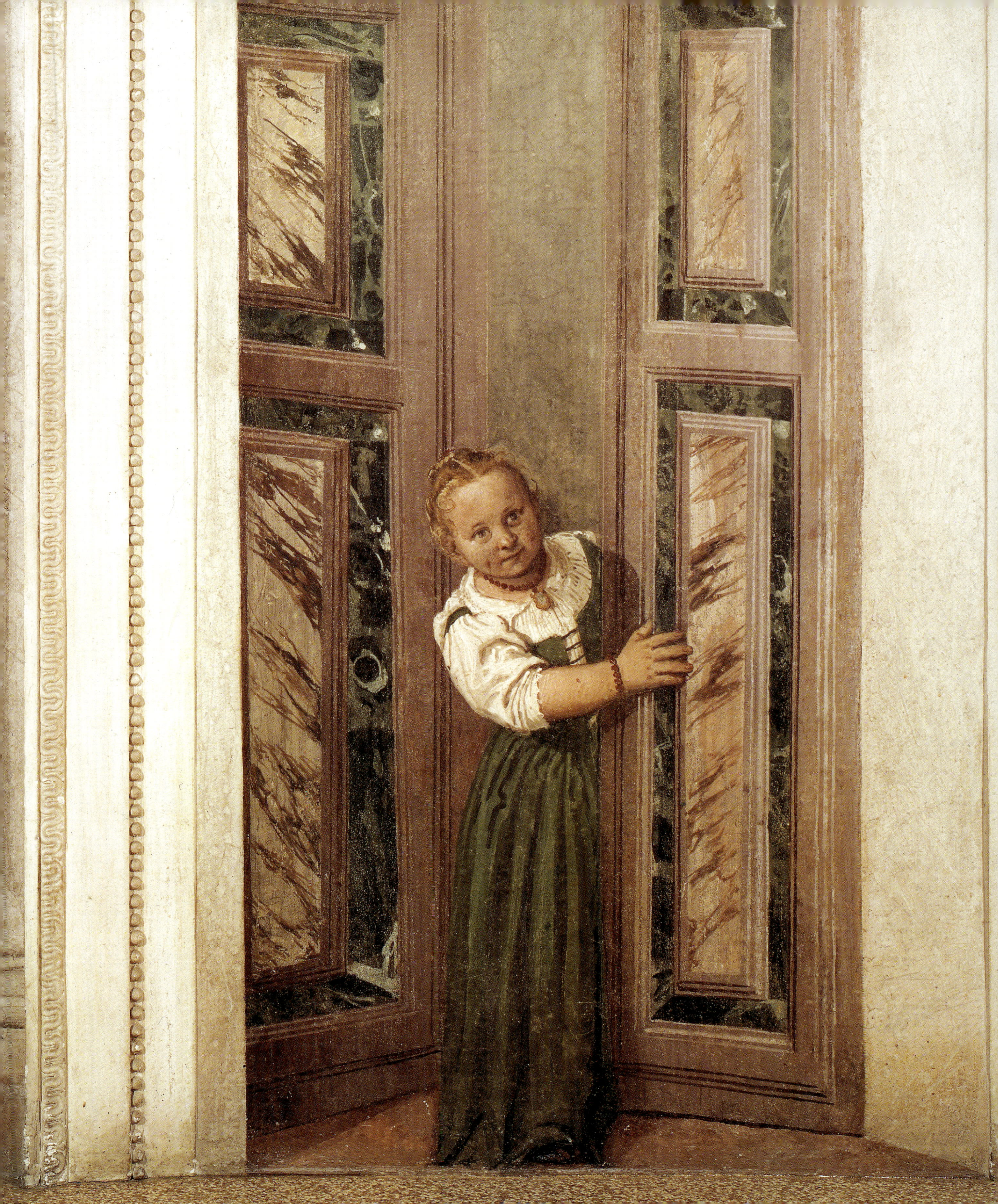

SECONDO. 51

LA SOTTOPOSTA fabrica è à Masera Villa vicina ad Asolo Castello del Triuigiano, di Monsignor Reuerendissimo Eletto di Aquileia, e del Magnifico Signor Marc'Antonio fratelli de' Barbari. Quella parte della fabrica, che esce alquanto in fuori; ha due ordini di stanze, il piano di quelle di sopra è à pari del piano del cortile di dietro, oue è tagliata nel monte rincontro alla casa vna fontana con infiniti ornamenti di stucco, e di pittura. Fa questa fonte vn laghetto, che serue per peschiera: da questo luogo partitasi l'acqua scorre nella cucina, & dapoi irrigati i giardini, che sono dalla destra, e sinistra parte della strada, la quale pian piano ascendendo conduce alla fabrica; fà due peschiere co i loro beueratori sopra la strada commune: d'onde partitasi; adacqua il Bruolo, ilquale è grandissimo, e pieno di frutti eccellentissimi, e di diuerse seluaticine. La facciata della casa del padrone hà quattro colonne di ordine Ionico: il capitello di quelle de gli angoli fa fronte da due parti: i quai capitelli come si facciano; porrò nel libro de i Tempij. Dall'vna, e l'altra parte ui sono loggie, le quali nell'estremità hanno due colombare, e sotto quelle ui sono luoghi da fare i uini, e le stalle, e gli altri luoghi per l'vso di Villa.

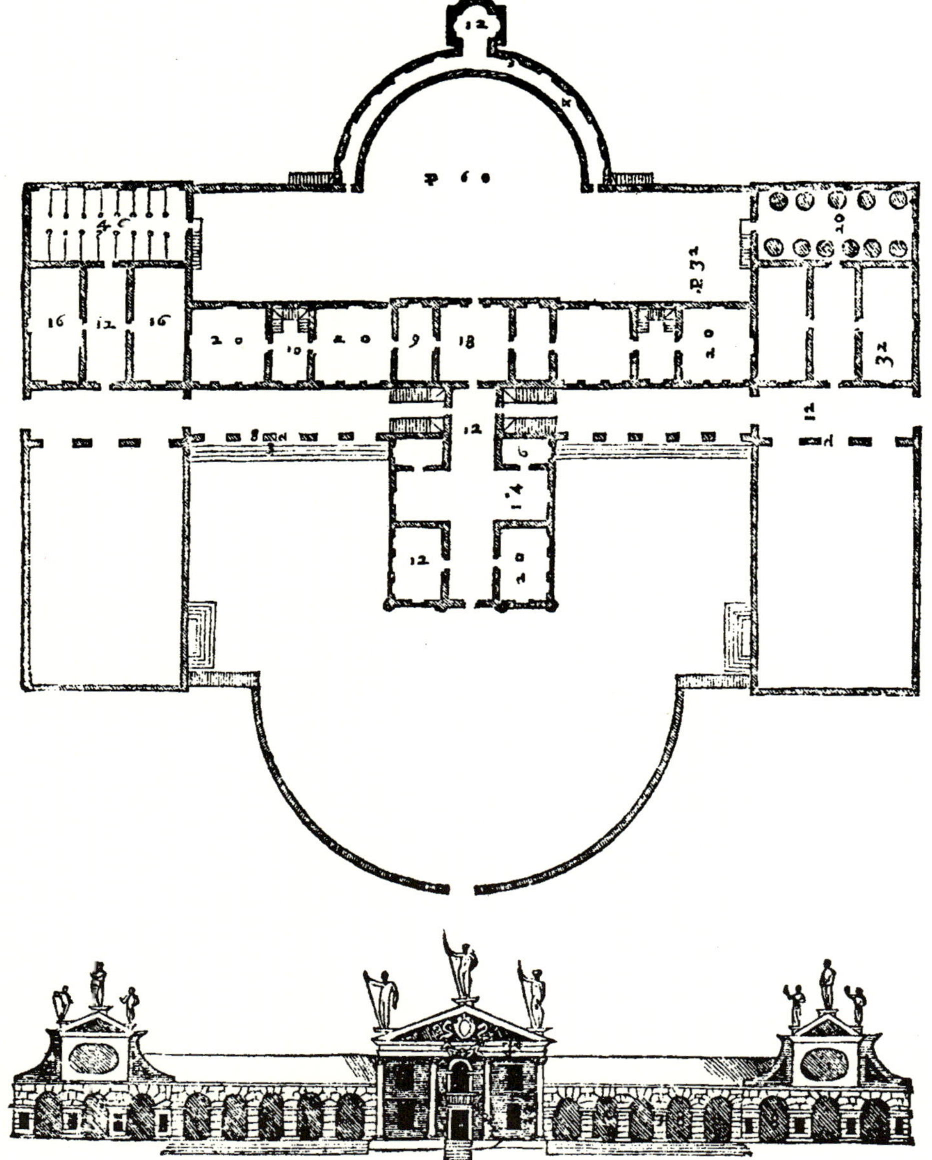

GG 2 LA SEGVENTE

63 Andrea Palladio
Description, Ground Plan and Prospect of the Villa Barbaro in Maser
Woodcut from: Andrea Palladio, *I quattro libri dell architettura*, Venice 1570, Lib. II, p. 51
Bayerische Staatsbibliothek, Munich

"The building below is in Maser, near Asolo, a Trevisan palace. It belongs to the honorable Daniele Barbaro and his brother Marcantonio. The part of the building that projects somewhat has rooms on two stories. The level of the upper rooms is the same as that of the rear court, where a fountain with countless plaster and painted decorations is hewn into the hill opposite the house. This fountain forms a pool used for fishing. From here the water is distributed. It runs to the kitchen and then, after watering the gardens to the right and left of the drive that gradually rises towards the house, into two fishponds with two drinking troughs on the public highway. From here it waters the kitchen garden, which is very large and full of excellent fruits and where sundry game is kept. The façade of the mansion has four columns of the Ionic order with the capitals of the corner columns being shaped on both sides. How these capitals should be made I will describe in the book about temples. On each side of the mansion are loggias with dovecotes at the end. Beneath are the wine cellars, the stables and other service buildings of the villa."

five rooms and the central hall in the main building's *piano nobile*, this concept of harmony is discernible time and time again.

To begin with, illusionistic fantasy landscapes in the central main room (ill. 64), framed by painted arcades and columns, establish a dialogue with those windows out of which one can see out onto the landscape of the nearer surroundings. These are joined, on the wall surfaces of the transept wing, by eight musicians (ills. 65, 66). Their significance is only revealed when one looks at the frescoes in the Sala dell'Olimpo. Contained within a circular cloud formation, the Muse Thalia, who is riding on a headless snake, forms the center of a painted planetarium (ill. 67). Assigned to her are Saturn, Jupiter, Mars, Apollo, Venus, Mercury and Diana, the gods of the starry sky with their respective signs of the Zodiac. A possible key to the interpretation of this iconographically unusual constellation is provided by a woodcut which Gafurius used in 1518 as an illustration in his treatise *De harmonia musicorum instrumentorum opus* and which anticipates central elements in Veronese's depiction. Both the music-making Muses in the central main room and the fresco (ill. 68) in the Stanza di Bacco (Bacchus Room) appear, according to this, to be alluding to the harmony of the spheres – the cosmic and harmonious sound, inaudible to man, created by the planets and their movements. The theory of the harmony of the spheres, which derives from the teachings of the ancient Greek philosopher Pythagoras (6th century B.C.) forms a central theme in Daniele Barbaro's edition of Vitruvius, and underlines the scholar's pronounced interest in astronomy. His ancestor, Ermolao Barbaro, had already devoted some treatises to this discipline. Daniele himself studied it intensively within the context of architectural theory. His portrait (ill. 58) testifies eloquently to this fact. In it, proportions and the orders of columns appear as fundamental elements of architectural work, next to a sphere, the model of the skies.

Other ceiling paintings by Veronese take the form of allegories in order to allude to love or the virtues of justice, moderation and strength, or appear as in the

64 *South-easterly View into the Cruciform Sala a Crociera of the Mansion*
Frescoes and plaster decoration
Villa Barbara, Maser

Painted Corinthian columns and "arcades", presumably carried out by Veronese's brother and assistant Benedetto Caliari, form a light architectural framework for the extraordinarily delightful *trompe l'œil* landscapes with small figures and classical buildings. A continuous plaster cornice provides an upper edge and three-dimensional wall articulation, and was – like the door frames – presumably done to a design by the painter. In 1648, Veronese's biographer Carlo Ridolfi was the first to identify the musicians as muses. A pair of them flanked each of the illusory doors in the "transept" vestibules through which visitors appear to enter the room. The final elements of the decoration are the *grisaille* equestrian scenes below, which are in the style of cameos.

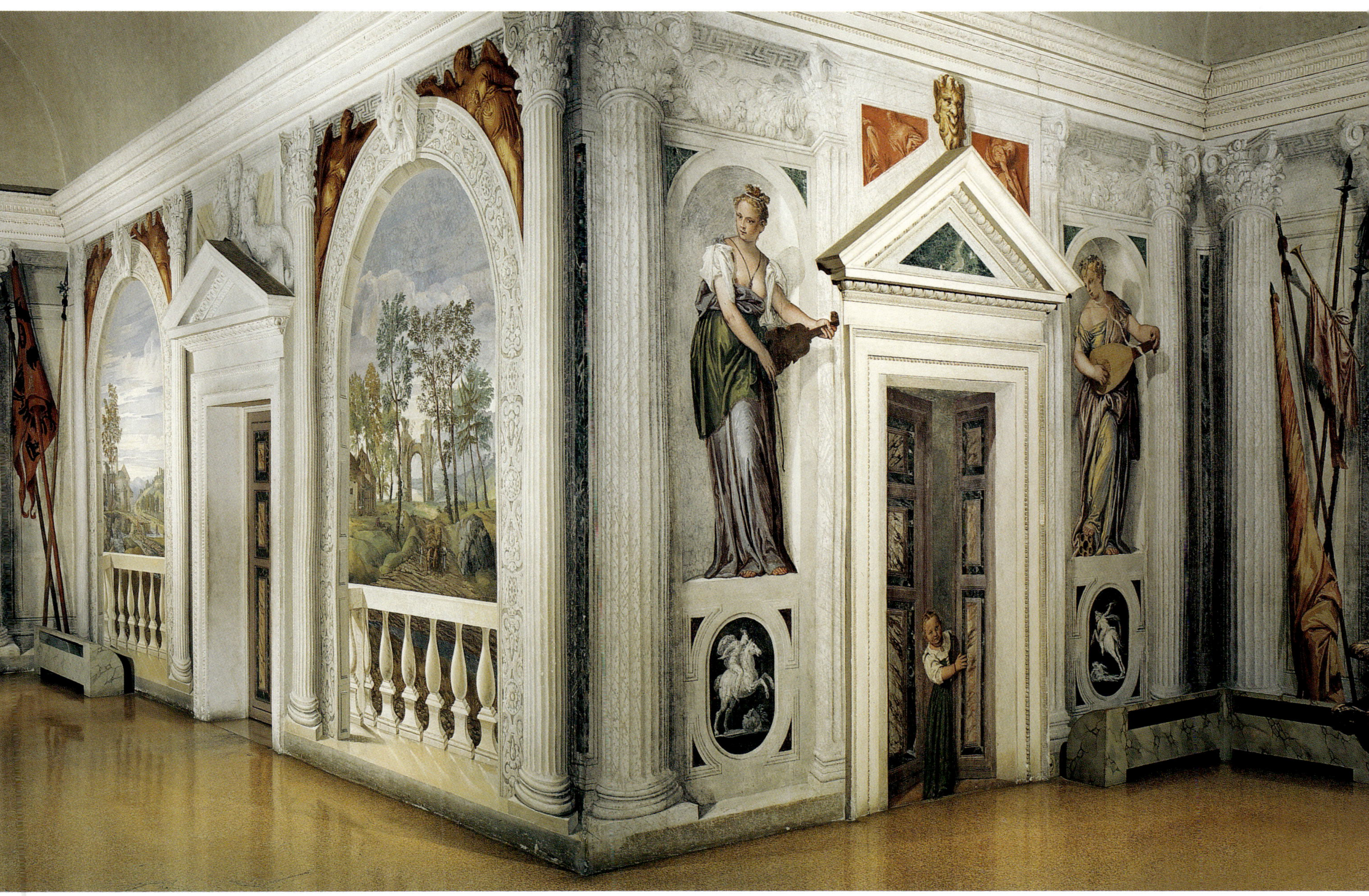

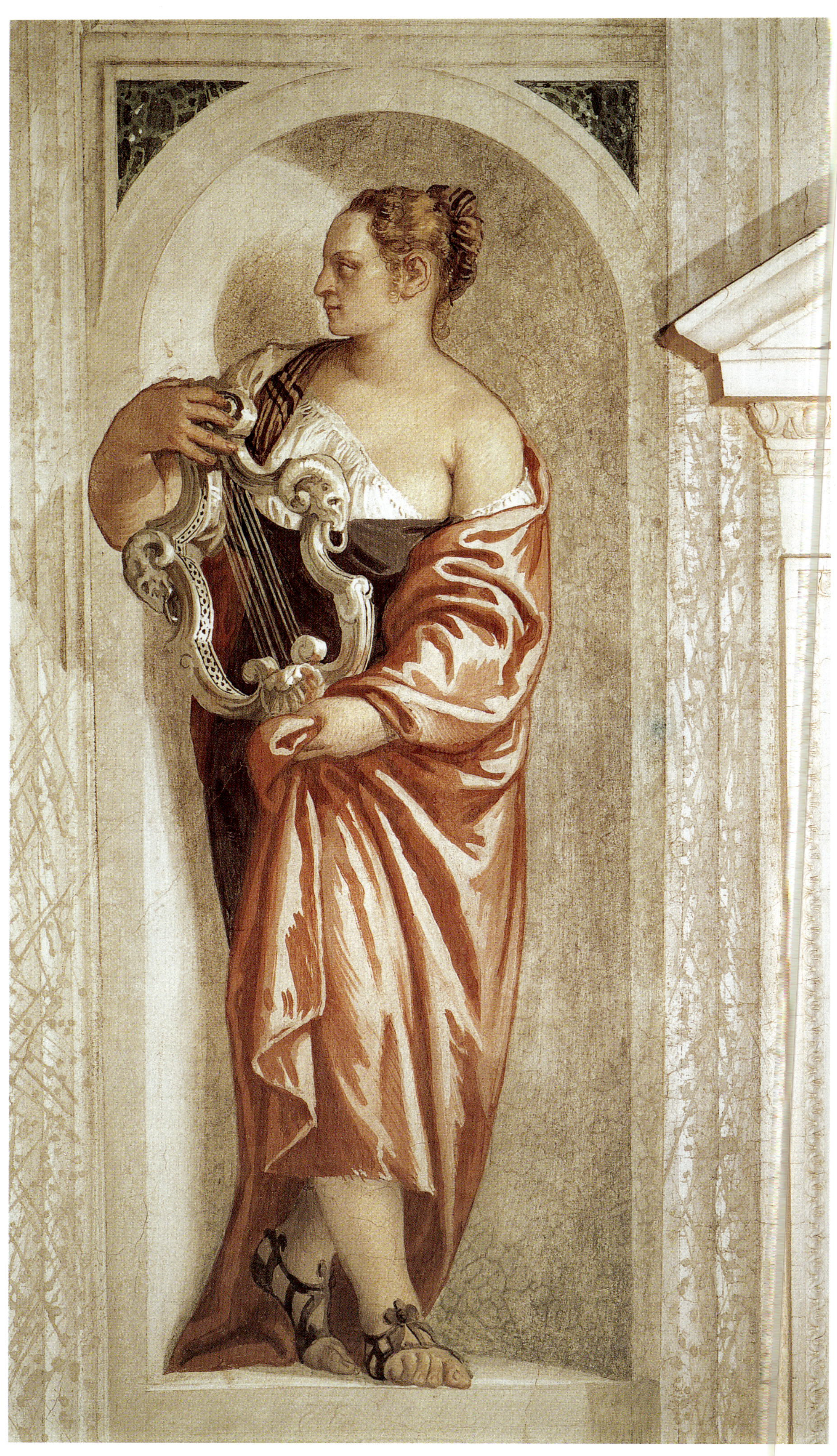

65 *Muse with Lyre*, c. 1560/61
Fresco
Villa Barbaro, Maser

As in most villas by Palladio, the interiors of the Villa Barbaro contain few architectural features as articulation, which is effected by paintings instead. The life-size Muses, who appear to be stepping out of niches, are part of the painted decoration as are the architecture, landscapes and the occasional children.

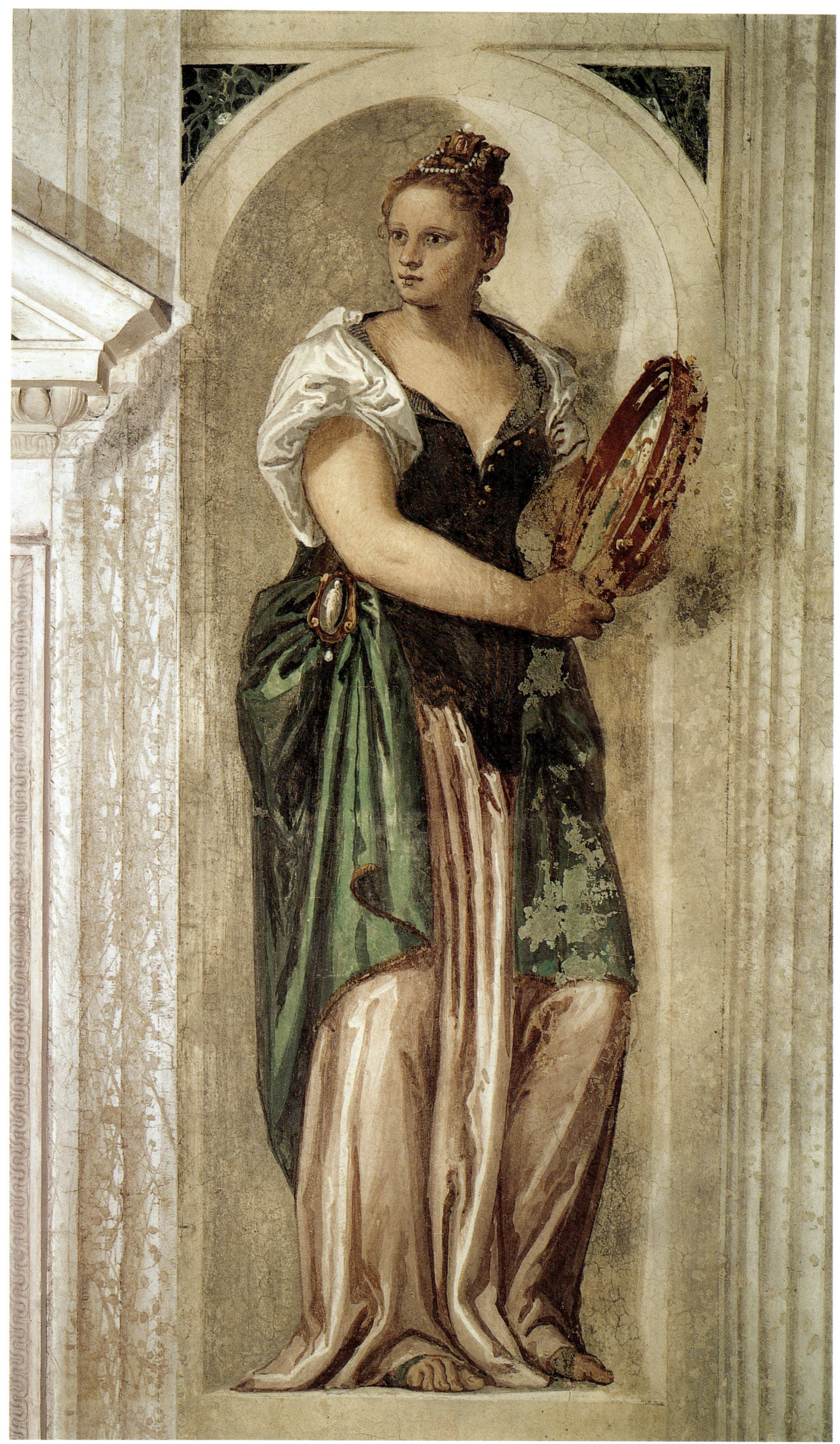

66 *Muse with Tambourine*, c. 1560/61
Fresco
Villa Barbaro, Maser

The eight music-making Muses stand in the "transept" of the Sala a Crociera at the Villa Barbaro as symbols of harmony, thematically closely related to the dome fresco in the Sala dell'Olimpo. Only there does Thalia, daughter of Apollo Musagetes, god of music and leader of the Muses, appear in a central position. The robes worn by the Muses owe their particular colorful attractiveness to the fall of light from the side.

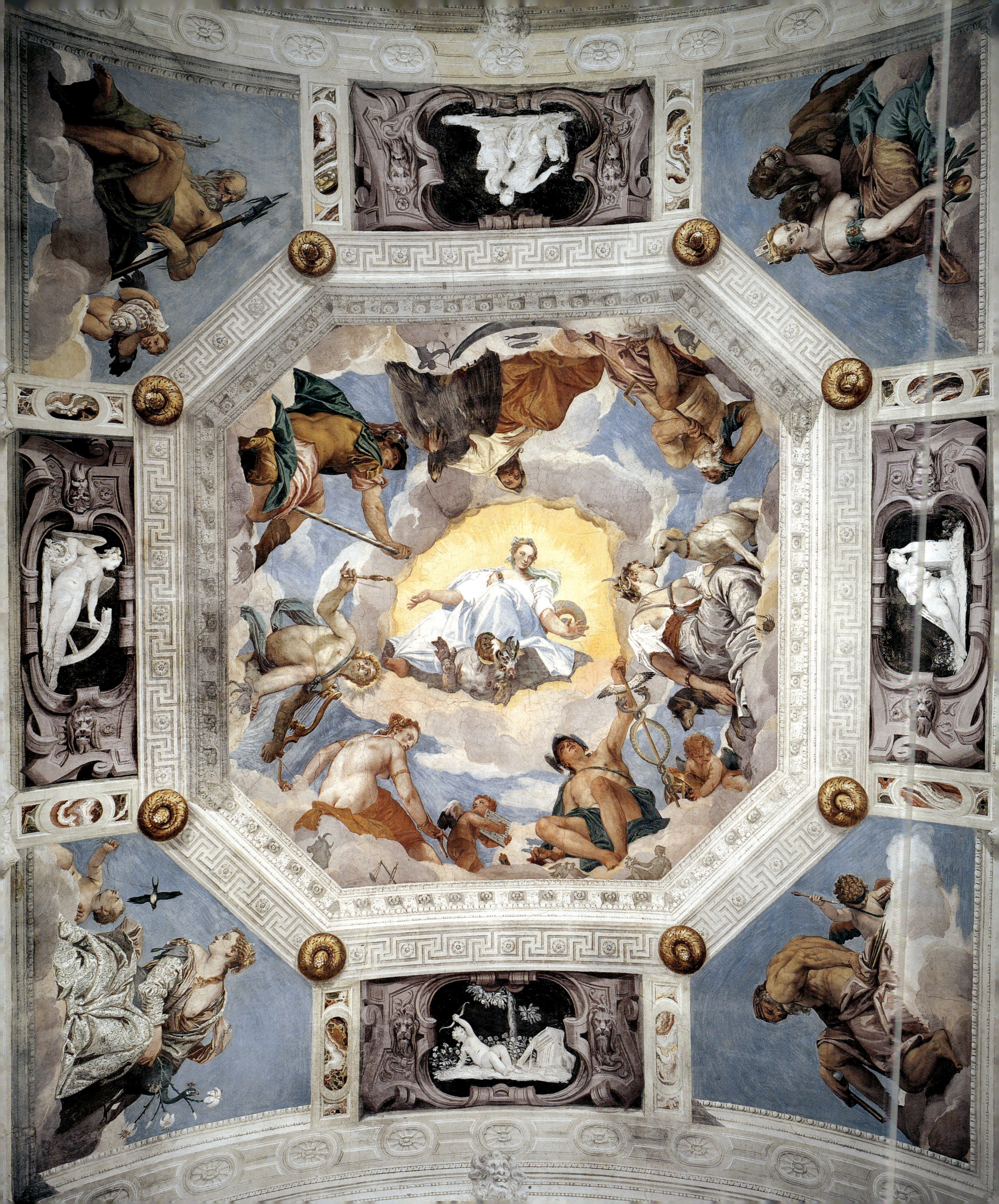

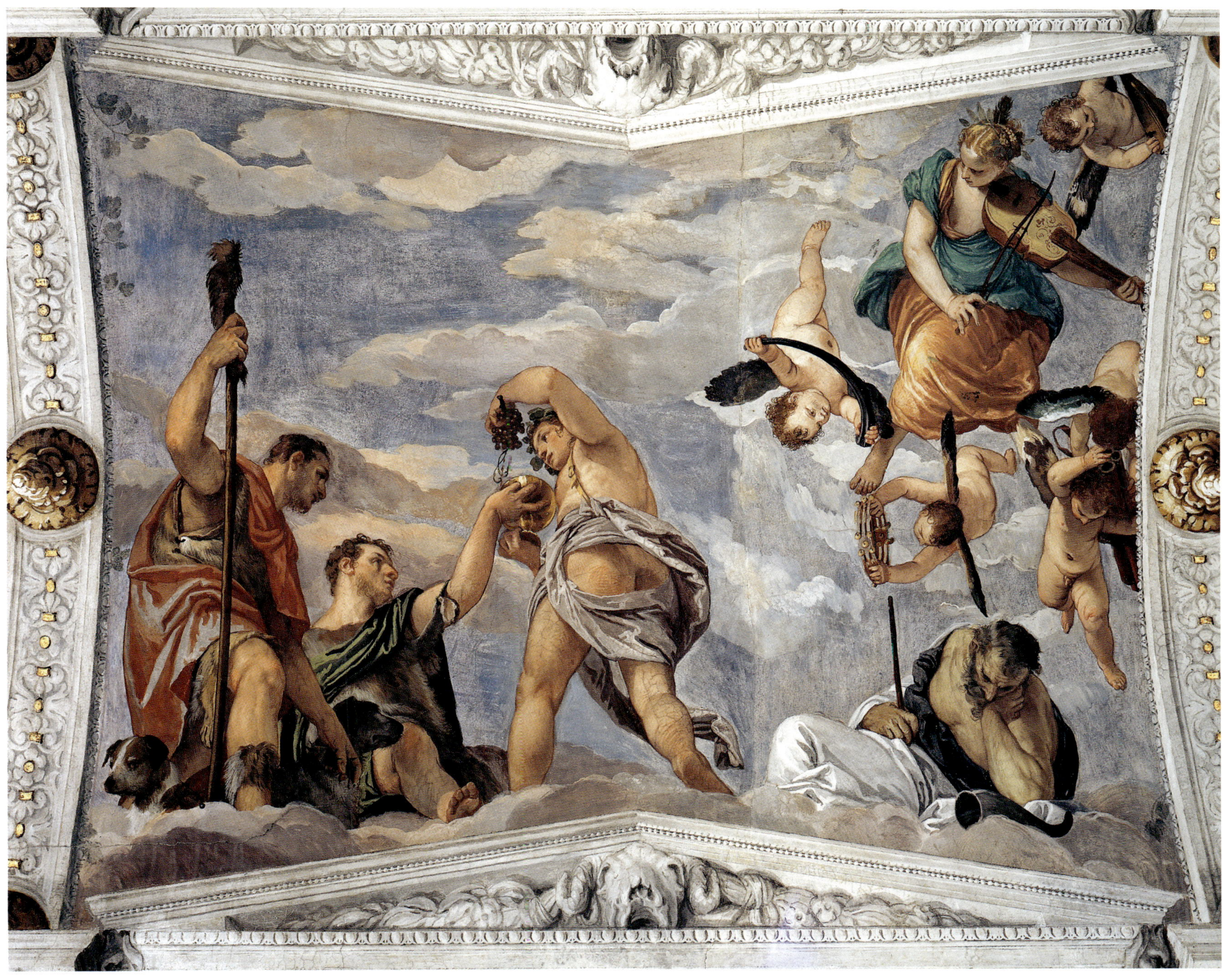

67 (opposite) *Sala dell'Olimpo*, c. 1560/61
Frescoes and plaster decoration
Villa Barbaro, Maser

This colorful fresco decoration of the Villa Barbaro reaches its climax in the Sala dell'Olimpo. The ceiling shows Saturn, Jupiter, Mars, Apollo, Venus, Mercury and Diana, the seven gods of the sky, gathered around the figure of a woman riding a headless snake, who has been interpreted, *inter alia*, as an allegory of divine wisdom. As Richard Cocke has explained, however, it could be Thalia, who in conjunction with the eight muses of the transept and the gods of the sky illustrates the real theme of the dome fresco, i.e. the harmony of the spheres. The adjacent pictorial fields in the octagon illustrate the elements of fire, earth, water and air, represented by figures of the gods Vulcan, Cybele, Neptune and Juno. In between, they include four allegories inscribed in cartouches.

68 (above) *Bacchus, Vertumnus and Saturn*, c. 1560/61
Fresco
Villa Barbaro, Maser

This ceiling fresco, which has lent its name to the room (Stanza di Bacco), has been variously interpreted. As a symbol of all-creative Nature, the vegetation god Bacchus, who is pressing the juice from grapes into a chalice, refers to the agricultural use of the villa. However, the combination with Saturn is unusual. Together with Bacchus, who appears here in the form of Apollo as leader of the muses, the old Roman god, lost in reverie as he listens to the music, seems to be an allusion to the harmony of the spheres.

69 *Nobleman in Hunting Attire*, c. 1560/61
Fresco
Villa Barbaro, Maser

Like the painted figures in the transepts of the Sala a Crociera, the nobleman returning from the hunt belongs to the contemporary viewer's world. East of the Stanza della Lucerna at the end of the suite of rooms, he enters the room through a *trompe l'œil* door.

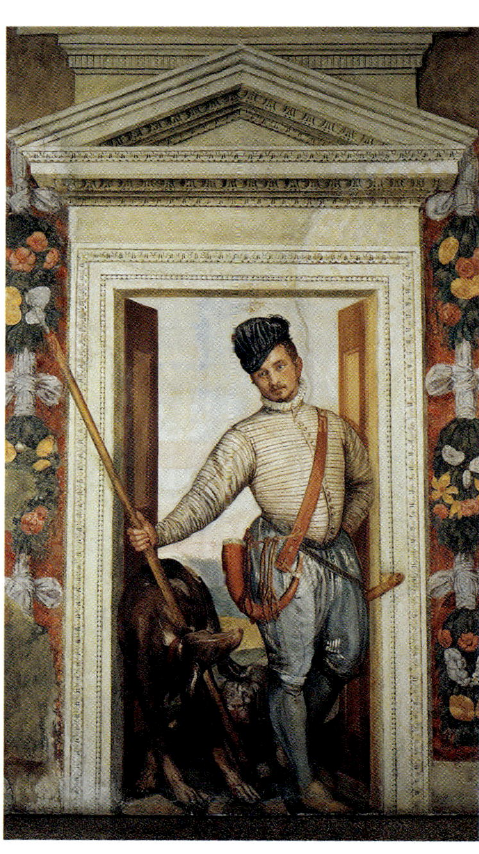

case of *Bacchus, Vertumnus and Saturn* (ill. 68) to be an allegorical reminder of the fertility of nature and the agricultural use of the villa. In general, mythological and secular elements combine quite unexpectedly with each other in many parts of the decorations. In the Sala dell'Olimpo, for example, it is Giustiniana Giustinian (ill. 71), the lady of the house and wife of Marcantonio Barbaro, who appears with her wet-nurse behind a painted balustrade, while on the other side of the room one of her two sons is studying a book. Right at the end of the row of rooms in the east wing, a *Nobleman in Hunting Attire* (ill. 69) steps out as if by chance through a painted door, while in the central hall an inquisitively sniffing dog before a painted balustrade tempts us, even today, to mistake it for the real thing. Apart from these references to everyday events in the villa's life, scattered religious depictions also form part of the fresco decorations. In the Stanza della Lucerna (Room of the Oil Lamps), the *Madonna della pappa* (ill. 70) quite evidently needs to be seen in combination with the allegorical ceiling fresco in the room, in which a personification of the Catholic faith is facing a beggar accompanied by a personification of Mercy. With an eloquent gesture, Religion indicates a snake twisted into a circle that is biting its tail, and in 16th-century heraldry this was a symbol of infinity. The moralizing tenor of the scene cannot be ignored. One cannot exclude the possibility that it could be indirectly linked with the Calvinistic tinges in the comments of the patriarch Giovanni Grimani on divine pre-ordination, which had caused disconcertment and became the object of an examination by the Papal Inquisition in Rome in 1561. In contrast to the position of the Calvinists, who considered love of one's neighbor to be solely a service to the glory of God, not to mankind, this iconographically unusual depiction speaks up, like a profession of faith, for the priority of the Catholic religion and a love of one's neighbor permeated by the eternal values of the faith, and once again it appears to confirm to what extent Daniele Barbaro had an overall influence on the creative process and the form of the frescoes.

Supported by his brother Benedetto Caliari (1538–1598), a painter who specialized in depicting architectures, Veronese developed a pictorial world in Maser that is unique in its quality and narrative density. As a fresco painter and master of spatial illusion, he unquestionably profited from the experiences he had gained in the church of San Sebastiano, for the wall paintings produced from 1558 for the clerestory area, above the gallery and in the spandrels of the choir arch had also been decorations that negated the pre-existing architectural structures and which formed a comparably imaginative union of ornamental, sculptural and architectural decorative forms. The actual protagonists in the pictorial world in the Villa Barbaro, ancient gods from classical mythology and allegories exemplifying human virtues, are components in a decorational program which was subject to rational principles of order and harmony, and whose choice of artistic methods corresponded to the demands of the time which had been imposed on contemporary painters by the art theoretician Lodovico Dolce. Thus, individual figures and architectural forms reflect a study of the classical period reformed by Raphael's work in Rome, and suggest that, during his work in Maser, Veronese was profiting from experiences which he had gained on the occasion of a visit to the Eternal City as part of the retinue of the Venetian ambassador Girolamo Grimani. The question of when this journey took place is very much open to speculation, especially as Grimani was in Rome on several occasions between 1555 and 1565. Nonetheless, if his later explanations to the Inquisition are to be believed, Veronese appears to have been acquainted with Michelangelo's *Last Judgment* in the Sistine Chapel even before it was overpainted by Daniele da Volterra (c. 1509–1566), meaning that he must have seen it before 1560. It is more than likely that he would have had an opportunity to study the decorations of classical villas during the course of this journey.

The illusionistic quality of the frescoes in Maser, the deceptive power of the painted architecture and figures, were first paid tribute to and praised by Carlo Ridolfi in 1648. Nevertheless, the competition between illusion and reality had already been keeping the contemporary art theoreticians of Venice busy. Hence the conception that painters were capable of achieving illusionistic effects with the aid of color had been passionately discussed in 1557 in the above-mentioned *Dialogo della pittura* by Dolce, using the example of the competition between the classical painters Zeuxis (c. 425 B.C.) and Parrhasius (c. 420 B.C.). According to Pliny (c. 23–79 A.D.), Zeuxis succeeded by means of his careful painting technique in reproducing grapes so realistically that birds flew up and began to peck at them. Parrhasius, meanwhile, had painted a curtain. When Zeuxis demanded that he pull the curtain aside so that he could see his competitor's picture, he was forced to acknowledge that it was a painted one (*Naturalis historiae*, XXXV, 65–66). For the Venetian Dolce, this anecdote was a metaphor that expounded how color and the way in which it was used could enable painted works to surpass their real-life models.

When this concept of the technique of painting was put into practice, it was necessary to pay attention to careful use of foreshortenings and sophisticated nuances in the skin tones, as well as reproducing the human figure in an appropriate manner. Taking another look at the central fresco in the Sala dell'Olimpo (ill. 67), it becomes clear that Veronese would have felt that his work was completely justified by Dolce's treatise. This is, of course, also true of the *varietà*, which, as Leon Battista Alberti had already pointed out, was one of the most important characteristics of a high-quality pictorial invention. With an eye to Raphael's function as a model, Dolce had updated the law of diversity in order to entrust it to contemporary painters as an alternative to the Mannerists' experienced style of painting. Veronese, who revealed that he was very familiar with Dolce's

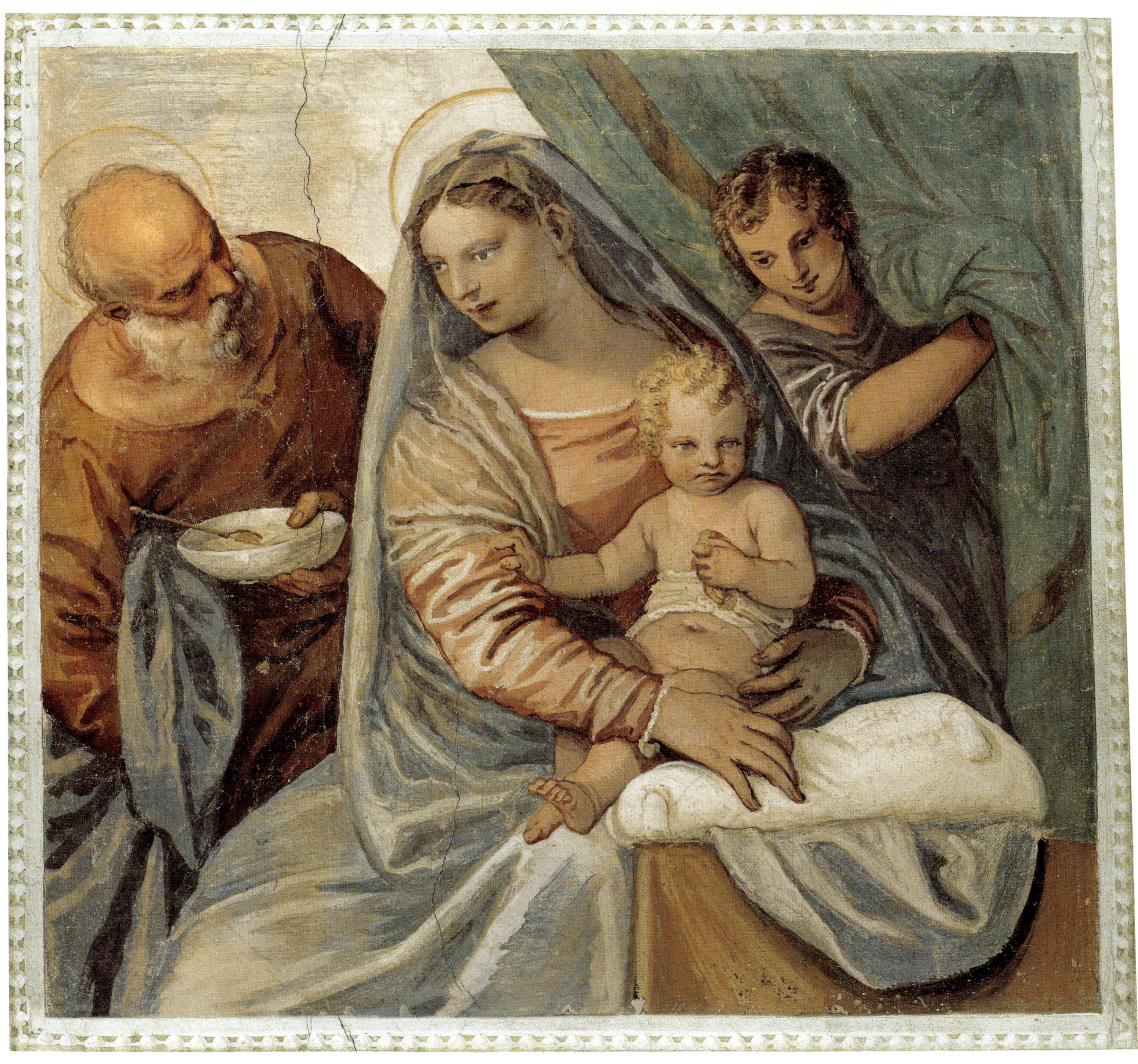

treatise on the occasion of his examination by the Inquisition in 1573, adopted these recommendations in Maser, and more: by turning the successfully tested principle of *varietà* into an artistic program, he made a decisive contribution to the further development and enrichment of Venetian painting.

70 *The Holy Family (Madonna della pappa)*, c. 1560/61
Fresco
Villa Barbaro, Maser

Like the Stanza del cane, the Stanza della Lucerna has a picture of the Holy Family as part of the iconographical program. Following Serlio (1475–1554) and his Christological interpretation of the use of Ionic with female saints, both rooms deploy Ionic columns. The *Madonna della pappa* stresses the role of Joseph as a provident paterfamilias, and is closely related thematically with the allegorical ceiling fresco, which symbolizes the precedence of the eternal values of faith.

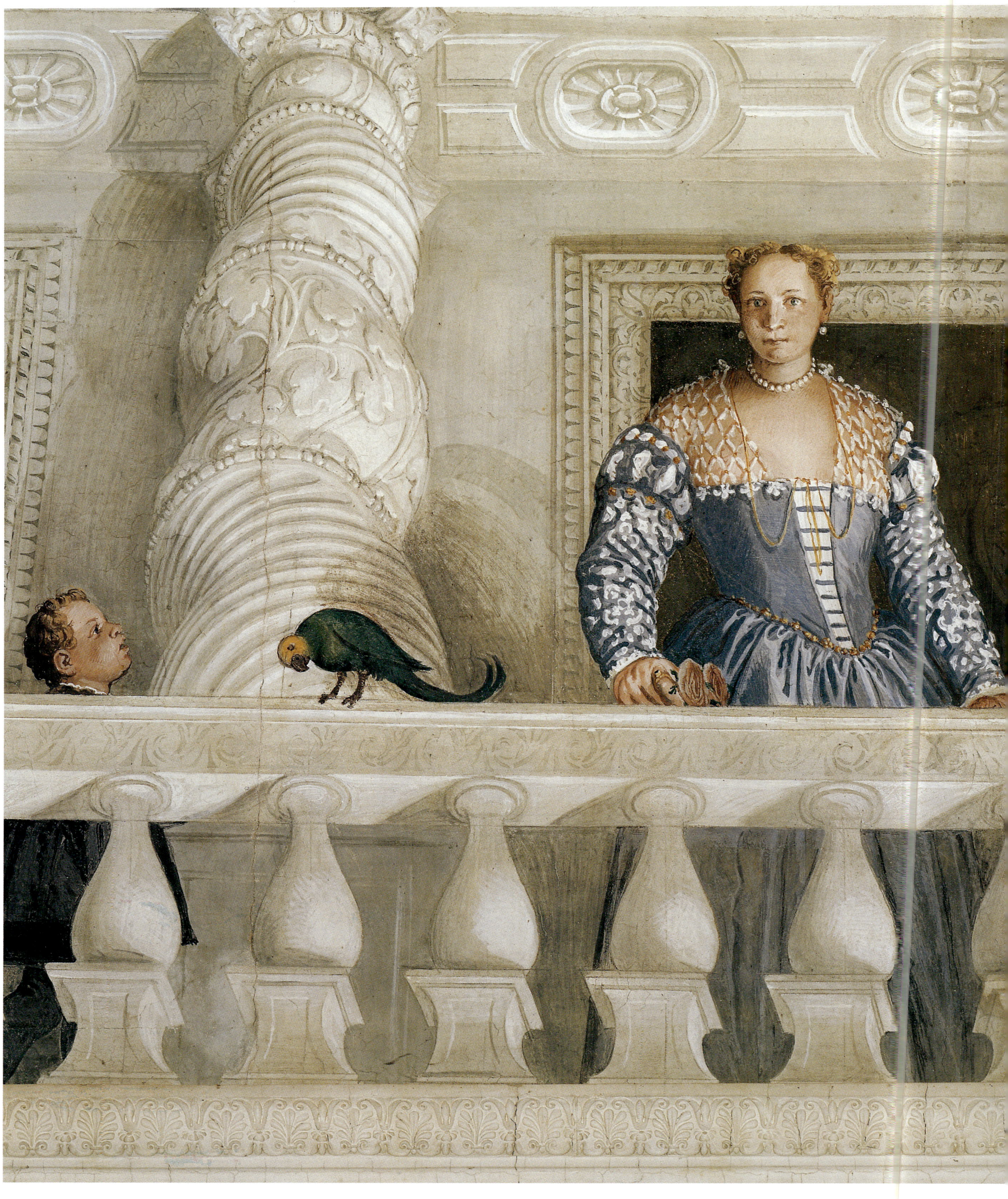

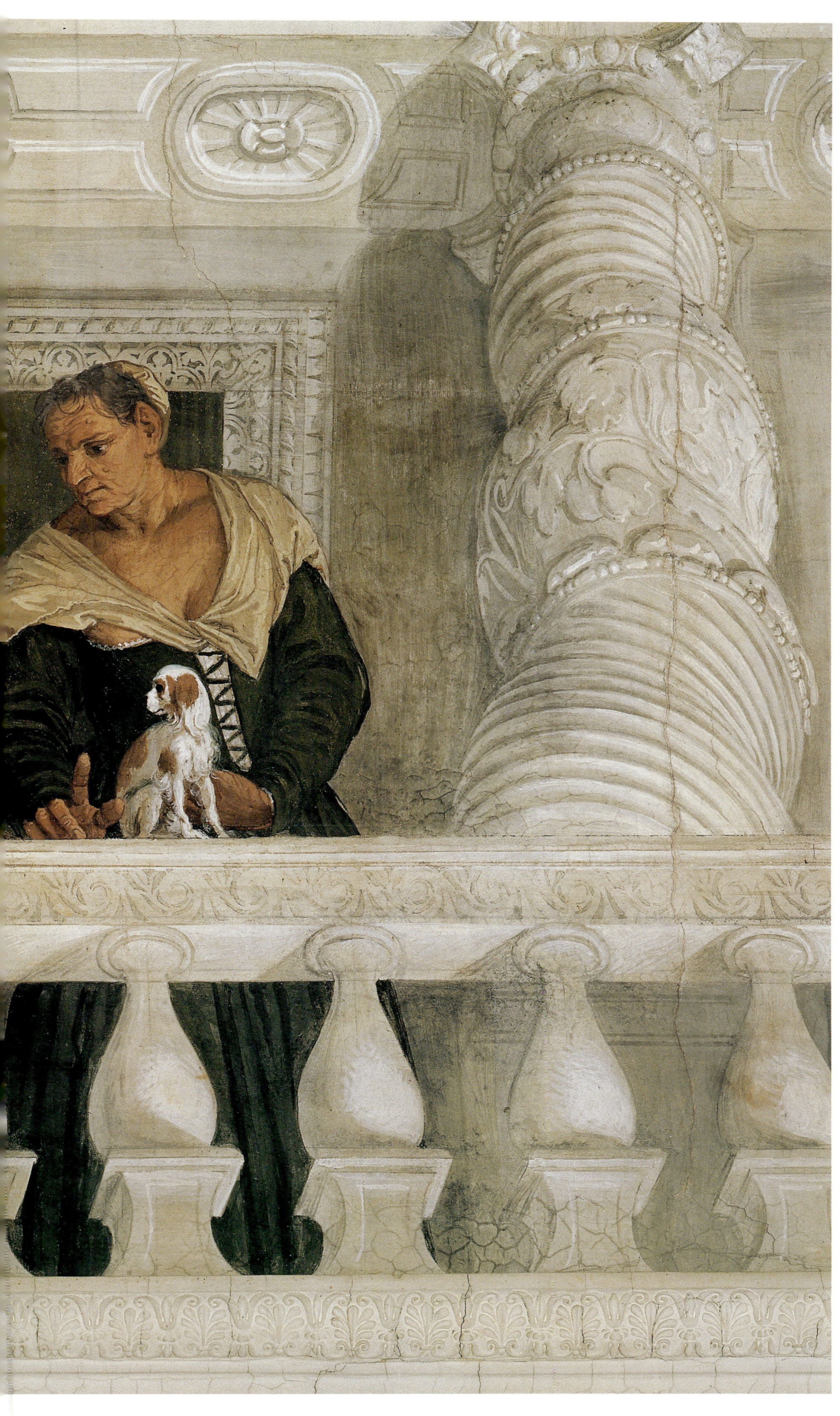

71 *Giustiniana Giustinian and her Nurse*, 1560/61
Fresco
Villa Barbaro, Maser

Dressed in the elegant dress of a Venetian noblewoman, the wife of Marcantonio Barbaro is shown alongside her nurse behind a balustrade. Both figures form part of the painted decoration in the Sala dell'Olimpo. Closer inspection of the figures reveals the very vigorous brushstrokes used by the painter. The gown of Giustiniana is made up of white dotted flecks of paint, which, in conjunction with the gleaming blue of the lengths of materials and the highlights, create an extraordinarily dashing effect.

A Program of Inventiveness

72 *Wedding at Cana* (detail of ill. 73)
Bride and groom

Since the 13th century, the Benedictine convent of San Giorgio Maggiore in Venice has served time and again as a refuge and home to secular and clerical personages of rank and stature. In the 16th century, the monastery was said to be among the most prosperous in the city, and it is therefore no surprise that the young Englishman, Thomas Coryat, touring Europe in 1608 to broaden his intellectual horizons, should describe the venerable monastery as the finest and richest in all Venice. Coryat's tour of the monastery included the refectory, which, with its *Wedding at Cana,* was considered one of the principal sights of the city. If we are to believe the monastic chronicle written in 1619 by Don Fortunato Olmo, kings and princes had clamored for copies of the picture. Certainly, it is the festive mood of the picture, set in a world very familiar to contemporary viewers, that must have prompted demands of this kind. On the left of the richly laden table, the groom and bride of the biblical wedding open the gently undulating procession of beautifully portrait-like heads, whose individual features constantly captured the imagination of viewers in the 18th century, and even occasionally induced romantic visitors to the refectory to see a portrait of the painter's own beloved in the bride.

At the beginning of the 1560s, Paolo Veronese was one of the leading painters in Venice alongside Jacopo Tintoretto and the old master Titian, and no less a figure than Vasari was to confirm, in 1568, the high regard in which he was held. The strength and self-esteem that had been continually growing made it easier for the painter to hold his own successfully against his established competitors, and left their mark on a scarcely comprehensible range of religious and secular history paintings.

After Veronese had provided proof in the Sala del Maggior Consiglio of the Doge's palace that he could, apparently effortlessly, fill even large picture planes with figures and architectural features, he went on to set new standards with his *Wedding at Cana* (ill. 73), painted for the Benedictine refectory of San Giorgio Maggiore in Venice. The painting which, like so many famous Venetian painted works, fell victim to Napoleon's art thefts in 1797 and was brought to France by sea, was commissioned on June 6, 1562 soon after the refectory, built by Andrea Palladio, was completed. The decisive factor must have been the good contacts with the Benedictine abbey of San Benedetto Po near Mantua, for which Veronese, helped by assistants, had shortly beforehand produced the *Consecration of St. Nicholas* (National Gallery, London) as well as two other large-format altar paintings. Don Andrea da Asola, who commissioned them, had been the abbot of the monastery of San Giorgio Maggiore since 1564, and it may therefore have been he who made sure that his portrait was added to the painting at a later date. While Ridolfi criticized the work in 1648 saying that the portraits of the clerics, which Paolo had been entirely obliged to include, did not harmonize properly with the other ideas drawn from his imagination, the sheer number of heads, some with portrait-like features, has repeatedly filled art experts and specialists with enthusiasm and challenged them again and again to determine the precise number of portraits. Even Vasari must have been fascinated when he saw the painting, covering 67 square meters of canvas, in 1566: two years later, when he wrote about it in his *Vite*, he praised the wealth of figures depicted in widely varying positions, and the lavish diversity of the garments. In addition, he particularly emphasized that the picture had been carried out in oil paints on canvas. But what at this time may have appeared highly unusual to the Florentine, who was used to works of comparable size being in the form of fresco paintings, had become a necessity in Venice due to the damp climate. Vasari unquestionably directed his attention mainly at the *varietà*, the wealth of figural and motif inventions, which on closer observation can be seen to be part of a comprehensive, precisely thought-out order.

Christ occupies the center of the wedding table, which was formerly a fictitious conclusion to the rows of tables at which the monks recalled the origins of the Eucharist at their daily meals. The events are framed by symmetrically arranged architectures and palace façades, carefully opening up the depth of the picture step by step, which are reminiscent of contemporary buildings by Andrea Palladio and Jacopo Sansovino, as well as the stage sets designed by the architect and theoretician Sebastiano Serlio (died 1554), in particular the *Scena Tragica* (*D'Architettura*, Lib. II). Their strong vertical lines correspond to the figure of the Lord who provides a calming, peaceful influence amidst those taking part in the meal. Because the parallel lines of the Doric colonnades converge on his head, the observer is positively forced to linger. The steward in charge of the banquet was also clearly highlighted compositionally. In his case, light has taken over the architecture's role in guiding one's gaze. Dressed in a valuable garment whose brocade decorations are shining in all their glory, he is on the right in the foreground looking at a goblet with the recently poured wine. While the steward already appears to suspect the miraculous transformation of the water into wine, on the left side a bearded Middle Eastern man, evidently the cupbearer, is bravely walking up to the bride and groom. Both figures form the corners of a triangle whose tip, once again, is the face of Christ.

Along the table and in the area of the higher-level terrace, Veronese has developed an almost unbelievable wealth of detail. Domestic servants bustling around busily, lavishly dressed servants, Levantines, musicians and spectators, containers and sideboards all interplay with the architectures to make a decisive contribution

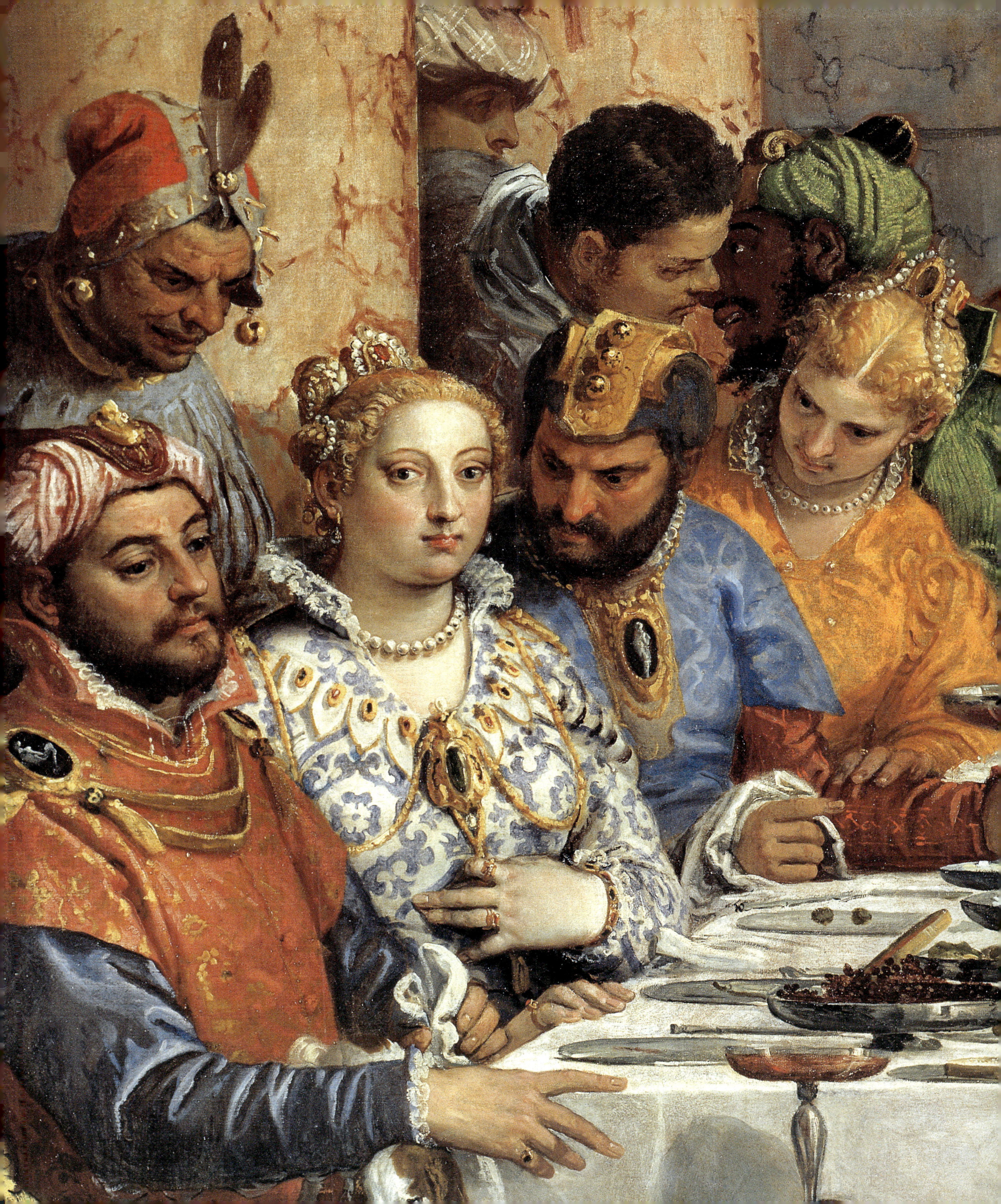

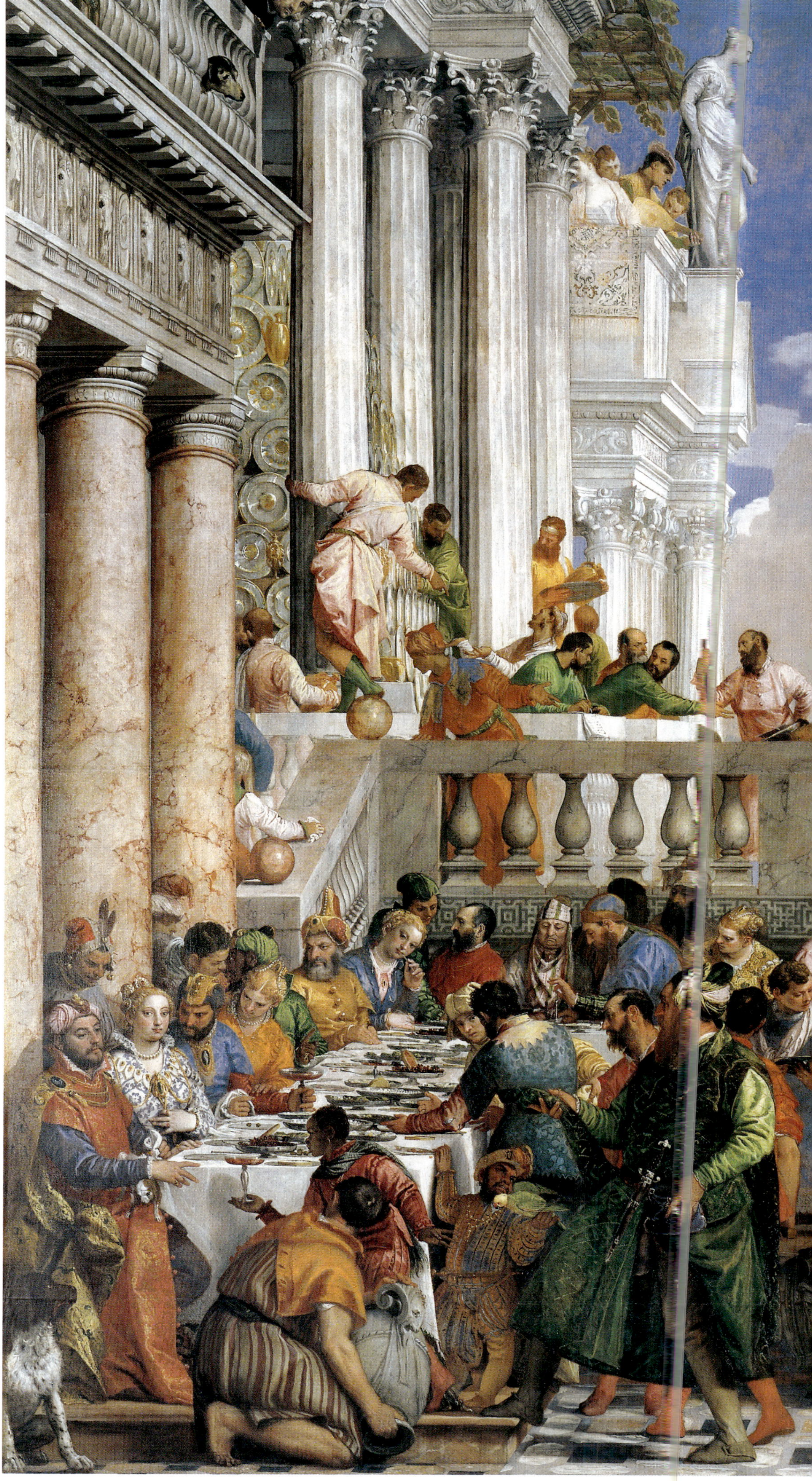

73 *Wedding at Cana*, 1562–63
Oil on canvas, 677 x 994 cm
Musée du Louvre, Paris

Covering a total area of about 67 square meters, the painting for the dining room of the Benedictine monastery of San Giorgio Maggiore in Venice depicts the biblical scene of the wedding at Cana (St. John 2, 1–11). When the wine ran out during the meal, Christ changed water into wine at the request of his mother Mary. Veronese moves the scene to a brightly lit terrace in front of imaginary Venetian palace façades. In the second half of the 16th century, the increased interest in rich subject-matter among painters and clients in Venice and the Veneto led to the simple core event (initially just the miracle of the wine) being gradually overlaid with lavish settings of more and more markedly realistic depictions of wedding gatherings. Yet in Veronese's painting, the compositional parallels with depictions of the Last Supper nonetheless manage to bring out the analogy between the transformation of the water into wine and sacramental wine into the blood of Christ.

The contract of June 6, 1562 specified both the exact size and the appropriate number of figures for the subject. As a precaution, Veronese was instructed to use only the best raw materials for his paints and not to omit the use of the finest ultramarine. As ultramarine, made from ground lapis lazuli, was highly expensive, the intention of this admonition was to circumvent the current practice whereby painters often short-changed their clients by using azure blue made from copper ore. The agreed fee for the painting was 324 ducats. While he was working on the picture on the island of San Giorgio, the artist had free board, and was promised a barrel of wine on completion of the picture. The monumental painting was finished 17 months later. Veronese probably had Benedetto Caliari with him as his assistant. Once famed as one of the principal sights of Venice and admired for centuries both north and south of the Alps as a masterpiece of Venetian art, the work remained influential into the 18th century. Looted by Napoleon, in the 19th century it was studied, copied and taken as a model by generations of French, German and English artists visiting the Louvre.

Among the interesting discoveries made during the restoration of the *Wedding at Cana* between 1989 and 1992 is the head of a Benedictine painted on paper and stuck *post hoc* on the canvas. This is possibly Andrea Pampuro, known as Andrea da Asolo, who became abbot of San Giorgio Maggiore in succession to Girolamo Scrochetto in 1564. The most expensive technical equipment has not been able to clarify whether the head – presumably carried out by an assistant of Veronese – replaced an already existing figure.

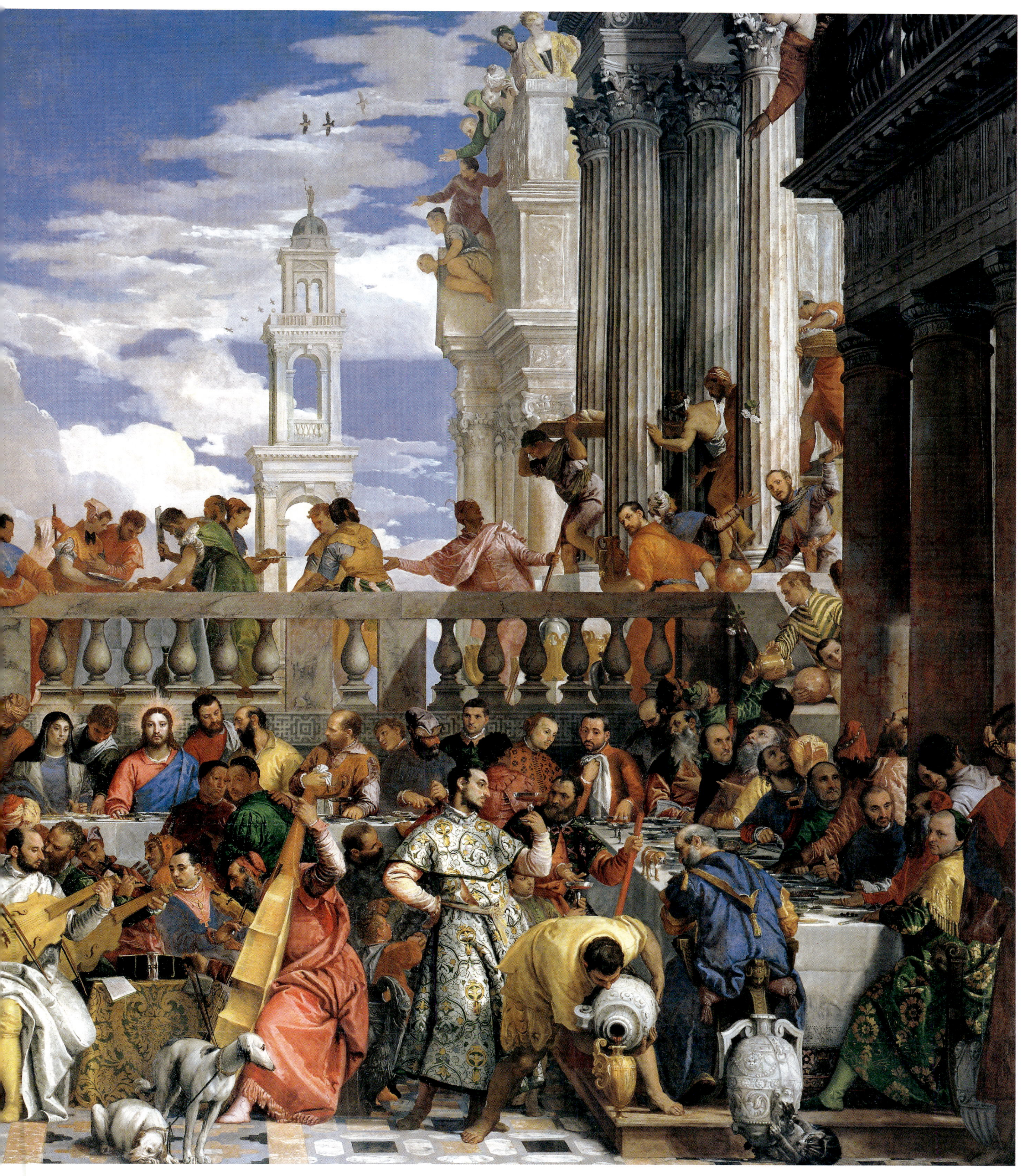

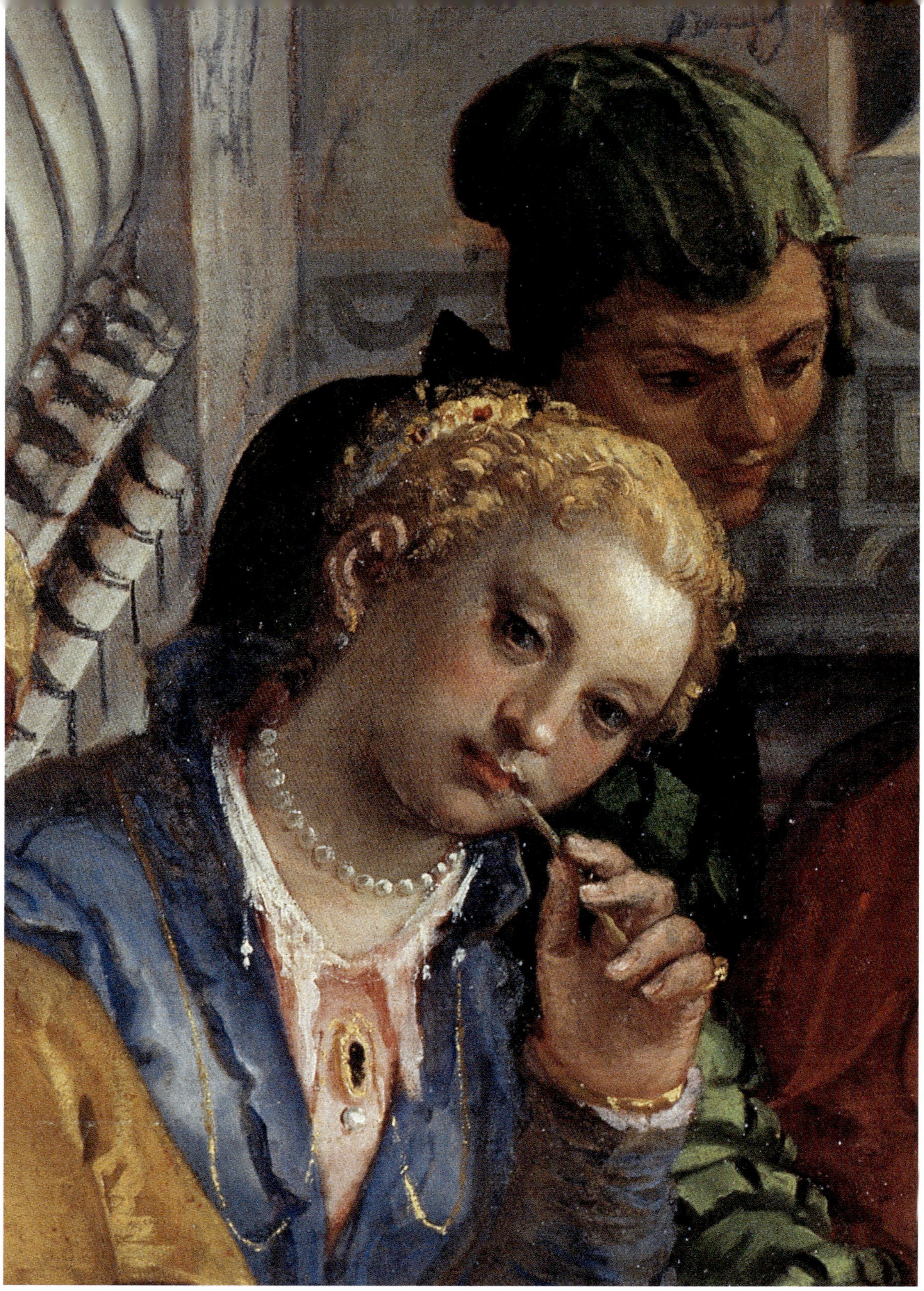

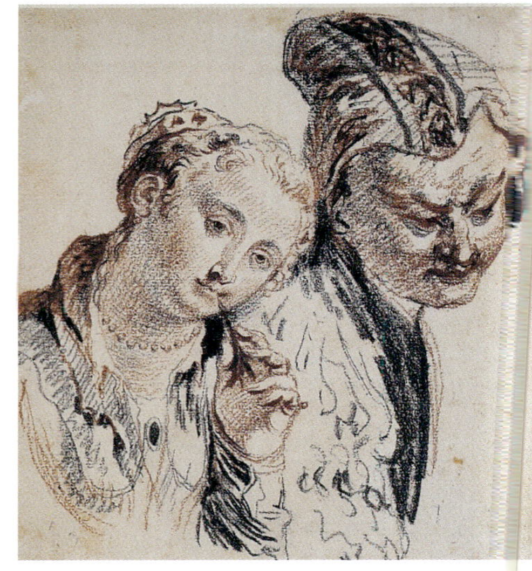

75 (above) Antoine Watteau (1684–1721)
Sketch with Two Figures, detail copy of Veronese, c. 1710–1715
Red and black chalk, 19.6 cm x 18.4 cm
Ashmolean Museum, Oxford

French painter and draftsman Antoine Watteau, who never visited Italy, became familiar with Veronese's *Wedding at Cana* (ill. 73) via a painted copy that belonged to the famous Parisian collector Pierre Crozat during his day. The pose of the two figures clearly appealed to Watteau's own sense of charm and grace.

74 (left) *Wedding at Cana* (detail of ill. 73)
Venetian woman

The blond Venetian woman on the left section of the table is using an ornate fork as a toothpick. For centuries, the figure caught the imagination of later painters, from Rubens to Watteau. In 1590, the Milanese painter and art writer Giovanni Paolo Lomazzo (1538–1600) used the example of this figure to highlight the Venetian painter's ability to give expression to various emotions and psychological states in the figures.

to the festive tenor of the scene. On the one hand, they are an expression of the painter's imagination, on the other, they reflect the narrative methods of certain elements in the Bible exegesis written by the man of letters Pietro Aretino who, in *L'humanità di Christo* (Venice, 1551), had, for his part, adapted the biblical story of the wedding at Cana into something magnificent. Finally, contemporary banquets may also have been a source of inspiration. During the course of the 16th century, incredibly sumptuous banquets repeatedly took place in Venice during the receptions of high dignitaries. For instance, Henry III of France (1551–1589) was honored with a feast in the Doge's palace in 1574 at which there were allegedly 3,000 guests. The scene was set with exquisite foods served on golden and silver dishes, and a large table in three sections which must have been similar to the one in Veronese's painting. The description of a feast in honor of the Duke of Mantua, for which we have the Venetian chronicler and historiographer Marin Sanudo (1466–1536) to thank, also inevitably evokes memories of Veronese's *Wedding at Cana* (ill. 73). Thus it is reported that curious spectators peopled the corridors and paths, and climbed onto beams and window ledges, even onto sculptures, in order to watch the festive event as closely as possible.

Given the wide range of invention, it is not surprising that the monumental painting was already being praised as his chief work during Veronese's lifetime and became a teaching aid. Figures such as the Venetian woman (ill. 74), who is gracefully bringing a dainty fork up to her mouth on the left side of the table, have stimulated painters' imaginations down the centuries. Antoine Watteau (1684–1721) had this motif in mind in a small sketch (ill. 75) which he executed in Paris c. 1710–1715 as the basis for a copy of the *Wedding at Cana*. Veronese's painting, which had already been meticulously copied by Johann König, a painter from Nuremberg, in the refectory of San Giorgio Maggiore, is by far the most frequently copied work in the Venetian painter's *œuvre*. Being mentioned in the same breath as Titian's famous *St. Peter Martyr* and called the "most beautiful picture in the world" in the 17th century, it was an important destination for visitors to Venice. The legends that inevitably grew up around this high regard were above all fed by the eloquence of the Venetian Marco Boschini. One of Veronese's most enthusiastic admirers, he laid the foundations between 1660 and 1674 for an anecdote with amazing public appeal and which continues to have an effect today. Thus, Boschini believed that the quartet of musicians (ill. 76) bore the features of Titian, Jacopo Bassano, Tintoretto and Veronese. As this further encouraged painters and culture-seeking travelers to visit the refectory, the Benedictines were eventually forced to counter the onslaught in 1705 by forbidding the production of copies.

76 *Wedding at Cana* (detail of ill. 73) Musicians

Between 1660 and 1674, Marco Boschini claimed that the musicians in the *Wedding at Cana* were portraits of the four most famous 16th-century Venetian painters. The man playing the viola da gamba he saw as Veronese, followed by Tintoretto, Jacopo Bassano and Titian. The surviving portraits of these painters contradict this theory, which gave rise to a series of legends. Ridolfi explicitly remarked in 1648 that the portraits of the clerics did not entirely blend with the other figures, who were creations of the imagination. Motifs emphasizing the center of the picture such as the raised knife of the servant carving a lamb on the raised terrace and the hourglass on the table have symbolic meaning and relate to the words of Christ to his mother: "My hour is not yet come" (St. John 2, 4).

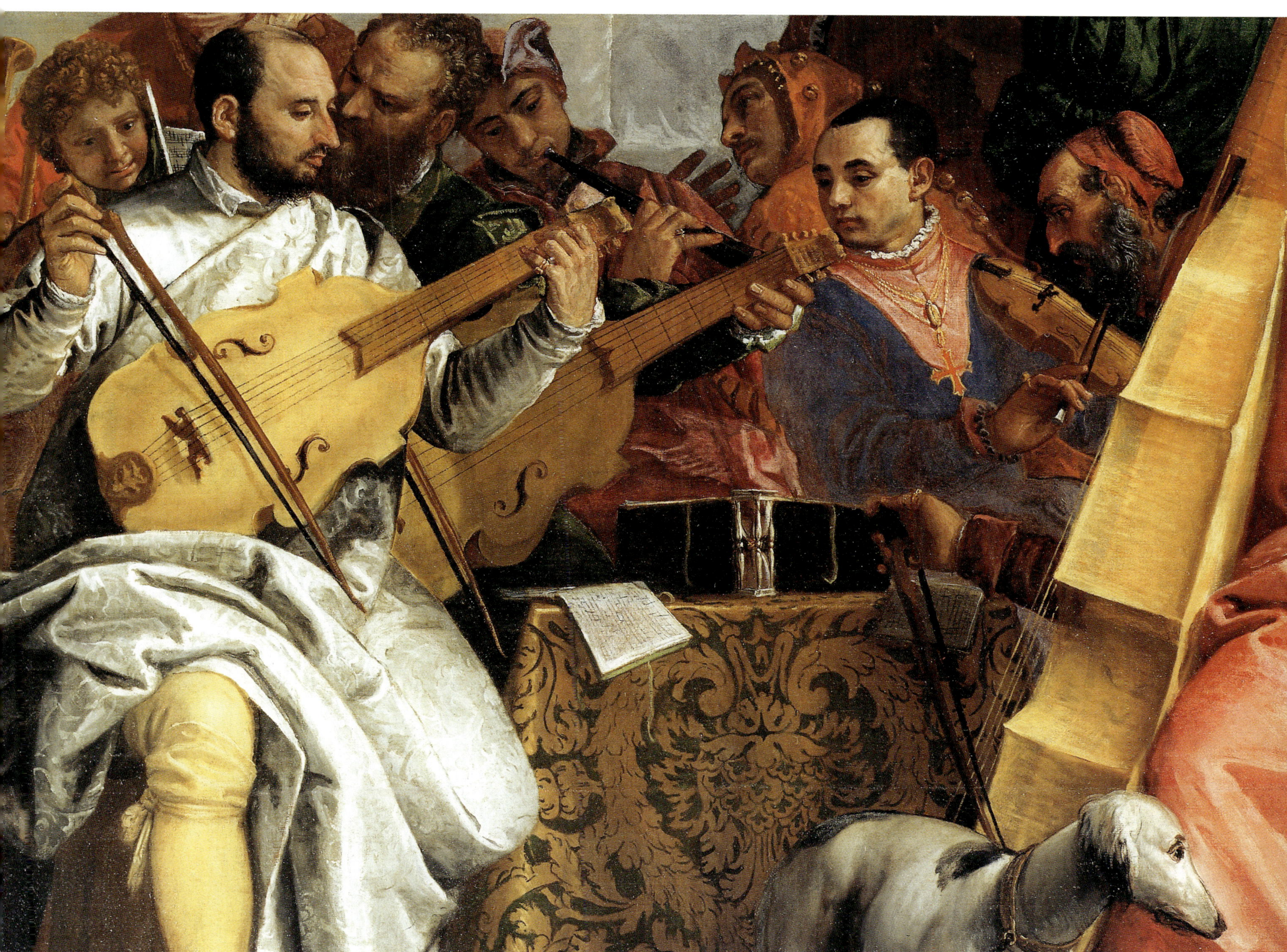

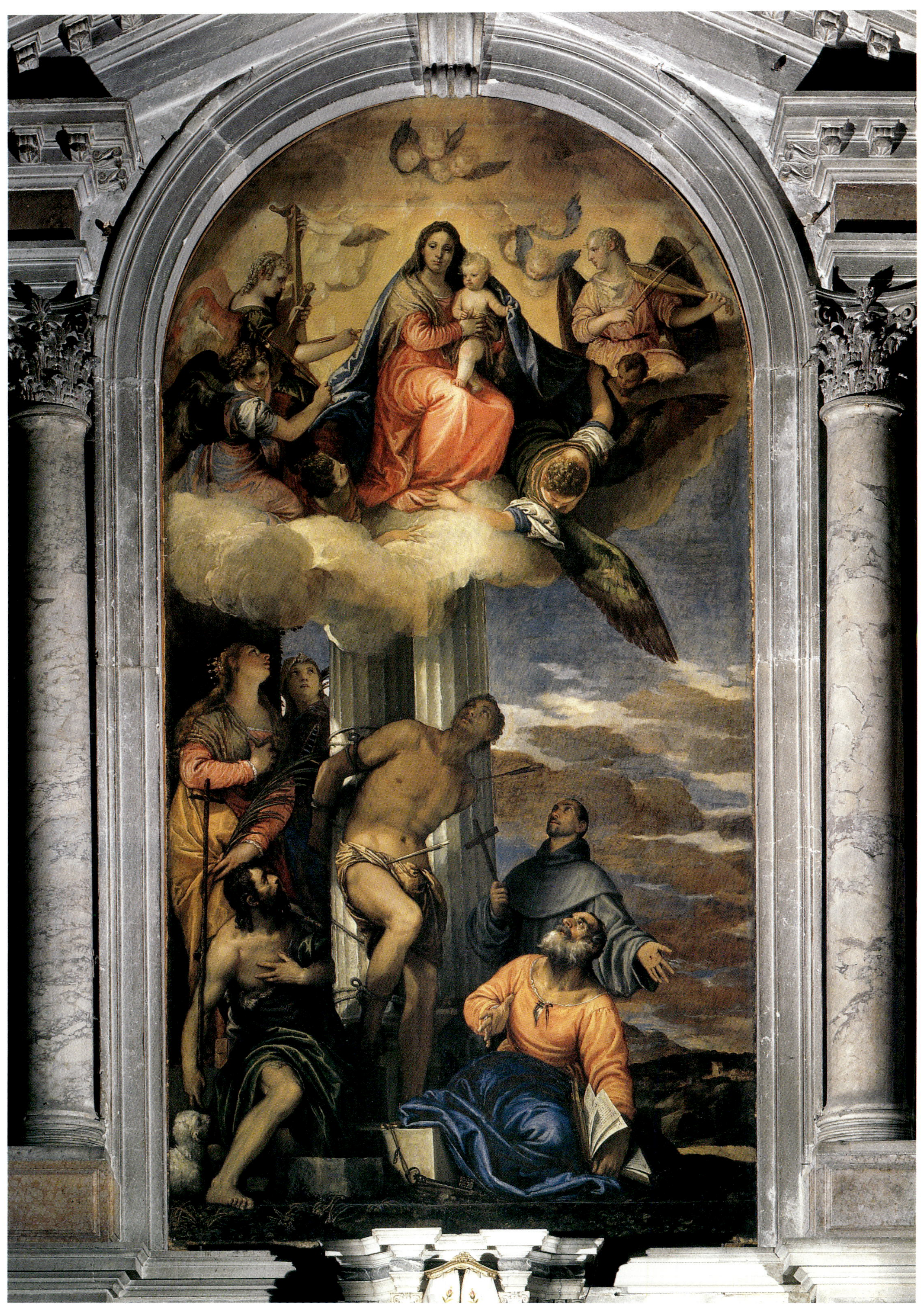

Boschini's romantically tinged notion, which evoked memories of the glorious history of Venetian painting, was evidently primarily an expression of the desire to create a symbolic illustration of the gift of *invenzione*, Veronese's creative ability to use colors in a play of forms indebted to the rules of musical harmony. Veronese for his part would scarcely have had the idea in his time of immortalizing himself so prominently in a religious history painting, and even less so within the circle of his painter colleagues, for the rivalry among Venetian painters was no secret. Albrecht Dürer's (1471–1528) correspondence testifies to the oppressive competitiveness among Venetian artists, and even if the rivalries which Vasari and Ridolfi later wrote about may, at least in part, be *topoi* in the genre of artists' anecdotes, there does appear to be a core of truth in certain reports. One need only remember the competition for the ceiling painting in the *albergo* of the Scuola Grande di San Rocco. In May 1564 agreement had been reached to involve some of the city's best painters in a competition, and Paolo Veronese, Andrea Schiavone, Guiseppe Salviati, Federico Zuccaro and Tintoretto had been asked to start by presenting a preliminary sketch. Tintoretto, who had already been passed over once in the prestigious competition for the ceiling paintings in the Libreria Marciana, presented the finished ceiling painting of the *Apotheosis of St. Roch* (Scuola Grande di San Rocco, Venice) one month later and without further ado made a gift of it to the brotherhood of St. Roch. As the clerics' rules made it their duty to accept donations and gifts, they did not hesitate long, and Tintoretto thus succeeded, by this crafty maneuver, to decide the competition in his favor.

Veronese did not need to fear any competition in the church of San Sebastiano. There was a long-standing relationship of personal trust between him and the prior of the monastery, who came from Verona; therefore there is a certain inevitability in the creation of the high altar with the *Madonna Enthroned with Saints Sebastian, Peter, John, Francis, Catherine and Elizabeth* (ill. 77), and the two wall paintings on either side showing the *Martyrdom of St. Sebastian* (ill. 78) and the *Martyrdom of Saints Mark and Marcellianus* (ill. 79). As with the organ case in the church, Veronese provided the design for the architecture of the high altar retable, which was executed between 1559 and 1561. In tried and tested imitation of Sebastiano Serlio and an antique *City Gate between Foligno and Rome*, a woodcut that appeared in the *Architettura* (Lib. III) first published in 1555, the pediment is once again completely filled by the large round arch. The particular charm of the altar painting, which is carefully matched to its architectural frame, is unquestionably the Apollonian figure of the titular saint who, tied to a column, has not given in to the suffering of his fate, but is leaning far forwards and gazing up in search of consolation at a cloud formation on which the Madonna is enthroned surrounded by angels making music.

Compared with the altarpiece, the theme of martyrdom becomes a dramatic event in the two paintings on the side walls of the choir, produced in about 1565. Brightly shining pictorial architectural features surrounded by light serve as decorative backdrops before which the scenes, full of figures and rich in detail, unfold in a horizontal format. The two works are stylistically similar to the *Martyrdom of St. George* (ill. 81), presumably produced shortly afterwards for the church of San Giorgio in Braida in Verona, insofar as they can offer some figural motifs of exceptional beauty. In the *Martyrdom of St. Sebastian* (ill. 78), the spectator's eye is captured mainly by the figure seen from behind on the right in the foreground. Leaning on a pilgrim's staff, it had appeared once before, about ten years previously, in the *Martyrdom of St. Giustina* (ill. 43), and now, differently dressed and slightly altered, it was being used as a *repoussoir* to direct the spectator to the central scene of the martyrdom. As a "beautiful" individual form it is part of a comprehensive order, for, by its position in the picture, the figure guides one's eyes to the *serliana* whose arch highlights the main scene, thus creating a picture within a picture. However, weaknesses are also apparent. The dense wall of figures of more or less uninvolved "extras" as well as individual heads that have been rather unsuccessfully incorporated in the picture make it clear that Veronese must have taken advantage of the aid of assistants. He had already been supported by his brother Benedetto and a certain Antonio when producing the ceiling paintings for the church of San Sebastiano. It is difficult to determine precisely their contribution, but given the wealth of commissions and duties during the course of the 1560s, there can be no doubt that Veronese was increasingly forced to establish his priorities and delegate certain tasks.

Apart from the above-mentioned works, other demanding large-scale altar paintings produced within a few years were the *Pala Marogna* for the church of San Paolo in Verona, and the *Pala di San Zaccaria* (ill. 82) for San Paolo in Venice. Together with *Christ Among the Doctors* (ill. 83), whose dating is also disputed and which was presumably carried out in the second half of the 1560s, they document the constantly growing reputation of the Venetian painter. The journey he made to Verona in 1566 on the occasion of his marriage to Elena Badile, the daughter of his former master, can therefore have been little more than a short breather, for the painter was increasingly being approached by private clients. As early as 1567 the impressive allegories *Omnia Vanitas* (Frick Collection, New York) and *Honor et Virtus post mortem floret* (ill. 117) were offered for sale in Venice, and shortly afterwards a commission from a member of the Pisani family, a venerable Venetian house, was to result in *The Family of Darius before Alexander the Great* (ill. 84).

The festive tone of this painting which, until it came to the National Gallery in London in 1857, was one of the most famous attractions in Venice, must have corresponded to a considerable degree to the cultural taste of the Venetian aristocracy. It embodies a convincing combination of those abilities of Veronese's in which the creative differences between his, Titian's and Tintoretto's works are most intensely evident. The beauty of the individual figures, coupled with the

77 *Enthroned Mother of God with SS. Sebastian, Peter, John, Francis, Catherine and Elizabeth*, c. 1564/65
Oil on canvas, 420 x 230 cm
San Sebastiano, Venice

The altarpiece for the choir of the church of San Sebastiano was presumably painted at the same time as the two lateral canvases in the gallery (ills. 78, 79). In doing the preliminary drawing for the architecture of the retable, Veronese worked once again as an architectural designer. The two female saints honor the memory of the founder Catharuza Cornaro and her executrix Liza Querini. Veronese's biographer Ridolfi, writing in 1648, thought he could discern the portrait of the client, Fra Bernardo Torlioni, in the figure of St. Francis.

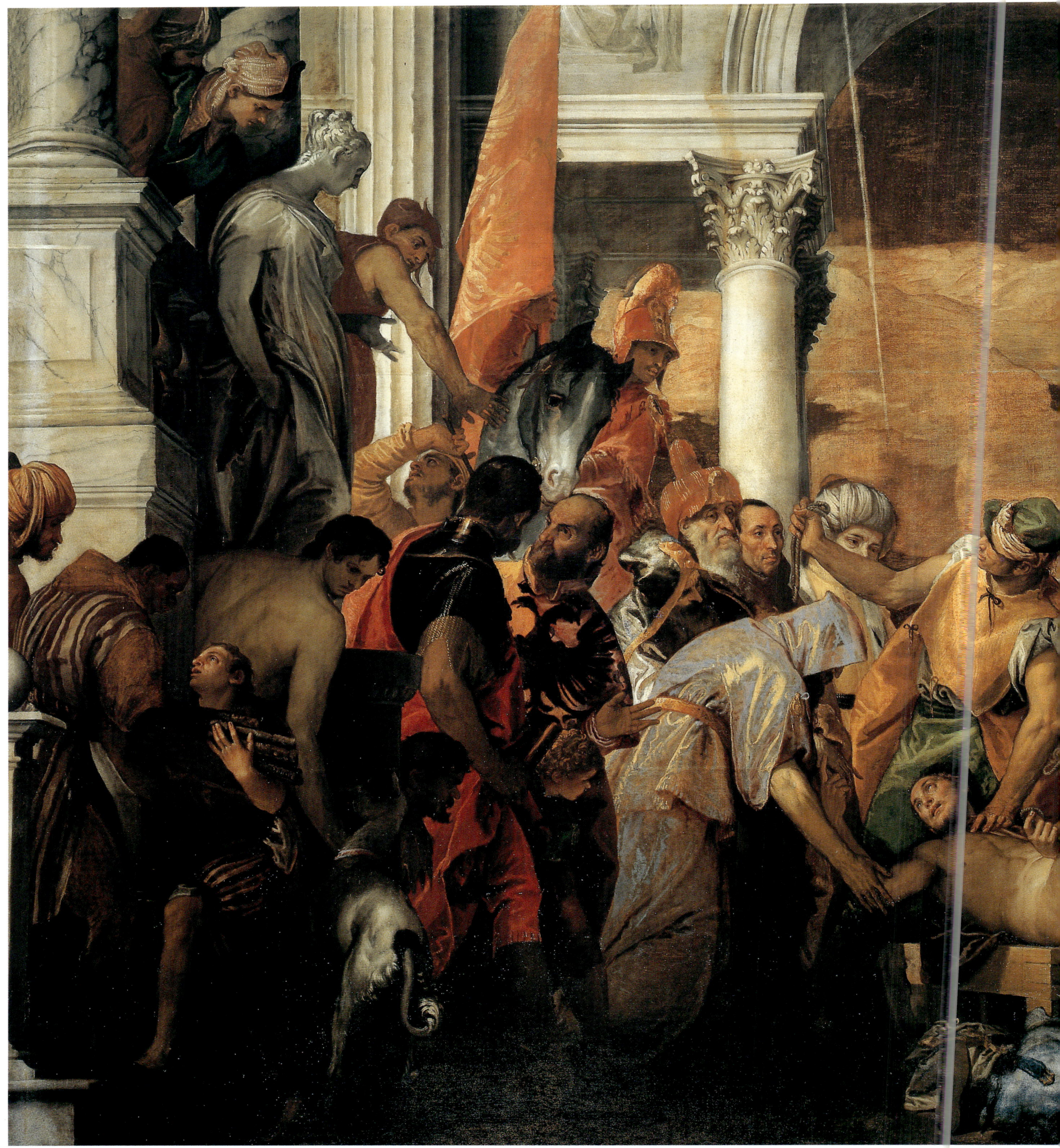

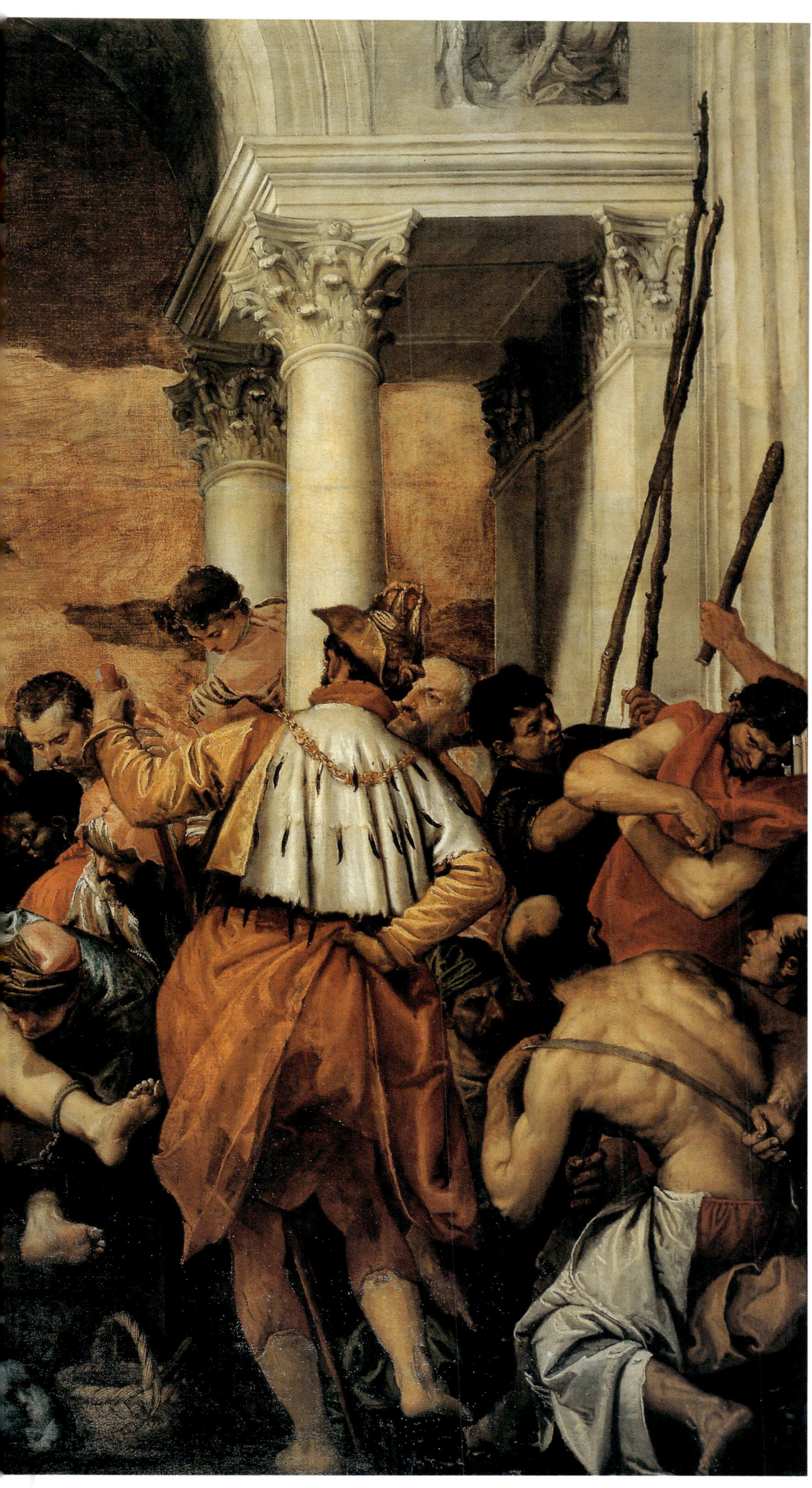

78 *Martyrdom of St. Sebastian*, c. 1565
Oil on canvas, 355 x 540 cm
San Sebastiano, Venice

This picture of the title saint suffering his gruesome fate bound to a frame is dramatically incorporated into the crowded detail of the composition. Compared with its counterpart, the choreography of the figures looks occasionally rather stiff and calculated. Moreover, some of the heads were clearly carried out by assistants. A specific feature of Veronese's technique is the combination of strongly contrasting oranges and greens.

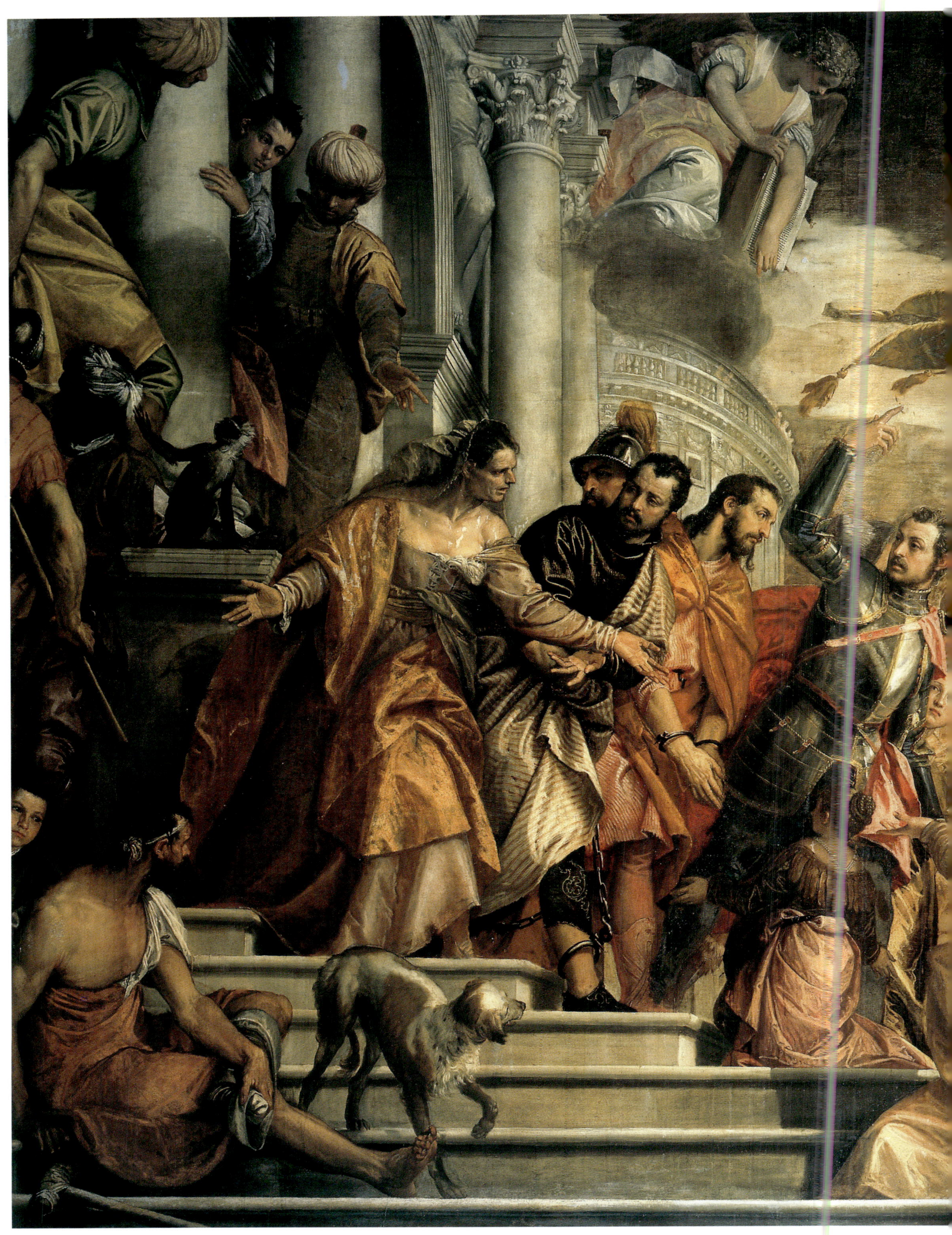

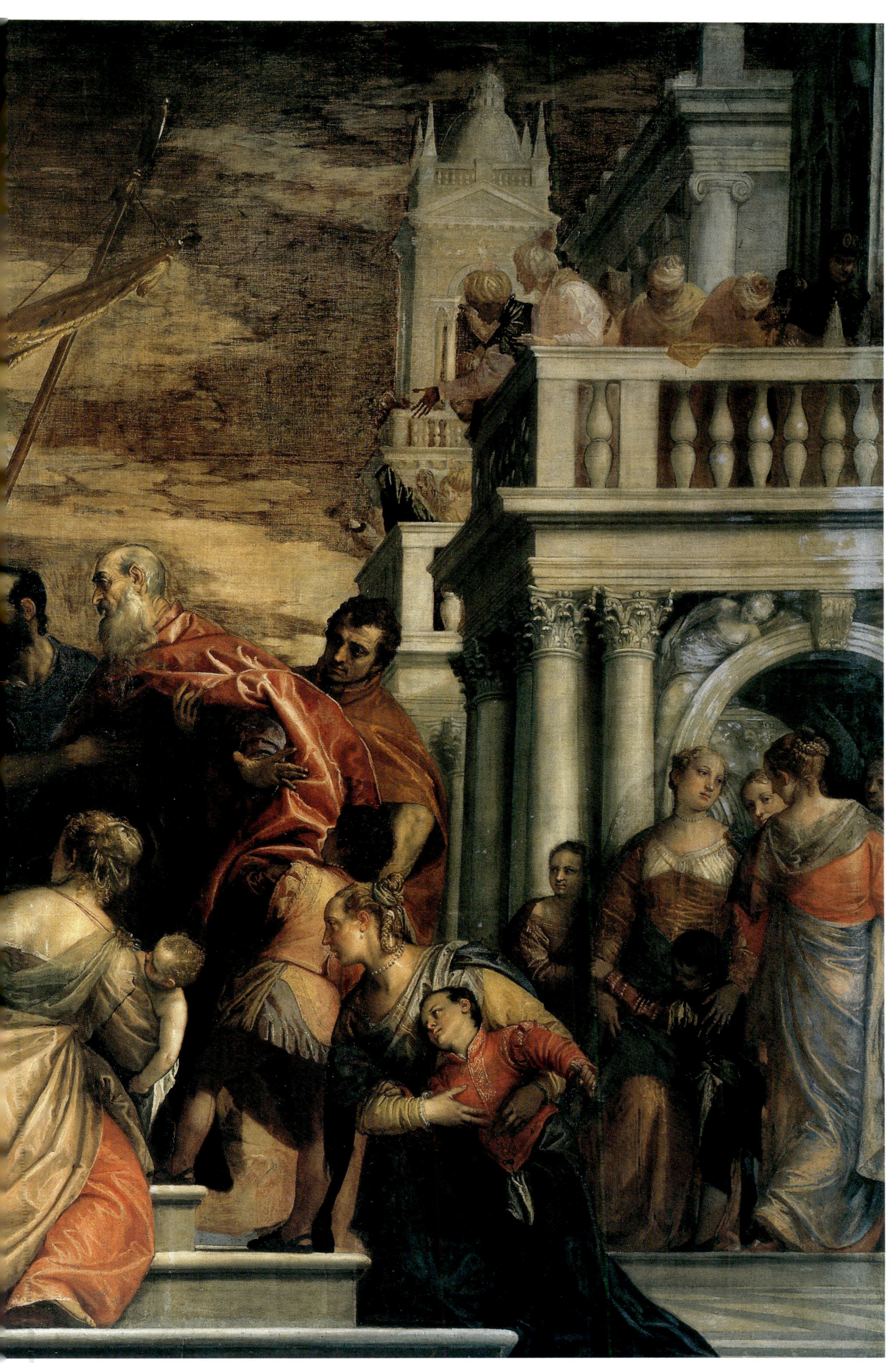

79 *Martyrdom of SS. Mark and Marcellianus*, c. 1565
Oil on canvas, 355 x 540 cm
San Sebastiano, Venice

The *Golden Legend* of Jacopo da Voragine tells the story of the brothers Mark and Marcellianus and the events before their execution in great detail. The attempts by their despairing parents to get the two martyrs, strengthened in their faith by St. Sebastian, to change their minds and abandon their faith is the subject of the crowded scene, which sticks very closely to the textual source. Idealized architecture conforming to the forms of Palladio and Sansovino provides the setting for the dramatic event. According to Ridolfi, the two paintings intended for the side walls of the "presbytery" were completed in 1565. This seems a credible date, and fits well with the report that Federico Zuccaro, who spent two and a half years in Venice from 1563, made drawings from both works.

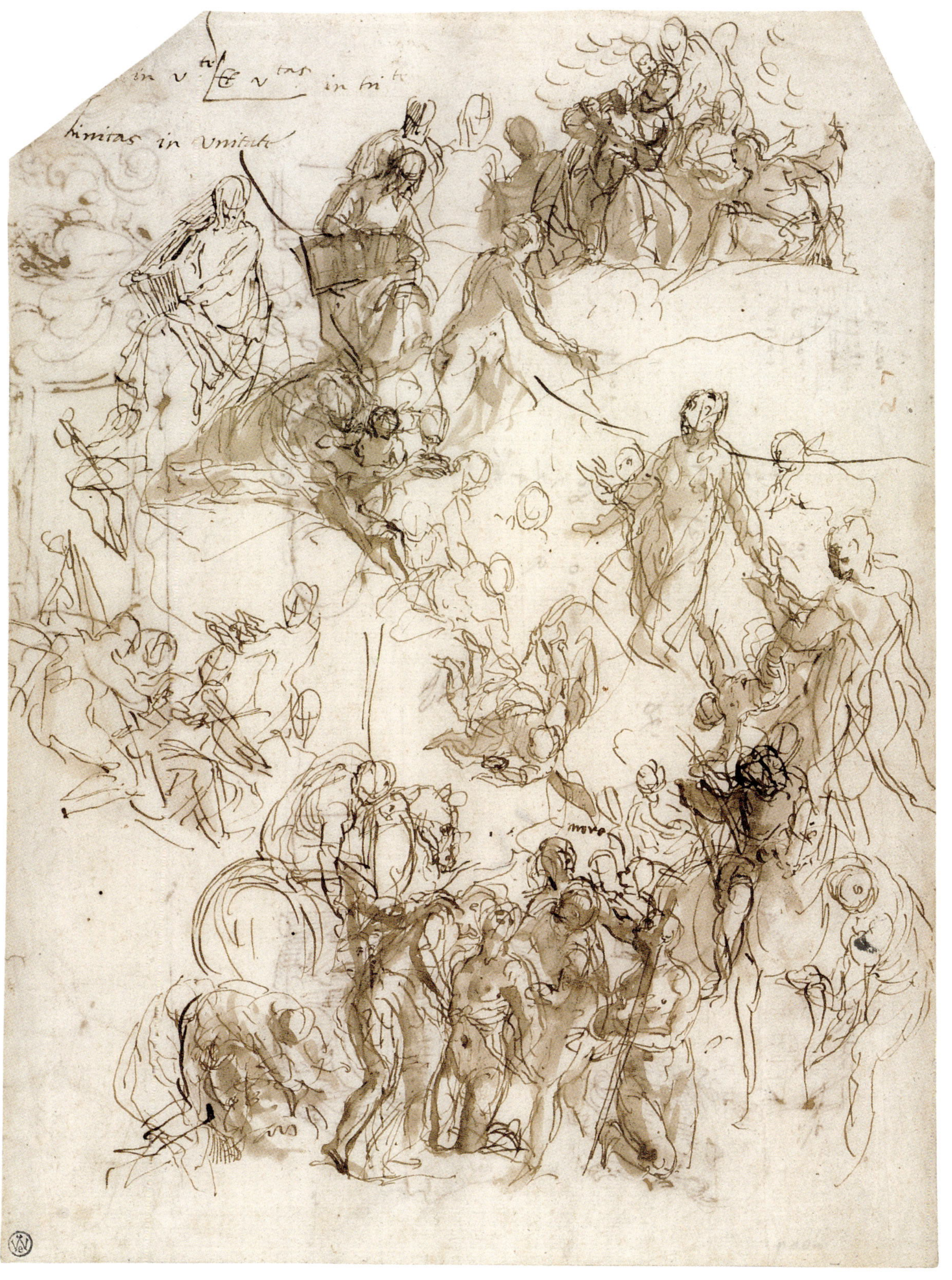

80 Sketch sheet with figure studies for the *Martyrdom of St. George*, c. 1564
Wash drawing, 28.9 x 21.7 cm
J. Paul Getty Museum, Malibu, California

Veronese was always very careful in his use of paper as a valuable raw material. When drawing, he used both front and back in many cases, working quickly with his pen to record his ideas. The inscriptions on the front of the sheet are also by the artist himself, noting *moro* (Moor) beside a figure that in the painted version appears to the left of the sword carrier, slightly turned away. A decisive change can be seen in the suggestive gesture of the kneeling saint. The gesture serves to reinforce the viewer's involvement in the scene, underlining the didactic function of the altarpiece.

81 (opposite)
Martyrdom of St. George, c. 1564
Oil on canvas, 426 x 305 cm
San Giorgio in Braida, Verona

Framed by a concave aedicule with double Corinthian columns, this large painting adorns Andrea Brugnoli's high altar of the church, the reconstruction of which materially involved Veronese's patron Michele Sanmicheli in 1552. Very probably Veronese was already working on a new altarpiece for the apse at that date. Two surviving *chiaroscuro* drawings and a copy appear to indicate the genesis of this first project. Only after the completion of the architecture of the high altar, i.e. soon after 1564, did work start on the iconographically unconventional altarpiece under the influence of Tridentine reformist ideas. It omits the gruesome torture of the martyrdom, concentrating instead on the saint's moment of intercession. Again, the central figure is incorporated in a group composition full of movement. The scene of the martyr's unclothing is exaggerated by the presence of the Madonna in a bank of clouds accompanied by SS. Peter, Paul and the cardinal virtues Faith, Hope and Charity.

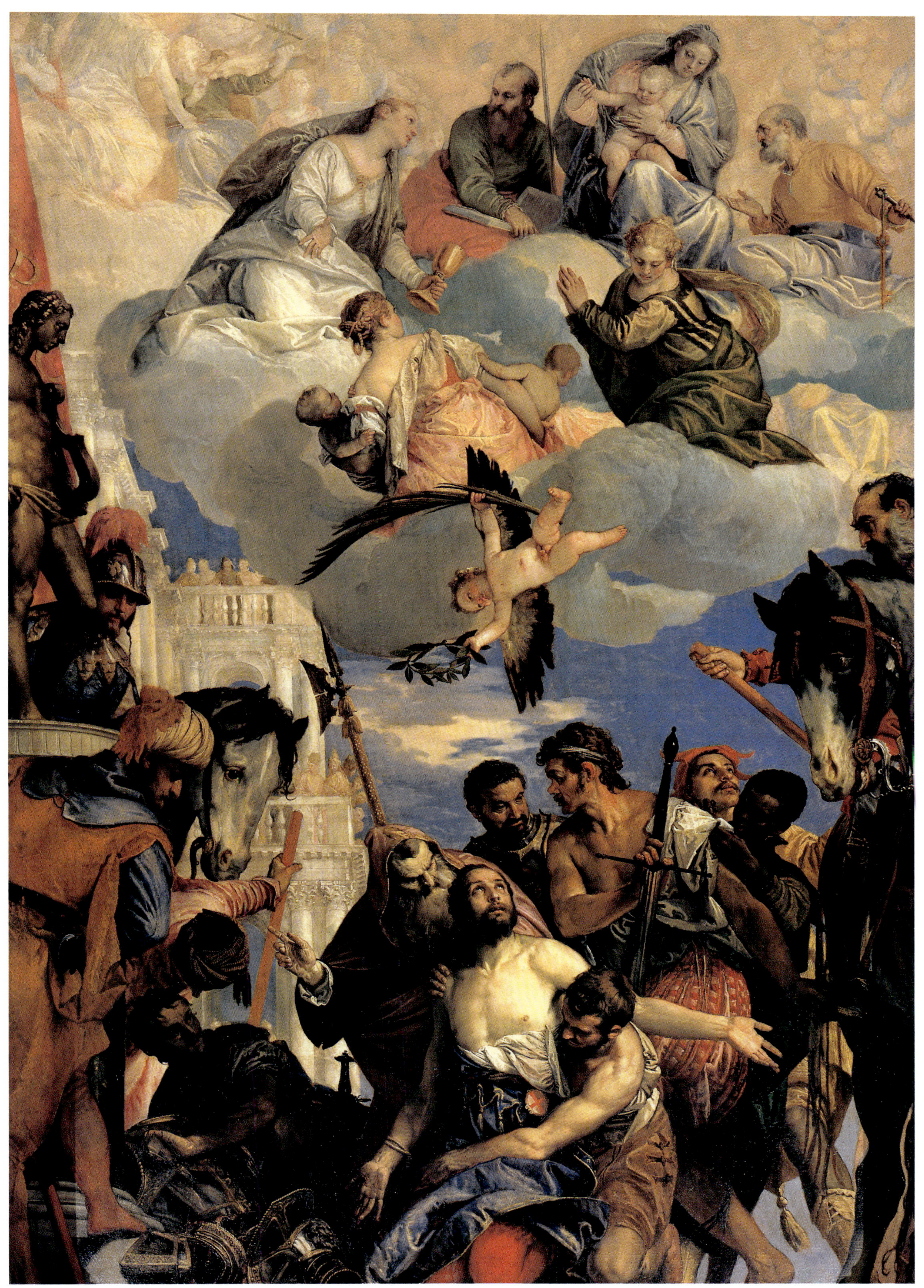

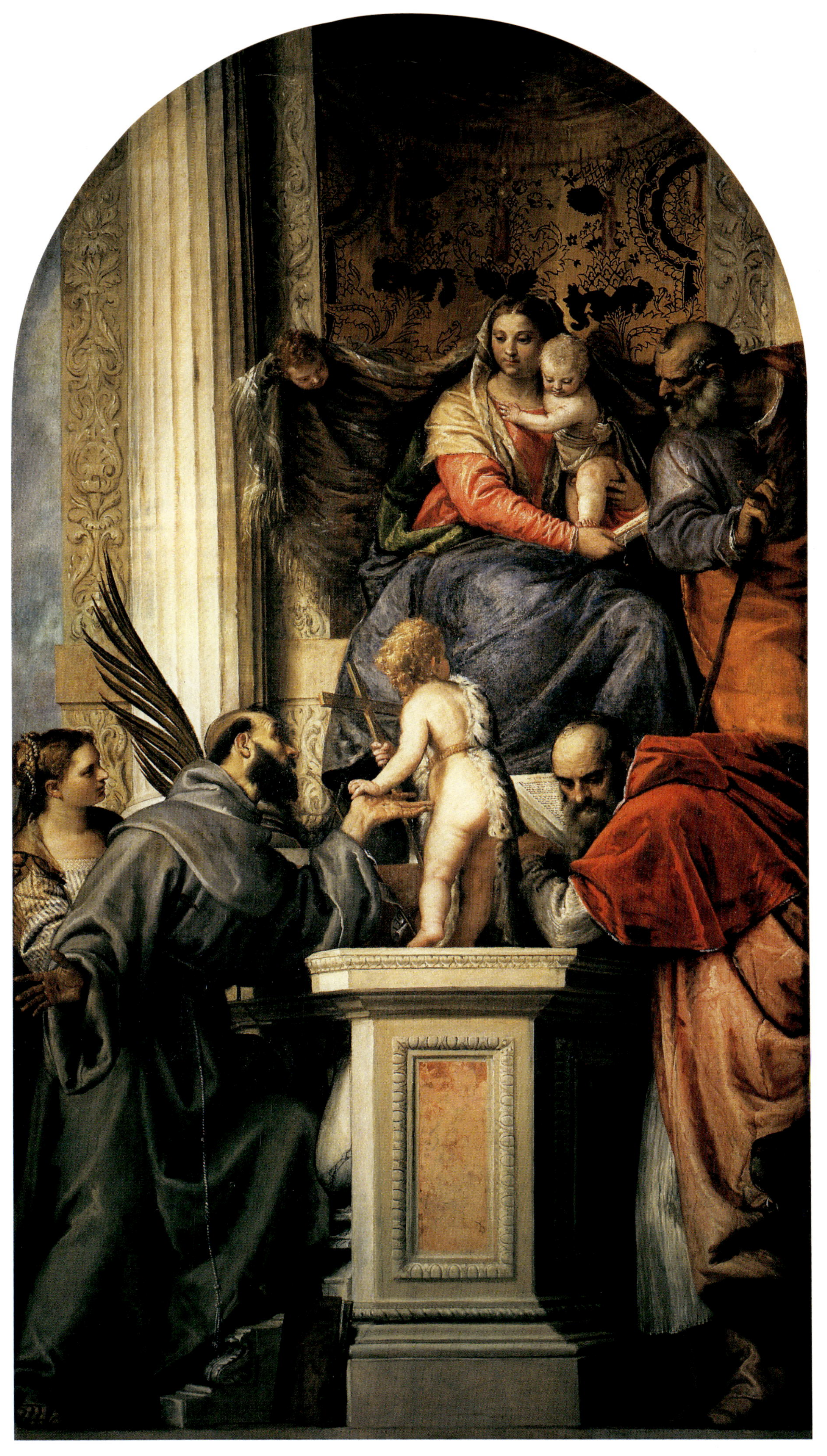

82 *Enthroned Madonna and Child, with the infant St. John the Baptist and SS. Joseph, Jerome, Justina of Padua and Francis (Pala di San Zaccaria)*, c. 1562–1564
Oil on canvas, 341 x 193 cm
Gallerie dell'Accademia, Venice

This altar painting is one of the principal works of the 1560s. It was originally part of the furnishings of the sacristy of the Venetian Renaissance church of San Zaccaria, and owes its commissioning to a gift by Francesco Bonaldo in 1562. Colors of unusual brilliance enrich the imaginative interplay of light and shade.

refined splendor of pictorial architectures flooded with light, set new standards and developed a degree of representation which filled Johann Wolfgang von Goethe (1749–1832) with enthusiasm when he visited the Palazzo Pisani-Moretta on the Canal Grande on October 8, 1786 specifically in order to see the picture. His admiration of the figures allowed him to generously overlook the historically incorrect costumes which, during the second half of the 17th century, had provoked criticism in the circles of French academic experts and had led Goethe to make the sober observation that a 16th-century story was intended. The story of Alexander, the victorious ancient general, was considered to be an example of magnanimous behavior, for after the Battle of Issus he had given the mother of Darius, the defeated Persian king, an honorable reception. This indeed provided excellent opportunities for identification, and it has therefore rightly been believed that a member of the Pisani family was intending the large history painting to be an allegory of virtue to act as a reminder of the military successes of one of his ancestors in battle against the Turks. The pictorial architecture, on the other hand, is idealized and forms a variation of the motif of the arcade with coupled demi-columns familiar from the *Martyrdom of Saints Mark and Marcellianus* (ill. 79), itself borrowed from the *loggetta* built next to the Campanile in St. Mark's Square by Jacopo Sansovino between 1537 and 1549.

Only on rare occasions did Veronese include actually existing buildings in his pictures. In the case of the *Adoration of the Virgin by the Coccina Family* (ill. 85), this very probably occurred at the express wish of the donor of the series of four paintings. In the background on the right appears the palace on the Canal Grande which the family, originally from Bergamo, probably commissioned from the Lombard architect Giovanni Giacomo de'Grigi (died 1572) in about 1560. It was depicted on a copperplate veduta (ill. 86) in about 1703 by Luca Carlevarijs (1665–1731), and little of its external appearance, at least, has changed to the present day.

This painting, created in about 1571, has an entire series of features in common with the picture of Alexander. Once again the painter developed the standing, seated and kneeling figures informally on a narrow stage, and in both cases it is the memorable aristocratic realism that gives the depictions their particular character. The Coccina picture (ill. 85) is fundamentally a secular group portrait dressed up as a private devotional picture. Thus, the right side of the composition is determined by the portraits of Alvise, Antonio and Zuanantonio Coccina with their wives and children. The family, which in the 16th century was one of the richest in the city, is commended to the Virgin by the three cardinal virtues of *Fides* (Faith), *Spes* (Hope) and *Caritas* (Charity). Screened by two mighty column shafts to

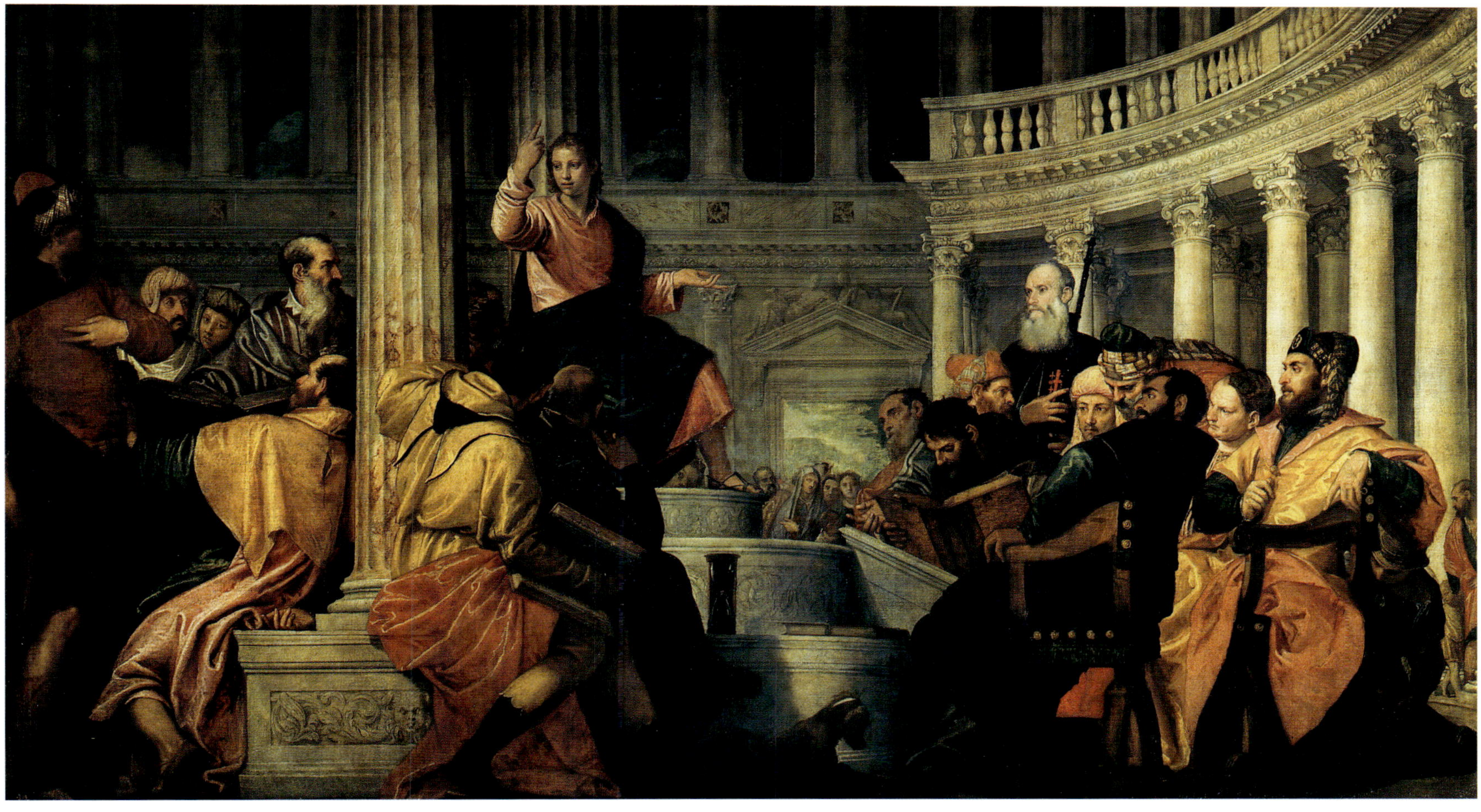

83 *Jesus among the Doctors*, c. 1566/67
Oil on canvas, 236 x 430 cm
Museo del Prado, Madrid

On the basis of the slightly damaged and fragmentary inscription *MDXLVIII* on the book block of the figure at Jesus's feet with its back to us, this painting has again been claimed as one of the painter's first works. This controversial dating is highly suspect when compared with the Mannerist style of early works painted in Verona such as the *Conversion of Mary Magdalene* (ill. 10) or the *Lamentation over the Dead Christ* (ill. 12). On the basis of the style and technique of a study for the figure with his back to us, carried out in black chalk (Sotheby's, London, 1970, no. 9), W. R. Rearick has recently proposed a dating of 1566/67. We know neither the name of the client nor the original destination of the picture, which is documented in 1686 in the Hall of Mirrors of the Alcázar in Madrid.

make others keep their distance, they form a calm conclusion on the left side, together with St. John and St. Jerome, of a composition which in formal terms is closer to a Doge devotional picture. With the addition of the *Bearing of the Cross*, the *Wedding at Cana* (ill. 87) and the *Adoration of the Magi*, the works presumably appeared in the form of a picture frieze and decorated a private room for devotions in the palace. In common with the altar painting, surviving only in the form of copies, that Veronese executed in about 1561/62 for the family's chapel in the Venetian church of San Francesco della Vigna, the ambitious sequence of pictures was evidently also part of a consistent strategy on the part of the family to establish themselves. The façade of the magnificent palace on the Canal Grande, conceived in imitation of the "al costume di Venezia" palace in Sebastiano Serlio's *Regole generali* (Venice, 1537, Lib. IV), had already conspicuously demonstrated the family's desire for *Repräsentation*. Originally from Bergamo, the Coccina were not a patrician family but nevertheless, being rich citizens (*cittadini*) and patrons of the arts, they responded self-confidently to

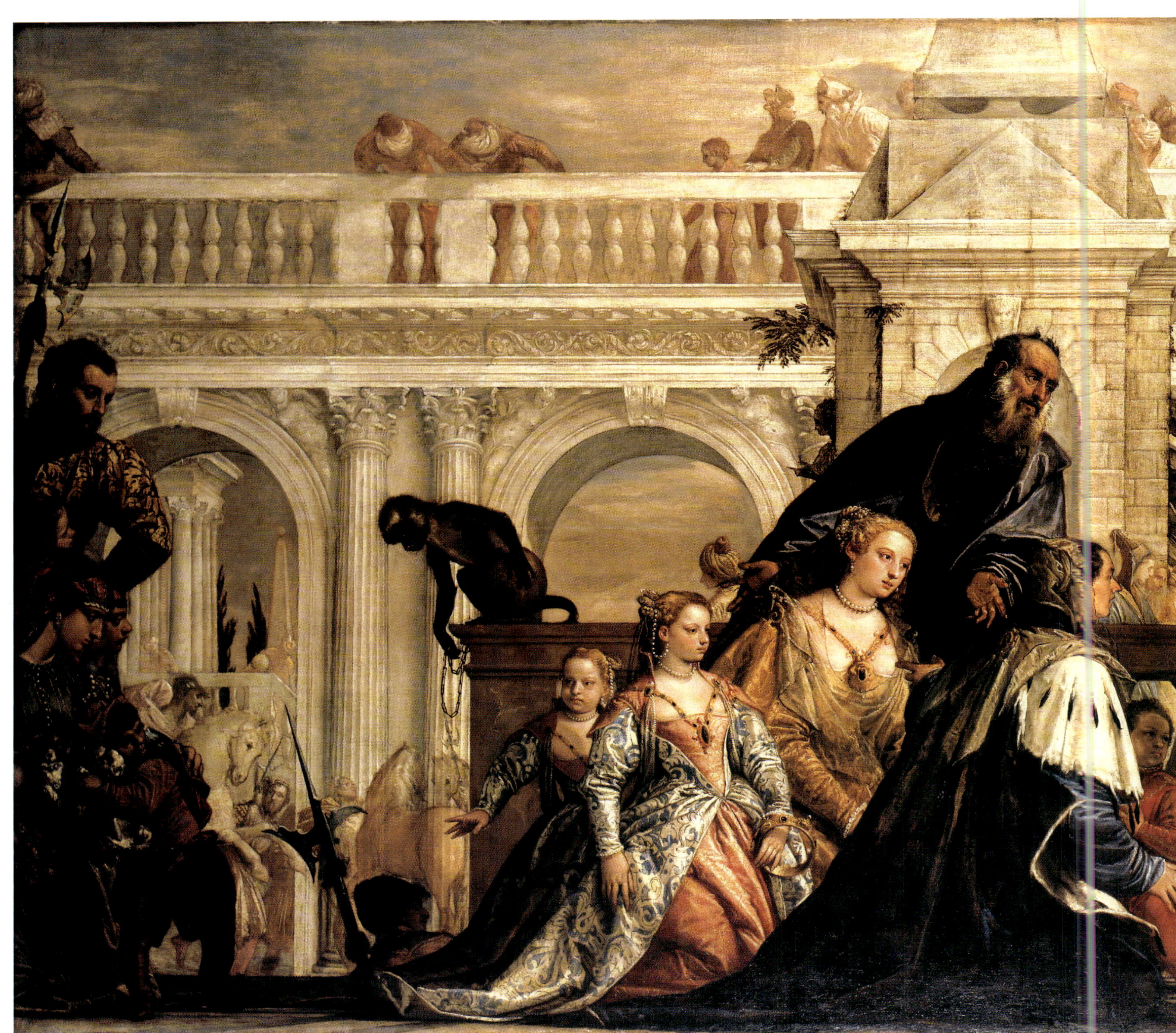

the values of the reigning aristocracy. For that reason, it is perhaps no coincidence that Veronese was their choice of history painter, for he enjoyed an outstanding reputation among the circles of the old established social and political elite of the city, and his idealized, often worldly pictorial environment reflected the refined cultural taste of the Venetian *nobili* to a particular degree. In the case of the Coccina family, social self-image unquestionably went hand in hand with the desire for the picture to be a *memoria* to record their piety for their contemporaries and descendants to see. The portraits of the clients which appeared in the *Adoration of the Virgin* (ill. 85), together with further portraits of members of the family hidden in the other pictures in the series, would not inevitably have offended against the Venetian custom of modesty, as their effect was achieved within the private context of the palace. Once again workshop assistants must have helped the painter execute them, though their collaboration was limited to technical tasks, for several surviving preliminary studies (ill. 89) demonstrate how carefully Veronese prepared individual figures and their arrangement.

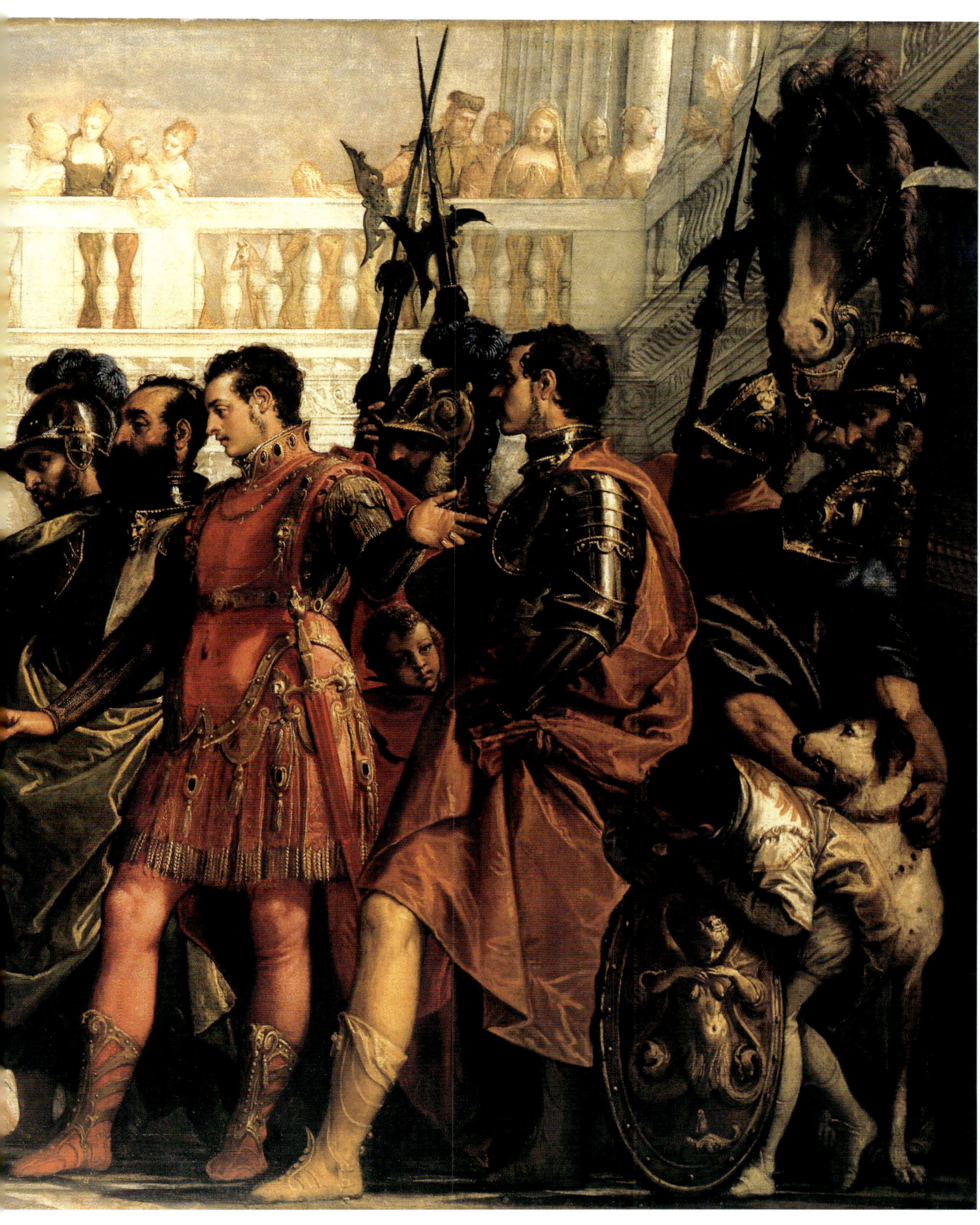

84 *The Family of Darius before Alexander the Great*, c. 1569–1571
Oil on canvas, 236 x 475 cm
National Gallery, London

When Alexander the Great was received by Sisygambis, mother of Darius, after the battle of Issus (333 B.C.), she mistook his companion Hephaistion for the victorious general. According to the ancient account, Alexander magnanimously put the royal parent at ease by saying: "He too is an Alexander." The history painting recalls the magnanimity of the great commander and ruler of antiquity in the form of a virtue allegory. As a quasi-private counterpart to the history paintings in the Doge's Palace, the picture presented the viewer with an example of a virtuous deed. According to Veronese's biographer Ridolfi, in 1648 the painting was in the possession of the Pisani in Venice. The suggestion, first made in 1862, that it had been painted for the Pisani's palazzo in Este is based on an anecdote told by the French art connoisseur Dézallier D'Agenvilliers. In 1762 he noted that the painter had painted the work at the Pisanis' country houses to thank them for their hospitality and left it behind as a gift.

Veronese's outstanding abilities in painting, the gift of *varietà* and *invenzione*, through which his art, in the eyes of contemporary art experts, had become second nature, was particularly suited to Baroque tastes and, in the 17th century, also gained him an outstanding reputation. When the Roman painter and architect Pietro da Cortona was reminiscing about his stay in Venice and visit to the Palazzo Coccina in the *Trattato della pitture e scultura. Uso et abuso loro*, written in conjunction with Pietro da Cortona in 1652, he confirmed of the cupbearer in the *Wedding of Cana* (ill. 87) that "he alone already deserves to be called a great and extraordinary wonder of art" (che quella sola merita d'esser nominata una grande, e straordinaria maraviglia dell'Arte). The extent to which this conviction evidently corresponded to the feelings and character of the age can be clearly gauged by the contemporary painter Mattia Preti's (1613–1699) depiction of the *Wedding at Cana* (ill. 91).

85 *The Adoration of the Virgin by the Coccina Family*, c. 1571
Oil on canvas, 167 x 414 cm
Gemäldegalerie Alte Meister, Staatliche Kunstsammlungen Dresden, Dresden

Along with three other pictures for devotional purposes, this painting originally formed part of the furnishings of the Palazzo Coccina (now Palazzo Papadopoli) on the Grand Canal. After Charles I of England had fruitlessly tried to obtain them in 1644, the pairs of pictures passed in 1645 to Francesco I d'Este in Modena. In 1746, his descendant Francesco III sold them to Augustus III, King of Saxony.

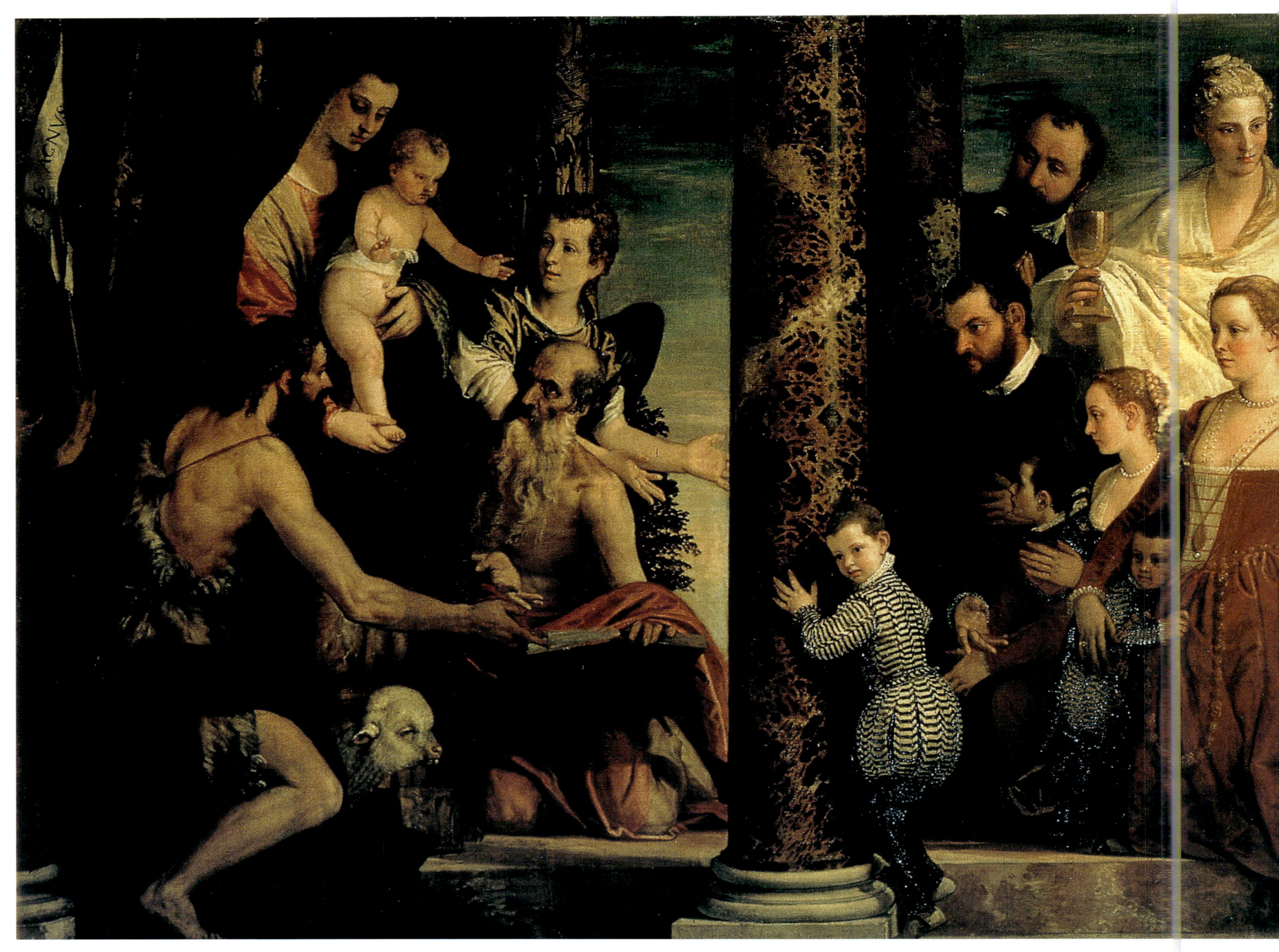

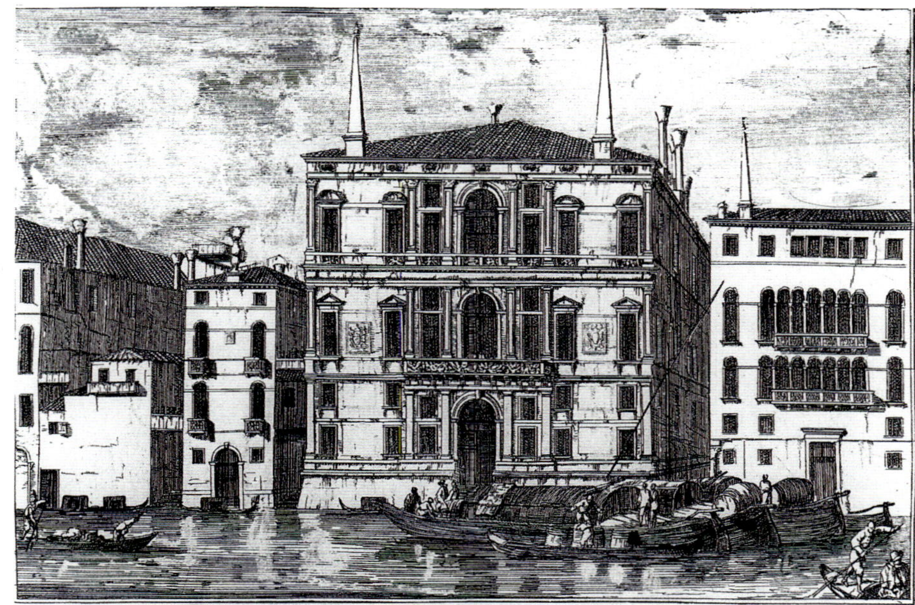

86 Luca Carlevarijs
The Palazzo Coccina on the Grand Canal, c. 1703
Etching, 183 x 290 (printing plate), from *Fabriche e vedute di Venetia*, 2nd ed., Plate 80
Bayerische Staatsbibliothek, Munich

Published in 1703 and containing a series of pictures of famous Venetian buildings, this book is considered an important contribution to the development of Venetian art of *veduta* in the 18th century. Among buildings considered worthy of inclusion by Carlevarijs was the Palazzo Coccina, which until 1645 contained four paintings by Veronese (now in Dresden). Built around 1560 by Giovanni Giacomo de'Grigi for Giovanni and Girolamo Coccina, the family palazzo was adjudged by Francesco Sansovino in 1581 to be one of the most splendid on the Grand Canal.

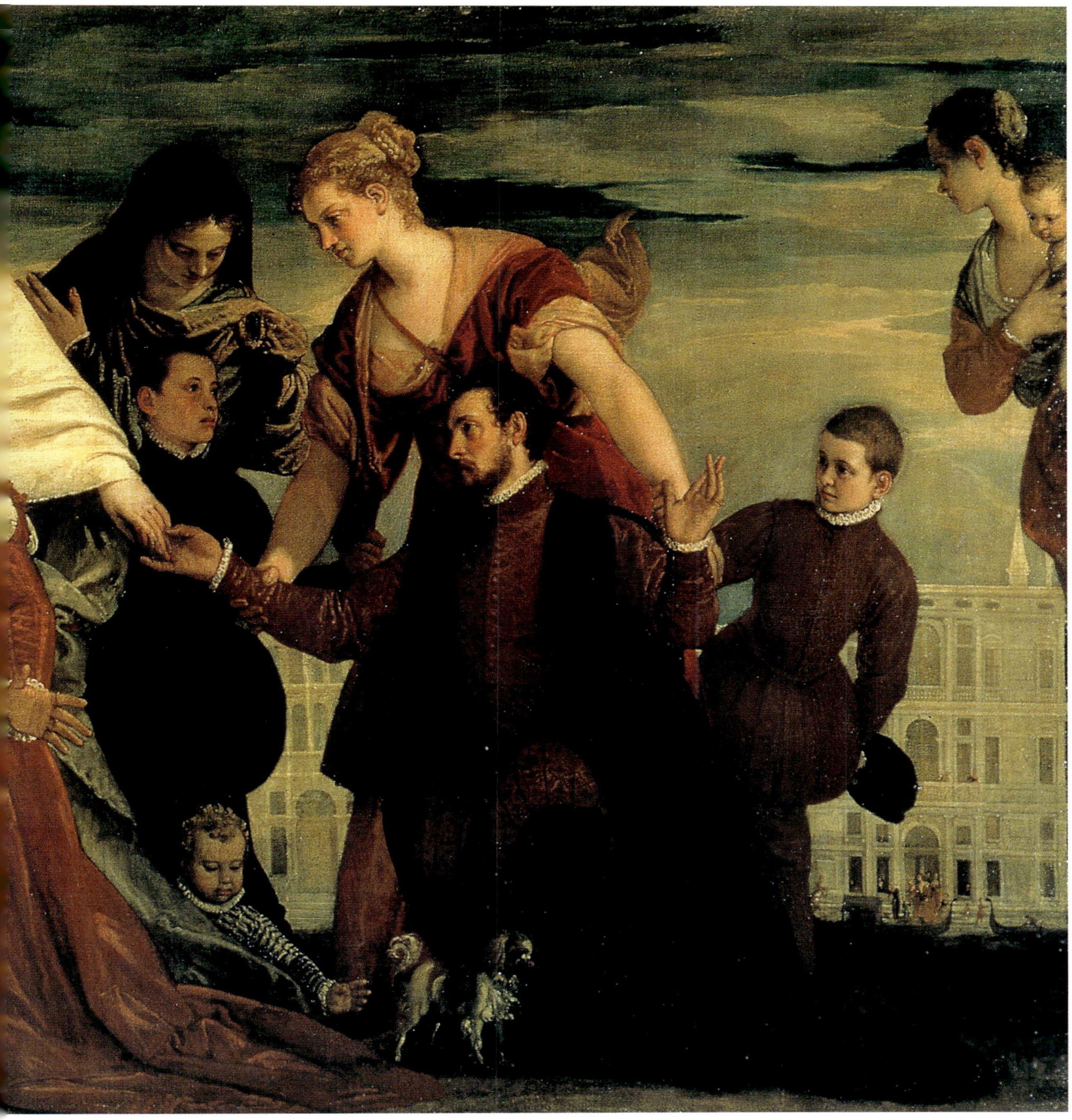

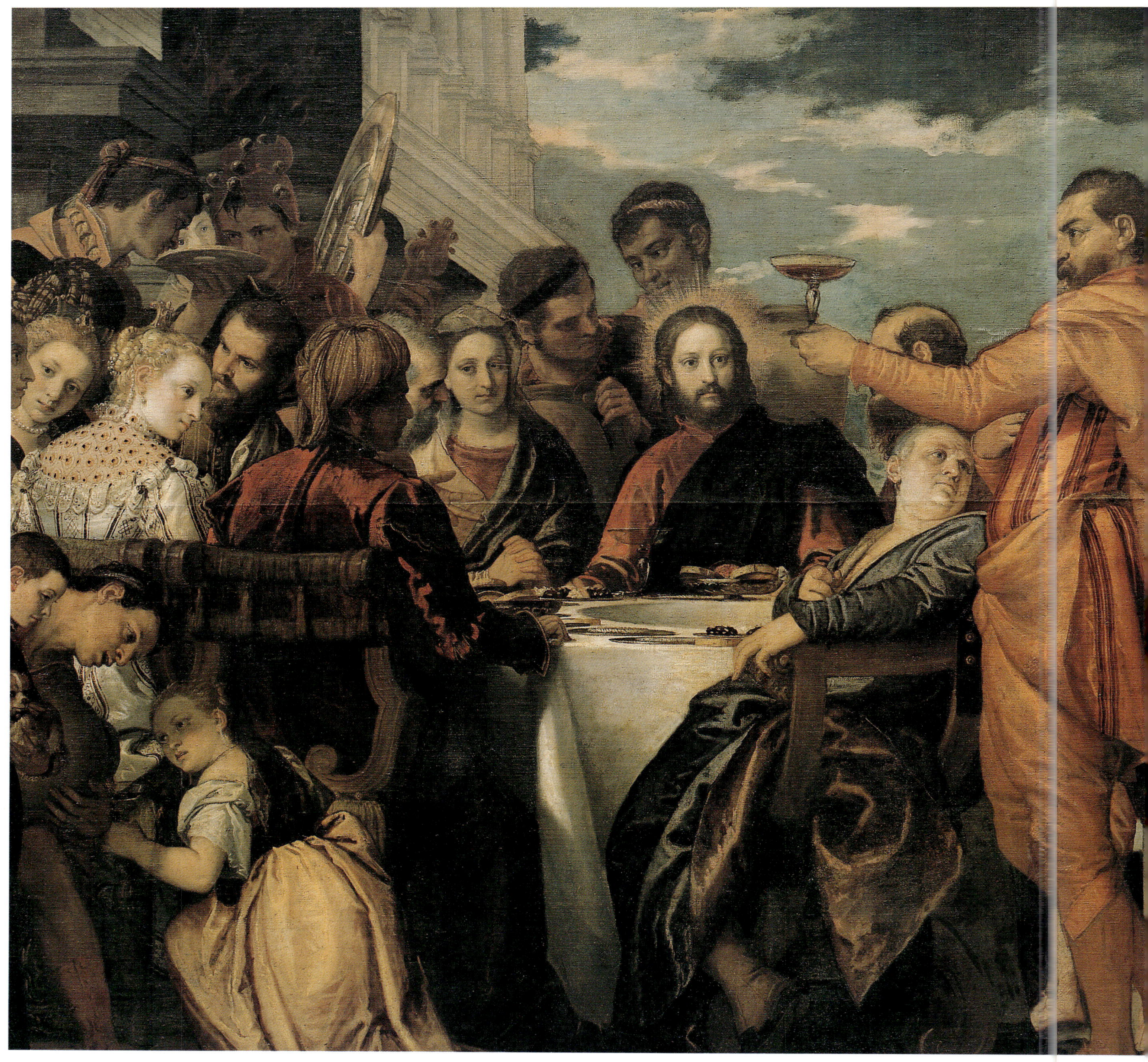

87 *Wedding at Cana*, c. 1571/72
Oil on canvas, 207 x 457 cm
Gemäldegalerie Alte Meister, Staatliche Kunstsammlungen Dresden, Dresden

This version of the wine miracle repeats a subject already painted by Veronese in 1562 (ill. 73). The structure of the work is far simpler here and more relaxed in its coloration, but nonetheless was considered in the 17th century as a perfect example of the artist's wealth of invention.

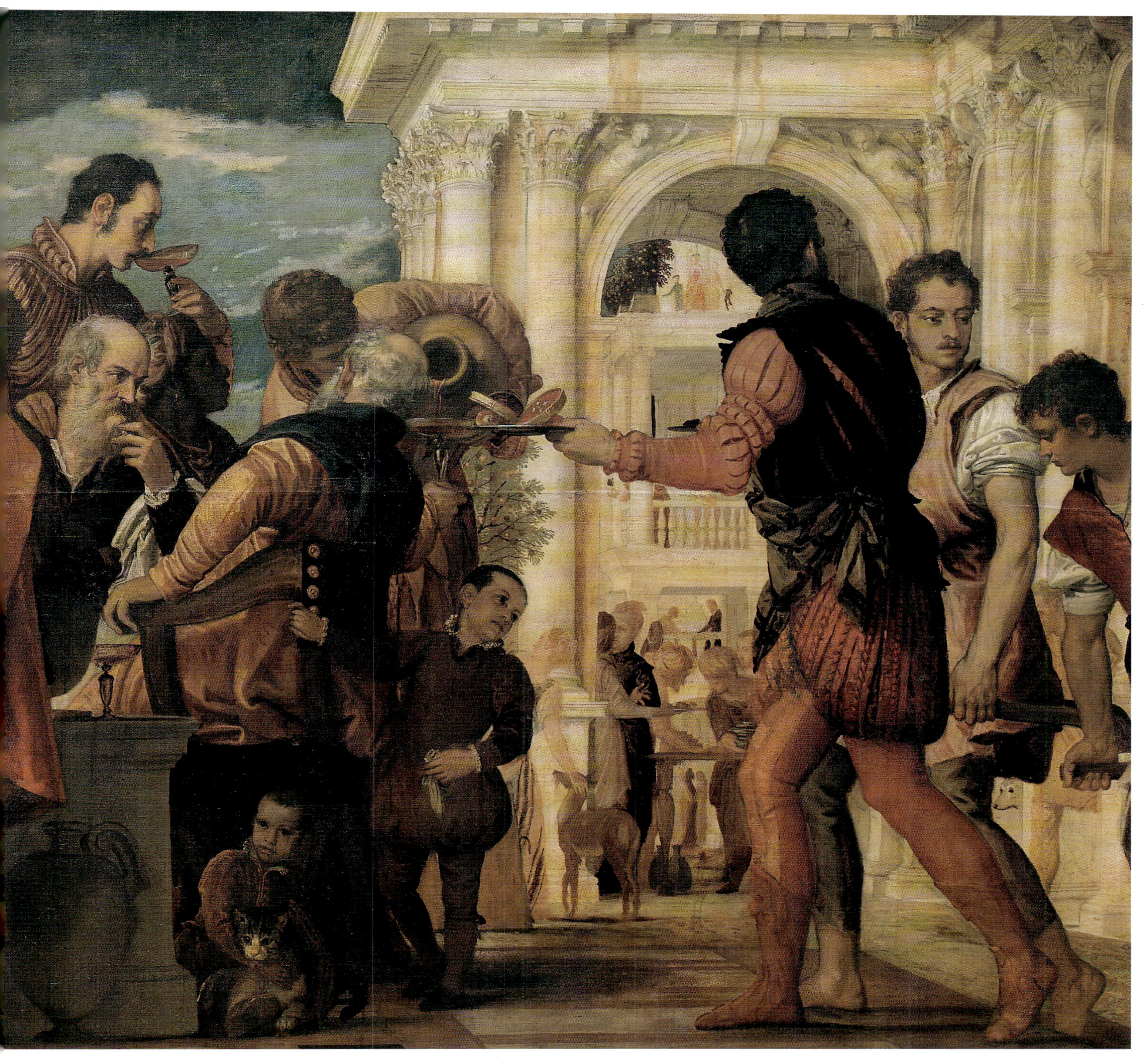

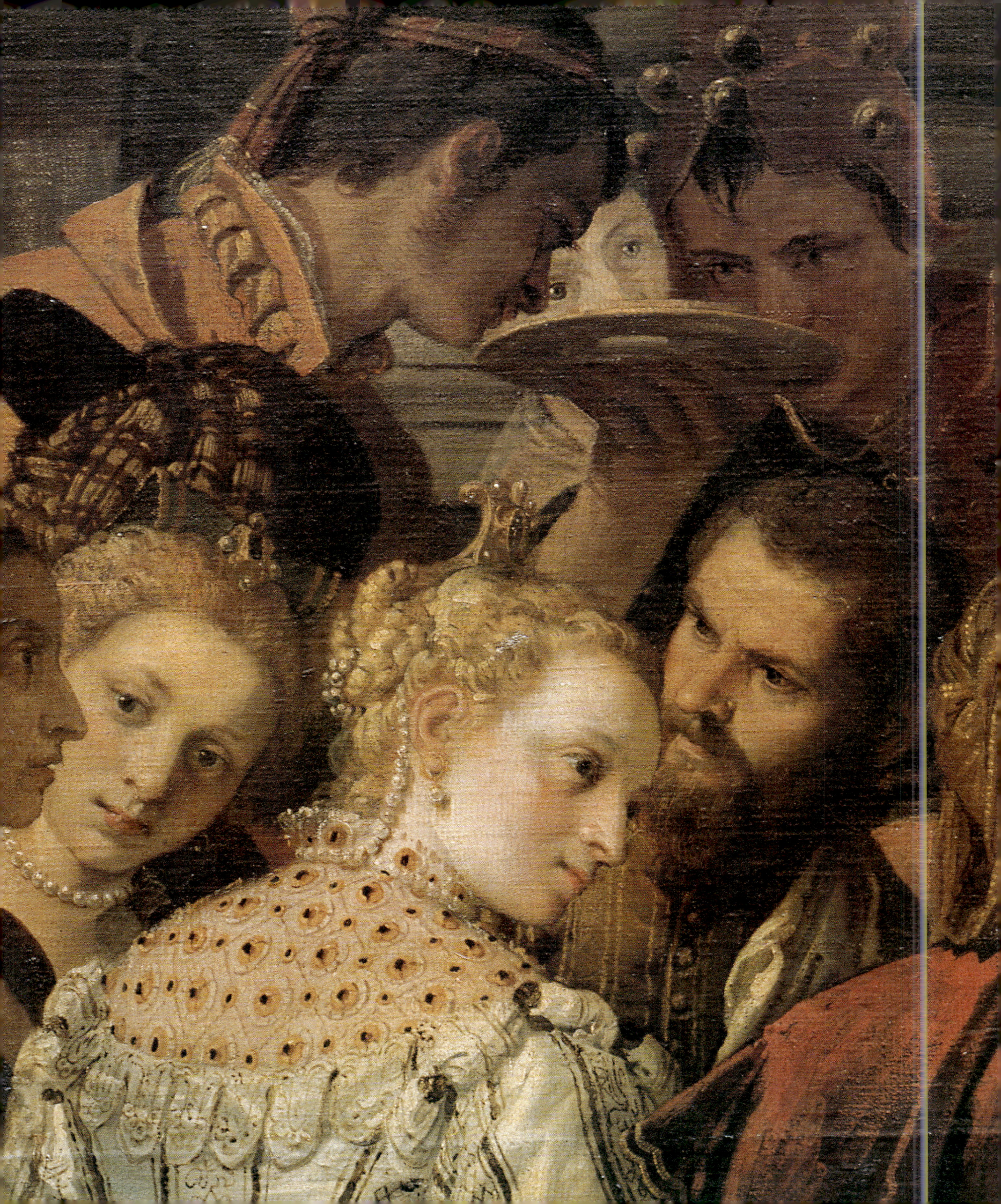

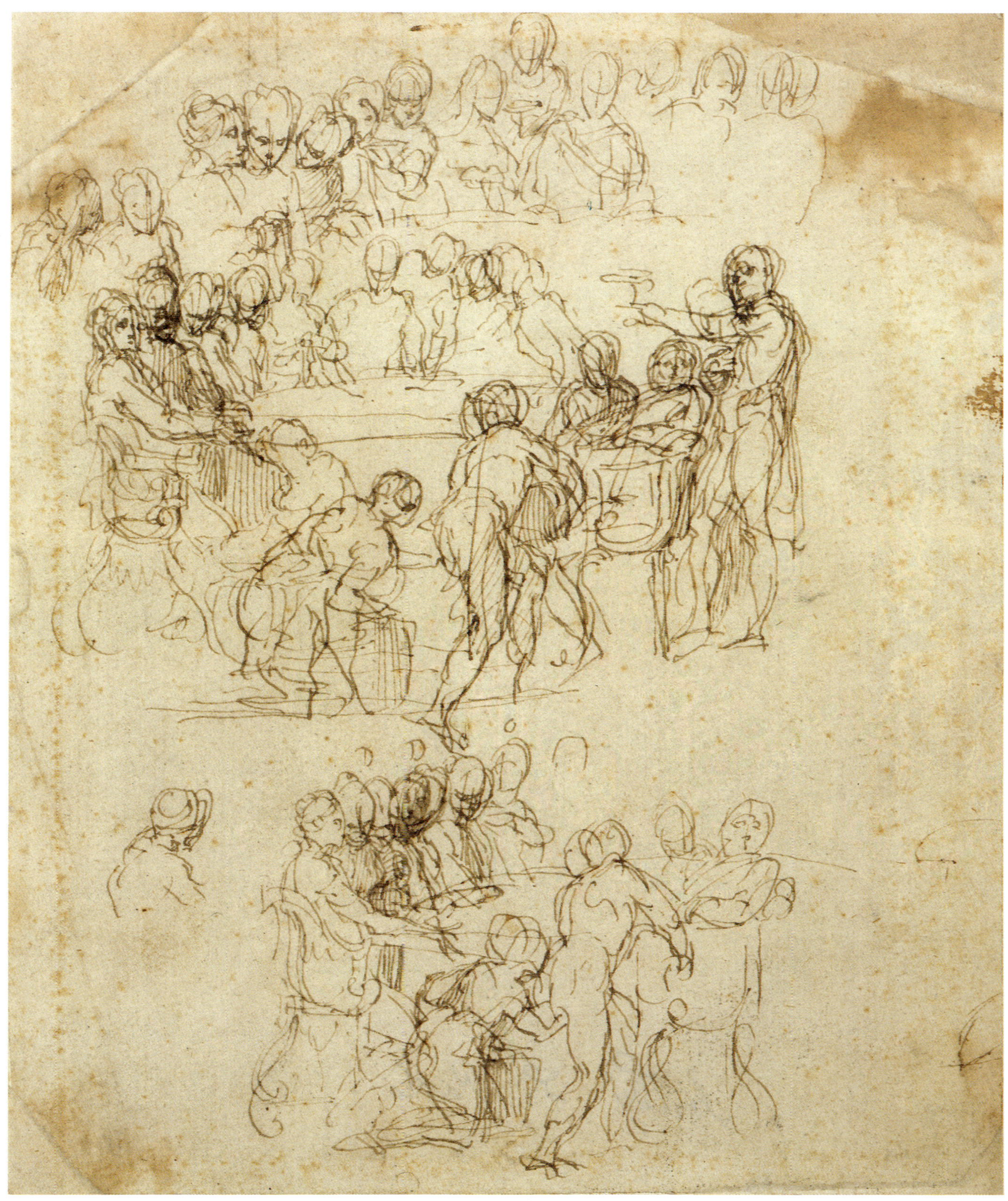

88 *Wedding at Cana* (detail of ill. 87)

The rich variety of inclined and conferring heads painted with great realism is characteristic of Veronese's painting. The artist repeatedly demonstrates his skills as a portrait painter even in his religious history paintings. Though Venetian patricians were required to outdo each other in modesty rather than in monuments, the introduction of discreet donor portraits was quite usual, and was justified on the grounds of demonstrating to the world the donor's piety. The delightful bride of the wedding, strongly highlighted by the artist, has enchanted connoisseurs and artists alike for centuries.

89 (above) Sketch sheet with studies for the *Wedding at Cana*, c. 1571
Pen drawings, 20.6 x 17.3 cm
Kupferstichkabinett, Staatliche Museen zu Berlin – Preussischer Kulturbesitz, Berlin

As one of a total of three sketches currently associated with the execution of the four Coccina pictures, this sheet brings together three different solutions for the grouping and arrangement of the wedding guests, in Veronese's typical drawing style. The figure of the wine-taster is already fleetingly pre-formulated in the central study. However, the painted version does not contain the figure with the jug familiar from the earlier version (ill. 73).

MATTIA PRETI AS ZEUXIS

In 1771, the art expert and librarian Antonio Maria Zanetti used the peculiar neologism "Paoleggiare", or "imitating Paolo", to describe a long-familiar phenomenon, using a painting by the Venetian painter Maffeo da Verona (died 1618) to illustrate it: a famous painting – he meant Paolo Veronese's *Wedding at Cana* (ill. 73) – inevitably gave imitators the idea of copying, quoting or varying it. The reproduction led the expert to remember the origins of certain motifs, and in favorable cases some of the esteem in which the admired model had always been held would, in scholarly discourse, be applied to the new work. Art theory has not always approved of such imitation. If one then turns one's attention to Mattia Preti's *Wedding at Cana* (ill. 91), it becomes clear what Zanetti was referring to at that time with his neologism "Paoleggiare", and what was meant when well-known art theoreticians of the 17th century advised painters, keeping in mind the selective imitation of nature, to make cautious use of the artistic property of others, like a bee that flies from flower to flower and carefully draws out the nectar.

When the painter Mattia Preti (1613–1699), born in Taverna in Calabria, arrived in Modena in 1651 in order to paint frescoes in the Capella delle Reliquie in the cathedral and San Biagio, he had long been familiar with Paolo Veronese's works. Pascoli and De Dominici for instance, the biographers of this painter who at first worked primarily in Rome, speak of a copy of a *Feast in the House of Simon,* which he carried out in Venice. Presumably created between 1643 and 1646 during the course of a journey through upper Italy, this work was formerly in the sacristy of the church of San Andrea della Valle in Rome. In Modena, Preti evidently once more made use of the opportunity to study Venetian painting. He unquestionably profited from the generosity with which Duke Francesco I d'Este (1610–1658) treated painters and art experts, allowing them access to his once famous collection of paintings in the Palazzo Ducale. It was here that the painter saw the *Wedding at Cana* (ill. 87), a work of Veronese's that he had probably already seen in Venice when it was still part of the furnishings of the Palazzo Coccina, and which had come into the Duke's possession together with three other pictures by the Venetian painter. The enormous esteem in which it was held is clear not only from reports in contemporary guides and treatises, but also from the painting in London. Thus Preti adopted both the cupbearer from Veronese's picture, seen raising his goblet to test the wine in the background on the right, and the bride, highlighted by a strong stream of light, in the *Wedding at Cana*. Even the woman taking part in the feast, who is partly cut off by the left side of the picture, is a motif drawn from the famous model, and the stylization of other figures, the manner in which the groups are formed and the conception of diverging head and body postures once again touch on characteristics of Veronese's, which during the second half of the 17th century were the preferred features with painters and experts associated with his large histories containing many figures. The festive tone of the depiction, the inclusion of pictorial architectures, the presence of the dog derived from the *Wedding at Cana* (ill. 73) in the Louvre and the figure seen from behind with a Moorish boy, are all elements that lead directly to Veronese, though they also show that the latter was already being viewed at a chronological distance, with the eyes of a Neapolitan painter who valued the works of Rubens (1577–1640) and Guercino (1591–1666) and who no longer considered the light-drenched pictorial spaces painted by the Venetian as an alternative to the dramatic light and dark of the Roman followers of Caravaggio (1571–1610) and his Neapolitan pupil Jusepe de Ribera (1591–1652). Preti used his models in a similar way to the ancient Greek painter Zeuxis when the latter was asked to paint a portrait of the beautiful Helen of Troy. According to Cicero in his treatise *De inventione*, Zeuxis (5th century B.C.) invited the girls in the surrounding area to his house and completed the work by selecting five of them as models and using only the most flattering part of each beauty's body in his painting.

Though Mattia Preti's painting is neither signed nor dated, it is generally agreed that it was painted between 1653 and 1659 in Naples and that, like the *Feast of Absalom* (ill. 90) which was also inspired by Veronese, it is one of the painter's main works. The most diverse stylistic methods were used in this work to create a memorable synthesis. In Veronese's case, it presupposes an intensive study of the *Wedding at Cana* (ill. 87), in part because a

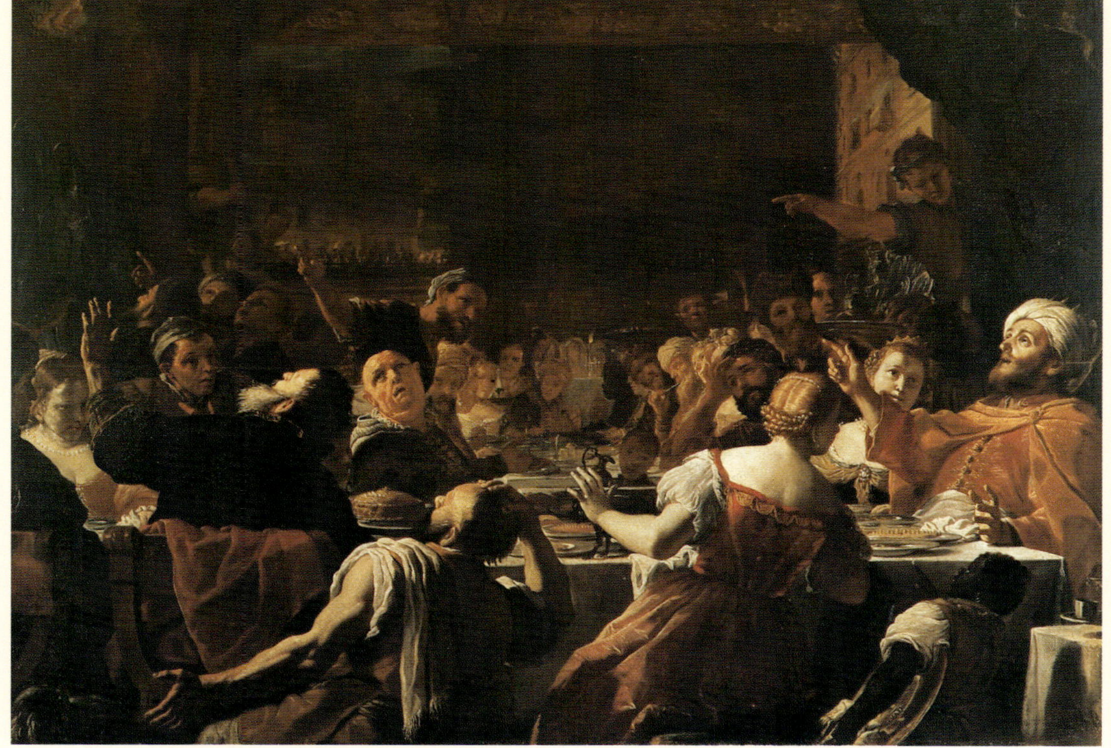

90 Mattia Preti
Absalom's Feast, c. 1653–1659
Oil on canvas, 202 x 297 cm
Museo di Capodimonte, Naples

The Feast was one of a series of four paintings that belonged to the furnishings of the palazzo of the Duca di San Severino Gruther in Naples in 1745. It probably served as a counterpart to *David Playing the Harp to Saul* (formerly Stair Sainty Matthiesen, New York), and in the 18th century it had already been compared with Veronese by Preti's biographer De Dominici, because of its magnificent painted architecture (*magnifica architettura*).

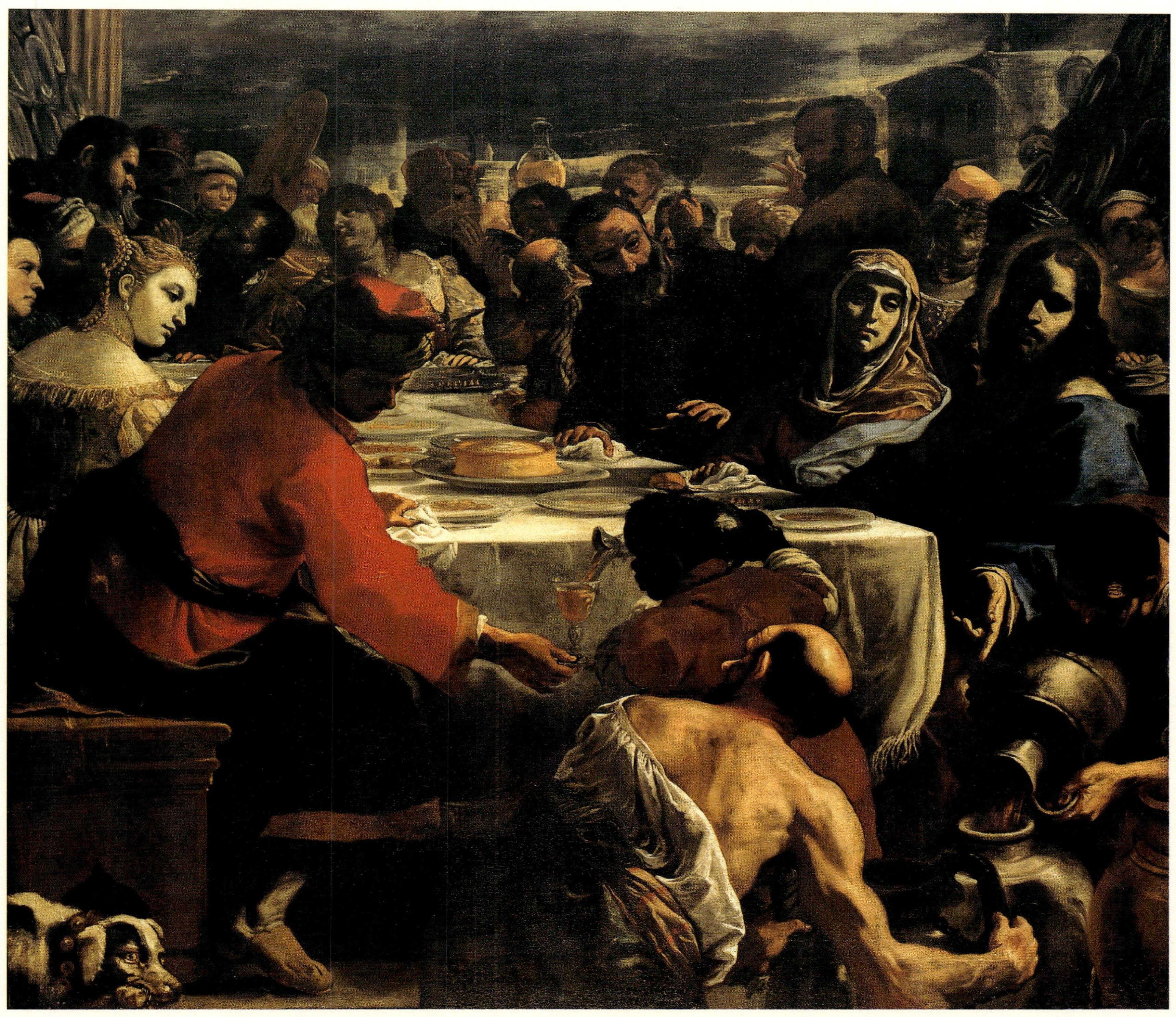

copperplate reproduction of the painting was not yet available at this point in time. Sketches or drawings of individual figures, which may have been produced in Venice or later in Modena, may have been used as memory aids by the painter and will have been a significant aid to him when he was required to carry out a commission of an unusual nature. It is reported that Gaspar de Roomer, a Flemish merchant living in Naples who was an art dealer and passionate collector of paintings and who already owned an homage to Veronese in the form of Peter Paul Rubens's large *Feast of Herod* (National Gallery of Scotland, Edinburgh), commissioned a painting from Preti and left the choice of theme to the painter. Even though other depictions of the theme were known by Bernardo de Dominici to be in the possession of Neapolitan collectors, it is the London painting, given the motifs it cites, that today probably provides the most pointed declaration of the painter's belief in Veronese. Newly discovered archives recently made it possible to prove that Gaspar de Roomer paid out the unusually high sum of 300 ducats to Preti on December 17, 1655. It is exceedingly tempting to assume that the painting in the National Gallery is one of the works that Roomer commissioned in 1655 and for which he paid such a high price.

91 Mattia Preti
Wedding at Cana, c. 1655
Oil on canvas, 203.2 x 226 cm
National Gallery, London

The painter Mattia Preti, who was based in Naples from 1653, became acquainted with Veronese's works in Venice and Modena. His high regard for them can be clearly discerned, especially in his own feast and banqueting scenes. This painting in London was very probably commissioned by Gaspar de Roomer, the hugely wealthy Flemish merchant who lived in Naples, and for whom Preti painted a lavish, crowded scene on a loggia in imitation of Veronese.

»Per ornamento, come si fa« – The Limits of Diversity

92 *Feast in the House of Levi* (detail of ill. 96)
Armed German mercenaries

The two *Landsknechte* (German imperial mercenaries) were among the features in this painting that brought Veronese before the Inquisition in 1573. When asked whether it seemed appropriate to him to introduce jesters, hard-drinking soldiers, dwarfs and other follies (*scurrilità*) in a depiction of the Last Supper, Veronese repeatedly declared during the course of the cross-examination that the figures concerned were outside the place where the supper itself was taking place and had been shown at a proper distance from Christ. Unquestionably, for once, the architecture served the painter and pictorial architect more than as a means of distinction. With Christ as the dominant figure, the central arch of the loggia ennobles the center of the picture. The subsidiary figures the Inquisition objected to are all confined to the steps at the sides. The size of the total canvas to be covered had made it necessary to introduce them, and Veronese himself was sure that he had acted in good faith and with a clear conscience. Iconographically unusual is the gesture of the apostle bending over the balustrade on the right a long way from the main event, to distribute bread from the Lord's table to the needy. This has been seen as an allusion to the distribution of the communion wafer at the Eucharist, citing in this connection the possible example of Tintoretto's *Apostles' Communion* in San Paolo, dating from 1570. There, children and beggars receive food from the Lord's table. However, in Veronese, the gesture seems to be intended to remind the Dominicans who commemorated the Last Supper during their shared daily meal in the refectory not to forget the obligation of charity.

On July 18, 1573 Veronese was summoned before the court of the Venetian Inquisition sitting in the Cappella San Teodoro near San Marco. Under the chairmanship of the Papal legate Giovanni Battista Dei and Giovanni Trevisan, the patriarch of Venice, charges were brought in the presence of the representatives of the Signoria, the "Savi dell' Eresia", Giacomo Foscarini, Niccolò Venier and Alvise Zorzi. The subject of the examination, carried out by the Inquisitor Fra Aurelio Schellino, was the charge that the inclusion of unseemly figures and motifs in the *Feast in the House of Levi* (ill. 96) in the refectory of Santi Giovanni e Paolo had infringed the proprieties, the law of appropriateness of artistic methods. What had happened? Let us start by briefly looking back.

The painter's predilection for giving particular attention to narrative and epic elements undoubtedly culminated in the large Feasts (*cene*). Even Carlo Ridolfi emphasized the huge amount of prestige which Veronese gained from these extraordinary pictorial inventions. Carried out between 1563 and 1573 for monasteries in Venice and Vicenza, it was in each case the local context that determined the huge format and particular form of the pictures. All of them were once attached to the walls at the end of monastery refectories where, supported by the use of symmetrical pictorial architectures, they created a loose painted extension of the real space. In the Barbaro and Soranza villas, Veronese had become sufficiently experienced in the mastery of large surfaces as a fresco painter. These experiences, following the monumental *Wedding at Cana* (ill. 73), were initially to leave their mark on the rather more modest *Feast in the House of Simon* (ill. 94) created in 1570 for the church of San Sebastiano. With both pictures, a new concept appeared to have arrived in the circles of certain Venetian ecclesiastical clients as to how religious feasts in refectories should look, for, just a short time later the Servites in Venice commissioned a depiction of the *Feast in the House of Simon* (ill. 93) from Veronese. More artistically ambitious and much clearer in its construction, the wall painting, which is almost 9 m. wide, varies the theme by introducing a semicircular pergola, which provides a view over an imaginative architectural landscape. The *Feast of Gregory the Great* (ill. 95), destined for the monastery of Madonna di Monte Berico near Vicenza, was another magnificent banquet scene painted in 1572 in Veronese's workshop in Venice. In common with all the other Feasts, this work appears neither simply decorative nor merely attempting to please. Quite the opposite: the arrangement and description of the participants in the feast who are dining within a colossal columned hall show how attentively the painter had studied the story of St. Gregory, upon which the depiction is based, in the *Legenda aurea* by Jacobus de Voragine (died 1298).

Inventiveness and *varietà*, however, do not reach their climax until the painting now known as the *Feast in the House of Levi* (ill. 96), which was commissioned by the Dominicans of Santi Giovanni e Paolo as a replacement for Titian's *Last Supper*, destroyed by a fire in the refectory in February 1571. It was this *Feast* which Veronese had to answer for before the Inquisition in 1573. The painting, a little more than 13 m. wide, offers a multitude of fully life-size figures; they are integrated into a festive three-part loggia conspicuously similar to the upper story of Jacopo Sansovino's Libreria Vecchia, though at the same time it is ultimately a variation of the emotive formula of the triptych which ultimately derives from ancient Roman triumphal arches. In place of the principle of increasing numbers, which still characterized the *Wedding at Cana* ten years before, there is now a clearly structured composition which allows the figures sufficient room to move. Christ once more occupies the center of the picture and, like St. Peter and St. John, is visually emphasized by the central arcade. Once again figures of exceptional beauty are presented on the pictorial stage. Thus, for instance, the steward in charge of the banquet (ill. 99), who is dressed in a shimmering garment, and whose physiognomy was, as early as the 18th century, quite rightly identified with the pseudo-antique *Bust of Vitellius* (Museo Archeologico Nazionale, Venice). Between 1525 and 1593 this imperial bust had been accessible to privileged painters in the Doge's palace, and was among others drawn by Veronese and Tintoretto. Nonetheless the steward was part of the group of figural inventions that appeared

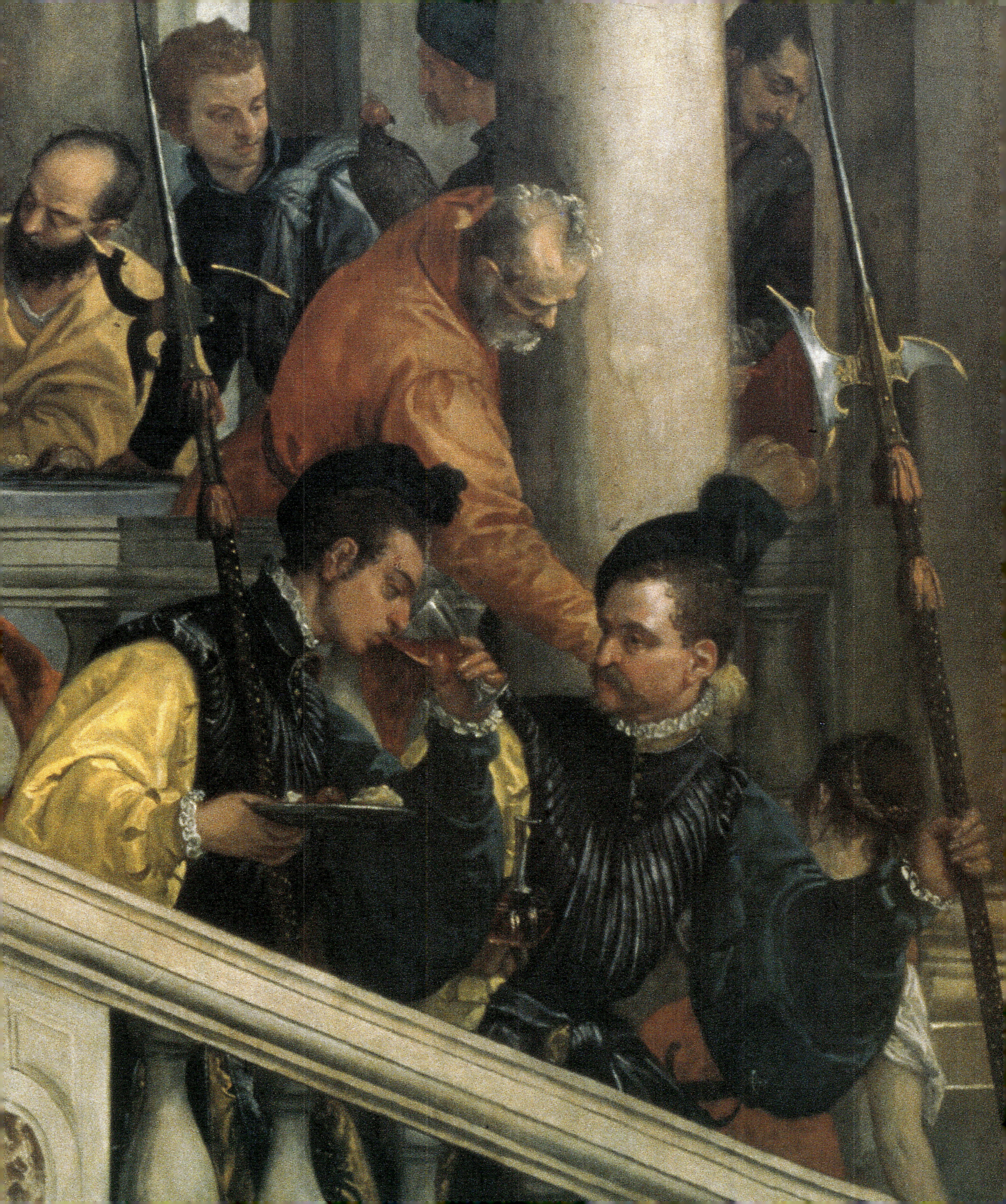

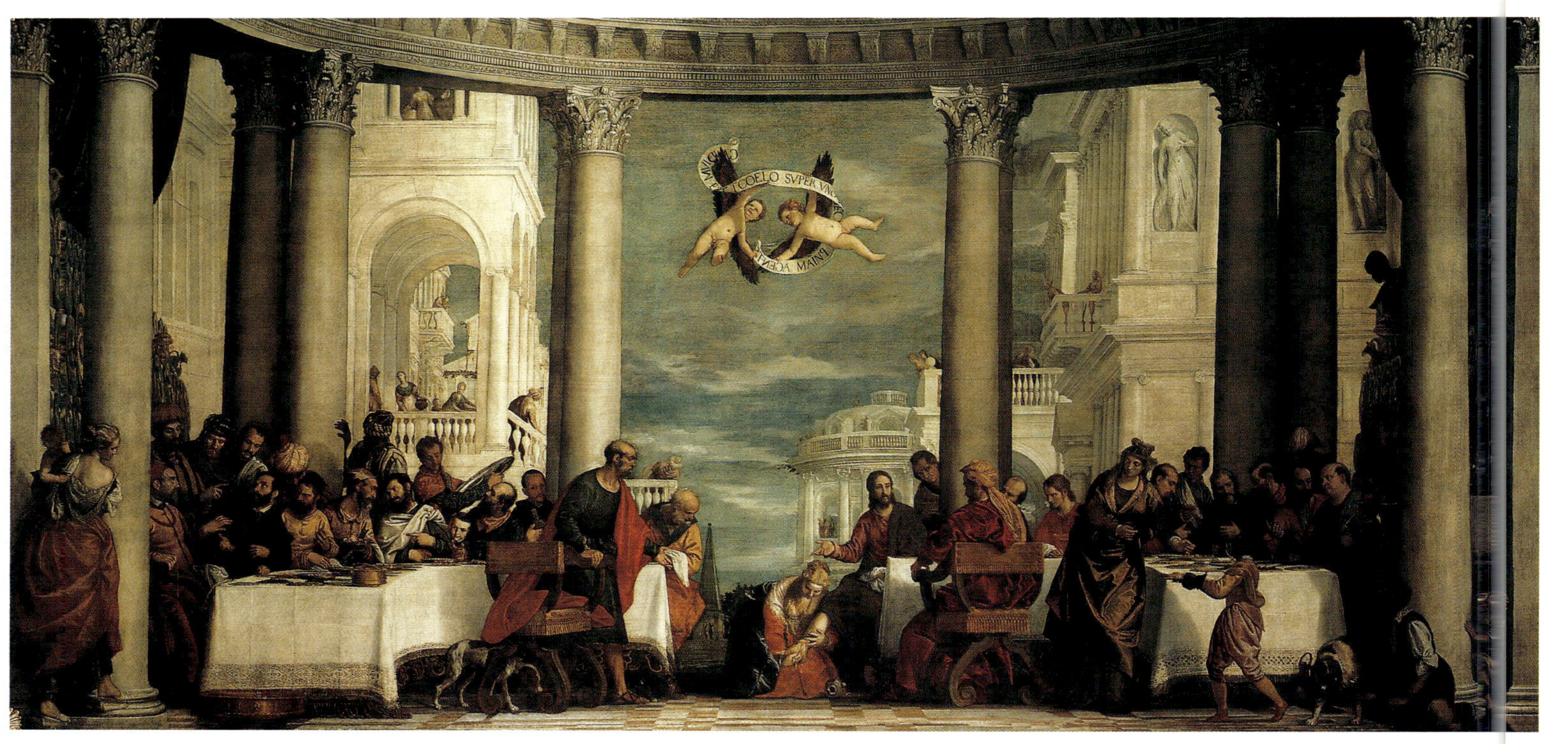
COELO SVPER

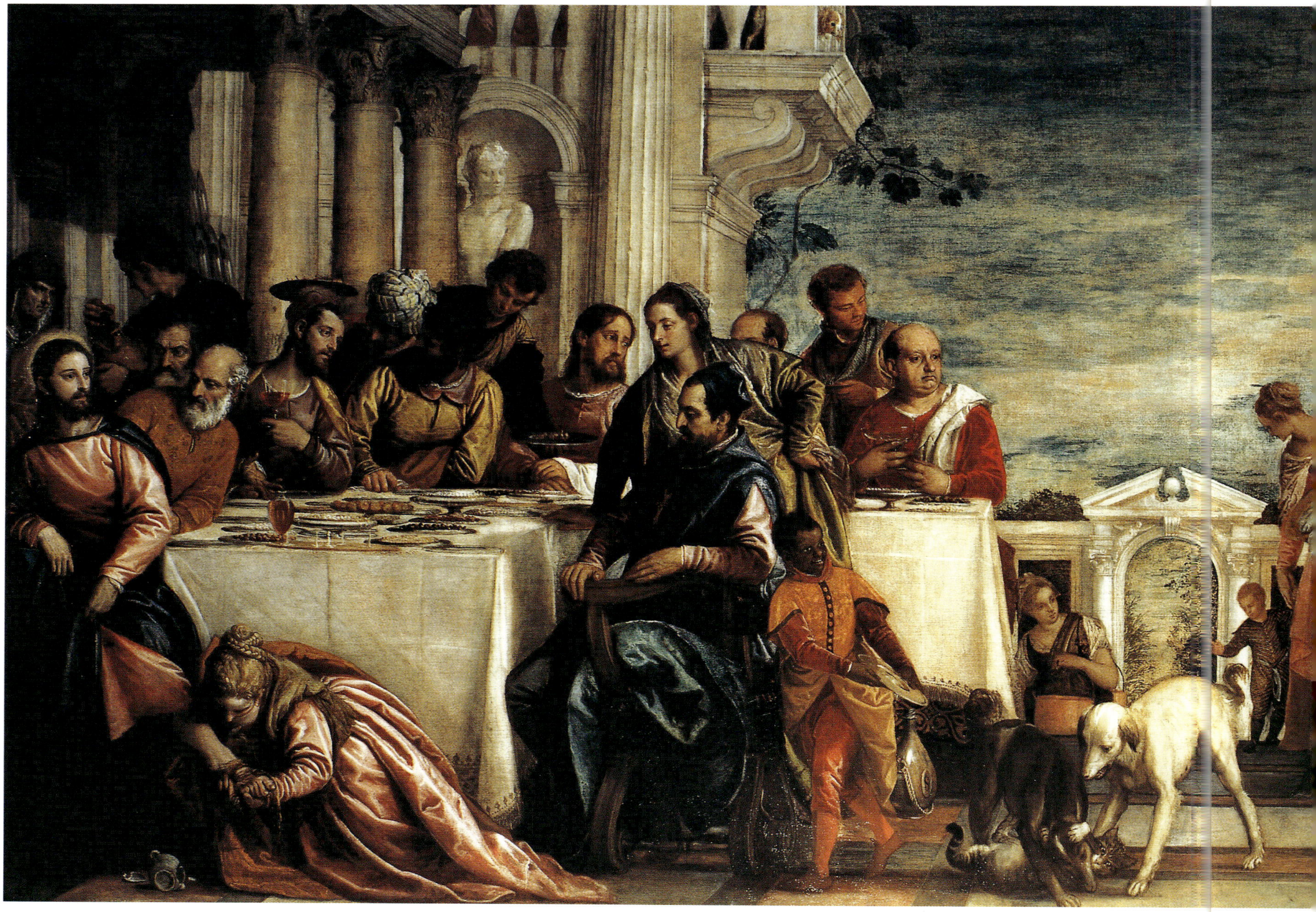

suspect to the Inquisitors in 1573. Asked about his tasks, Veronese replied: "A carver of meats (*scalco*) who I thought had come there for his amusement to see how things were done at table there." While the suspicious tribunal initially accepted this information, it was just a short time later that the decisive questions were posed about the significance of the servant with the bleeding nose, armed German mercenaries drinking wine and the dwarf-like jester with a parrot (ill. 98). However, both Veronese's reply, "For decoration, as one does" (Per ornamento, come si fa), the reference to the extensive *ornamento* which, given the enormous picture plane, had become a necessity, met with just as little understanding as his attempt to appeal for the freedom of the arts, in imitation of a familiar quotation from the poet Horace. In the eyes of the Inquisition the figures with which they found fault could by no means be part of the household of the owner of the hall in which the Last Supper took place, and thus – addressing themselves to the painter – they openly voiced what, apart from the initial disputes about the theme of the depiction, must have been the actual reason for the summons: "Do you not know that in Germany and other places devastated by heresy, they have a habit of filling their pictures with foolish things to degrade the affairs of the Holy Catholic Church and to make fun of it, in order to teach unsuspecting or ignorant people false doctrine?" Only a few years after the conclusion of the Council of Trent (1545–1563), which had been convened as a response to the Protestant Reformation in order to provide clear standards for theology and proclamations of faith, this was evidently an opportunity to make an example, for the Inquisition very rarely became involved in questions of theology relating to art. In Florence in 1557, it had had a picture by the painter Sandro Botticelli (1444/45–1510), on which a man suspected of heresy was depicted, covered up without further ado, and in the early 1560s Daniele da Volterra was commissioned in Rome to wrap numerous nude figures in the *Last Judgment* by Michelangelo in the Sistine Chapel in painted cloths; Veronese in turn was required to alter the queried depiction within three months at his own expense in such a way as was suited

93 (opposite)
Feast at the House of Simon, c. 1570–1572
Oil on canvas, 454 x 874 cm
Musée national du Château, Versailles

The picture intended for the refectory of the Venetian monastery of Santa Maria dei Servi forms a logical development of the Milan *Feast* (ill. 94). Magnificent architecture reminiscent of contemporary work by Palladio and Jacopo Sansovino frames and articulates the crowded scene. In the early 1660s, numerous princely collectors vied for the picture, which in 1664 was finally given by the Serenissima to the French King Louis XIV as a politically motivated gift.

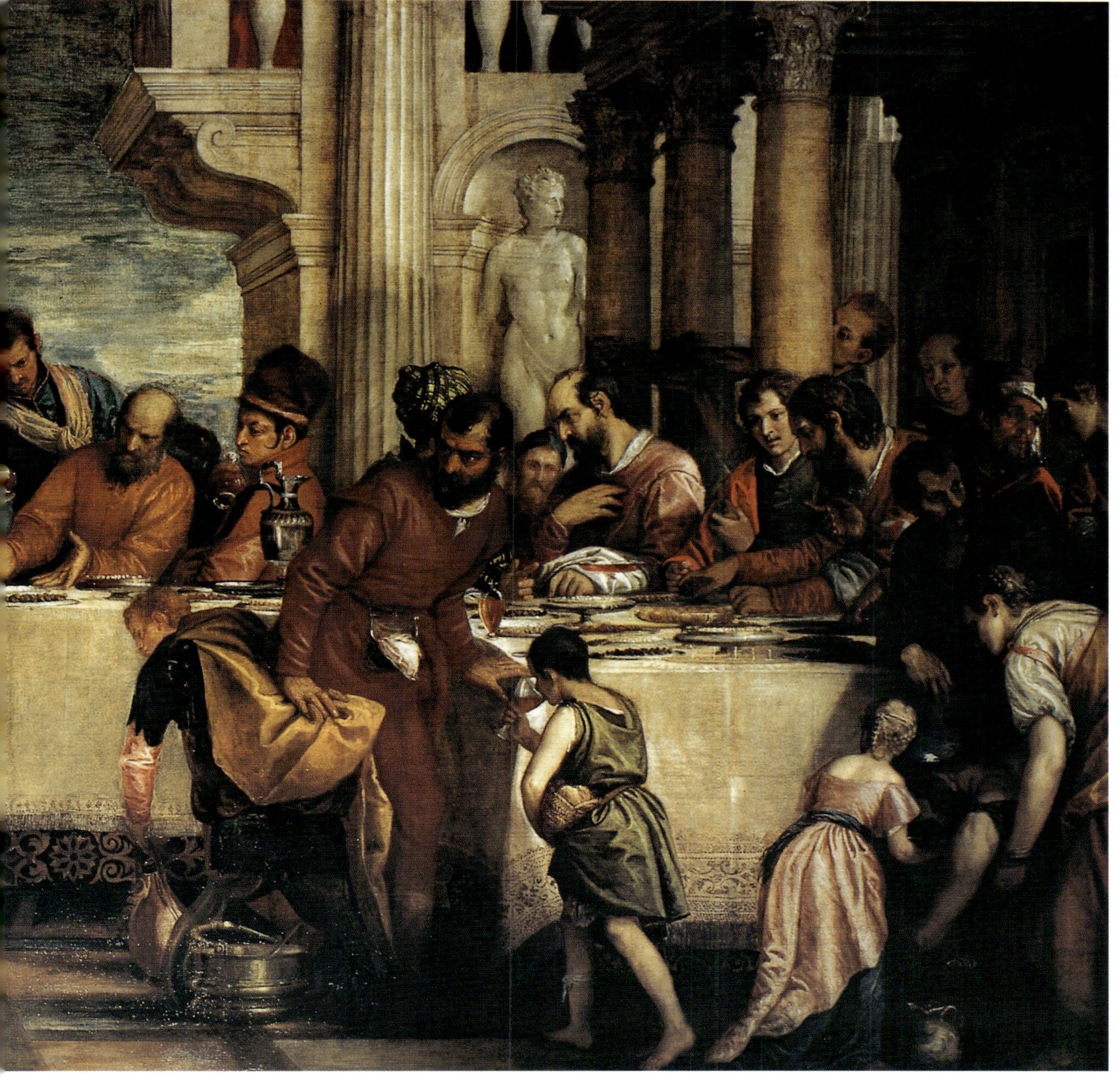

94 *Feast at the House of Simon*, c. 1567–1570
Oil on canvas, 275 x 710 cm
Pinacoteca di Brera, Milan

Veronese's biographer Ridolfi dates this painting to 1570. Until 1817, it hung in the dining room of the Jeronymite monastery of San Sebastiano in Venice. Weaknesses in the depiction of individual heads result from the involvement of assistants.

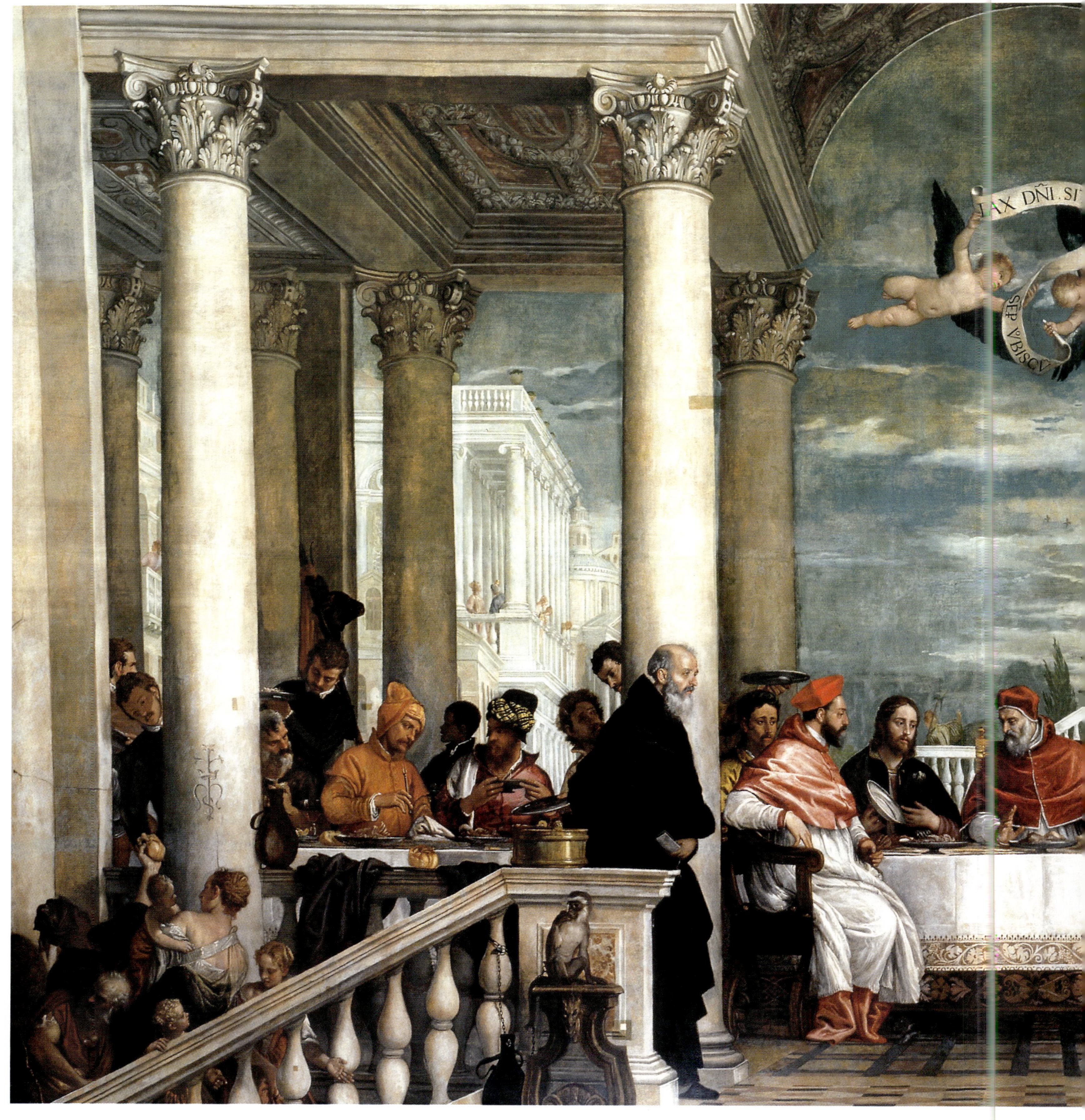

95 *Feast of Gregory the Great*, 1572
Oil on canvas, 477 x 862 cm
Basilica di Monte Berico, Vicenza

This is the only one of the monumental Feasts still in the position it was originally intended for, though seriously damaged by Austrian soldiers in the 19th century. Once again, the painter uses great imagination to develop an ideal architectural landscape, which acts as a light-filled foil to offset the vivid colors in their dramatic brilliance. A feature of all the feast pictures by the Venetian painter is that he dispenses with strict central perspective. Instead, the broad format always incorporates several focal points.

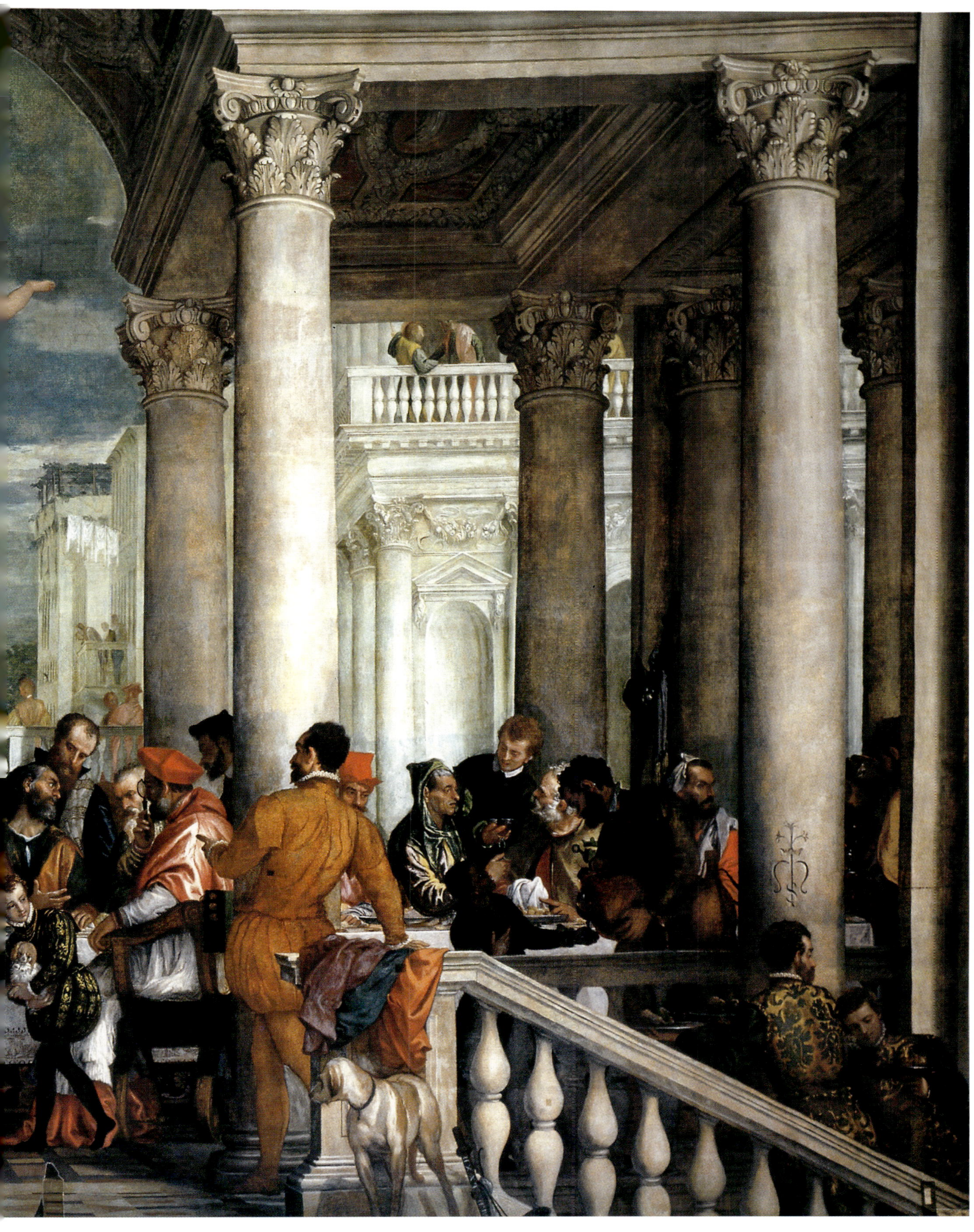

96 (following double page) *Feast in the House of Levi*, 1573
Oil on canvas, 555 x 1,310 cm
Galleria dell'Accademia, Venice

Commissioned by the Dominicans of SS. Giovanni e Paolo in Venice, the painting gets its present title from the painter's brush with the Venetian Inquisition. Individual figures and motifs had caused offense, so that accusations of heresy were voiced aloud during the cross-examination.

The original subject of the enigmatic picture is controversial. Veronese himself added to the confusion in no small measure by saying that it was "… a picture with the supper that Jesus Christ celebrated with his disciples in the house of Simon."

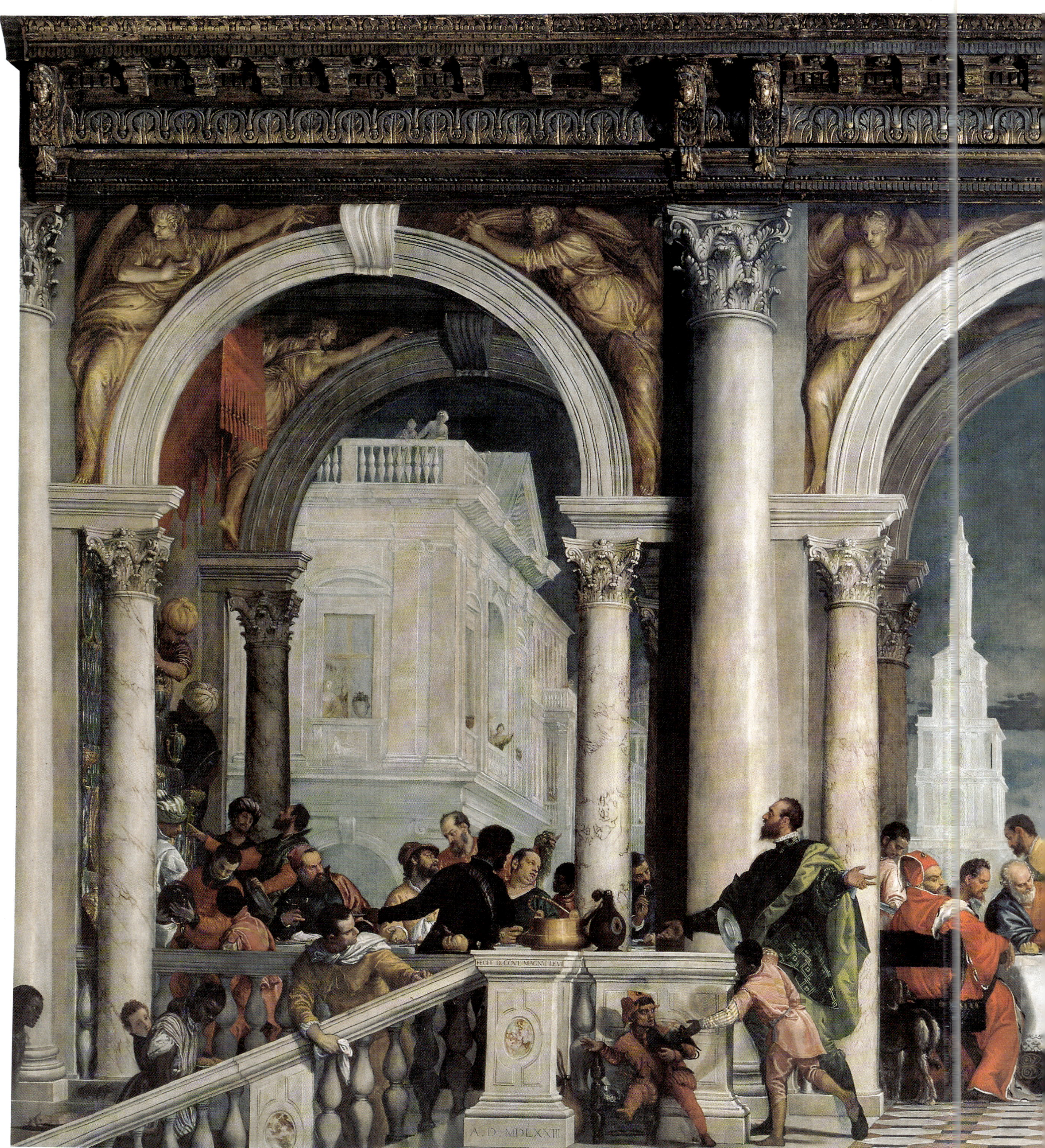
FECIT D. COVI. MAGNU. LEVI
A. D. MDLXXIII.

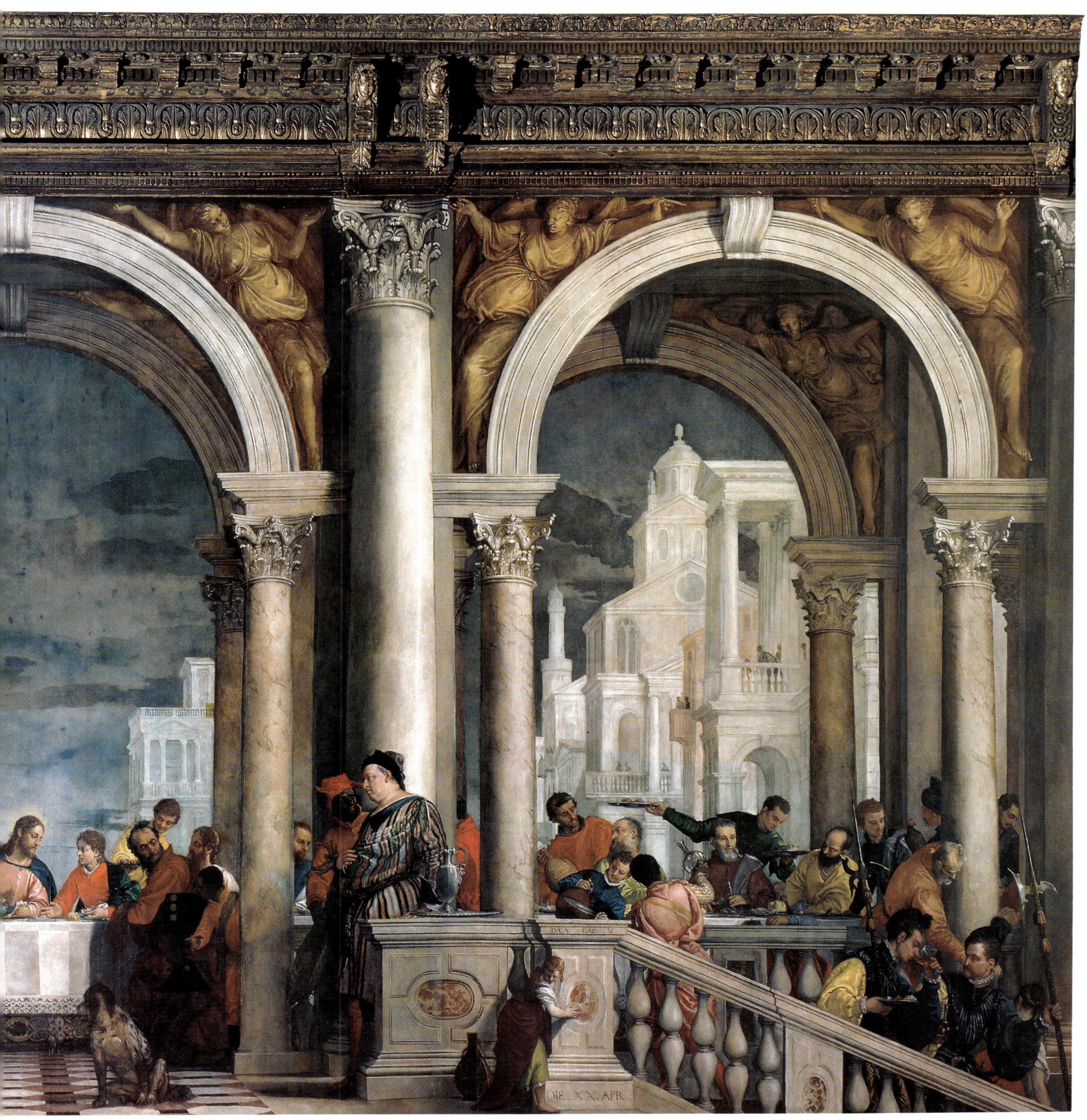
LVCÆ CAP. V.
DIE . XX . APR .

to the Last Supper. It is known that the Venetian painter very cleverly avoided reworking the incriminating details. Only the title of the picture was altered, and the Latin inscription "FECIT.D. COVI. MAGNV. LEVI – LUCÆ CAP.V." which is visible at a distance still documents the apparently effortless transformation of the depiction from the *Last Supper* into the *Feast at the House of Levi*.

The record of the proceedings (ill. 97), which is kept in the State Archives in Venice, documents the hearing in the form of a dialogue and is among the most interesting historical documents relating to Venice's art history. Evidently set down in writing by a clerk who was insufficiently familiar with the material, the contradictory wording of central passages of the text continues to make it difficult to arrive at a final clarification of the disputed question of the original theme of the picture. Everything had begun with the prior of Santi Giovanni e Paolo. He had approached the Inquisition with a complaint and had subsequently been ordered to see that the painter produced a Mary Magdalene instead of a dog. Stating that such a figure could not be added there, Veronese politely but firmly rejected the prior's demand and it went on from there. His reputation was not damaged by the case, which was the only one of its kind in Venice. By 158[illegible] at the latest Giovanni Trevisan, who had been present at the trial in his capacity of patriarch, received *Saints John the Evangelist, Peter and Paul* (San Pietro di Castello, Venice), a large altar painting in the form of an atmospheric landscape picture, and the Doge Marino Grimani took delivery of the *Adoration of the Shepherds with Saints Jerome and Augustine*, a work mainly carried out by members of Veronese's

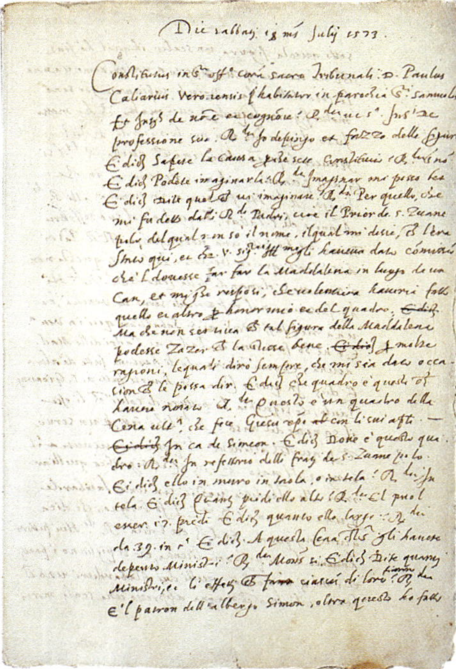

97 (below) *Minutes of the Trial of Paolo Veronese by the Inquisition*, 1573
Santo Ufficio, Processi, Busta no. 33, page 1
Archivio dello Stato, Venice

The minutes are five pages long, and record the trial in dialogue form. In the judgment of the Inquisition tribunal, the painter had breached decorum by including unseemly figures and motifs in the Last Supper painting for the refectory of SS. Giovanni e Paolo. Instructed to correct the painting concerned within three months, Veronese's only reaction was to add an inscription changing the scene to the *Feast in the House of Levi* (ill. 96). The document remained unknown until 1867, when it was discovered and published along with other trial documents by the French archivist Armand Baschet.

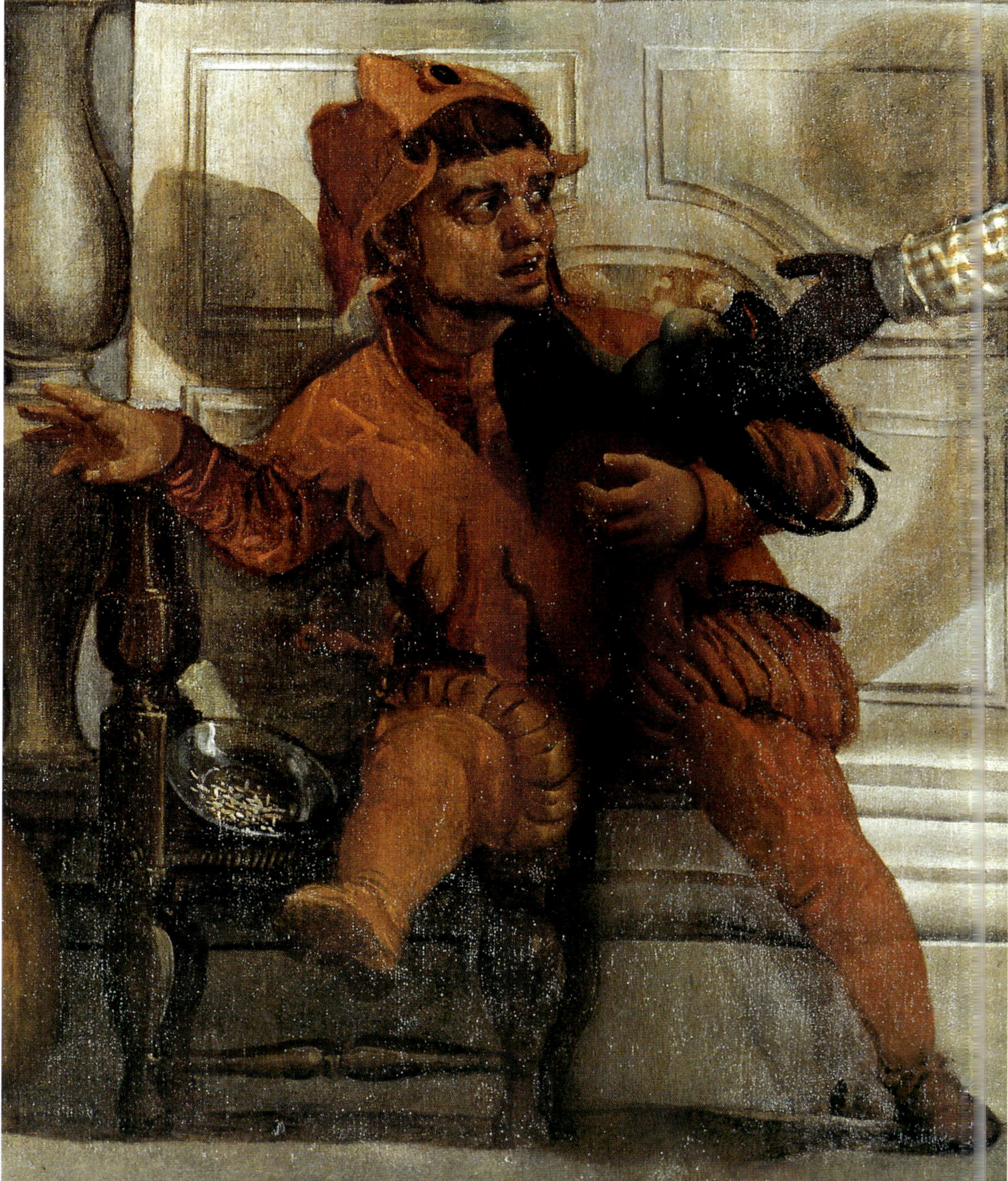

98 *Feast in the House of Levi* (detail of ill. 96)
Dwarf jester with parrot

The colorful dwarf jester with a parrot was among the motifs that the painter sought fruitlessly to justify to the Inquisition in 1573 by referring to the need to fill the canvas with decorative forms (*per ornamento*).

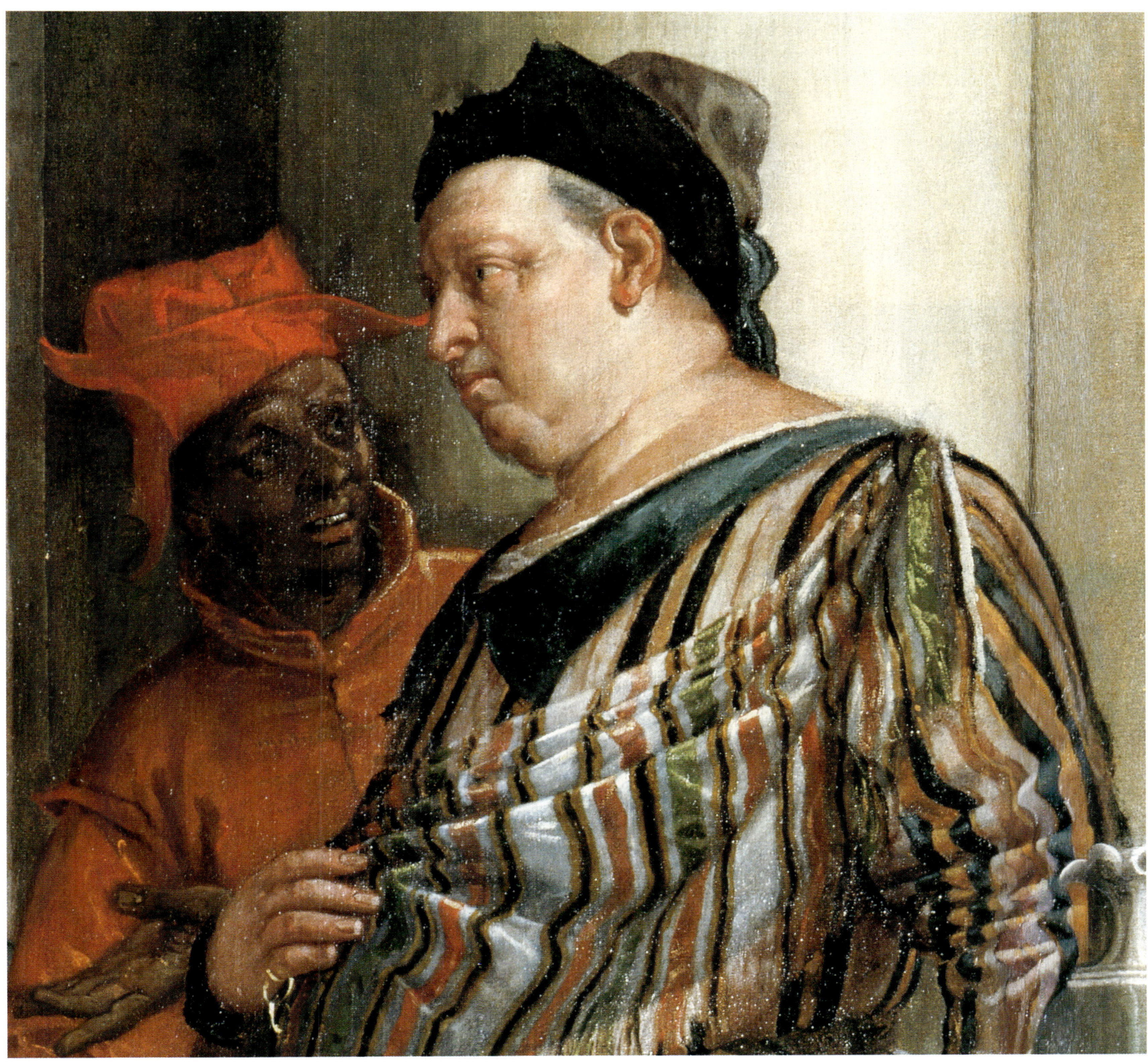

workshop, in Venice in November 1583; these are just two of numerous other respected patrons who expressed the high esteem in which they held the painter by commissioning works.

As pictorial tasks that were closely tied in to the particular local contexts of monastery refectories, and for which there was only a very limited demand in Venice and the Veneto during the last third of the 16th century, the large religious Feasts remained a specialty of Veronese and his workshop until the completion of the *Feast in the House of Levi* (ill. 96), which forms both a climax and a break. While an entire series of large-scale depictions containing many figures were produced for the Serenissima after 1573, towards the end of his career the painter's artistic vocabulary became increasingly economical and concentrated.

99 *Feast in the House of Levi* (detail of ill. 96)
Master steward

The memorable head of the master steward suggests close study of the pseudo-classical *Vitellius* bust (Museo Archeologico Nazionale, Venice), which Cardinal Domenico Grimani sent to Venice from Rome in 1523. Like Tintoretto, Veronese had made a drawing of the bust (British Museum, London), which had been on display in the Doge's Palace from 1525. There may have been a cast of the emperor's bust among the plaster casts documented as being owned by Veronese's heirs.

Triumph and Fame

100 *Religio and Fides*, c. 1575–1577
Oil on canvas, 320 x 200 cm
Sala del Collegio, Doge's Palace, Venice

The central painting of the ceiling of the Sala del Collegio, along with the *Neptune and Mars* (ill. 102) and *Venetia between Justitia and Pax* (ill. 103), symbolizes in allegorical form the Republic of Venice's claims to political power. It also reminds the Council of its specific obligations, one of which was monitoring matters of faith. Although a fixed written program for the ceiling has not survived and the putative authorship of Marcantonio Barbaro cannot be proven, it is assumed that the painter was forced to follow the requirements of the clients in terms of content and presentation.

In 1575 and 1577, disastrous fires devastated the decorations in the Sala del Collegio, the Sala del Maggior Consiglio and the Sala dello Scrutino, among other halls in the Doge's palace. For a number of years, the refurbishment of these rooms provided a rich field of activity for Veronese, his colleagues who were themselves becoming increasingly important, and many other well-known Venetian painters and their workshops. Directed by Andrea da Ponte and perhaps even with the assistance of Andrea Palladio and Marcantonio Barbaro, a new program of decorations was immediately developed for the Sala del Collegio, the Great Council's conference hall. Payments made to Veronese prove that work commenced in December 1575. The decoration of the gilded *soffitto* (ill. 101), which was carried out entirely under his direction, comprises three large paintings framed by polychrome satellite pictures and six histories carried out using the *chiaroscuro* technique. As painted self-portraits of Venice, the allegories with their Latin inscriptions reflect the political and religious self-image of the Republic and its virtues. *Neptune and Mars* (ill. 102), for instance, symbolizes the "ROBUR IMPERII" of the military and naval power of Venice, while *Religio and Fides* (ill. 100) and *Venetia between Justitia and Pax* (ill. 103) point to the just and peaceful rule of the state in general and the work of the Council (Collegio) in particular. Finally, in dialogue with the Venetian virtues of Strength, Faith and Justice, the *chiaroscuro* histories finally present exemplary themes from Greek and Roman history. A feature of the main pictures is the remarkable clarity of formal idiom. Figures that are sculpturally strongly shaped, complicated, and yet with restrained movements, contrast effectively with the shining blue of the sky. As in the ceiling paintings of the church of San Sebastiano, painted architectural features are once again used, though columns and pediments only appear as backgrounds in the picture fields of the Virtues. By providing the figures with support and suggesting spatial depth, they also form the basis for rich color contrasts.

Directly following the decoration of the ceiling, which was probably largely completed by 1577, Veronese produced a further work for the Republic in the same location in the form of the *Votive Picture of Doge Sebastiano Venier* (ill. 104). As the only surviving votive picture of a Doge produced by the painter, the history painting mounted above the throne of the head of state forms a prelude to an impressive number of similar depictions. Framed by painted Ionic columns and two *grisailles*, which depict St. Sebastian, the Doge's patron saint, and St. Justina, the patroness of the Battle of Lepanto, the composition fills the entire front wall of the Sala. In the presence of his former companion Agostino Barbarigo, St. Mark and Venetia, Sebastiano Venier (died 1578) appears as a *miles christianus* kneeling before St. Justina and the personification of Faith, who in turn guides us in the direction she is looking, towards Christ, the king of the world. Venier had been the captain in charge of the victorious Venetian fleet at the Battle of Lepanto (1571), and was therefore part of a politically motivated allegory whose intention was to celebrate the successful defense of the Christian faith by the Serenissima. Interestingly, Veronese's *modello* (British Museum, London) initially intended a quite different pictorial solution. Here, the central figure of Venetia, watched by St. Mark enthroned on a cloud, is paying tribute to Venier's services by crowning him, and thus the moment of the Doge's investiture is of prime importance in determining the tenor of the depiction. A report written by Francesco Sansovino corresponds with this original version; in 1581 he evidently only knew the pictorial program that had been specified in writing, and not Veronese's votive painting which, as has been assumed accordingly, did not take on its present shape until between 1582 and 1584.

It is surely no coincidence that preliminary drawings and *modelli* survive for an entire series of projects connected to the painter's work in the Doge's palace. Here, the artistic liberties that he had defended so bravely before the Inquisition in 1573, and the demand to be able to decorate pictures at his own discretion, had presumably from the start been subject to tighter limits due to prescriptions regarding content and the existence of iconographical programs. Even if today it is still hard to decide to what extent the painters engaged in the work were able to add their own artistic features, the

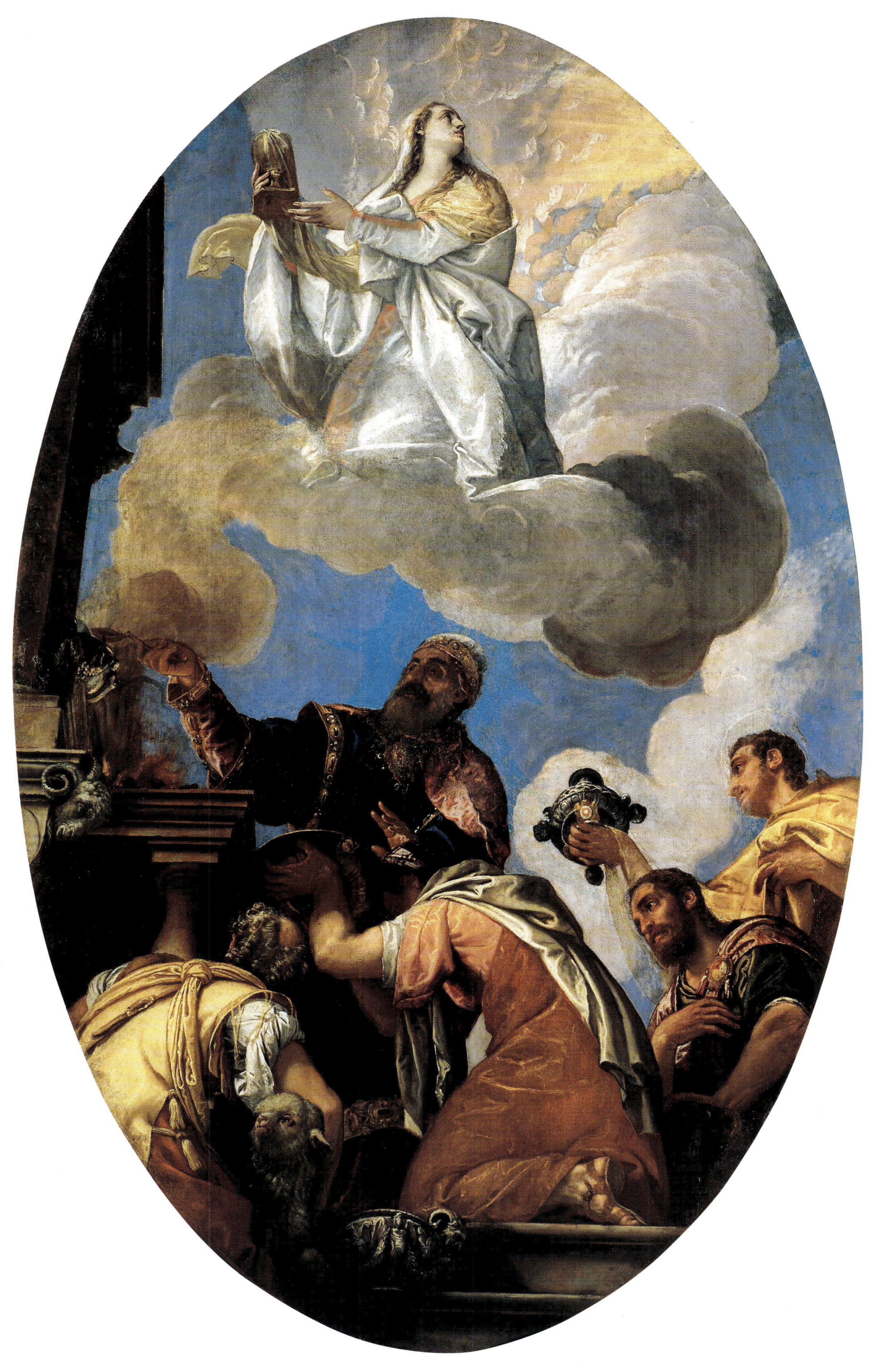

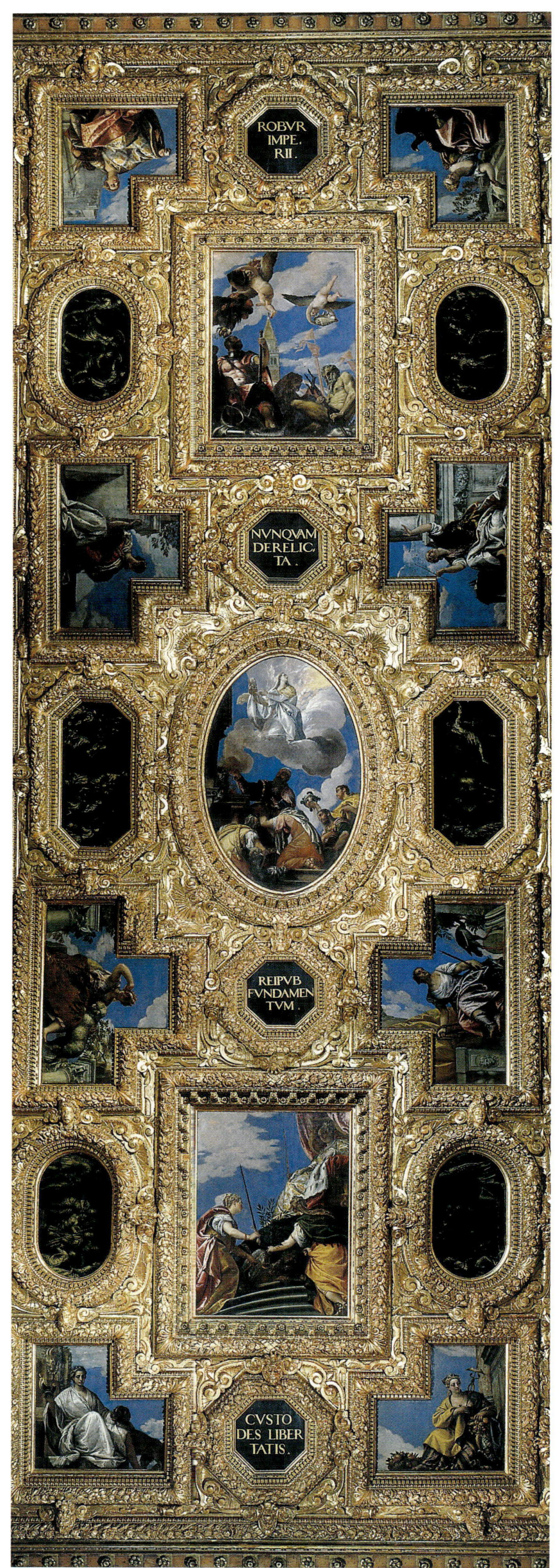

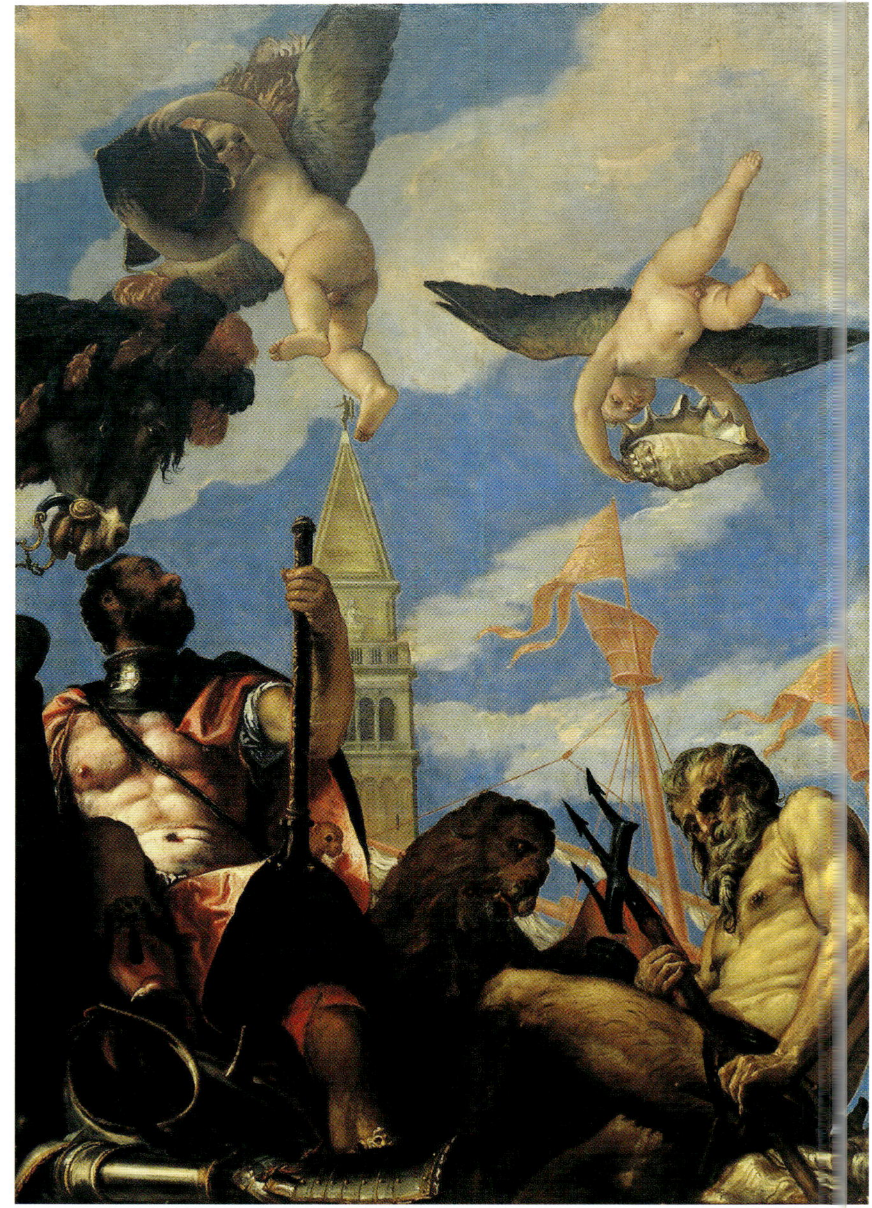

102 (above) *Neptune and Mars*, c. 1575–1577
Oil on canvas, 250 x 180 cm
Sala del Collegio, Doge's Palace, Venice

The painting is one of the three principal ceiling pictures (cf. ill. 101). It is flanked by allegories of moderation, industry, simplicity and magnanimity. The figures of Mars, the god of war, and the sea god Neptune allude to the power of Venice on land and sea.

101 (left) Paintings by Veronese in the gilt wooden ceiling
Sala del Collegio, Doge's Palace, Venice

The fire in the Doge's Palace in 1574 also destroyed the decoration in the Sala del Collegio. Restoration work commenced immediately, and Veronese was commissioned to do the ceiling paintings.

103 (opposite)
Venetia between Justitia and Pax, c. 1575–1577
Oil on canvas, 250 x 180 cm
Sala del Collegio, Doge's Palace, Venice

Flanked by the allegories of gentleness, fidelity, vigilance and prosperity (ill. 101), this ceiling painting presents the personifications of Justitia and Pax before the throne of Venetia. Again, this is a political allegory symbolizing the just and peaceful rule of the Republic of Venice.

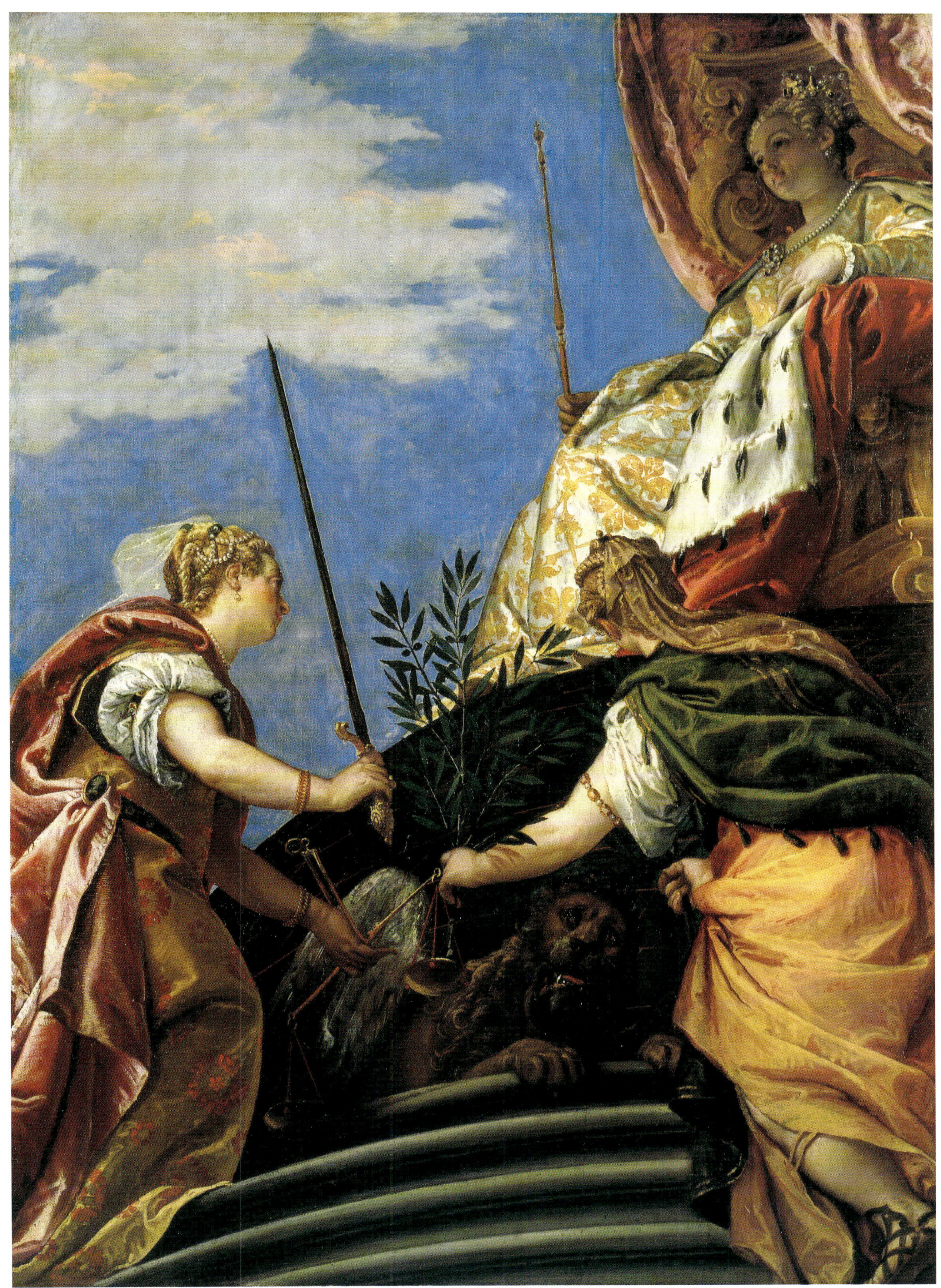

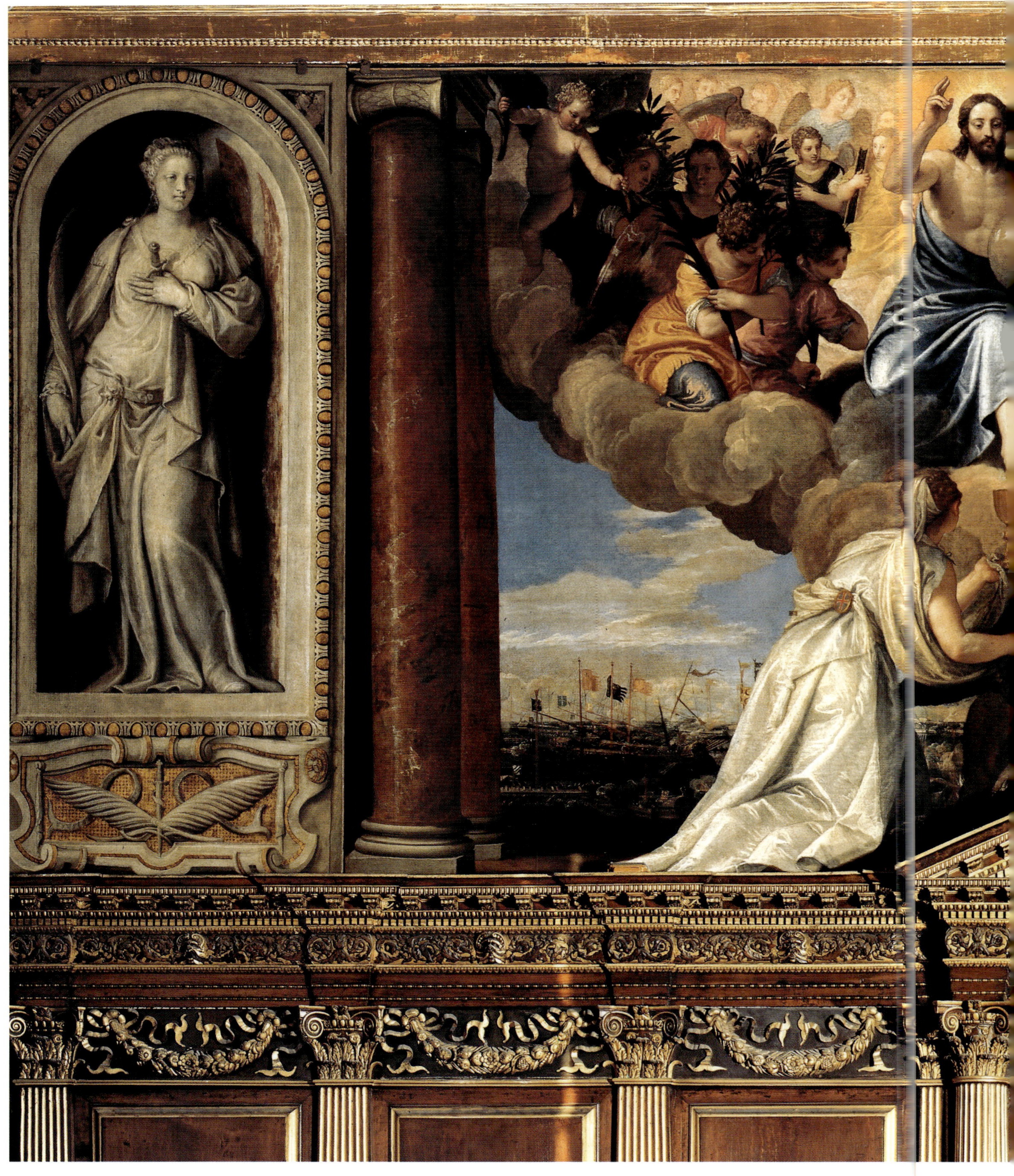

104 *Votive picture of Doge Sebastiano Venier*, c. 1581/82
Oil on canvas, 285 x 565 cm
Sala del Collegio, Doge's Palace, Venice

This painting commemorates the sea battle of Lepanto (1571) and the military successes of the Venetian captain general Sebastiano Venier, who was elected Doge in June 1577 and died only a year later. Unlike the *modello* (British Museum, London), which still shows the Doge being crowned by Venetia, the final version – presumably dating from post-1581 – emphasizes his role as the defender of Christian faith in the service of the state.

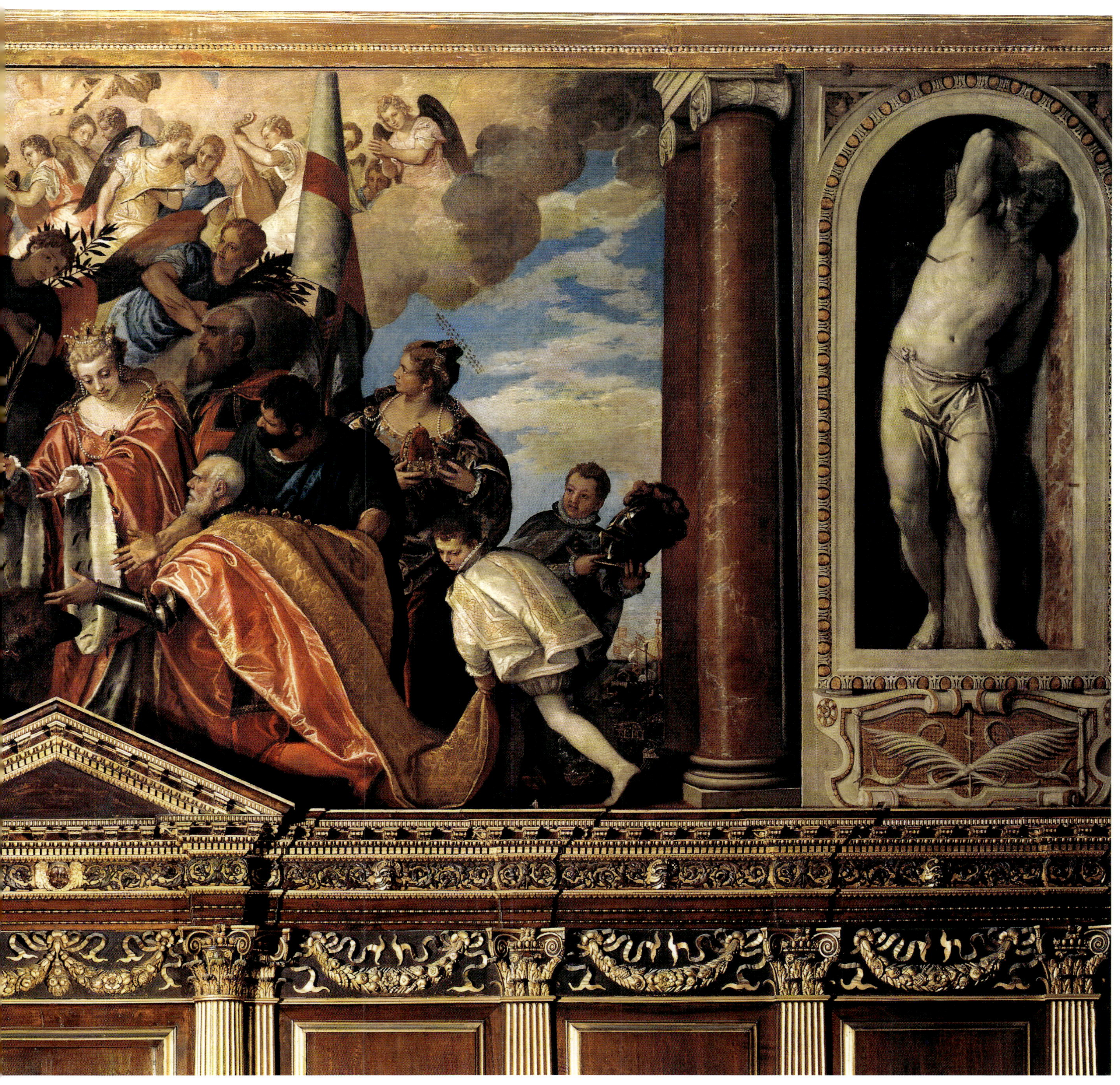

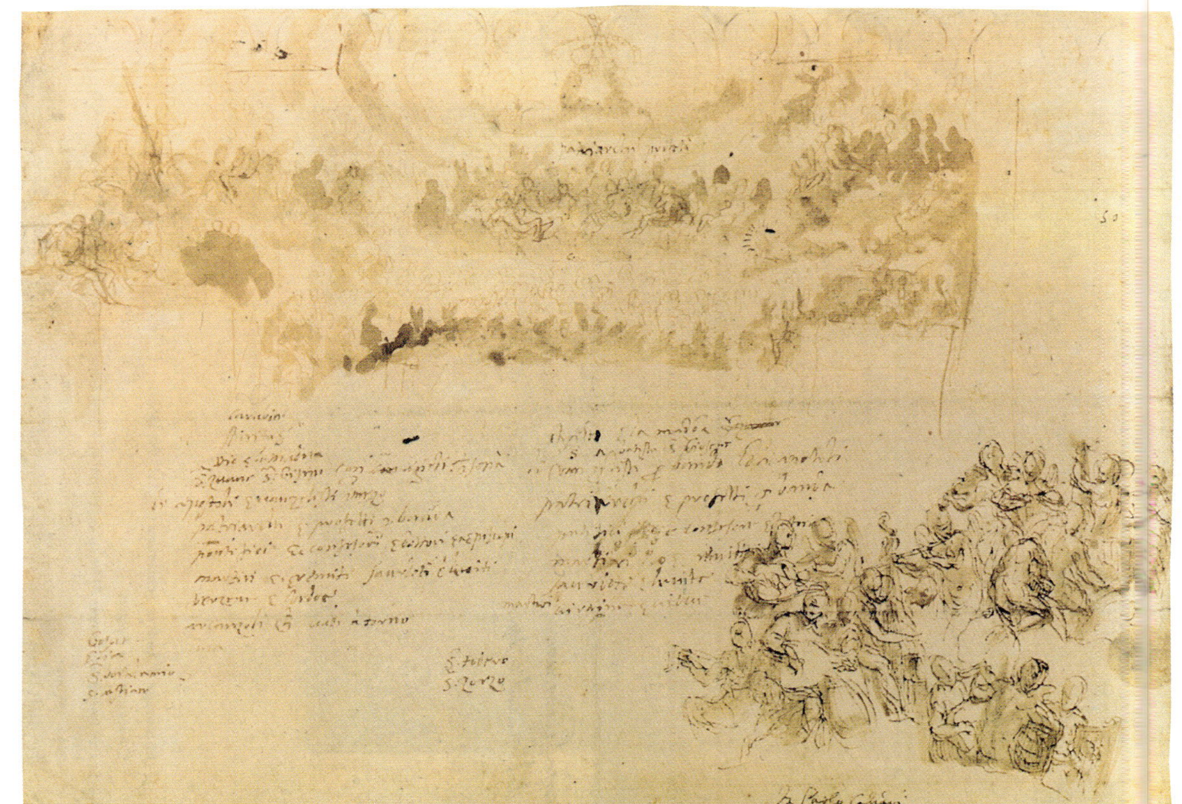

105 Sketch page with a compositional study and figure studies for *Paradise*, 1579–1582
Pen drawing, 22 x 31.4 cm
Formerly Christie's, Monaco, 1993, no. 19

This page of sketches only recently turned up in the art trade. It relates to the competition on behalf of the Signoria for the refurnishing of the main wall of the Sala del Maggior Consiglio in the Doge's Palace. Previously only three drawings with preliminary studies for individual pictures were known. The upper half of the sheet shows a drawing in Veronese's customary rapid hand indicating the planned overall composition. Notes in his own handwriting explain individual motifs, and possibly relate to the iconographical program of the picture.

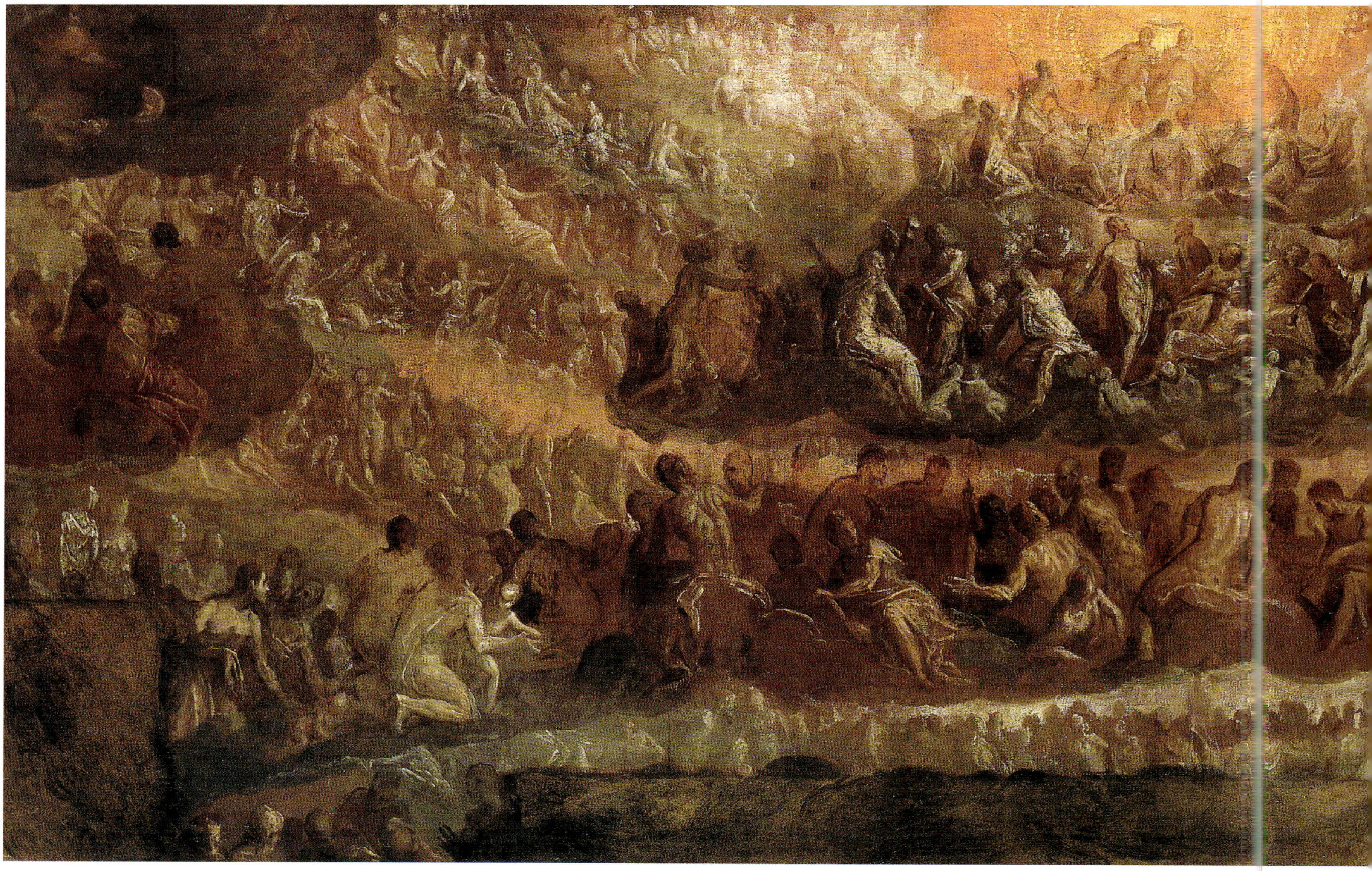

existence of *modelli* in many cases argues that the clients, who were endeavoring to remain in control, had a say in these matters. It is therefore no surprise that Veronese was once again taking part with his designs in what was probably the Serenissima's most prestigious project.

The equally complicated and exciting story of the competition for the refurbishment of the main wall in the Sala del Maggior Consiglio, and the desire to replace the *Coronation of the Virgin* created in the 1360s by the Paduan painter Guariento (fl. 1338–c. 1370) with a new up-to-date work, began to take shape in about 1560. It was evidently also intended to involve Federico Zuccaro, who stayed in Venice between 1563 and 1565, for he delivered two drawn plans during the late phase of the planned renovations and stated years later that the continuing conflict with the Turks had delayed the start of the work. Not until after the great fire, between 1579 and 1582, were various painters finally invited to submit their inventions (*inventioni*). Due to surviving *modelli*, we now know that Palma il Giovane, Francesco Bassano, Jacopo Tintoretto, and Paolo Veronese took part in the competition. The latter prepared for the project by making numerous drawings (ill. 105) and an oil sketch (ill. 106). After lengthy consultations the commission for painting *Paradise* was given to Veronese and Francesco Bassano. When Girolamo Bardi published a description of their painting in Venice in 1587, he knew the task and the program, but not the picture itself, for the latter had still not been produced by this point as the two painters were unable to come to any agreement between themselves. When Veronese died a year later, the aged Tintoretto was chosen in his place, and he in turn delivered further *modelli* and finally, around 1592 and in collaboration with his son Domenico and Palma il Giovane, completed what is probably the largest painting in the world.

At the beginning of the 1580s, Veronese delivered the boldest sample of his abilities as a ceiling painter in the form of the *Triumph of Venetia* (ill. 107), set in the heavy gold frame on the ceiling of the Sala del Maggior Consiglio above the seats of the Doge and his municipal authorities. Once again based on a drawn *modello* (Lord Harewood Collection, Leeds), this was a "proto-Baroque" pictorial invention and, on account of its perspectival arrangement, the carefully considered compositional structure of the three groups of figures, the shining colors and the skillful distribution of light and shade, it was soon one of the most famous works in the city. The upward viewpoint with its sense of depth,

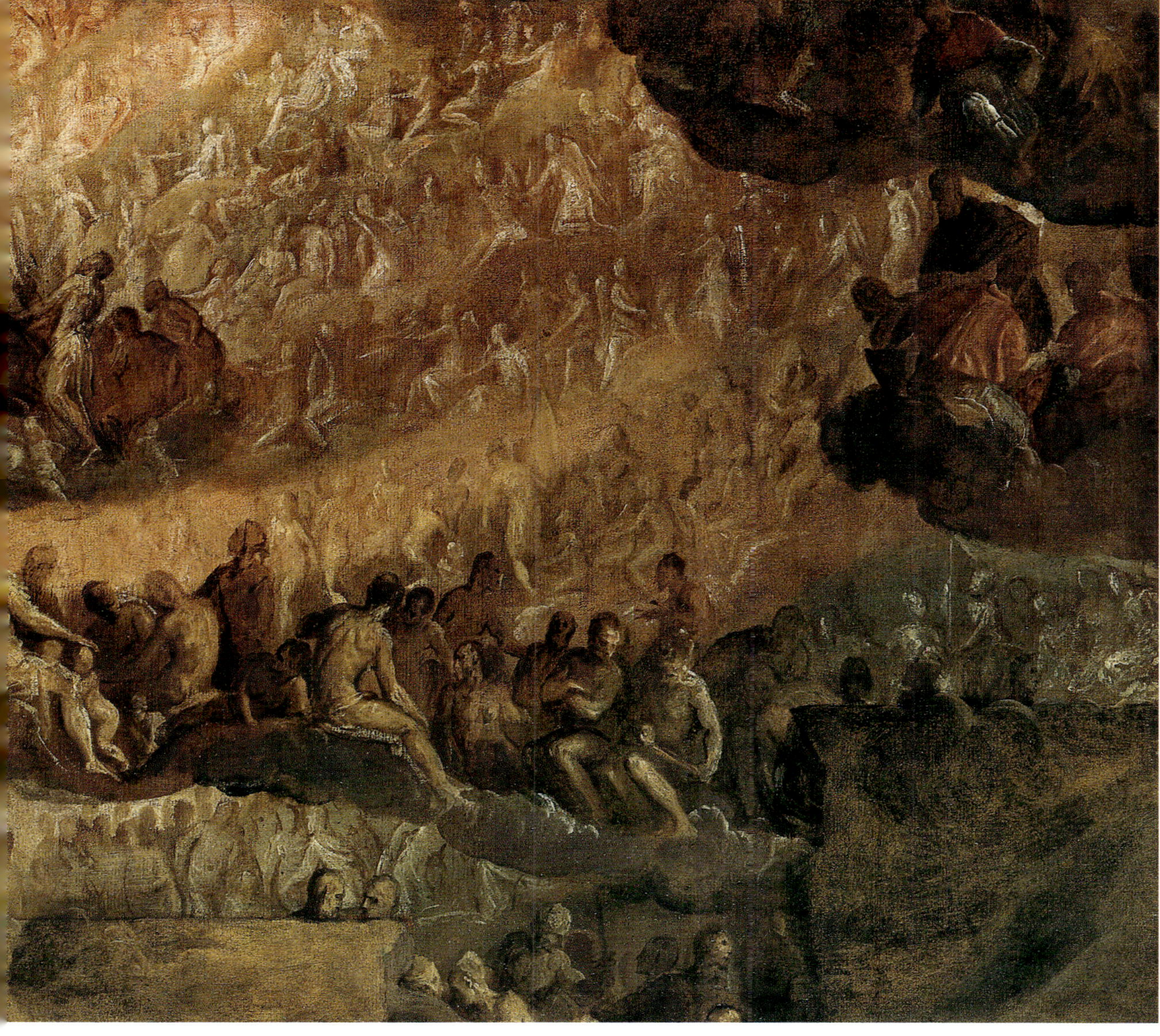

106 *Paradise*, c. 1579–1582
Oil on canvas, 87 x 234 cm
Musée des Beaux-Arts, Lille

In all probability, the great *modello* was the decisive factor in enabling Veronese and Francesco Bassano to qualify successfully for the job of painting the monumental painting on the main wall of the Sala del Maggior Consiglio in the Doge's Palace. The ambitious project was delayed, however, and when Veronese died in 1588, the Signoria transferred the important commission to Tintoretto.

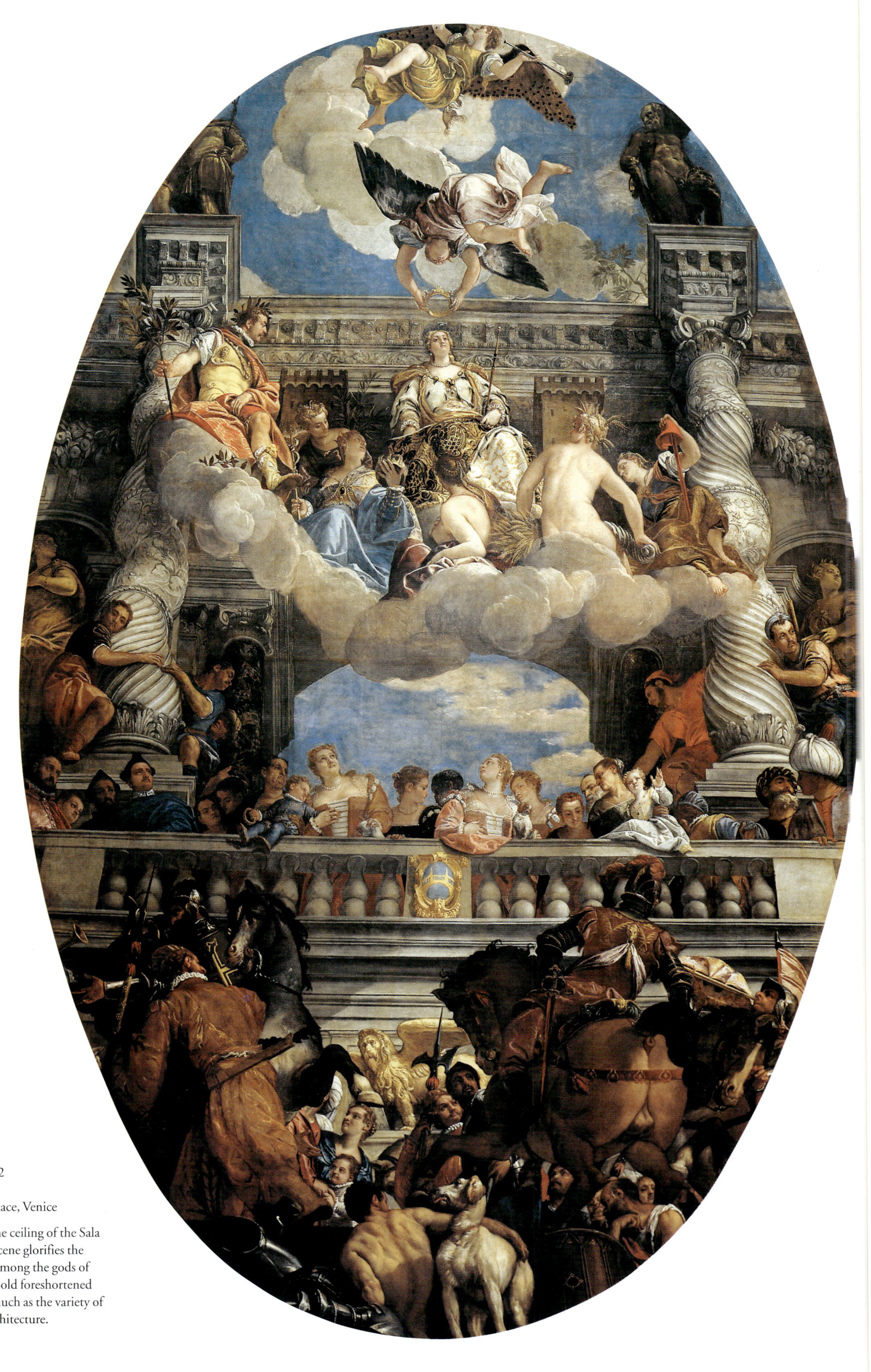

107 *Triumph of Venetia*, c. 1579–1582
Oil on canvas, 904 x 580 cm
Sala del Maggior Consiglio, Doge's Palace, Venice

As one of the three great pictures for the ceiling of the Sala del Maggior Consiglio, this crowded scene glorifies the enthroned personification of Venetia among the gods of Olympus as a symbol of eternal rule. Bold foreshortened perspectives catch the viewer's eye as much as the variety of figures and splendor of the painted architecture.

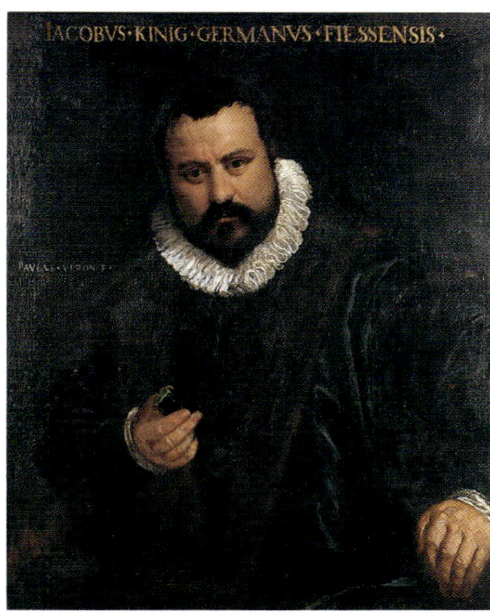

108 (above) *Portrait of Johann Jakob König*, c. 1575–1580
Oil on canvas, 83 x 73.5 cm
Národní Muzeum, Prague

The Füssen-born goldsmith and art dealer Johann Jakob König (c. 1536–c. 1600) visited Venice several times after 1571. As a highly regarded jeweler, he was later in the service of the Emperor Rudolph II in Prague. An inventory of his paintings drawn up in 1603 lists numerous portraits, including self-portraits by Tintoretto and Veronese. The self-assured König had had himself immortalized by both artists. In the Veronese picture, the gesture and rotation of the body gives the impression of a momentary snapshot reminiscent of the psychological portraits of Lorenzo Lotto (d. 1556), who worked in Venice in the 1520s.

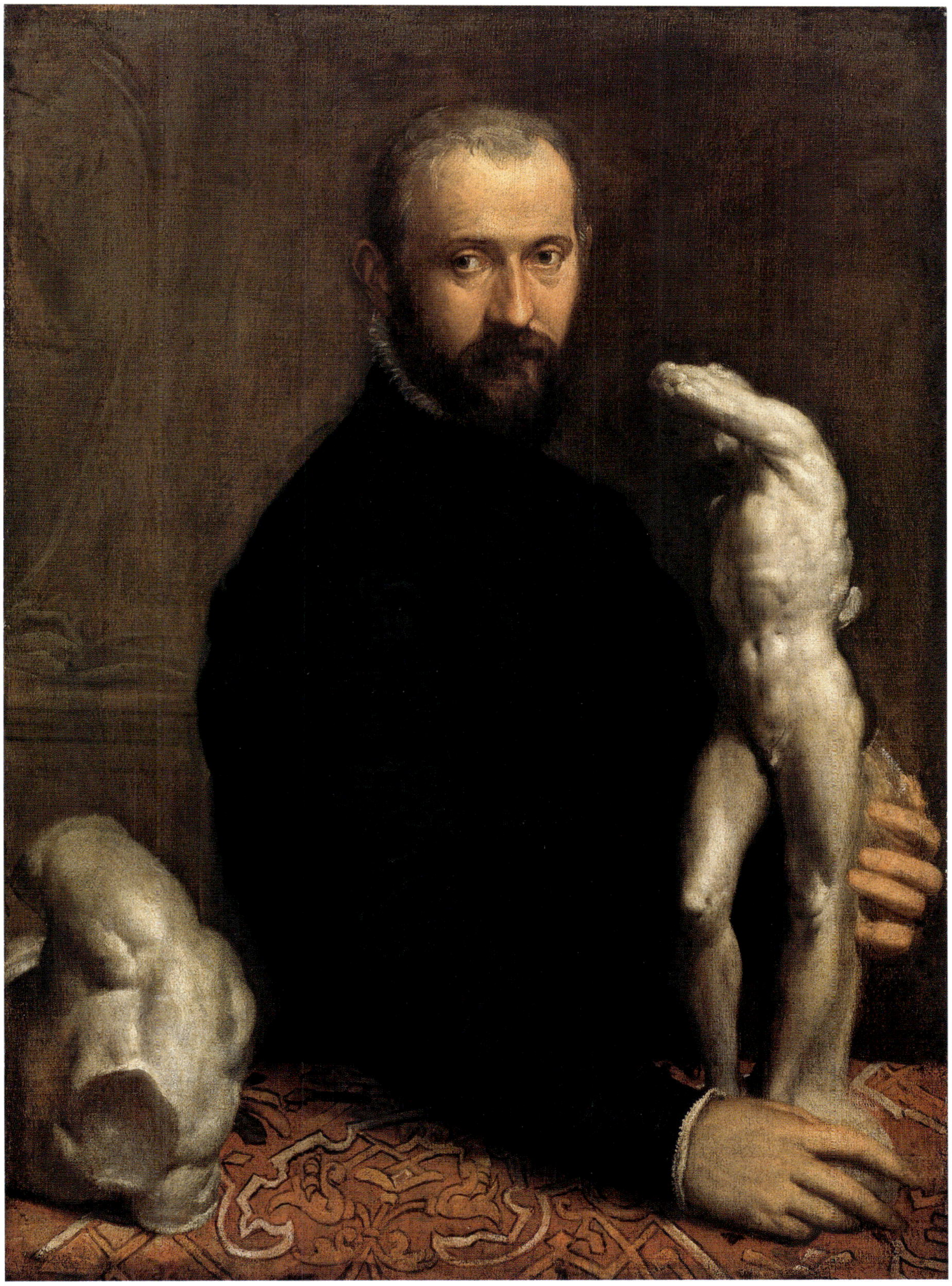

109 (right) *Portrait of Alessandro Vittoria*, c. 1575
Oil on canvas, 110 x 77 cm
Metropolitan Museum of Art, New York

There are good reasons for the identification with the Venetian sculptor Alessandro Vittoria (c. 1525–1608). Vittoria had already had his portrait painted in 1552/53 by the Lombard painter Giovanni Battista Moroni. Comparisons with that picture (Kunsthistorisches Museum, Vienna) and the bust he himself executed for his tomb before 1595 in the Venetian church of San Zaccaria leave no doubt as to the subject's identity. The sculptor grasps the *modello* of a statuette with both hands. It closely resembles a bronze of St. Sebastian by him in the Metropolitan Museum.

the *di sotto in sù*, had at this point in time already been tried out on several occasions, and with great success, by Veronese. It was this work, however, described as a "machine" in the 18th century due to its complexity, that introduced structural methods in the field of ceiling painting which had a lasting effect far beyond Venice, right into the Alpine region of southern Germany, and which were revived in the works of the Venetian painter Giovanni Battista Tiepolo (1696–1770) in the ingenious and graceful shape of Venetian Rococo. As a ceiling painter in the Sala del Maggior Consiglio, Paolo Veronese once more played a decisive part in the formation of a politically motivated and specifically Venetian national iconography. Venetia, the state personified, is enthroned like a queen before the backdrop of a triumphal fantasy architecture on a band of clouds. The patriotically charged program, developed with the substantial involvement of the Venetian *nobili* Giacomo Marcello and Giacomo Contarini and the cleric Girolamo Bardi, confronted

110 Marcantonio Raimondi
The Vision of St. Helena, copy of Raphael (?)
Copper engraving, 15.6 x 9.3 cm
Kupferstichkabinett, Staatliche Museen zu Berlin – Preussischer Kulturbesitz, Berlin

Marcantonio Raimondi (d. 1534), the real founder and main representative of the Italian High Renaissance graphics industry, copied many drawings by Raphael. This small sheet, which like many works by him is neither signed nor dated, may have been produced around 1511 in Rome, when painter and engraver collaborated very closely.

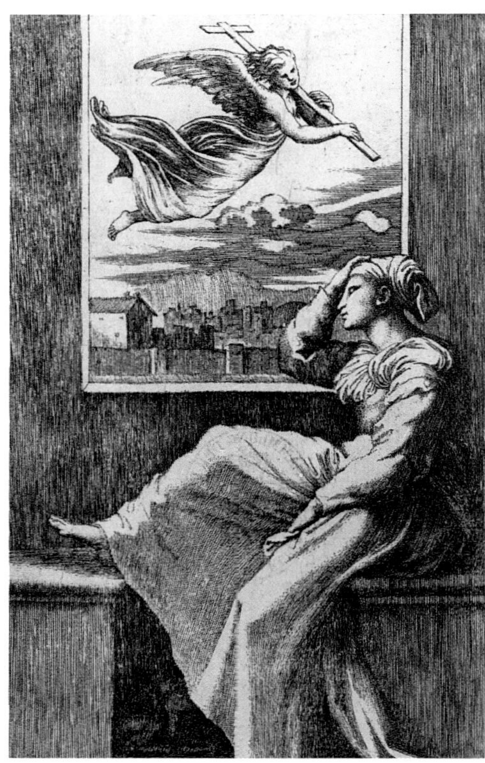

111 (opposite) *The Vision of St. Helena*, c. 1575–1578
Oil on canvas, 197.5 x 115.6 cm
National Gallery, London

Flavia Julia Helena (d. c. 329), the mother of Constantine the Great, made a pilgrimage to Jerusalem, so legend tells us, to find the Cross of Christ, which had appeared to her in a dream. In 1648, Veronese's biographer Ridolfi mentions another picture on the same subject in the Contarini collection in Padua, but it is not impossible that the London picture was already in Rubens's possession in Antwerp in 1642. Veronese did very few single-figure pictures. Raimondi's engraving (ill. 110) forms the starting point for the impressive, simply structured composition, which is wholly imbued with the humanized view of the saint.

the painter with clear prescriptions about content: he was to depict Venetia enthroned over city and countryside, an allusion to the world-ruling Roma, being crowned by a Victoria, the goddess of victory, accompanied by the seven Virtues and the four Seasons. In addition, he was to include a crowd in festive mood in the picture. Both in the plan and on the ceiling painting, Veronese omitted the four Seasons. Moreover, on the oval painting Eloquence and Strength appear in the form of statues of Mercury and Hercules, which suggest that, despite their prescriptions regarding content, the clients were quite willing to permit the painter to add his own features.

Apart from this official task for the Serenissima, Veronese, during the course of the 1570s, had already carried out numerous altar and devotional paintings and a series of portraits; in many cases the identity of the people depicted in the latter remains unknown, with the exception of the Venetian sculptor *Alessandro Vittoria* (ill. 109) and the goldsmith and jeweler *Johann Jakob König* (ill. 108), who was born in Füssen, Germany. In addition, there are allegories and mythologies; for a while these were even the preferred theme of the painter and his productive workshop. As early as the Coccina pictures there had been signs of a change in palette. Bright daylight had been replaced by an evening atmosphere. In the *Virtues* (ill. 101) on the ceiling of the Sala del Collegio the painter used a clear and almost classical formal language. The simple yet very convincing formal composition of these allegories is echoed in the unusual single-figure picture of the *Vision of St. Helena* (ill. 111) in London's National Gallery. The original purpose of the painting, whose existence can first be proven in Amsterdam in 1681, is unknown. Surprisingly, in this composition Veronese made a conspicuously direct use of a copper engraving on the same theme (ill. 110) by Marcantonio Raimondi (died 1534), which in turn appears to derive from a model in Raphael's circle. This adaptation of an engraving, so untypical of the painter's late work and with a directness unique in his *œuvre*, may have been carried out at the request of the unknown client, for even at an advanced age Veronese was evidently quite willing to take on tasks of a comparable nature. Thus, such a sensation was caused in Venice by a portrait of Bianca Capello (died 1587), the Grand Duchess of Tuscany, painted by Scipione Pulzone (before 1550–1598) and exhibited in 1586 by the Venetian *nobile* Francesco Bembo, that copies were commissioned from Tintoretto, Bassano, Palma il Giovane and Veronese. In Veronese's case, this portrait – which no longer exists – was still in the possession of his heirs in 1682, and there is some suggestion that the still surviving portrait of her husband Francesco I de' Medici (Staatliche Kunstsammlungen, Kassel), who died in 1587, was produced by Paolo Veronese himself and that it was once a pendant to the other work. At the beginning of the 1580s Veronese returned to the theme of St. Helena (ill. 112). The portrait-like, anthropomorphized conception still characteristic of the intimate London version is now overlaid with the pathos of the staging. Before the backdrop of a valuable curtain and a column architecture cut off by the edge of the picture, the dreaming empress's garment, overabundantly decorated with brocade, develops an independent existence against which the figure itself and the actual message of the picture struggle to assert themselves. Its format suggests that its function was that of a private devotional picture, but the supposition that a respectable Venetian patrician had her patron saint in mind when donating the picture must remain a matter for speculation.

Veronese's successes and his huge productivity between 1560 and 1588 rely, to a not inconsiderable degree, as has already been mentioned on several occasions, on collaboration with members of his family and assistants. Following the example of Titian, Tintoretto and the Bassani, he started running a well-organized workshop from an early stage, and, to begin with his younger brother Benedetto Caliari, and later his sons Gabriele (1568–1631) and Carletto (1570–1596) among others, worked as his assistants. As the "Haeredes Pauli", Veronese's artistic heirs, the latter two continued running the workshop after their father's death, completed unfinished paintings and, during the course of their own commissions, incorporated the motifs and compositional ideas of their famous master, with a greater or lesser degree of spontaneity, in works ranging from free translation to straightforward copies. In a letter to Giacomo Contarini, who commissioned a complex allegorical painting, Benedetto himself described the nature of their collaboration in a few words: "*da me dissegnato, da Carlo abotiato e da Cabriel finito*". According to this, a preliminary sketch produced by Benedetto had been transferred to canvas by Carlo. Gabriele finally had the task of carrying out the painting. The "Haeredes Pauli" were of course able to make use of an extensive body of pen, chalk and *chiaroscuro* drawings, of *ricordi* and *modelli* with wide-ranging functions, that Veronese had used as materials for his work during his life and some of which at least remained in the possession of the family until 1682.

Informative insights into the studio's manner of working can be gained from various reports by Veronese's well-informed biographer, Carlo Ridolfi. Thus he writes about his own master Antonio Vassilacchi, who in the early 1570s on occasion worked in Veronese's workshop, describing how the former together with other assistants copied paintings and drawings by the master. In addition, Vassilacchi owned a collection of drawings in Veronese's own hand which were presumably used often enough as models and aids in his own projects. The fact that this practice played an important part in the running of the workshop is echoed in the *Vita* of Parrasio Micheli (before 1516–1578), who occasionally worked with Veronese and who quite openly used a drawing by the latter, now in the British Museum, in his *Worship of the Body of Christ* (San Giuseppe, Venice). It is therefore not surprising if Veronese's own works, such as the *Christ and the Centurion* (ill. 114) and the *Finding of Moses*

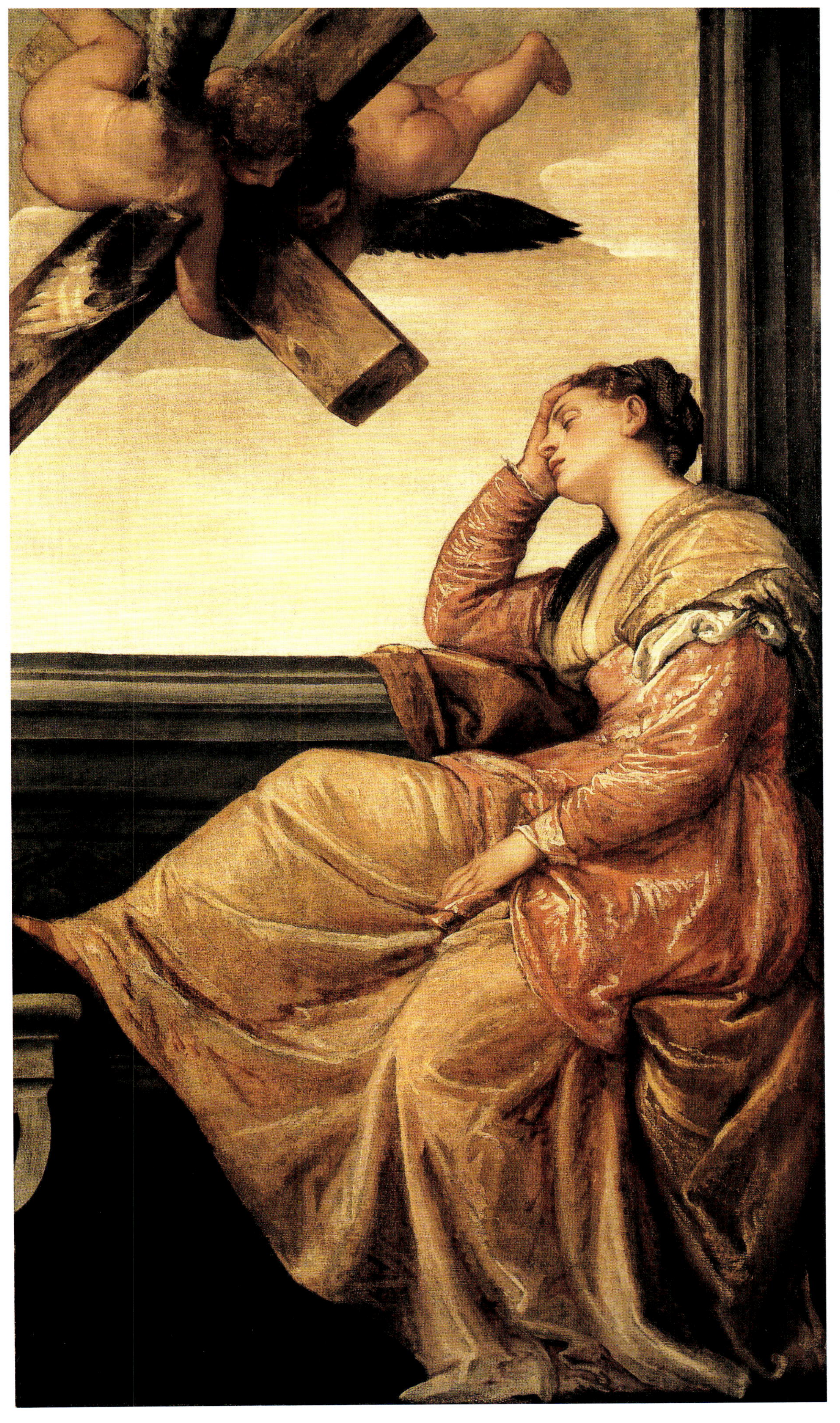

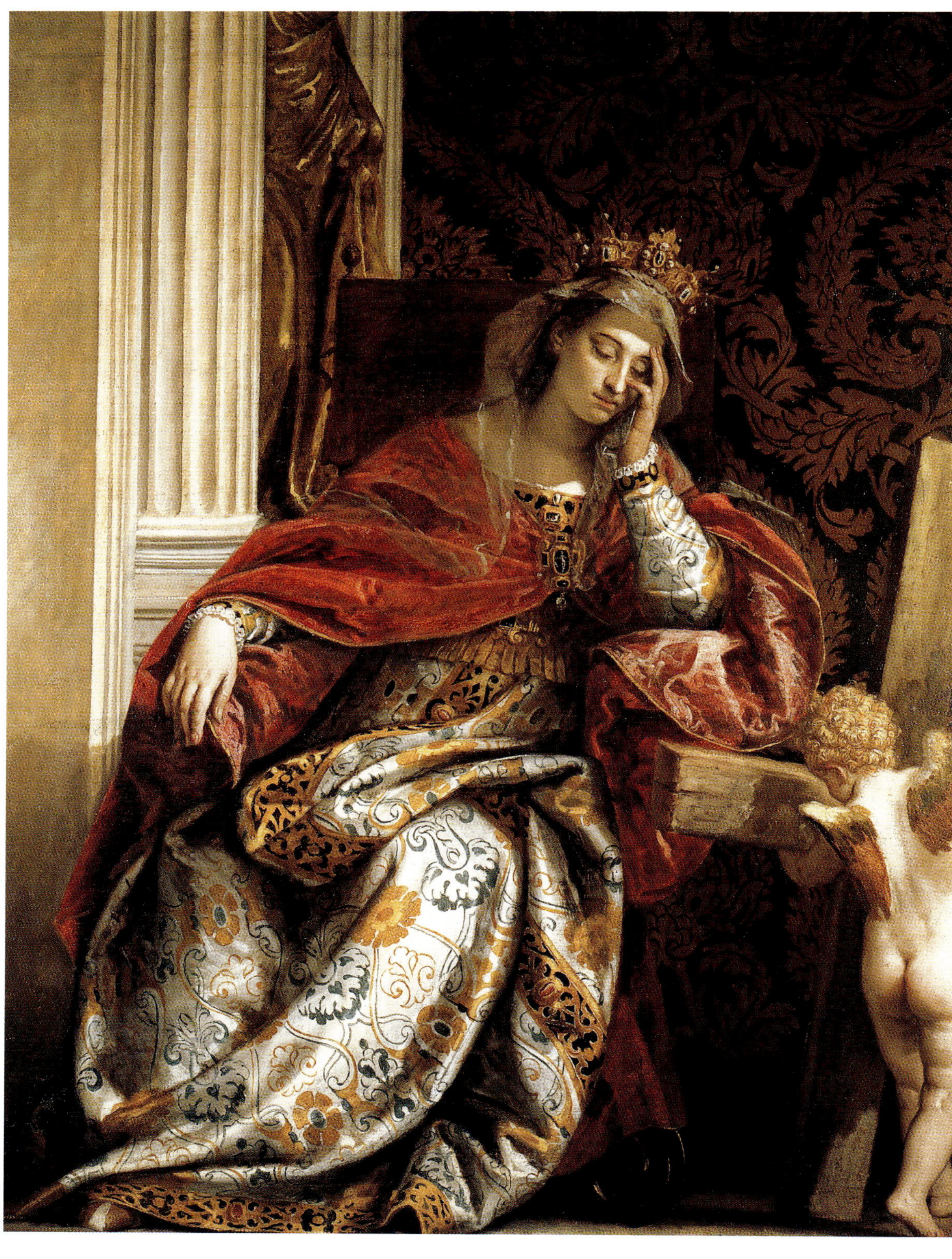

112 *The Vision of St. Helena*, c. 1580/81
Oil on canvas, 166 x 134 cm
Pinacoteca Apostolica Vaticana, Vatican, Rome

Veronese's second version of the subject of St. Helena is quite different both artistically and in content. St. Helena is now crowned and wearing the splendid dress of an empress. Brightly gleaming columns with a statue between them ennoble the location of the event. However, in comparison with the London picture (ill. 111) the choreography of the picture is rather superficial and calculated. The dating of the picture remains problematic. In her dress, she seems a figure taken wholly from the repertoire of the Feasts. Only the powerful color contrasts and selective distribution of light, which resemble most closely the figure of *Judith* (Kunsthistorisches Museum, Vienna), generally dated to around 1582/83, justify the late dating.

(ill. 113) were varied or copied by painters working in his workshop. This development was accelerated due to the Venetian painter's constantly growing obligations, as well as the rapidly increasing demand in the last quarter of the 16th century, as a result of his fame, for paintings among royal clients.

Veronese's depictions of biblical themes, and above all his allegories and mythologies, were extremely sought after – and not merely in Venice where a gap in the market had been created by the death of the aged Titian (died 1576). The *Annunciation* (ill. 116), signed and dated 1583 and nonetheless carried out with the assistance of his workshop, was sent to Spain the same year it was completed. His high regard for the almost 5 m. high painting may have led King Philip II (1527–1598), who had been employing various Italian artists since 1567, to summon Veronese to Spain in order to give him further work in the Escorial – an invitation which the latter will surely have declined in view of his advanced age, so that the Titianesque *Annunciation* will probably have remained the only painting by Veronese in the royal collection until the painter Diego Velázquez (1599–1660), during the course of his second Italian journey, bought the magnificently colored mythologies showing *Venus and Adonis* (ill. 115) and the *Death of Procris* for Philip IV (1605–1665).

113 (opposite)
The Finding of Moses, c. 1580
Oil on canvas, 50 x 30 cm
Museo del Prado, Madrid

This small painting, which probably came from the collection of Charles I of England, is one of the earliest and best versions of an Old Testament subject inspired by the works of the painter Bonifazio de'Pitati (d. 1553). Several replicas in Veronese's own hand are known, together with a number of variants and sundry derivations carried out with the help of the workshop. The scene is a river bank in a highly atmospheric landscape. The story tells of an infant boy left out in a basket on the Nile, who is found by Pharaoh's daughter and brought up by her as her own son, Moses. The bridge and city are reminiscent of Verona. When Marco Boschini repeatedly describes Veronese in the 17th century as the treasurer of painting and compares his works with jewelry, this is the picture that seems to be meant by the metaphor. The delicately nuanced interplay of light and shade, achieved with a fine brush, unfolds to produce the glowing effect of brilliant jewels.

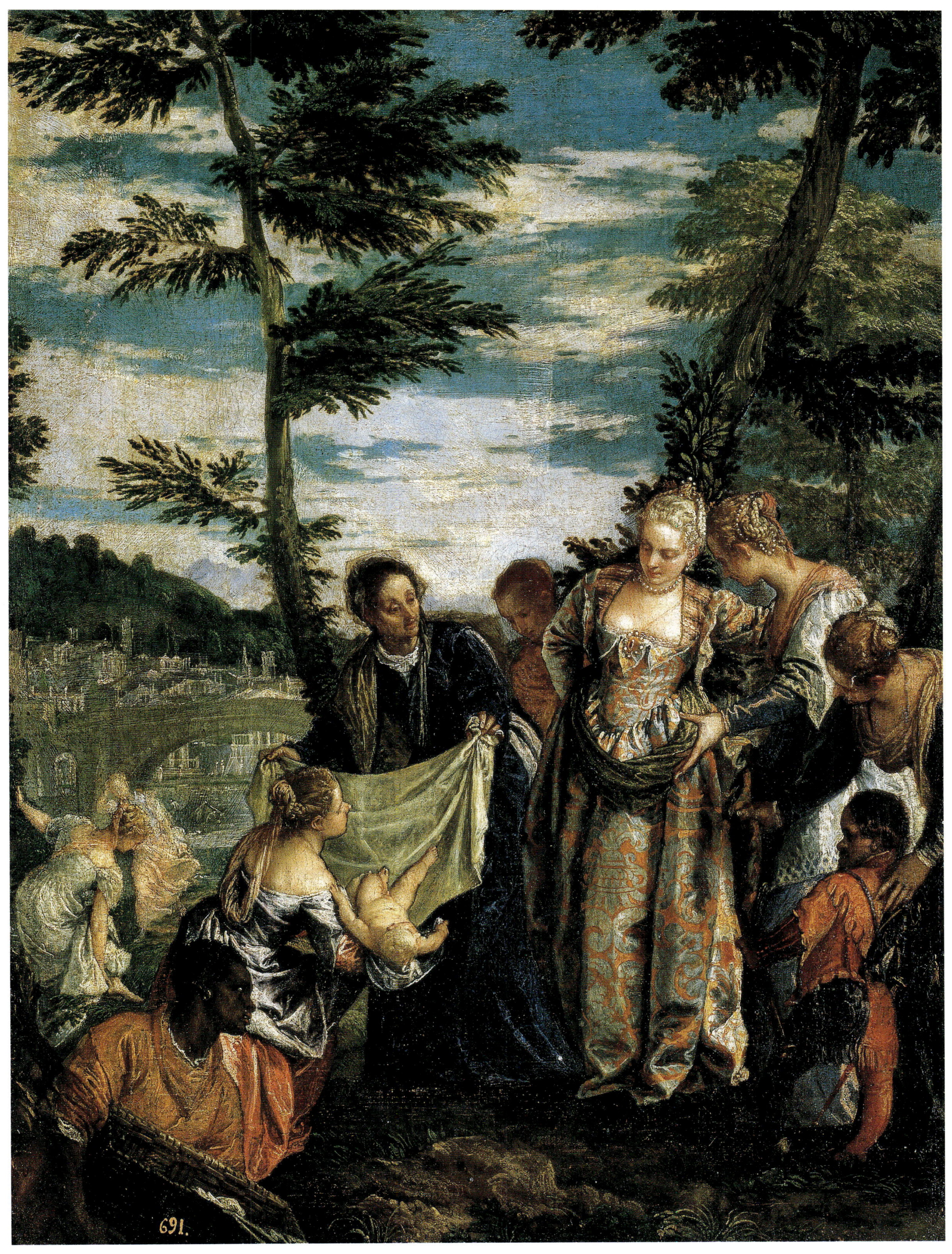
691.

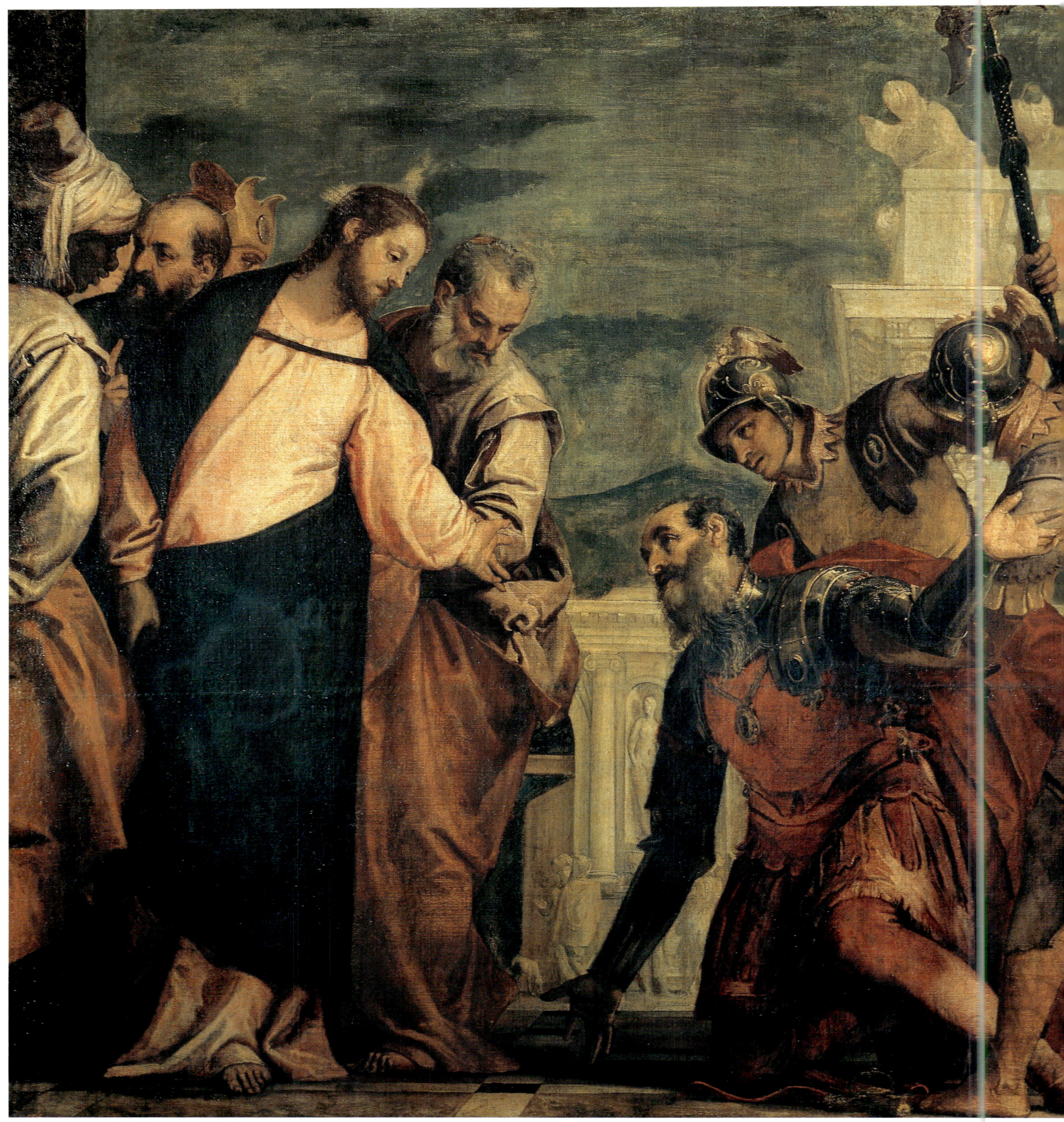

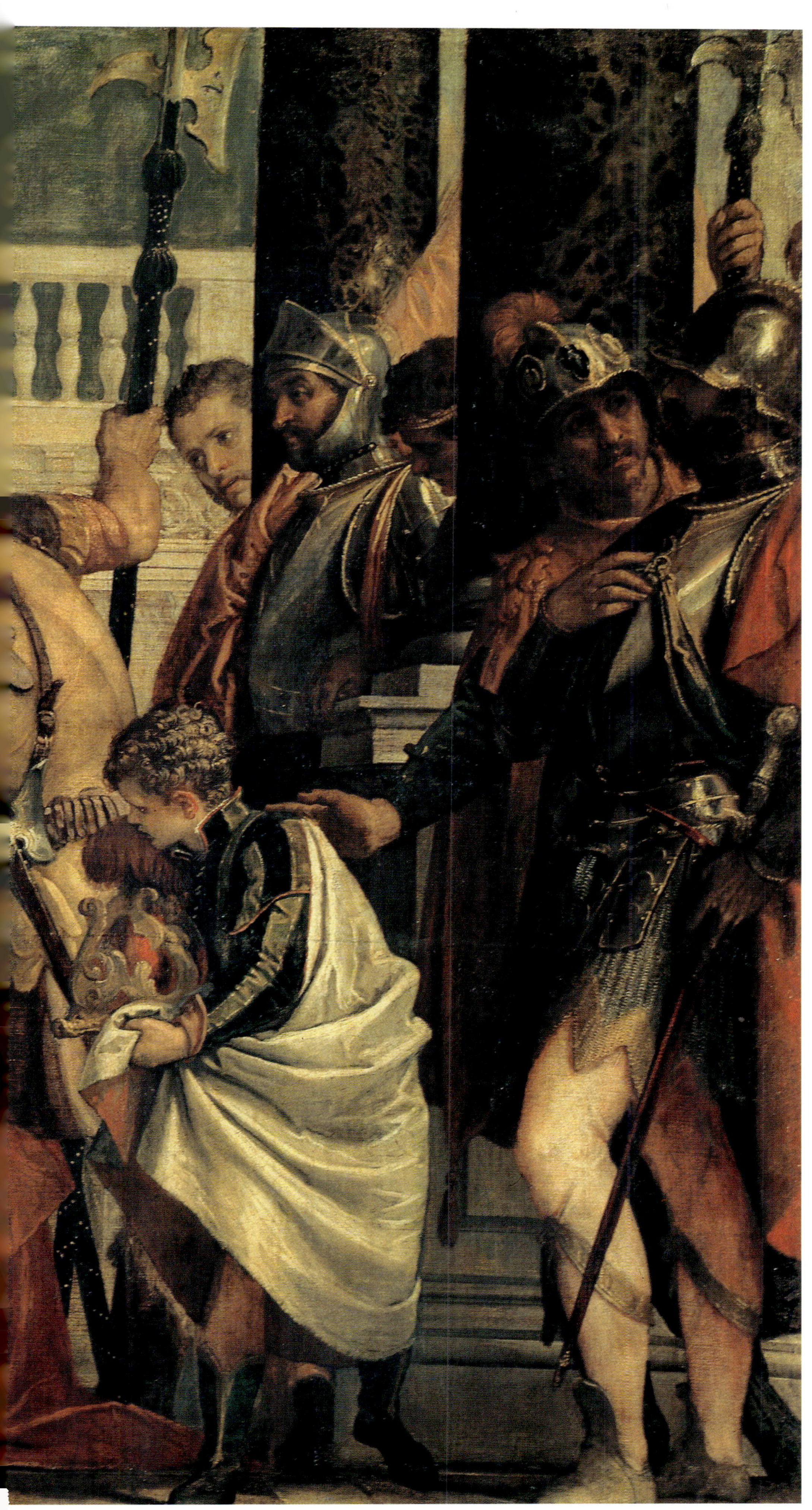

114 *Christ and the Centurion* , c. 1570–1572
Oil on canvas, 192 x 298 cm
Museo del Prado, Madrid

The popularity among clients of this theme of Veronese's is proved by no fewer than four different workshop versions, which in their turn became models for further copies and variations. The signed and dated (1587) picture on the same subject that now belongs to the furnishings of the Venetian church of Sant'Angelo Raffaele shows how compelling Veronese's approach was for his nephew and colleague Alvise Benfatto del Friso (c. 1544–1609).

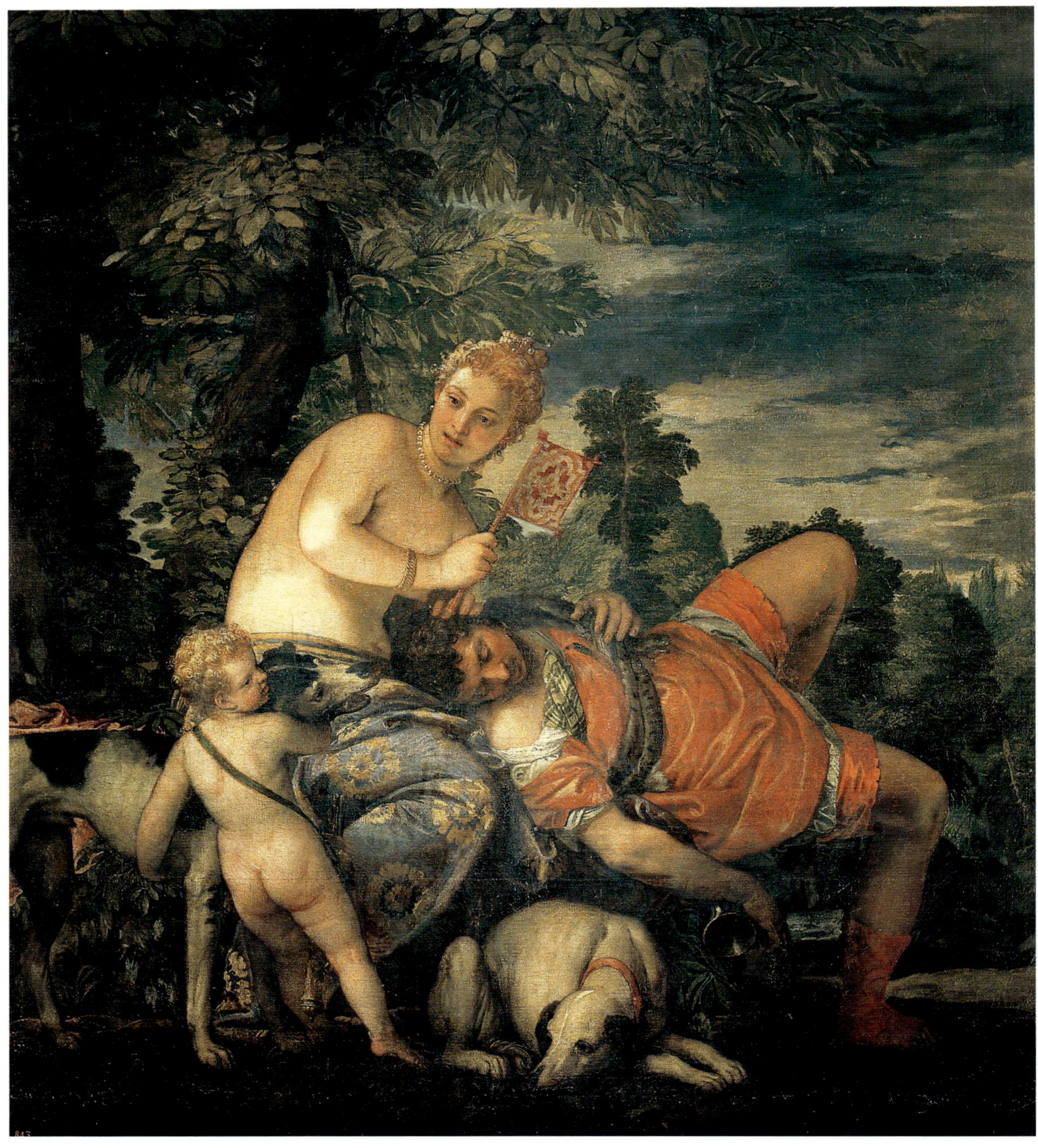

115 *Venus and Adonis*, c. 1580–1582
Oil on canvas, 212 (162) x 191 cm
Museo del Prado, Madrid

Later extended at the top, this work was originally a counterpart to the *Death of Procris* now in the Musée des Beaux Arts in Strasbourg. Both mythologies were first mentioned in *Il Riposo*, a tract published by Raffaello Borghini in 1582, and presumably executed some time between 1580 and 1582. The scene is an atmospheric wooded landscape with the classical lovers in the foreground. The brilliant colors and wealth of detailed subject-matter are typical of the late Veronese.

Veronese painted a depiction of the *Finding of Moses*, a subject very popular in collectors' circles, for Duke Guglielmo Gonzaga (died 1587) in Mantua, and Duke Carlo Emanuele I of Savoy (1562–1630) was another nobleman in Italy who took particular pleasure in this pictorial theme. The young duke commissioned four large paintings for his residence; they were largely carried out by assistants in accordance with the master's plans and were delivered to Turin in about 1582. As early as 1584, the Holy Roman Emperor apparently possessed two mythologies by Veronese, *Mars, Venus and a weeping Cupid* and a *Venus*, but apart from the fact that it has not been possible to identify reliably either painting to this day, it is questionable when the account written by Raffaello Borghini refers to Emperor Maximilian II (1527–1576) or to his son and heir Rudolph II (1552–1612) in Prague. The latter ascended to the imperial throne in 1576. An ambitious collector and client with an understanding of art, Rudolph II entertained a particular love of complicated allegories and erotic "allusions"; the Mannerist painter Hans von Aachen (1552–1615), Joseph Heintz the Elder (1564–1609) and Bartholomäus Spranger (1528–1579), who were in his service, all played a significant part in formulating them. Even though his role as Veronese's patron is unclear, at the beginning of the 17th century the Venetian painter was represented in the famous gallery in Prague Castle by several mythological depictions in the form of allegorical fables, including the two impressive paintings of *Omnia Vanitas* and *Honor et Virtus post mortem floret* (ill. 117), which had been offered for sale to Duke Albrecht V of Bavaria as early as 1567 and had probably come into the possession of Rudolph II through the mediation of the antiquarian Jacopo Strada.

Charles de Croy (died 1612) also proved to have a lucky knack as a collector. He was an ambassador of Philip II, and during a stay in Venice in 1595 he

116 *Annunciation* (detail, lower half of picture), 1583
Oil on canvas, 470 x 206 cm
Patrimonio Nacional, Real Monasterio de San Lorenzo de El Escorial, Madrid

Signed and dated 1583, this painting reached the Escorial in the same year, where it was originally intended for the altar of the main chapel. However, the dimensions were not right, so a smaller work by Pellegrino Tibaldi (1527–1596) was used instead. Veronese's brother may have assisted with the picture, but the soft, fluid movements of the Archangel Gabriel and the complexity of the figural composition in the upper half suggest that Veronese himself was largely responsible.

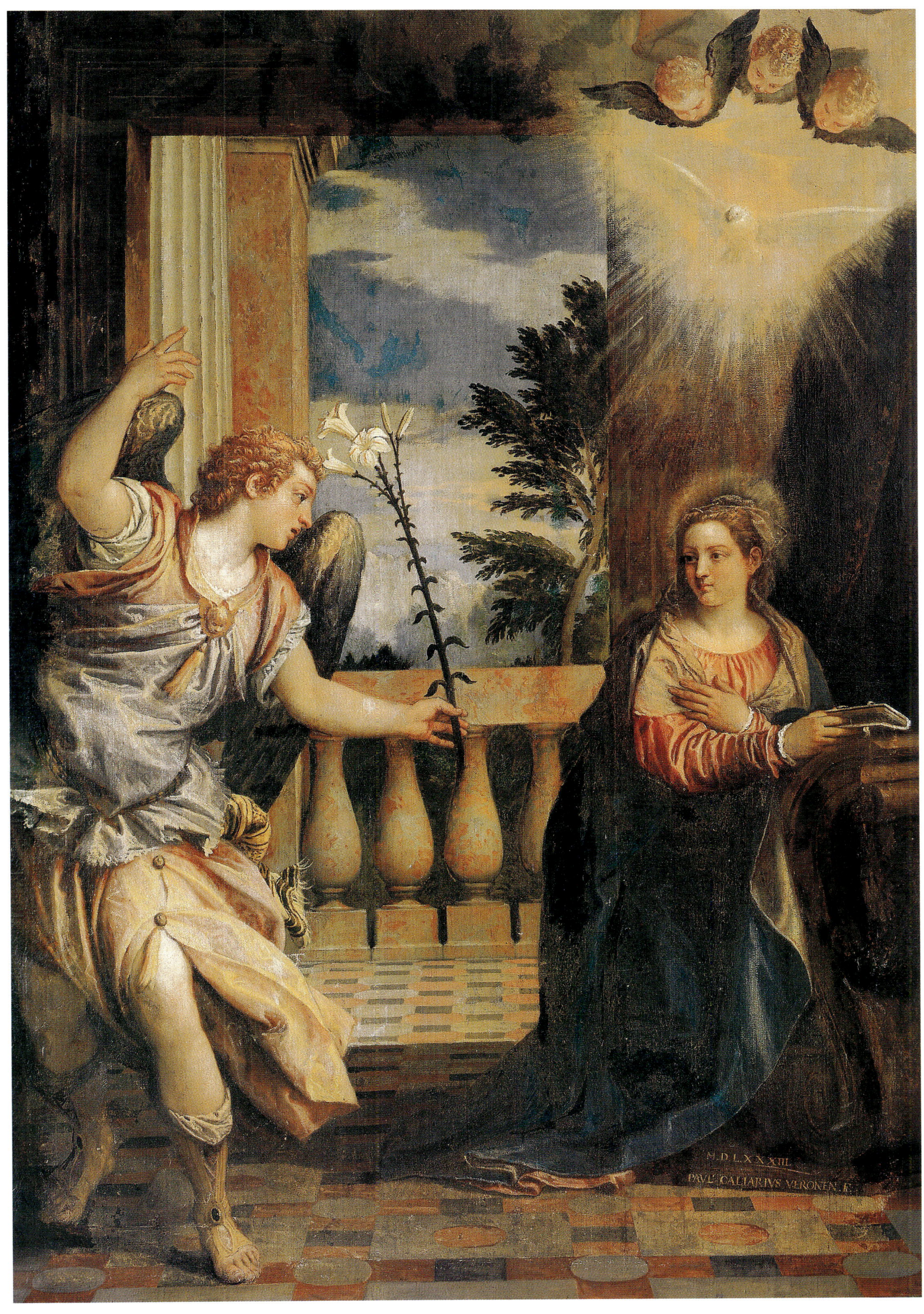
M.D.LXXXIII.
PAVL. CALIARIVS VERONEN. F.

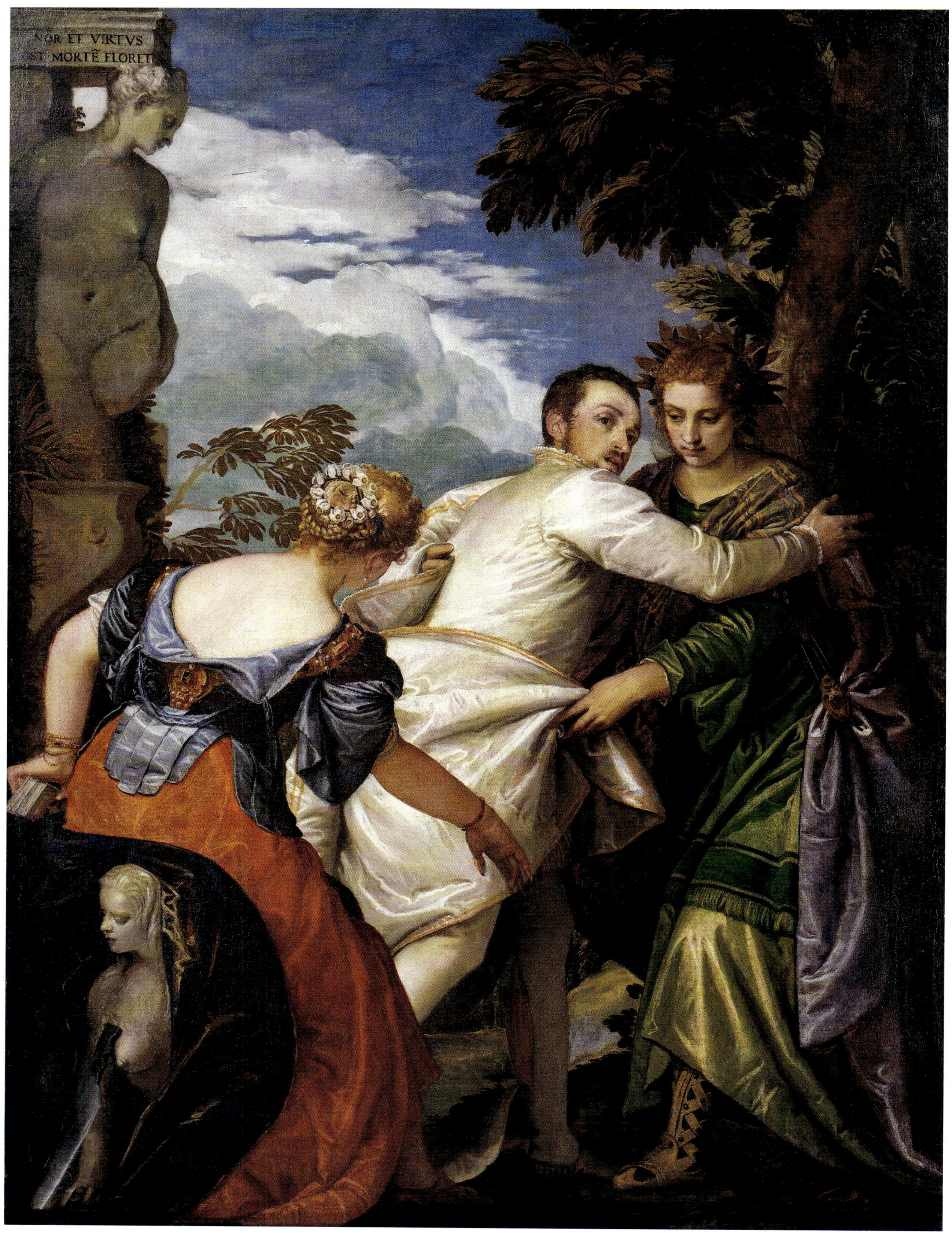
NOR ET VIRTVS
MORTÊ FLORET

118 *Mars, Venus and Cupid*, after 1580
Oil on canvas, 165 x 124.5 cm
National Gallery of Scotland, Edinburgh

Veronese and colleagues from his workshop treated the subject of Venus – particularly popular among collectors – several times from the mid-1560s. Marked variations in quality, considerable weaknesses in the disposition of the figure of Mars, and the existence of a drawing by Veronese squared off with chalk (British Museum, London), in which Venus and Cupid are pre-formulated in sketch form, indicate a workshop piece produced under Veronese's supervision.

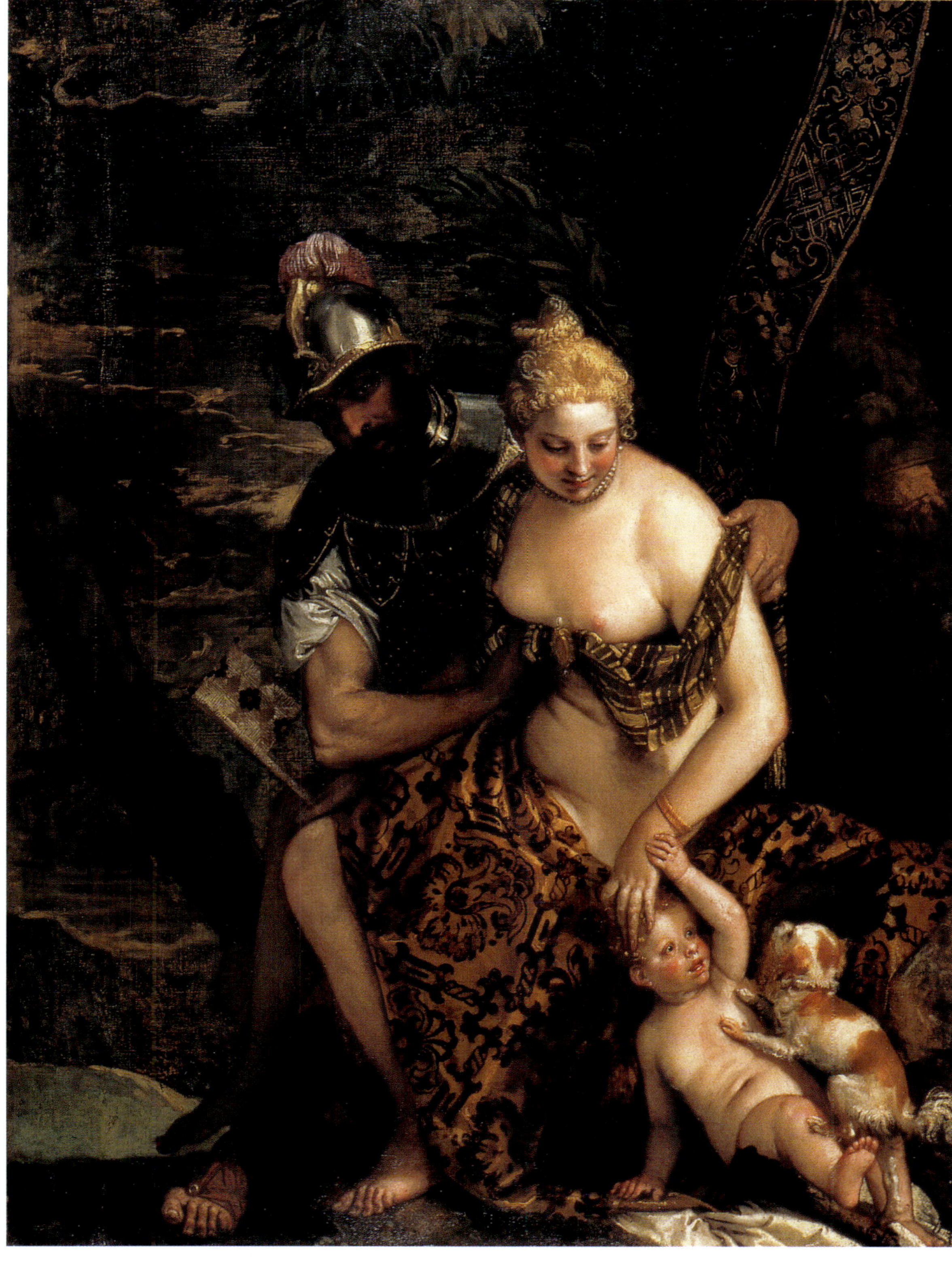

117 (opposite)
Honor et Virtus post mortem floret, before 1567
Oil on canvas, 219 x 169.5 cm
Frick Collection, New York

Marked top left with the inscription *(HO)NOR ET VIRTVS / (P)OST MORTE(M) FLORET*, this picture is also described as *Hercules between Virtue and Vice*, alluding to the story told in Hesiod when Hercules meets two beautiful women at a fork in the road. The youthful hero of the allegory is an elegantly clad Venetian in white silk garments, who was taken at the end of the 17th century, when the picture was in the collection of Queen Christina of Sweden in Rome, to be a self-portrait of the artist. Unhesitatingly he turns to Virtue, who is crowned with a laurel wreath. Drops of blood on his ripped leg covering testify to the fruitless attempt by Vice – Lust and Pleasure, in the long run the death-bringing opponent of Virtue – to hold back the man of honor and win him over.

succeeded in purchasing a total of eleven works by Veronese and his workshop. This sequence of pictures consisted of a cycle of ten paintings of almost identical measurements and one individual work depicting scenes from the Old and New Testaments; in about 1619, the paintings were bought in Brussels by Balthasar Gerbier for the Duke of Buckingham and came to England, only to change hands once more in Antwerp around 1648. Archduke Leopold William, the Spanish king Philip IV's (1605–1665) governor of The Netherlands from 1647 to 1656, was considered an ardent admirer of Veronese and Venetian painting of the Cinquecento and finally brought the valuable series of paintings to Prague; but only for three of the works produced in about 1585, the other eight of which are now kept in the museums of Vienna and Washington, was this the end of a long journey.

Veronese's successes in Venice, and his fame and recognition in the circles of royal collectors at the end of his artistic career, can by no means conceal the fact that he was not admitted to the pantheon of the most famous Italian painters until the 17th century, at a point in time when Venetian painting of the Cinquecento was enjoying considerable prestige in the most important European art centers. In Venice Marco Boschini (1613–1678), who worked as a copper engraver, artistic man of letters, tourist guide and occasional art agent, passionately described the atmosphere in a few words. In his *Carta del navegar pitoresco* which appeared in 1660, he compared the collectors staying in Venice to hunters who were eagerly setting out their nets and would spend any amount of money in order to carry off the city's painted treasures. When he wrote this he must have been thinking mainly of Veronese's works, for, due to Carlo Ridolfi's writings and some of his own as well as through reproduced engravings, prominent main works had become well-known in many places north of the Alps. Charles I of England (1600–1649), Christina of Sweden (1626–1689), Archduke Leopold William (1614–1662) to whom Boschini dedicated his *Carta* – all these, followed by well-known or lesser-known dukes, patricians and wealthy merchants such as the Reynst brothers from Amsterdam, bought paintings by the Venetian painter who had, in the meantime, achieved classical status. On many occasions, however, wealthy admirers of paintings that could not be moved or were not for sale had no other choice than to make do with workshop replicas, contemporary copies or imitations. Often enough works of this nature were bought in the belief that they were by Veronese himself, and even accepted experts of the subject-matter such as the painter Pietro da Cortona, who during his time bought an "apocryphal" Veronese for Cardinal Alessandro Bichi, were not immune against unwelcome surprises. If, given the constantly in-creasing demand, originals were no longer available, copies came into their own. Recently, attention has been drawn to Francisco Gómez de Sandoval y Rojas, the Duke of Lerma (1552–1625), a Spanish collector in King Philip III's (1578–1621) circle, who by 1607 at the latest had no less than six copies after Veronese and two works by the painter himself in his La Ribera residence near Valladolid; they very probably included the painting *Mars, Venus and Cupid* (ill. 118), now in Edinburgh, that was given to Charles I in 1623 on the occasion of his visit to the Spanish court.

While Veronese's mythological heroes and heroines shine out in full light, the religious works of his late period are, in many cases, characterized by a clear reduction of means. In individual cases such as *Christ in the Garden of Gethsemane* (Pinacoteca di Brera, Milan), landscapes and night scenes gain importance, and moving works such as the *Crucifixion* (ill. 119) in the Louvre and the *Pietà* (ill. 120) in St. Petersburg, which was presumably produced in about 1581 and of which several versions are known, appear permeated by a new, apparently private devotion.

Carefully balanced light and dark effects determine the tone of one of the last and most important works produced by the painter, who died during the night of April 19–20, 1588. *The Miracle of St. Pantaleon* (ill. 121), created for the Venetian church of the same name, is apparently determined entirely by the use of color. In a vertical format, the altarpiece uses the most economical means to develop its narrative of the miraculous healing of a child by Pantaleon, a doctor who was later denounced to the Emperor as a Christian by envious healers and had to suffer a terrible martyrdom. The picture is determined by the red cloak trimmed with fur worn by the saint who is stepping forward from a sparsely lit rear courtyard. With gently undulating lines, he creates a connection to the two boys and the donor of the picture, Bartolomeo Borghi. Colorful half-shadows indicate the transitions between individual forms and make it possible to guess why Veronese was, for several centuries, celebrated as the colorist *par excellence* and, on occasion, is even described as the Impressionists' pioneer.

The French painter Eugène Delacroix (1798–1863), who was one of the first artists to profit from the Louvre's new function as a place of learning and who from the start was a passionate admirer of Veronese's painting, enthusiastically wrote about the Venetian painter's painting technique, which he studied on several occasions in the form of copies. Thus it says in his diary for November 3, 1850: "Paolo Veronese flattens the half tone of light and that of shadow. I have ascertained from my own experience that this process itself produces an astonishing illusion. It confines itself to connecting both by a gray shade which is only applied dry in certain places. Equally he places the most powerful and transparent shade of gray, which forms the border between the shadow and gray tone, above it lightly." While, during the course of the 19th century, art critics ceaselessly complained about superficial displays of splendor and the neglect of the spiritual at the expense of the material world, it was almost without exception painters who were able to keep an unprejudiced point of view when looking at Veronese's works. One of their number was no less a figure than Paul Cézanne (1838–1906), who became ecstatic about the *Wedding at Cana* (ill. 73) when he paid a visit to the Louvre: "That is painting. Every piece, the whole, the corporeality, the color values, the composition, the shudder, everything is there ... All one sees is a large colorful undulation – of what ... That is what a picture should first provide, a harmonious warmth, a chasm into which one's gaze immerses itself." Veronese was, of course, not interested in recording fleeting visual stimuli. Rather, he was concerned with looking into the colorful and material essence of armor, brocade cloth, rocks, of translating the visible world of objects into colors in order to utilize them in an ideal painterly picture arrangement. When Cézanne finally concluded that Paolo Veronese "painted as we see", his theme echoed one of the Venetian painter's central artistic qualities.

119 *Crucifixion*, c. 1582
Oil on canvas, 102 x 102 cm
Musée du Louvre, Paris

It is debatable whether this picture (which once belonged to the Cologne-born Paris banker Everard Jabach (1610–1695) but by 1683 at the latest was in the possession of the French king Louis XIV) is identical with a picture on the same subject described by Marco Boschini in the Casa Garzoni in Venice in 1660.

The arrangement of the crosses links the picture with an incomparably more dramatic *Crucifixion* painted for the Venetian church of San Nicolò della Lattuga (Gallerie dell' Accademia, Venice). Both works display the same glowing colors and the occasional borrowing from Tintoretto. Particularly memorable is the shrouded figure in the yellow robe, which is often identified as Mary Magdalene, but is more probably Synagoga, the personification of Judaism.

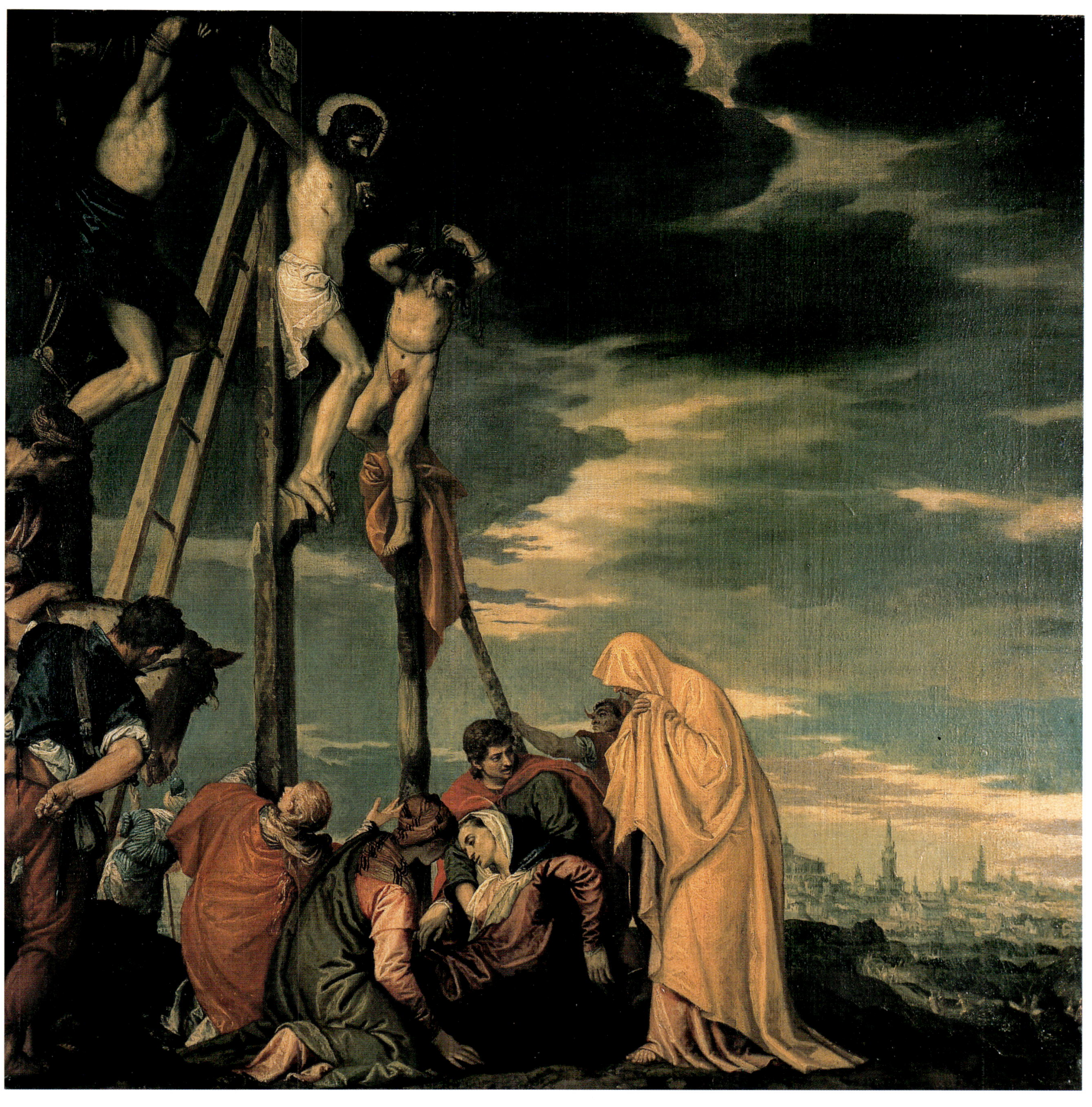

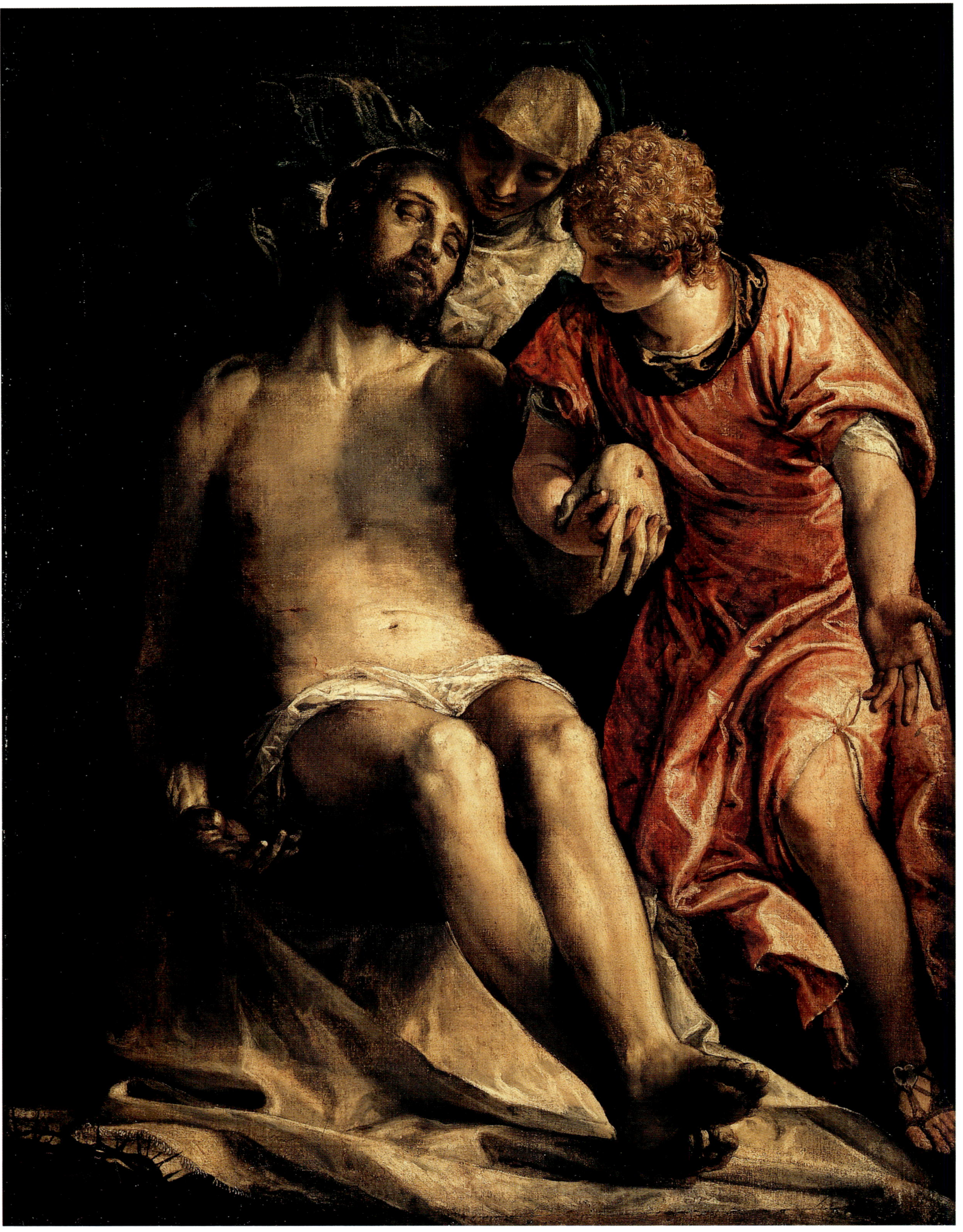

121 *The Miracle of St. Pantaleon*, 1587
Oil on canvas, 277 x 160 cm
San Pantaleon, Venice

This altarpiece, which is excellently preserved, is one of the last that can be attributed definitely to Veronese. Bartolomeo Borghi, who originally commissioned the painting for the main altar of the church, is seen solicitously holding a sick boy. St. Pantaleon, the miracle-working physician, is about to perform an act of healing on the boy. The brightly lit torso on the right is clearly imitated from the Hellenistic sculpture of *Silenus* (Museo Archeologico Nazionale, Venice), which came from the Grimani collection and was certainly known to Veronese.

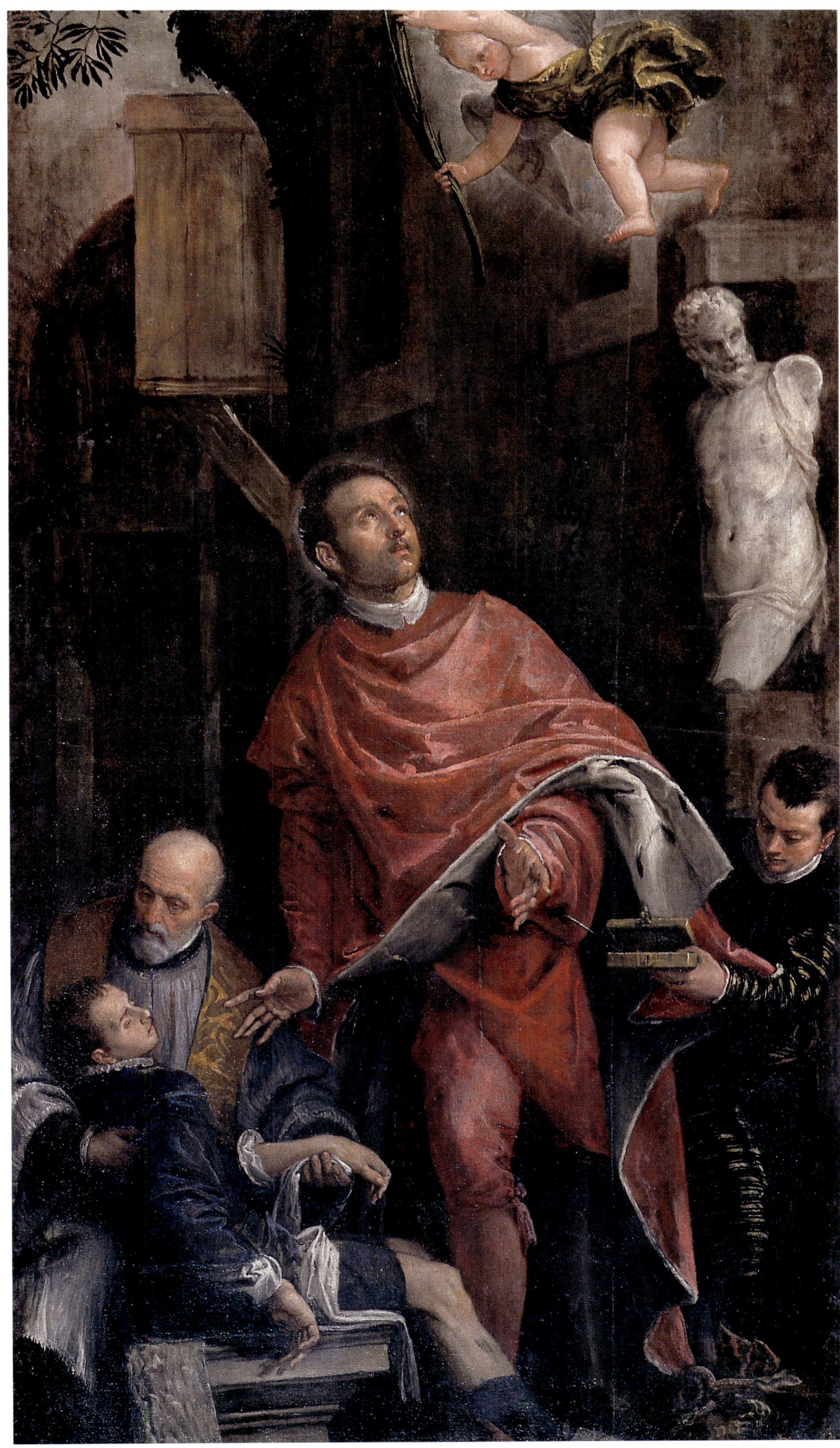

120 (opposite) *Pietà*, c. 1581
Oil on canvas, 147 x 111 cm
Hermitage, St. Petersburg

An engraved copy dated 1582 by Agostino Carracci is the first documentary evidence of this picture, which was intended for the church of SS. Giovanni e Paolo in Venice. Apart from Christ, it shows only Mary and an angel, against a dark background. The figural composition is notable for its severe closedness of forms, with the drama lying in the interplay of the expressive heads. The innovative quality of the devotional picture is underlined by the existence of several weaker replicas and variants carried out at a later date by Benedetto Caliari and colleagues from the workshop.

CHRONOLOGY

1528 Paolo is born in Verona in the district of San Paolo, the second eldest son of the stonemason Gabriele di Piero and his wife Caterina.

1538 Birth of Benedetto Caliari, his brother and later colleague.

c. 1539 Entry to the workshop of the Veronese painter Antonio Badile, first mentioned as his student and assistant in May 1541. Afterwards presumably trained for a while with Giovanni Caroto.

1551 Works in the Villa Soranza near Castelfranco as a protégé of the architect Michele Sanmicheli. First public appearance in Venice with the *Pala Giustinian* for the chapel of the same name in the church of San Francesco della Vigna.

1552 The *Temptation of St. Anthony* is commissioned by Cardinal Ercole Gonzaga for the cathedral in Mantua.

1554–1556 In Venice Veronese plays a decisive part in the decoration of the Sale del Consiglio dei Dieci (Sala della Uedienze, Sala della Bussola and Stanza dei Tre Capi).

1555 Veronese moves to Venice. First use of the name "Paulo Veronese" in the contractual agreement for the apartment in the Santi Apostoli district. Bernardo Torlioni, the prior of San Sebastiano in Venice, commissions "Paulo Caliaro Veronese" to produce the ceiling painting in the sacristy. Between 1555 and 1570, numerous other paintings and illusionistic frescoes are produced on the ceiling and side walls of the nave, and in the choir and refectory.

1556–1557 In Sansovino's Libreria Vecchia, Veronese once again provides proof of his abilities as a ceiling painter: with the tondo showing the allegory of *Music* he emerges as the victor from a competition between a total of seven painters. Works alongside the sculptor Alessandro Vittoria as a fresco painter in the Palazzo Trevisan in Murano.

1559 Probable start of a journey to Rome as part of the retinue of the Venetian ambassador Girolamo Grimani.

1560 – 1561 Painting in the Villa Barbara in Maser by Andrea Palladio.

1562 On January 7, commissioned for the large-format painting of *Frederick Barbarossa Kissing the Hand of the Antipope Victor IV*, which was destroyed in 1577 during a fire in the Sala del Maggior Consiglio in the Doge's palace.

1562–1563 The *Wedding at Cana*, in the refectory of the Benedictine monastery of San Giorgio Maggiore in Venice, is the first of the monumental sacred feasts.

1566 On April 17, in Verona, he marries Elena Badile, the daughter of his former master.

1567/1570 Birth of his sons Gabriele and Carletto Caliari.

1572 On April 29, Veronese is paid for the *Feast of Gregory the Great* in the refectory of the monastery of Madonna di Monte Berico in Vicenza. In Venice, he moves to the Calle di Ca' Mocenigo in the parish of San Samule.

1573 The *Last Supper* in the refectory of the Dominican monastery of Santi Giovanni e Paolo in Venice causes offense. Veronese is summoned before the Inquisition and required to justify himself. A compromise solution is a change in title to *Feast at the House of Levi*.

1575 He stays in Padua together with Benedetto Caliari. Completion of the *Martyrdom of St. Justina* for the high altar of the monastery church of the same name. The plague is raging in Venice.

1575–1582 Paintings for the ceilings and walls of the Sala del Collegio and Sala del Maggior Consiglio, which were destroyed by fire in 1574 and 1577.

1585 Veronese declines an invitation to work for the Spanish king in the Escorial.

1587 Commissioned by Bartolomeo Borghi, he creates the *Miracle of St. Pantaleon* for the Venetian church of the same name.

1588 Veronese dies on April 19 at the age of 60 after being ill for eight days with pleurisy and a fever; he is buried in the church of San Sebastiano.

GLOSSARY

Accademia degli Incamminati (Ital. "academy of those making their way"), private academy founded in Bologna in the early 1580s by Agostino (1557–1602), Annibale (1560–1609) and Ludovico Carracci (1555–1619). Its teaching called for the recollection of the great examples of the Italian Cinquecento (Raphael, Michelangelo, Correggio, Titian, Veronese) and attached particular importance to the study of models and nature.

Accademia degli Infiammati (Ital. "academy of the enlightened"), humanist academy founded in Padua in university circles, to which important commentators, philosophers and men of letters belonged.

Aedicule (Lat. *aedicula*, "little house"), framing of portals, windows and niches using two columns, pillars or pilasters supporting an entablature and a triangular or segmental arch pediment.

Allegory (Gk. *allegoria*, from *allegorein*, "say something differently"), visual depiction of abstract terms, contents or contexts, usually based on literary concepts. The main means employed are figures, actions and symbols; in the 19th century, allegories frequently appeared in sculpture form in connection with buildings and monuments.

Arcade (Fr. *arcade*, "strainer arch", from Lat. *arcus*, "bow" (weapon)"), an arch or series of arches resting on supports at either end.

Architrave (from Gk. *archein*, "start, rule", and Lat. *trabs*, "beam"), a main beam resting on supports such as columns that carries the weight of the upper building. It can be structured using fascias, usually three stepped horizontal divisions.

Battle of Lepanto, naval battle during the course of which the 208 ships belonging to the Holy League gained a decisive victory on 7 October 1571 over the 210 ships of the Ottoman Turkish fleet on the edge of the Gulf of Corinth.

Camera Obscura (Lat. "dark chamber"), initially a usually portable casing with a hole (aperture) instead of a lens or mirror, used as a drawing aid for perspectival compositions by landscape, architectural and veduta painters. It consists of an opaque box with a small opening through which the rays of light are focused so that they produce an inverted small mirror image on the far side.

Cardinal Virtues (Late Lat. *cardinalis*, "key issue"), the four basic virtues of Temperantia (temperance), Fortitudo (fortitude), Prudentia (prudence/wisdom) and Justitia (justice) adopted in Christian ethics from the Greek philospher Plato (427–347 B.C.). Gregory the Great (540–604 A.D.) added the three so-called divine or theological virtues of Fides (faith), Caritas (charity/love) and Spes (hope). Based on this group of seven, the Christian system of virtues was further expanded during the high Middle Ages.

Carnations (from Lat. *carnis, caro*, "flesh"), the shade of color by which naked human skin is reproduced in paintings, usually using a mixture of white and red.

Catholic Reformation or **Counter Reformation**, term in ecclesiastical history referring to the reform of the entire Church which was widely believed to be necessary as early as the late Middle Ages. Reform programs, such as those passed by the Councils of Constance (1414–1418) and Basle (1431–1437 and 1448) or the 5th Lateran Council (1512–1517), did not achieve any lasting results. Not until the Protestant Reformation were the Pope and Roman Curia forced to take specific action against abuse of position, declining moral standards, the selling of indulgences and excesses in the worship of saints and relics. With the *Laetere Jerusalem* (1544) bull, Pope Paul III (1534–1549) was responsible for the convocation of the Council of Trent which, in three separate sessions between 15445 and 1563, started the process of inner reform in the Church.

Chiaroscuro Painting (Ital. "light–dark"), structural method used in graphics (the art of drawing and printing) and painting in which strong light and dark effects are used to contrast with each other. It is frequently used to dramatize the events in the picture and create plasticity.

Cinquecento (Ital. "500"), term used in Italian art history for the 16th century, and also a stylistic term. As such, it does not refer to the art of the entire 16th century, but specifically to the High Renaissance as opposed to the Quattrocento, the Early Renaissance.

Clerestory, a row of windows in the upper part of the wall of a basilica's nave (main aisle).

Colonnade (Fr. *colonnade*), row of columns with a straight entablature and no arches.

Congregation (from Lat. *congregatio*, "gathering, community"), a close community of monasteries within the same monastic order.

Consiglio dei Dieci (Ital. "Council of Ten"), established in 1310, the highest political decision-making body in Venice. Its members were elected for a fixed term by the Senate, the Venetian parliament of noblemen. While the Doge ranked above the Council, he had to use considerable personal power if he wanted to win against them.

Council of Trent, *see* Catholic Reform.

Devotional Picture, usually small-format picture for the silent devotion of an individual worshipper or a community.

Di sotto in sù (Ital., "from the bottom upwards"), method of depiction seen from below in extreme foreshortening, usually applied in ceiling paintings.

Disegno (Ital. "drawing"), drawing, design, sketch; beyond the literal meaning of the word, the term was, particularly during the Renaissance, the subject of extensive discussions on art theory, and in its extended sense included the conceptual area of the artistic idea and the significant compositional principles used when putting a creative notion into practice (Vasari).

Eucharist (from Gk. *eu*, "good", and *charis*, "grace, thanks"), thanksgiving; the sacrament of the Last Supper with bread and wine, the climax of the Christian service.

Example (Lat. *exemplum*, "example"), in the fine arts, a depiction which usually presents the moral actions of the picture's hero in historical conflict situations, to be considered a model of virtue by the observer.

Exegesis (Gk.), explanation and interpretation of pieces of writing, in particular the Bible.

Faun (Lat. *faunus*), ancient Roman god of nature, protector of shepherds, farmers, fields and livestock. Equated with the Greek god Pan, he is frequently depicted with a goat's legs and horns.

Fluting, vertical concave grooves along the shaft of a column, pillar or pilaster. They can be connected to each other by sharp edges or separated by fillets.

Frontispiece (Fr. *frontispice*, "front [of a building], title page"; Med. Lat. *frontispicium*; from Lat. *frons*, "forehead", and *spicere*, "look"), here: decoration on the title page of a book.

Gentiluomo (Ital.), Italian term for a man with a gentlemanly disposition.

Grisaille (from Fr. *gris*, "gray", and *grisailler*, "paint gray"), gray on gray painting; manner of painting which deliberately omits grades of color and uses only stone colors, shades of brown, or gray. It is particularly suited to imitating sculptural works in paintings.

Heraldry, area of research focusing on the origins and interpretation of emblems (symbols).

Heresy (from Gk. *hairesis*, "the elected, way of thinking"), in the classical age denoted the choice of a particular school of thought. In Christianity, the term increasingly meant opinions held in opposition to the orthodox doctrine.

History (Lat. *historia*; Gk. *historia*, "knowledge, news"), genre of paintings in which religious or historical events are the subject of the picture.

Inquisition (Lat. *inquisitio*, "examination, investigation"), medieval ecclesiastical institution for hunting down heretics and criminals; from 1231 papal Inquisitors (mainly Dominicans and Franciscans) were appointed. Pope Gregory IX (1227–1241) and the collection of decrees published in 1234 made the Inquisition a papal institution ("Sanctum Officium"), and it was later extended to include other offenses such as magic, witchcraft and fortune-telling.

Investiture (Lat.), process by which an ecclesiastical or secular dignitary is appointed to his office.

Ionic Order, one of the classical order of columns that was used during the Renaissance; its characteristics are a capital with curled volutes on either side.

Jeronymites, congregation of hermits named after St. Jerome of Stridon which followed the Augustinians' rule with additions from St. Jerome's writings. Their main tasks were spiritual welfare and academic work.

League of Cambrai, alliance against Venice lasting from 1508 until 1510 between Pope Julius II (1443–1513), Emperor Maximilian I (1459–1519), Ferdinand of Aragon (1452–1516), Louis XII of France (1462–1515) and some Italian states.

Legenda aurea (Lat. "golden legend"), collection of legends about saints compiled by the Dominican Jacobus de Voragine (1228/29–1298). From the Middle Ages onwards it was an important source text in Christian art.

Loggetta (Ital.), small loggia: open arcaded walkway supported by columns or pillars.

Mannerism (from Fr. *manière*, "manner"; and Lat. *manuarius*, "of the hands"), period of European art falling between the Renaissance and the Baroque, from about 1520/1530 until 1620. In Mannerism, the harmonious ideal forms, proportions and compositions developed during the Renaissance were in part reversed. Thus, characteristic features of the style include increased dynamics in the pictorial scenes, elongated human bodies and anatomically inconsistent positions, extremely complicated compositions, irrational and very theatrical lighting and a use of color that was no longer restricted to the object it represented.

Miles christianus (Lat. "Christian soldier"), term used for military service on behalf of Christ and the Church, though it can also mean spiritual arms.

Modello (Ital. "model, pattern"), 1. the mature design, usually on a small scale, of a painting or sculpture which can be used to consult with the client. 2. Model which stays in the workshop to be used to produce several copies of a commissioned painting. 3. Sculptural aid in a painter's studio.

Nobile (Ital.), patrician. The aristocratic families comprised a good 4 per cent of the Venetian population. The male members of the families were in charge of guiding the Venetian state.

Nymphaeum (Gk.), series of classical fountains dedicated to the nymphs, Greek goddesses of Nature.

Observance (from Lat. *observantia*, "observation"), following the rule of a monastic order.

Pala (Ital. "panel"), altarpiece or a sculptural or painted altar decoration. Usually pointed or rounded at the top.

Patriarch of Aquileia, official or honorary title of some Roman Catholic archbishops. In the 5th century, almost all of Venetia and Istria, western Illyria and Noricum were subject to the metropolitan power of Aquileia. In 568 the incumbent patriarch (title first proven to exist in 558–560) fled from the Langobards to Grado, upon which the Langobard diocesan bishops elected their own metropolitan in 607. From then onwards, two patriarchies existed: the Byzantine Grado and the schismatic Langobard Old Aquileia. In 1238 the patriarch of Aquileia moved his residence to Udine. In 1418–1420, Venice conquered Aquileia's secular territory and in 1451 the patriarchy of Venice was founded. From then onwards the patriarch's see was always occupied by Venetians.

Pendant (Fr. "hanging"), corresponding, related counterpart, such as paintings connected by motif, decoration or theme, such as the portraits of a married couple.

Pergola (Ital.), open arbor consisting of pillars or columns, usually entwined with plants.

Peristyle (Gk. *peristylon*), the columned hall surrounding a courtyard or square.

Piano nobile (Ital.), or *bel étage*, the main floor of a building, usually above the ground floor, containing the public rooms.

Pilaster (Ital. *pilastro*; from Lat. *pila*, "pillar"), rectangular wall pillar used to structure a wall surface which normally only projects slightly and consists of a base (bottom), shaft (central part) and capital (head). It is frequently fluted, i.e. the shaft is decorated with vertical grooves.

Pliny the Elder (23/24–79 A.D.), born Gaius Plinius Secundus, Roman author. The only one of his works that has survived is a *Naturalis historiae* (history of nature) in 37 volumes, in which for the first time all natural phenomena were presented in an encyclopedic and organized fashion.

Portico (Lat. *porticus*, "columned hall"), usually open porch supported by columns or pillars on the main entrance side of a buildings. Frequently supports a pediment.

Presbytery (Gk. *presbyterion*, "Council of Elders"), or choir, the raised space at the end of a church's nave which contains the high altar and is reserved for members of the clergy.

Provenance (from Lat. *provenire*, "come from"), origins, of a piece of art for example.

Refectory (Med. Lat. *refectorium*; from Lat. *reficere*, "remake"), monastic dining hall.

Repoussoir (from Fr. *repousser*, "push back, scare off"), term used for figures or objects such as tree stumps or architectural fragments depicted in the foreground of a picture, which are often used to create an illusion of depth and guide the observer towards the main events.

Retable (Fr. *retable, rétablir*; Lat. *retabulum*, "rear wall"), structure behind or on the rear side of the altar table with a sculptural or painted altarpiece.

Ricordo (Ital. "memory"), drawing or sketch of an already existing work.

Rustication (Lat. *rustica*; from *rusticus*, "rural, rustic"), stonework whose blocks have been given a rough finish on the front sides.

Sacra conversazione (Ital. "sacred conversation"), type of depiction of the Madonna in the dignified companionship of several saints. The term is misleading as no actual conversation is taking place.

Sala (Ital.), hall, large room.

Satyr (Gk. *satyros*), Greek nature demigod, a two-legged horse in human form with a horse's ears, tail and hooves. Occasionally also depicted with a goat's feet and horns. He is a boisterous, lecherous companion of Dionysus, the Greek god of wine and fertility.

Serenissima (Ital.; abbreviation of *La Serenissima Repubblica Venezia*, "the most serene republic of Venice"), term, in use since the Middle Ages, which describes the splendor and dignity of Venice and is, at the same time, an expression of Venetian self-confidence.

Serliana or Venetian window, architectural motif invented by Donato Bramante (c. 1440–1514) and named after Sebastiano Serlio (1475–1554), and also called a Palladio motif. It consists of an arrangement of columns surrounding three lights, with the center pair of columns joined by a semicircular arch. The lights on either side finish with a straight entablature at the height of the bottom of the arch.

Servite (Lat., Med. Lat.), member of a mendicant order founded in 1233.

Signoria (Ital. "sovereignty"), from the late Middle Ages, the guiding council or government of Italian cities. Usually a single family presided over it.

Soffit (Lat., Ital.), wooden ceiling decoration.

Spandrel, triangular area of stone or brickwork. Spandrels are, for example, produced when arches are surrounded by rectangles. Pendentives are formed in buildings with domes and take the shape of curved triangles at the transition point from the square ground plan to the vaulted dome.

Stanza (Ital.), room.

Terraferma (Ital. "firm land"), the mainland forming part of the Venetian Doge's sovereign territory, i.e. the strip of coastline immediately next to the lagoon,

Tondo (Ital. "sphere, plate"; from Lat. *rotundus*, "round"), circular painting or relief (sculptural method of depiction on a surface).

Torsion (Lat.), twisting; altered form of solid bodies by contradictory twisting motions.

Triclinium (Lat.), 1. dining room in Roman houses, 2. dining hall for pilgrims in monasteries.

Tympanum (Gk. "eardrum, drum"), arched area above a portal or the area within a pediment.

Vasari, Giorgio (1511–1574), Italian architect, painter and art author. His *Lives* of Italian artists, published in 1550 and 1568, are among the most important source texts in art history.

Venus, Roman goddess of spring and gardens, closely connected to concepts of grace and charm; later equated with Aphrodite, the Greek goddess of love.

Vestibule (Lat. *vestibulum*, "forecourt"), the anteroom or entrance hall of a building. In ancient Roman dwellings, the vestibule was situated before the entrance to the house.

Vita (Ital. "life"), life; literary narration of the life of a famous person.

Votive image (Lat. *votivus*, "praised, dedicated"), a sculpture dedicated to a saint or god in gratitude for being saved from danger, supported in a petition, or having one's prayers answered.

SELECTED BIBLIOGRAPHY

Exhibition catalog: *The Art of Paolo Veronese – 1528–1588*, ed. William R. Rearick, National Gallery of Art, Washington 1988.

Exhibition catalog: Veronese e Verona, ed. Sergio Marinelli, Museo di Castelvecchio, Verona 1988.

Exhibition catalog: *Paolo Veronese – Disegni e dipinti*, ed. Alessandro Bettagno, Fondazione Giorgio Cini, Vicenza 1988.

Paolo Veronese: Restauri, ed. Giovanna Nepi Scirè (Quaderni della Soprintendenza ai Beni Artistici e Storici di Venezia, 15), Venice 1988.

Richard Cocke: *Veronese's Drawings. A catalogue raisonné, London 1984*

Richard Cocke*:* *Veronese*, London 1980.

Philipp Fehl: "Veronese and the Inquisition. A study of the subject matter of the so-called 'Feast in the House of Levi'," in: *Gazette des Beaux-Arts*, no. 58, 1961, pp. 325 – 354.

Erik Forssman: "Über Architekturen in der venezianischen Malerei des Cinquecento", in: *Wallraf-Richartz-Jahrbuch*, no. 29, 1967, pp. 105 – 139.

Joachim Gasquet: *Cézanne*, Berlin 1930.

Massimo Gemin (ed.): *Nuovi studi su Paolo Veronese* (Techné 8), Venice 1990.

Diana Gisolfi Pechukas: "Two oil sketches and the youth of Veronese", in: the *Art Bulletin*, no. 64, 1982, pp. 388 – 413.

Huse, Norbert, Wolfgang Wolters. *The Art of Renaissance Venice: Architecture, Sculpture and Painting, 1460–1590.* Translated by Emund Jephcott. Chicago: University of Chicago Press,1990.

Jürg Meyer zur Capellen and Bernd Roeck (eds.): *Paolo Veronese. Fortuna Critica und künstlerisches Nachleben (studi/Schriftenreibe des Deutsches Studienzentrum in Venice, 8)*, Sigmaringen 1990.

Kuno Mittelstädt (ed.): *Eugène Delacroix. Dem Auge ein Fest. Aus dem Journal – 1847–1863*, Frankfurt am Main 1988.

Terisio Pignatti and Filippo Pedrocco: *Veronese*, 2 vols, Milan 1995.

Andreas Priever: *Vorbild und Mythos – Die Wirkungsgeschichte in der 'Hochzeit zu Kana' Paolo Veroneses (Studi/Schriftenreihe des Deutschen Studienzentrums in Venedig, 16)*, Sigmaringen 1997.

Rearick, William R. *The Art of Paolo Veronese, 1528–1588*, Washington: National Gallery of Art; Cambridge, England: Cambridge University Press, 1988.

Carlo Ridolfi: *Le maraviglie dell' arte ovvero le vite degli illustri pittori veneti e dello stato*, Venice 1648. Ed. Detlev von Hadeln, 2 vols, Berlin 1914/1924.

Mark W. Roskill, *Dolce's 'Aretino' and Venetian Art Theory of the Cinquecento*, New York 1968.

Wolfgang Wolters: *Der Bilderschmuck des Dogenpalastes. Untersuchungen zur Selbstdarstellung der Republik Venedig im 16. Jahrhundert,* Wiesbaden 1983.

PHOTOGRAPHIC CREDITS

The publishing house and publisher wish to thank the museums, collectors, archives and photographers for permission to reproduce the works illustrated and their cooperation in the production of this book.

© Archiv für Kunst und Geschichte, Berlin (43, 56, 57) – photo: Erich Lessing (13, 48/49, 78/79, 94/95, 133); © Archiv für Kunst und Geschichte, Berlin – photo: Cameraphoto (42 top); © Archivio della Stato, Venice (110 left); © Archivio Fotografico del Museo Correr, Venice (6, 11); © Art Collections of Prague Castle, Prague (121 left); © Ashmolean Museum, Oxford (80 right); © Bayerische Staatsbibliothek, Photostelle, Munich (30, 62, 66, 95 top); © Bibliotheca Hertziana, Max-Planck-Institut, Rome (31); © Bildarchiv Preußischer Kulturbesitz, Berlin – photo: Jörg P. Anders (99, 122); © The Bridgeman Art Library, London (42 bottom, 131); © Cameraphoto-Arte, Venice – photo: Piero Codato (17 bottom, 24, 26, 34, 35, 39, 40, 41, 46, 54 left, 55, 82, 86/87, 106/107, 108/109, 114 left, 115, 124, 135); © Christie's Images, London (53 right, 118); © Fotoflash, Venice (25 right); © Fotostudio dal prà, Montagnana (45); © The Frick Collection, New York (130); © The J. Paul Getty Museum, Malibu (88); © Graphische Sammlung Albertina, Vienna (17 top); © The Metropolitan Museum of Art, Gwynne Andrews Fund, 1946 (46.31) – photo: 1982 The Metropolitan Museum of Art, New York (121 right); © Musée des Beaux-Arts et de la Dentelle d'Alençon, Alençon (54 right); © Vatican Museums, Rome – photo: P. Zigrossi (113); © The National Gallery, London (16, 92/93, 101, 123); © The National Museum of Western Art, Tokyo (19); © Nicolò Orsi Battaglini, Florence (8); © Oronoz, Madrid (63, 125); © The Pierpont Morgan Library/Art Resource, New York (64); © RMN, Paris – photo: Daniel Arnaudet (21), Michéle Bellot (22 right, 38, 53 left), Gérard Blot (27, 104 top); Hervé Lewandowski (118/119); © Rijksmuseum, Amsterdam (61); © Sächsische Landesbibliothek, Abt. Deutsche Fotothek, Dresden (9); © SCALA group S.p.A., Antella/Florence (14, 15, 20, 23, 25 left, 33, 36, 37, 50/51, 59, 65, 68, 69, 70, 71, 72, 73, 74/75, 84/85, 89, 90, 91, 100, 104/105, 114 right, 116/117, 120, 126/127, 128, 129, 134); © Staatliche Kunstsammlungen Dresden, Gemäldegalerie Alte Meister, Dresden – photo: Klut, Dresden (96/97); © Szépmüvészeti Múzeum, Budapest – photo: 80/93, András Rászó (58); © The Walters Art Gallery, Baltimore (22 left); Yale University Art Gallery, New Haven (18)